Issues in Political Theory

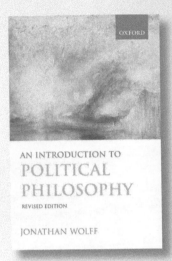
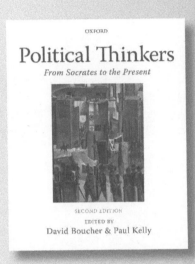
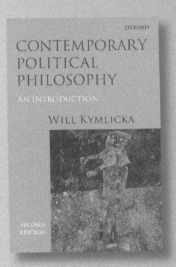

Issues in
Political Theory

Third edition

Edited by
Catriona McKinnon

OXFORD
UNIVERSITY PRESS

UNIVERSITY PRESS

Great Clarendon Street, Oxford OX2 6DP,
United Kingdom

Oxford University Press is a department of the University of Oxford.
It furthers the University's objective of excellence in research, scholarship,
and education by publishing worldwide. Oxford is a registered trade mark of
Oxford University Press in the UK and in certain other countries

© Oxford University Press 2015

The moral rights of the author have been asserted

1st edition 2008
2nd edition 2012
Impression: 4

Published in the United States of America by Oxford University Press
198 Madison Avenue, New York, NY 10016, United States of America

British Library Cataloguing in Publication Data
Data available

Library of Congress Control Number: 2014946119

ISBN 978-0-19-968043-6

Printed in Great Britain by Ashford Colour Press Ltd, Gosport, Hampshire

For Bria and Caelan

Acknowledgements

Thanks are due to my husband, Matt Pittori, for his encouragement as I went around the block for the third time, and to my lovely children who put everything in the right perspective. I would like to thank Jeremy Williams for his continued great work in updating the Online Resource Centre and—for the first time—his provision of stimulating new case studies for the book itself. I am grateful to the team at Oxford University Press—in particular, my editor Martha Bailes—for their unflappable professionalism and support. Finally, I am very grateful to my stalwart and evolving gang of contributors for their outstanding chapters in this new edition.

New to this edition

- New chapters on crime and punishment, power, and war and intervention, with cases on international crime, Afghanistan and the War on Terror, and racialized inequality in the USA.
- New cases on mosque-building in Europe, conscription, deliberative polling, and torture and counter-terrorism.
- Key thinkers boxes embedded within the text, so that you can build your understanding of the figures behind the ideas as you learn.

Contents

List of case studies

Notes on the contributors

Gillian Brock is Professor of Philosophy at the University of Auckland in New Zealand. Her most recent work has been on global justice and related fields. Her books include *Global Justice: A Cosmopolitan Account* (Oxford University Press, 2009) and *Debating Brain Drain* (with Michael Blake; Oxford University Press, 2015). She is the editor or co-editor of a number of volumes including *Current Debates in Global Justice*; *The Political Philosophy of Cosmopolitanism*; *Necessary Goods: Our Responsibilities to Meet Others' Needs*; *Global Health and Global Health Ethics*; and *Cosmopolitanism versus Non-Cosmopolitanism: Critiques, Defenses, Reconceptualisations*.

Tom Campbell is a professorial fellow in the Centre for Applied Philosophy and Public Ethics (CAPPE), Charles Sturt University, Australia. He is a visiting professor in the School of Law, King's College, London, and has been Professor of Jurisprudence at The University of Glasgow and Professor of Law at the Australian National University. He is the author of *The Legal Theory of Ethical Positivism* (Dartmouth, 1996) and *Justice* (Palgrave-Macmillan, 2001).

Clare Chambers is University Senior Lecturer in Philosophy and Fellow of Jesus College, University of Cambridge. She has previously held posts at the University of Oxford and the London School of Economics, and has twice been a Visiting Scholar at the University of California, Berkeley. She is the author of *Sex, Culture, and Justice: The Limits of Choice* (Penn State University Press, 2008) and, with Phil Parvin, *Teach Yourself Political Philosophy: A Complete Introduction* (Hodder, 2012), as well as articles and chapters on liberalism, feminism, multiculturalism, equality, autonomy, and radical theories of social construction. She is currently working on the state regulation of marriage.

Thomas Christiano is Professor of Philosophy and Law at the University of Arizona. He has been a fellow at the Princeton University Center for Human Values, the National Humanities Center, All Souls College, and Australian National University. He is the author of *The Rule of the Many* (Westview, 1996) and *The Constitution of Equality* (Oxford University Press, 2008) and articles on moral and political philosophy. He is editor of *Politics, Philosophy and Economics* (Sage). His current research is on global justice and international institutions, human rights, fair exchange, democracy, and the foundations of equality.

Helen Frowe is Wallenberg Academy Research Fellow in Philosophy at Stockholm University, where she directs the Stockholm Centre for the Ethics of War and Peace. She is the author of *The Ethics of War and Peace: An Introduction* (Routledge, 2011) and *Defensive Killing: An Essay on War and Self-Defence* (Oxford University Press, 2014).

Anna Elisabetta Galeotti is Full Professor of Political Philosophy at the Università del Piemonte Orientale. She has spent several years as a research fellow in various institutions abroad, including Cambridge University, the European University Institute in Florence, the Institute for Advanced Study in Princeton, the Centre for Ethics and Public Affairs of St Andrews University, and the Safra Foundation Center for Ethics of Harvard University. She has worked on toleration for many years, and has published three books and many essays, including *Toleration as Recognition* (Cambridge University Press, 2002) and 'Female circumcision' (*Constellations*, 14, 2007). She is currently writing a book on self-deception and democratic politics.

Axel Gosseries is a professor at the University of Louvain (UCL, Belgium) and a permanent research fellow at the Fonds de la Recherche Scientifique (FNRS, Brussels). He is the author of one monograph on intergenerational justice in French (Aubier, 2004) and the co-editor of three, including *Intergenerational Justice* (with L. Meyer; Oxford University Press, 2009). He has published some fifty articles and chapters in such journals and volumes as the *Canadian Journal of Philosophy*; the *Journal of Political Philosophy*; *Politics, Philosophy and Economics*; *Loyola of Los Angeles Law Review*; *International Economic Review*; and *Economics and Philosophy*.

Keith Hyams is Associate Professor of Political Theory and Interdisciplinary Ethics at the University of Warwick. He has held visiting positions at the Universities of Toronto, Oxford, and Louvain. He has published articles on consent, distributive justice, and the ethics of climate change.

Dale Jamieson is Professor of Environmental Studies and Philosophy, and Affiliated Professor of Law at New York University. He is the author of *Ethics and the Environment: An Introduction* (Cambridge University Press, 2008). He is currently writing a book on how to live with climate change.

Catriona McKinnon is Professor of Political Theory at the University of Reading. She is the author of *Liberalism and the Defence of Political Constructivism* (Palgrave, 2002), *Toleration: A Critical Introduction* (Routledge, 2006), and *Climate Change and Future Justice: Precaution, Compensation, and Triage* (Routledge, 2011). She is writing a book on climate change as an international crime against future people.

Monica Mookherjee is a Senior Lecturer in Political Philosophy at the University of Keele. She is the author of *Women's Rights as Multicultural Claims: Reconfiguring Gender and Diversity in Political Philosophy* (Edinburgh University Press, 2009) and the editor of *Democracy. Religious Pluralism and the Liberal Dilemma of Accommodation* (Springer, 2010). She is currently writing a book on the application of the human capabilities approach to theories of multiculturalism.

David Owen is Professor of Social and Political Philosophy at the University of Southampton. He has also been Visiting Professor in Politics and in Philosophy at the JW Goethe University, Frankfurt am Main. He is the author of *Maturity and Modernity* (Routledge, 1994), *Nietzsche, Politics and Modernity* (Sage, 1995), and *Nietzsche's Genealogy of Morality* (Acumen, 2007) and has co-edited volumes including *Multiculturalism and Political Theory* (Cambridge University Press, 2007) and *Recognition and Power* (Cambridge University Press, 2007), as well as writing articles on a wide range of topics. He is currently working on issues in the ethics of migration.

Massimo Renzo is Associate Professor of Philosophy at the University of Warwick. He has been a fellow at the Australian National University, Osgoode Hall Law School and the Murphy Institute at Tulane University. He works primarily in legal and political philosophy. His main research interests are in the problems of political authority, international justice, and the philosophical foundations of the criminal law.

Jonathan Riley is Professor of Political Economy and Philosophy at Tulane University. He is the author of *Liberal Utilitarianism* (Cambridge University Press, 1988), *Mill: On Liberty* (1998; 2nd edn, Routledge, 2014), and *Mill's Radical Liberalism* (Routledge, 2014), as well as of more than eighty articles in peer-reviewed journals and volumes. He is currently completing a book on agonistic value pluralism and liberal democracy.

Jeremy Williams is a Birmingham Fellow in Philosophy at the University of Birmingham. His work spans political philosophy and bioethics, and he has previously authored articles on abortion, procreative ethics, and decisional rights in bodily materials.

Jonathan Wolff is Professor of Philosophy at University College London. His books include *An Introduction to Political Philosophy* (Oxford University Press, 1996; 2006), *Disadvantage* (with Avner de-Shalit; Oxford University Press, 2007), *Ethics and Public Policy: A Philosophical Inquiry* (Routledge, 2011), and *The Human Right to Health* (Norton, 2012).

Guided tour of textbook features

This book is enriched with a number of learning tools to help you navigate the text, build your understanding of the key issues in political theory, and show you how theory can be applied to real-world cases. This guided tour shows you how to get the most out of your textbook package.

Reader's guide

Power is central to any understanding of politics but what roles does the concept of power play in such an understanding, and what different modes of power can be distinguished? Recent political theory has seen a variety of views of power proposed, with these views having significantly different implications for conceptualizing the scope and form of political activity. Two main views concerning power are the locus of contemporary debate. The first, 'agency-centred' view, emerges in the Anglo-American debate that follows discussions of community power in American democracy. The second, 'non-agency-centred' view, emerges from the post-structuralist work of Michel Foucault. At stake, in the debate between them, are how we distinguish between injustice and misfortune, as well as how we approach the issues of freedom and responsibility.

Reader's guides

Reader's guides at the beginning of each chapter set the scene for upcoming themes and issues to be discussed, and indicate the scope of the chapter's coverage.

- **Affiliation:** Being able to live with and toward others; to recognize and show concern for other human beings; to engage in various forms of social interaction. Having the social bases of self-respect and non-humiliation. Not being discriminated against on the basis of gender, religion, race, ethnicity, and the like. ➡ See Chapters 3 and 7.
- Other species: Being able to live with concern for and in relation to animals, plants, and the world of nature. ➡ See Chapter 11.
- Play: Being able to laugh, to play, to enjoy recreational activities.
- **Control over one's environment:** Being able to participate effectively in political choices that govern one's life. ➡ See Chapter 4 Being able to have real opportunity to hold property. Having the right to seek employment on an equal basis with others.

The capability view has been extremely influential in at least two ways: first, it has been

Cross-references

Clear in-line cross-references help you to make links between ideas in different chapters.

KEY THINKERS

Plato (427–347 BC)

Plato was a classical Greek philosopher and a pupil of Socrates, whose life and thoughts he recounts in many of his early writings. Among Plato's central ideas was the thought that behind everything we experience are as-yet-unknown 'forms'—that is, abstract universal representations of the types and properties that we experience. Perhaps Plato's best-known work is *The Republic* (360 BC; 1974), in which he sets out his vision for a utopian society. Such a society would have a rigid caste system, with farmers and traders at the bottom, warriors in the middle, and philosopher-rulers with their philosopher-king at the very top. Plato famously claimed that '*Unless philosophers become rulers, or rulers study philosophy, there will be no end to the troubles of men*'.

Boxes

Key concepts boxes provide you with detail on the core principles that make up the big ideas, while **key texts** boxes direct you to major works of political theory, and **key thinkers** boxes provide biographical context to some of the most influential theorists and philosophers. **Key points** boxes summarize what is covered in each main section and are a useful revision aid.

CASE STUDY

The contest over purpose-built mosques in Europe

In recent decades, Muslim communities coming from many different African and Asian countries have steadily been growing throughout Europe. In all European countries, religious freedom is acknowledged to be a fundamental right, usually embodied in Constitutions. Thus, the building of appropriate places of worship for Muslims would be expected as the obvious consequence of their residency in European countries. But this is not the case. While the so-called 'garage or backyard mosques' multiply, the resistance over the construction of purpose-built mosques, with or without the minaret, is widespread and has produced intense political conflicts in many cities including Cologne, Copenhagen, and Milan, often becoming an issue in national politics (Allievi, 2010). The controversy over mosque building raises two questions of toleration. First, is the mosque

Case studies

Each chapter ends with an extended case study to show how political theory can be used to understand some of the most hotly debated topics in contemporary politics.

Questions

A set of carefully devised questions has been provided to help you assess your understanding of core themes and to reflect critically on the main ideas.

FURTHER READING

■ Bellamy, A. (2008) 'The responsibilities of victory: *Jus Post Bellum* and the just war', *Review of International Studies*, 34: 601–5 Bellamy's paper outlines the history of *jus post bellum* and argues that we ought not to regard it as part of just war theory.

■ Frowe, H. and Lang, G. (eds) (2014) *How We Fight: Ethics in War*, Oxford: Oxford University Press This collection of ten essays explores theoretical issues relating to *jus in bello*, including the doctrine of double effect, non-combatant immunity, and the distribution of risk between combatants and non-combatants.

■ Frowe, H. (2011) *The Ethics of War and Peace: An Introduction*, New Abington: Routledge Frowe's introduction to just war theory focuses on contemporary debates concerning the moral equality of combatants, non-combatant immunity, the moral status of terrorists, and the legitimacy of humanitarian intervention.

Further reading

Take your learning further by using the reading lists at the end of each chapter to find the key literature in the field, or more detailed information on a specific topic.

Web links

At the end of each chapter you will find an annotated summary of useful websites to help you with further research.

Glossary terms

Key terms appear in bold in the text and are defined in a glossary at the end of the book to build understanding as you work through the text and to aid you in exam revision.

Guided tour of the Online Resource Centre

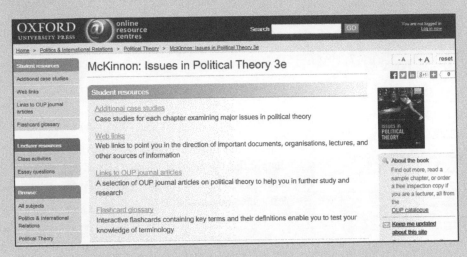

www.oxfordtextbooks.co.uk/orc/mckinnon3e/

The Online Resource Centre that accompanies this textbook provides students and lecturers with ready-to-use learning and teaching materials. These resources are free of charge and designed to maximize the learning experience.

The case studies and exercises on the Online Resource Centre have been updated by Jeremy Williams of the University of Birmingham.

For students

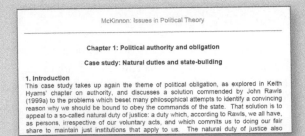

Additional case studies

Each chapter is accompanied by an additional case study to show how theory can be used to examine major issues in political theory, demonstrating the relevance of political theory to politics in practice.

Additional annotated web links

Web links have been provided to point you in the direction of important documents, organizations, lectures, and other sources of information on political theory.

Links to OUP journal articles

Links to OUP journal articles

The articles cited below are relevant to the content in *Issues in Political Theory*. Some give background information on the subject as a whole, while others build on information in specific chapters.

Leif Wenar, <u>Original acquisition of private property</u>, Mind 107/428, 1998.
Background information

Brad Hooker, <u>Rule-Consequentialism</u>, Mind XCIX/393, 1990
Background information

Philippa Foot, <u>Utilitarianism and Virtues</u>, Mind XCIV/374, 1985.
Background information

A selection of OUP journal articles on political theory has been compiled to help you in further study and research.

Flashcard glossary

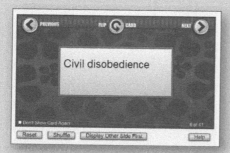

Interactive flashcards containing key terms and their definitions enable you to test your knowledge of terminology.

For registered adopters of the textbook

Chapter 10

Class activities

Organize the class or seminar for a debate. Have one side propose one of the following motions:

1. 'Showing respect for cultural sensitivities requires limits on freedom of speech.'

2. 'Animal welfare must not be compromised because of religious dietary requirements.'

3. 'Religion has no place in the public school system.'

4. 'Minority rights are antithetical to equality.'

Weekly assignments

Prepare a short presentation for your class or seminar *on* one of the following questions:

1. How can we decide who speaks for a cultural group? Why does this question matter?

2. How should the state respond to illiberal minorities under its jurisdiction?

3. Are there any good reasons why the gay community can't claim rights as a minority culture?

Class activities, weekly assignments, and essay questions

A suite of questions and activities that encourages class debate has been provided for use by instructors in tutorials, seminars, and assignments.

Introduction

CATRIONA McKINNON

→ **Chapter contents**

- What is political theory?
- Plan of the book
- Political theory and the real world

What is political theory?

'Political theory' is the study of how we should live together in society. Given that there are many aspects to social life and social cooperation, there are many dimensions to political theory. Broadly, there are two overlapping sites of enquiry: relations between people and institutions within state boundaries, and relations between states on the international stage.

Starting with political and social relations within state boundaries, a long-standing and foundational line of enquiry focuses on why individuals should accept the political **authority** of the state, what its limits are, and how those who wield the power of the state should come to do so. Have we all consented to have this power exercised over us? If so, when, and how, was it given? If we have not consented to it, is the state illegitimate and may we reject its edicts? Must we be bound by a constitution enacted before we were born? If we should, and do, accept the state, what are its limits? May the state monitor our movements, communications, and interactions with others without our knowledge? May it require us to serve—militarily or otherwise, in times of war or peace—on pain of punishment? On what authority does the state inflict punishment on members who perform crimes, and what form may punishment take? And what is the best way in which to choose the group that has its hands on this immense power? Most people in democracies now reject the principle of hereditary rule—but why is **democracy** preferable? Why not benign dictatorship instead? And what makes a state democratic?

State institutions provide the basic framework within which people live: these institutions set the terms of social interaction by in some respects limiting, and in other respects expanding, the possibilities for people acting on and with one another. A further function of these institutions is to divide up the benefits and burdens of cooperative activity: who should get the spoils and who should pay the costs? We also need to know when and how we may defend ourselves against one another: what limits should be placed on how people may treat one another and what penalties can be imposed on members of society who transgress these limits? Further, how should people relate to one another within these limits? May those different from us in beliefs and practices be condemned and shunned? And how should those among us who are dependent—the infirm, the ill, the old, and children—be treated? Who is responsible for their care and what form should that take? And what do we owe as a matter of justice to people in the future, and in the past? Still further, we need to know how we should organize ourselves in the smaller groupings of society to which we all belong at some point in our lives. How should families operate? What obligations do employers have to their employees? Should classes and castes be abolished? And how, if at all, do voluntary groupings—religions, pressure groups, trade unions, etc.—help us to live together well?

Beyond what goes on within states are a set of questions related to how states ought to relate to one another. Ought any principles of social cooperation and justice that are justified within state borders be extended to apply to all states everywhere? Are there minimum standards—perhaps related to human rights—which morally bind all states, regardless of their differences? What are the responsibilities, if any, of the developed to developing states? How may a state act, unilaterally or multilaterally, towards any state that threatens it? What are the conditions under which war is just? And, in the age of globalization and looming dangerous climate change, how ought states to mobilize in order to tackle, collectively, serious threats that no one state can tackle on its own?

These categories of enquiry are loosely demarcated: answers given to questions in one category very often affect answers to questions in another. For example, if we believe that all people are equal in virtue only of their humanity and that, as such, each deserves an equal distribution of the benefits and burdens of social cooperation, then we will have to work hard to assert that the mere fact that a person is a citizen of a rich country makes him or her more deserving of the benefits that attach to that membership than someone unfortunate in being born in a poor country. Furthermore, many political theorists argue that the way in which intra- and inter-state questions have been addressed in the history of political theory has failed to take proper account of features of the human condition that are fundamental to an accurate understanding of what it is that political institutions have to respond to. The following four facts in particular have salience. First, that human beings live on a bounded planet containing limited resources, and have nowhere else to go: this truth raises questions of how human beings and their political institutions ought to relate to the environment. Second, that human beings are divided into two sexes: this makes questions of how the sexes relate to one another—in particular, questions about the power that men wield over women—foundational in political theory. Third, that human beings, at any point in time, are part of a chain of generations stretching backwards and forwards in time, and that all future generations are entirely vulnerable to any present generation: this makes the temporal legacy of political institutions central to thinking about their character and justification. And finally, the inequalities and effects of power on human social and political relations, and an understanding of how power can be exercised over people in subtle and multifarious ways should inform assessment of political institutions and social relations in domestic and global contexts.

Plan of the book

The chapters in the book are loosely grouped to reflect the three sites of activity in political theory just described.

- **Chapters 1–7** discuss problems of political obligation, liberty, the limits of toleration, the nature of democracy, requirements of equality and social justice, the concept of crime and approaches to punishment, and the promise and problems of multiculturalism. The focus in these chapters is on issues that most commonly arise within the boundaries of states.

- **Chapters 8–10** explore problems that cross state borders, and in some cases call into question the moral legitimacy of those borders; through exploration of 'just war theory' they also address the moral principles governing inevitable armed conflicts between states.

- **Chapters 11–14** introduce approaches to features of the human condition that theories addressing intra- and inter-state relations must be sensitive to. Many of the theoretical approaches canvassed here are relatively recent arrivals in mainstream political theory and reflect unprecedented degrees of interconnection between people across the globe and an increased awareness of the fragility of human life on Earth and the extent to which some groups of people are vulnerable to others.

The topics of the chapters in this book have been chosen to reflect key sites of activity in the discipline of normative political theory as it stands today—in particular, with an eye to the most important, visible, and influential strands in political theory over the last fifteen years. The concepts and issues discussed in them have framed—and have themselves been informed by—the political discourse and practice of the late twentieth and the beginning of the present centuries. The book has also been written specifically bearing in mind the practical nature of political theory, the way in which political theory always aims to change the world, while connecting with its realities. To this end, each chapter is accompanied by a detailed case study, in which the theoretical themes and questions posed in the main chapter are explored and probed at a practical level. The case studies show how political theory can be put to use in analysing and critiquing hotly debated aspects of politics in the world today. They should encourage the reader to try out such analysis and critique, on topics he or she cares about, using the concepts and strategies of argument to be found in the chapters. Political theory is a dynamic, exciting subject, with the potential to change people's minds and thereby change the world. Putting theory into practice in the case studies shows many ways in which this might happen.

Political theory and the real world

How do political theorists think about the questions described so far? Very often, a distinction is made between **normative** and **descriptive** thinking in order to address these issues. Normative thinking is thinking in terms of how persons, society, or the world ought to be; descriptive thinking aims to present a picture of how persons, society, and the world actually are. In this way, descriptive thinking can be said to mirror the world, while normative thinking aims to change it.

Political theory is a normative subject: political theorists tell us how people ought to interact, the sorts of laws we ought to pass, what it means for democratic systems to function well, etc. In order to make such normative claims, political theorists must assume certain empirical facts. For example, a background descriptive assumption made by theorists of **distributive justice** is that the conditions to which their principles apply are those of a moderate scarcity of goods, to be contrasted with abundance and with extreme scarcity (each of which would, in different ways, make distributive justice redundant).

The normativity of political theory often prompts those coming to it for the first time to be sceptical about the extent to which it speaks for political problems as they are found in the real world. This scepticism commonly takes one, or a combination of, the following forms:

a) Because all values are relative to particular cultures and traditions, and given that all arguments in political theory draw on values, any argument in political theory can be sound only in a particular cultural context.

b) Many of the moral imperatives created by political theories are such that people—and, by extension, collective agents such as states—will not comply with them. This makes political theory redundant as a guide to political practice.

c) Many arguments in political theory assume idealized conditions which do not exist in the real world. In that case, political theory is utopian.

Let me address each of these ways of turning away from normative political theory.

First, relativism. There are many varieties of relativism, and some have a degree of sophistication that does not justify the rejection of normative political theory (Baghramian, 1994). The (crude) form I shall address here is this:

1. Values, and practices justified by reference to them, fundamentally differ across place and culture.

2. Therefore, there are no value-related practices that have universal legitimacy; that is, there are no value-related practices which are required of people in all places and all cultures.

3. Therefore, we ought never to require of people that they desist or alter their value-related practices.

There are at least two fundamental mistakes in this line of reasoning. The first problem relates to the move from (1) to (2): the fact that there is a diversity of value-related practices in the world does not establish that there are no value-related practices justified across all contexts. Perhaps humankind has just not discovered these practices yet. The irrelevance of diversity to establishing the possibility of universally justified value-related practices can be seen by considering how total convergence on a set of such practices is not sufficient to show them to be universally justified: this is a major message of Orwell's *1984*. Second, the argument is self defeating (Williams, 1972): it has as its conclusion (3), a universally binding requirement to engage in a value-related practice (viz. abstaining from making requirements of others) which it denies the existence of in its premise (2).

Next, let us examine the claim about the practical redundancy of political theory, given facts about human nature. According to Estlund (2011), there are at least three ways to read the claim that human nature blocks requirements delivered by political (and moral) theory. Let us imagine that P denotes voluntarily shrinking one's personal carbon footprint in order to promote global greenhouse gas emissions reductions, so as to tackle climate change in line with principles of global justice that allocate the costs of mitigation disproportionately to industrialized nations. This requirement of a theory of climate justice might be resisted by an appeal to human nature in three ways:

1. First, with the claim that people <u>cannot do</u> P.

2. Second, with the claim that people <u>will not do</u> P.

3. Third, with the claim that people <u>cannot will</u> P.

If a political theory delivers requirements that it is logically, conceptually, or nomo-logically impossible for people to satisfy—for example, if it required them to change the past—then that theory would be practically redundant in the sense captured by (1) above. However, no political theories do this and, in the example of greenhouse gas emissions reductions, there is no such impossibility.

Turning to (2), as Estlund puts it, '[t]*o show that a standard will not be met might count against people's behaviour rather than against the standard*' (Estlund, 2011: 209). There are all sorts of explanations for why people will not do what they ought to do—*inter alia* greed, laziness, ignorance, fear—but none of these are in themselves sufficient to defeat a requirement that they behave otherwise. In the climate change example, the fact that people will not reduce their own personal carbon footprint (perhaps because of how this would reduce their access to luxury goods) does nothing to show that they are not required to do this. To expect any political theory simply to mould its requirements to what people will in fact do would be to deprive political theory of any radical and progressive potential.

Turning to (3), the claim here might be that political theories require people to do things that they cannot will themselves to do, and for that reason have no traction in the real world in which people cannot bring themselves to behave in ways required of them by political theories. In response to this, Estlund reflects that being unable to bring oneself to do something does not show that one cannot do that thing (Estlund, 2011: 213): at most, it shows that the person has a weakness or some other deficiency of will. But (someone might object) if this is true of all human beings—and so is, to that extent, human nature—then surely a political theory is asking people to do what they cannot do, and for that reason is to be rejected. In response, Estlund invites consideration of the following scenario:

> Suppose people line up to get your moral opinion on their behaviour. Bill is told that his selfishness is indeed a motivational incapacity, but that it does not exempt him from the requirement to be less selfish. But behind Bill comes Nina with the same query. Again, we dispatch her, on the same grounds as Bill. Behind Nina is Kim, and so on. Since each poses the same case, our judgement is the same. The line might contain all humans, but that fact adds nothing to any individual's case... I take this to show the following rather significant thing: even if a large dose of selfishness is part of human nature, this does not refute theories of justice that require people to be less selfish than that.

(Estlund, 2011: 220–1)

Finally, let me consider the claim that normative political theory is unacceptably uto-pian. It is true that much normative political theory involves the articulation and defence of ideals; for example, of democracy, equality, or justice. But from the fact that a theory has this focus, it does not follow that it bears no relation to the real world. Indeed, these ideals might be necessary in order for us to act politically in the world at all. For example, the ideals of political theory could stand as measures of the moral desirability of a range of practical options—for example, related to policies or institutions—all of which lie within a feasible set (Swift, 2008). That is, the ideals of political theory could step in when the feasi-bility considerations of social science run out. Or, the ideals of normative political theory might be thought of as the endpoint of a journey, where 'non-ideal' theory and the social sciences address how to get there (Robeyns, 2008). That is, the ideals of political theory guide the direction of travel for more non-ideal enquiries.

Of course, there is much more that could be said about the place of normative political theory in real-world politics but I hope to have shown that the three sceptical sets of reflections discussed earlier are, at best, the beginnings of lines of enquiry, not the end.

To sum up, the aim of this book is to ensure that the reader gains a firm grasp of the basics of contemporary political theory, while being given a sense of its dynamism and its potential to connect with political practice in exciting and surprising ways. Although the chapters progress in the way outlined, the book is not linear and has multiple points of entry. Readers should feel free to dip into the book at any point, and then follow up the featured cross-references to thematically connected chapters for a deeper understanding of associated debates and related issues. The topics and questions of political theory are not free-standing and independent of one another: themes criss-cross, and debates in one area can be fruitfully enhanced by those in another. The cross-references will indicate points for which this is particularly the case.

Making arguments in political theory is not a matter of 'making it up as you go along'. There are ways of arguing that are better or worse than others, and arguments may have more, or less, informed content. This book shows such arguments in action and reveals the difference that good arguments in political theory might make to the world we know. Familiarity with these methods, and the deep understanding of the key concepts of political theory that reading this book will deliver, will equip readers with a conceptual toolbox that enables them to address their own arguments to real-world political problems.

1

Political authority and obligation

KEITH HYAMS

✔ Reader's guide

Why should we obey the law? Should we always obey the law, regardless of what it requires us to do, or should we obey only just laws? Can the authority that governments claim for themselves be justified? Do governments have to meet certain criteria in order rightfully to claim this authority? In this chapter, we will look at the various approaches that political theorists have taken to answering these questions. As well as reviewing arguments in favour of political authority and obligation, we will also consider anarchist positions, which claim that we are not obliged to obey the law. To illustrate these themes, the case study explores military conscription as a problem of political obligation.

Introduction

The starting point for many of the issues discussed in this book is the state. How should political representatives be chosen? How much should the state tax us and how should it spend that tax? When should the state go to war? How should the state control our borders? Before moving on to these questions in later chapters, one question suggests itself before all others: why should we have a state at all? Why should we, human beings born into a world that is ruled everywhere by this state or that, acquiesce in the power of those states? Why should we accept the **authority** that they claim for themselves and why should we obey their laws?

Questions about political authority and obligation require us to delve into **normative** issues—issues about what we *should* do and about what principles we *should* follow. In order to justify political authority and obligation, we need to identify normative principles that can ground our case. But we also need to address **descriptive** issues—issues that are about how the world is or how the world would be if something were to happen. We need to know whether obeying the laws set and enforced by our governments *would* be the best way in which to follow the normative principles that we identify. Consider, for example, the claim that we should obey the law because, if we do not do so, then society will collapse into chaos. This claim implies an argument with two premises:

- a normative premise, which says that we have a duty not to let society collapse into chaos; and

- a descriptive premise, which says that, if we do not obey the law, then society will collapse into chaos.

 KEY CONCEPTS

Authority

To have authority in the practical sense is not merely to have power over someone. To have power over someone is to have at one's disposal the means to make that person do something— but authority requires something more: that the person subject to the authority have a certain 'pro' attitude towards the person or institution that claims authority. Authoritative directives are obeyed not because those who obey them are fearful of punishment, but because those who obey them think that the directives *should* be obeyed by virtue of their issuing from the authority.

Together, these two premises entail the conclusion that we have a duty to obey the law. In order to challenge this conclusion, people might question either the normative premise or the descriptive premise. They might ask normative questions: do we really have a duty not to let society collapse? Why should I believe that we have such a duty? Or they might ask descriptive questions: why will society collapse if I do not obey the law? Are there no other ways in which we could prevent society from collapsing other than by obeying the law? Might we not, for example, set up anarchist self-governing federations instead?

The following sections will discuss various arguments in support of the claim that we have a duty to obey the law. In order to assess these arguments, you should try to work out on what normative and descriptive premises they rely, and how plausible you think those premises are.

Consent

Perhaps the most important historical justification for political authority and obligation is what is often called **consent theory** (or **contract theory**). Consent theorists claim that we should obey the law because we have consented to do so. Consent theory is a type of **voluntarism** because it says that our obligation to obey the law derives from a voluntary undertaking on our part.

Consent theory is often associated with the seventeenth-century English philosophers Thomas Hobbes and John Locke, and with the eighteenth-century French philosopher Jean-Jacques Rousseau. But the thought that we have consented to obey the law was first given currency by the Greek philosopher Plato, in his dialogue 'Crito' (360 BC; 1892). Plato recounts how Socrates was condemned to death by an Athenian court for corrupting the minds of the youth with his ideas. Whereas Socrates' friends urge him to escape, Socrates himself refuses to flee and stays to drink the fatal hemlock. Socrates argues, among other things, that his long residence in Athens constitutes an agreement to obey the laws of Athens. By living in Athens he has, in other words, consented to obey the law. He must therefore respect the court's verdict and submit to his execution.

 KEY THINKERS

Plato (427–347 BC)

Plato was a classical Greek philosopher and a pupil of Socrates, whose life and thoughts he recounts in many of his early writings. Among Plato's central ideas was the thought that behind everything we experience are as-yet-unknown 'forms'—that is, abstract universal representations of the types and properties that we experience. Perhaps Plato's best-known work is *The Republic* (360 BC; 1974), in which he sets out his vision for a utopian society. Such a society would have a rigid caste system, with farmers and traders at the bottom, warriors in the middle, and philosopher-rulers with their philosopher-king at the very top. Plato famously claimed that '*Unless philosophers become rulers, or rulers study philosophy, there will be no end to the troubles of men*'.

Consent theorists make two claims. First, they claim that, by consenting to obey the law, each of us can impose on ourselves an obligation to obey the law. Second, they claim that we have, in fact, consented to obey the law. The first of these claims has generally been regarded as uncontroversial; it is the second claim that has provoked one of the liveliest

KEY CONCEPTS

Consent

When someone consents to something, he or she either takes on a duty to do a particular thing or permits others to do a particular thing. Consent is important not only to politics but also to a whole range of contexts. We talk, for example, about whether sex was consensual, about consenting to some medical treatment, and so on. As Hurd writes (1996: 123): '*Consent turns a trespass into a dinner party; a battery into a handshake; a theft into a gift; an invasion of privacy into an intimate moment; a commercial appropriation of name and likeness into a biography.*'

and most enduring debates in the history of political thought. As the eighteenth-century Scottish philosopher David Hume wrote:

> My intention here is not to exclude the consent of the people from being one just foundation of government where it has place. It is surely the best and most sacred of any. I only pretend, that it has very seldom had place in any degree, and never almost in its full extent.
>
> **(1748; 1947: 219)**

What, then, about the consent theorist's claim that we have consented to obey the law? When are we supposed to have consented? How did we consent? To whom did we consent? With the possible exception of new immigrants to certain countries, few of us will ever have said or written anything explicitly stating that we hereby consent to obey the law. So on what basis do consent theorists claim that we have consented to obey the law? And even if some of us have consented, have we all? Have women consented to a largely male dominated state? Or is consent theory, as Pateman (1988) has claimed, really just a cover for the subordination of women by men in the name of the state?

Tacit consent

Modern consent theorists follow Locke (1690; 1924) in making a distinction between **express consent** (also sometimes called **explicit consent** or **active consent**) and **tacit consent** (also sometimes called **implicit consent** or **passive consent**). Express consent is the type of consent that we give when we expressly announce—in speech or in writing—that we consent to something. Tacit consent, on the other hand, refers to more subtle forms of consenting within which no express announcement is made. Consent theorists argue that the fact that most of us have never said or written anything indicating our consent to obey the law shows only that we have not *expressly* consented to obey the law; it does not show that we have not *tacitly* consented to obey the law. Furthermore, they argue, we *have* tacitly consented to obey the law, by doing things such as voting in elections and even just by residing in a particular geographical territory (see Box 1.1).

Considerable confusion surrounds the distinction between express consent and tacit consent. That express consent is exemplified by acts such as uttering a statement of consent or signing a document is clear enough; what is not clear, however, is what such acts are supposed to exemplify and to what type of acts they are opposed. The distinction most often appealed to in this connection is a distinction between consent by action and consent

---

BOX 1.1 THE CASE OF WEST PAPUA

What would it take for an entire population expressly to consent to be governed by a particular government? According to the Indonesian government, the population of West Papua—the western half of the island that also includes Papua New Guinea—consented to its authority in 1969, the date of an event that it calls the 'Act of Free Choice'. Yet West Papuan independence activists point out that the act involved only 1,026 tribal leaders who were hand picked by Indonesia and coerced into agreeing to the authority of the Indonesian government over West Papua (see Saltford, 2003). The West Papuan activists further claim that this coerced act of consent continues to be used as a pretext for an unjustified military occupation of their country that has seen widespread **human rights** abuses and genocidal tactics used against the indigenous Papuan population.

---

by omission: express consent means consent by doing something, whereas tacit consent means consent by not doing something. On this interpretation, an example of tacit consent would be remaining silent when the chair of a meeting announces that all who do not speak up at a particular time will be deemed to have consented to a particular proposal. The obvious problem with this interpretation is that at least one of the acts that consent theorists claim is tacit consent to obey the law—voting—is an act, rather than an omission. Thus, although the distinction between consent by action and consent by omission might help to illuminate the variety of ways in which consent can be given, it is not particularly relevant to arguments for consent theory.

In order to unlock the distinction that *is* relevant to these arguments, consider the types of act that count as express consent: saying 'I consent to X', signing a document, etc. These are all fairly trivial acts that serve no particularly useful purpose other than in their role as consent. If these acts were not to count as consent, there would rarely be any reason to perform them—and there is a good reason for this. Suppose that acts of express consent could include useful acts such as eating, playing football, breathing, and telling someone one's name—acts that we might well have a reason to perform other than in order to consent. In such a scenario, we would end up consenting to things not because we wanted to consent, but because we could not avoid consenting in order to eat, play football, etc.—or we would have to refrain from performing these useful acts in order to avoid consenting. If, on the other hand, only acts with no useful role are selected to serve as acts of express consent, then we do not have to avoid performing useful acts in order to avoid consenting. With this restriction in place, we can be sure that when someone performs an act of consent, he or she does so because he or she wants to consent and not merely because he or she wants to perform that act.

The problem for consent theorists is that the two acts that they want to say are acts of consent to obey the law—voting and residing—are both useful acts. As such, they cannot count as acts of express consent without running into the problem just discussed. Tacit consent provides a way out, however, because acts of tacit consent *can* be useful acts. But (and it is a big 'but') not just any acts can qualify as tacit consent. An act can only qualify as tacit consent if it would normally be prohibited to the person who consents, because someone has a right that they not perform the act without thereby consenting. The right holder grants an exemption from the prohibition only on condition that, when the act is performed, consent is automatically given. So, for example, a customer in a restaurant tacitly consents to pay for his or her meal by eating the meal. Unless eating the meal counts as consent to pay for the meal, then he or she should not have eaten it. The dish belongs to the owner of the restaurant and he or she has a moral right that, unless the customer thereby consents to pay for the meal, he or she should not eat it.

Why the requirement that acts of tacit consent must be acts that would be prohibited unless specified as consent? Because this requirement allows us to get around the problem that arises, as we saw earlier, with useful acts counting as consent. Acts of tacit consent are acts that the person who consents would not have been permitted to perform anyway, had the act not been specified as consent. As such, he or she has nothing to lose by that act being specified as an act of consent. The customer at the restaurant, for example, does not lose out if eating a meal at the restaurant counts as tacit consent to pay for the meal. Had the customer not been permitted to eat the meal as an act of tacit consent, he or she would not have been permitted to eat the meal at all.

In order to determine whether residing and voting can count as tacit consent to obey the law, it is therefore important to ask whether these things would otherwise be prohibited to us because the state has a moral right that we not do these things without thereby consenting. If the state does not have such a right, then it cannot treat our doing these things as consent to obey the law.

A second important question that we must ask in order to determine whether these supposed acts of consent succeed in placing us under a duty to obey the law is: was the consent given freely? Or rather: was the consent given *freely enough* to be effective in placing us under a duty to obey the law? Theorists differ in their views about just how freely consent needs to be given in order to be effective. At the very least, most theorists agree that coerced consent—that is, consent performed under threat of harm—is ineffective. Suppose, for example, that you are mugged in the street. The mugger holds a gun to your head and tells you that if you do not hand over your wristwatch, he will shoot you. You might consent to hand over your wristwatch, but your consent is ineffective. You do not give the thief any right to keep the wristwatch. The wristwatch remains yours and you are entitled to try to reclaim it.

Residence as consent

Both Plato and Locke (see Box 1.2) claim that residence in a particular geographical territory counts as consent to obey the laws of that territory. (Locke claims that even travelling through a geographical territory counts as consent to obey its laws.) To some readers, this might seem to be an entirely natural claim: if we do not like the laws of the country in which we live, then we are free to leave and live elsewhere. If we choose to stay, then we have consented to obey the laws of that country. But are we really free enough to leave for our continued residence to count as effective consent? Even if we set aside those states that forcibly prevent their citizens from leaving, many of us would have to leave behind our friends, family, culture, and work, etc. in order to move elsewhere. So you might well question whether, if we choose not to make these sacrifices, our continued residence can really count as free and effective consent. Hume (1748; 1947) famously argued that our residence in a territory no more counts as effective consent than does the presence on board a ship of a man who was carried on board while asleep. Rousseau (1762; 1968), on the other hand, insists that when the state does not impede our exit, then our continued residence is free enough to count as effective consent. But he accepts that when we are forced to stay in a country by a coercive state, our residence does not count as effective consent.

That is one reason why some theorists have questioned whether residence in a country can count as consent to its laws. Another reason appeals to the thought that, as we saw earlier, the state can only treat our residence as tacit consent to obey the law if it has a moral right that we not reside in the country without thereby consenting. It is not easy to see why the state would have a right that we not live within its borders unless we consent to obey its laws. Many people own the land on which they live and seem therefore to have a prima facie right to live on that land without submitting to anyone's rules. We cannot simply assume that the government, as the authority that presides over the land, has a right to determine who can live within its borders. To do so would beg the very question that we wish to answer: *why* should we regard the authority that the government claims for itself as legitimate? It looks, then, as though the residence version of consent theory cannot succeed without relying on some prior justification for political authority that does not appeal to tacit consent. If such a justification can be found, then political authority will already have been shown to be legitimate and consent then becomes redundant.

BOX 1.2 PLATO, LOCKE, HUME, AND ROUSSEAU ON RESIDENCE AS CONSENT

And if any one of you wishes to go to a colony, if he is not satisfied with us and the city, or to migrate and settle in another country, none of us, the laws, hinder or forbid him going whithersoever he pleases, taking with him all his property. But whoever continues with us after he has seen the manner in which we administer justice, and in other respects govern the city, we now say, that he has in fact entered into a compact with us, to do what we order.

(Plato, 360 BC; 1892: 41)

Every man that hath any possession or enjoyment of any part of the dominions of any government doth hereby give his tacit consent, and is as far forth obliged to obedience to the laws of that government, during such enjoyment, as any one under it, whether this his possession be of land to him and his heirs for ever, or a lodging only for a week; or whether it be barely travelling freely on the highway; and, in effect, it reaches as far as the very being of any one within the territories of that government.

(Locke, 1690; 1924: 177)

Can we seriously say that a poor peasant or artisan has a free choice to leave his country, when he knows no foreign language or manners, and lives, from day to day, by the small wages which he acquires? We may as well assert that a man, by remaining in a vessel, freely consents to the dominion of the master; though he was carried on board while asleep, and must leap into the ocean, and perish, the moment he leaves her.

(Hume, 1748; 1947: 221–2)

After the state is instituted, residence implies consent; to inhabit the territory is to submit to the sovereign. [Footnote:] This should always be understood to refer only to free states, for elsewhere family, property, lack of asylum, necessity or violence may keep an inhabitant in the country unwillingly, and then his mere residence no longer implies consent either to the contract or to the violation of the contract.

(Rousseau, 1762; 1968: 153)

Voting as consent

A second act that some consent theorists have argued is tacit consent to obey the law is voting in a democratic election. John Plamenatz, for example, writes that '*where there is an established process of election to an office, then, provided the election is free, anyone who takes part in the process consents to the authority of whoever is elected to the office*' (1968: 170). Of course, not everyone in the world has the opportunity to vote in a democratic election, and even among those who do, many choose not to exercise it. But can we at least say that citizens of democratic states who do cast their vote have freely consented to obey the law?

Recall again the requirement that the state can treat an act as an act of tacit consent only if it has a moral right that we not perform the act without thereby consenting. This requirement seems to pose less of a problem for the voting version of consent theory than it did for the residence version. The state sets up and runs elections for the benefit of those who participate in them, using its own ballot boxes and voting slips. As such, it seems plausible that the state does have a right that people not vote if they do not thereby consent to obey the law.

Now recall the requirement that consent must be free and uncoerced in order to be effective. The voting version of consent theory seems even more problematic than the residence version in this respect. The problem is that whether or not we choose to vote, we will all be forced to obey the law anyway. We do not really have the choice to abstain from the political and legal arrangements of our country altogether. As such, some who would prefer to opt out altogether, if they were able, will choose to vote nevertheless. They will reason that if they are going to be forced to obey the law regardless, they might as well at least be forced to obey the laws of the party that they least dislike.

Is a vote cast under such circumstances free and uncoerced? Consider the following analogy: a man holds a gun to your head and demands either your wallet or your wristwatch. You would prefer to keep both your wallet and your wristwatch, but because you do not have that option, you choose to give him your wristwatch. Did you freely consent to give away your wristwatch? That seems unlikely. You simply chose the lesser of two evils, and there is a strong case for treating your consent as coerced and therefore ineffective. Likewise, when the state gives us a choice between being governed by this party or that, we may choose the least worst option by voting for the party that we least dislike. But if such a vote counts as consent, then it is, like the giving of the wristwatch, coerced consent. And as we saw earlier, whatever theorists may think about the influence of other forms of unfreedom on consent, everyone agrees that coerced consent is ineffective. In short then, voting cannot count as effective consent to obey the law, at least until those who do not vote are permitted to disobey the law.

Hypothetical consent and normative consent

Perhaps in contemplation of the problems that beset attempts to show that we have consented to obey the law, some thinkers, from Hobbes (1651; 1996) onwards, have adopted the alternative claim that we would, if the state did not already exist, set up a state and consent to obey its laws. This is sometimes called **hypothetical consent** (or a hypothetical contract)—consent that we *would* give in an imagined situation that does not match reality.

A key challenge for hypothetical consent theorists is to show why it matters what we *would* do rather than what we have, in fact, done. It is easy to see why our actual consent to obey the law should bind us to the law, but why should our hypothetical consent bind us to the law? The worry, as Ronald Dworkin puts it, is that '*a hypothetical contract is not simply a pale form of an actual contract; it is no contract at all*' (1977: 151).

Hypothetical consent theorists have tried to respond to this challenge in a number of different ways. Central to these responses is often the claim that, by looking at hypothetical consent, we can determine what it would be rational for us to agree to, even if we were purely self-seeking (for example, Hobbes, 1651; 1996; Gauthier, 1986). But again, one might reasonably challenge the hypothetical consent theorist to explain why we should care what it would be rational for us to do, when, in reality, we might prefer to act irrationally. If the hypothetical consent theorist replies along the lines of, 'because it is in your best interests to do what it is rational to do', then it looks like his or her argument for political authority and obligation appeals to the benefits that the state brings, rather than on the moral importance of consent.

An interesting recent development in consent theory is Estlund's idea of 'normative consent'. Estlund (2007) points out that consent to something immoral is often ineffective. He suggests that perhaps immoral refusal to consent to something can also be similarly ineffective, such that it fails to prevent the person in question from being bound to do the thing that they immorally refuse to consent to. He gives the example of a passenger on a stricken airplane who refuses to participate in a collective effort that will save many passengers if, and only if, all passengers participate in the effort. Surely, Estlund notes, the refusing passenger can be compelled to comply with the effort even though he withholds his consent to do so. Similarly, Estlund suggests, perhaps those who do not consent to obey the law can be compelled to do so, because it is wrong of them to withhold their consent to do so.

☆   **KEY POINTS**

- Consent theorists claim that we should obey the law because we have consented to do so.

- Consent theorists rely on the Lockean notion of tacit consent. Tacit consent has been interpreted in different ways, but is most usefully interpreted as consent by doing something that you would not otherwise be permitted to do, because someone has a right that you not do that thing without thereby consenting.

- Some consent theorists argue that residence in a geographical territory counts as tacit consent to obey the law. One objection to this claim is that we are not free enough to leave our country of birth for our residence to count as effective consent. Another objection suggests that residing on one's own land is not a prohibited act and cannot therefore count as tacit consent.

- Some consent theorists argue that voting in a democratic election counts as tacit consent to obey the law. But as long as those who do not vote are forced to obey the law despite their abstention, it seems reasonable to treat voting as coerced and, therefore, ineffective consent.

- Hypothetical consent theorists argue that we *would* consent to set up a state and obey the law if the state did not already exist. The difficulty for hypothetical consent theorists is to explain why it should matter morally what we would do, rather than what we have, in fact, done.

- Estlund's idea of 'normative consent' expresses the thought that sometimes one's immoral refusal to consent to something can fail to prevent one being bound to do the thing anyway.

Fairness

The theorist H. L. A. Hart argues that if we accept a benefit, then it is only fair that we should reciprocate and give something back. In the present context, if we enjoy the protection of police and armies, if we use roads, hospitals, schools, and other government-run services, then we should reciprocate by obeying the law. Not to do so would be unfairly to free ride on the efforts of others.

> [W]hen a number of persons conduct any joint enterprise according to rules and thus restrict their liberty, those who have submitted to these restrictions when required have a right to a similar submission from those who have benefited by their submission.
>
> **(Hart, 1955: 185)**

In other words, those who have willingly sacrificed their liberty, in order to make possible the benefits provided by the state, have a right to expect that the rest of us, who also receive these benefits, do the same.

An important objection to this view, first put by Nozick (1974: 90–5), denies that we can become duty-bound to reciprocate for benefits that we have not requested. Suppose that any group *could* place you under an enforceable obligation to take part in its project, simply by foisting benefits on you regardless of how much you want those benefits. This would, Nozick argues, unfairly curtail your freedom to choose in which projects to involve yourself so as best to promote those ends that you deem worth promoting.

Nozick gives the example of a neighbourhood in which some people decide to start an entertainment programme over a public address system. The initiators of the programme draw up a list of everyone in the neighbourhood, which includes you, and assign everyone a day during the year on which each person is to run the programme. No one except the organizers is asked whether they want to participate, but everyone in the neighbourhood hears the broadcasts. When your day comes, having enjoyed the entertainment programme thus far, the organizers expect you to run the programme for the day. Nozick argues that this is unfair and that you have no duty to show up. All of the pleasure that you derived from the broadcasts over the past year might still not be worth the pleasure that you would derive by spending the day doing something else. No one other than you has a right to decide how you should use your time and resources to best promote the ends that you deem worth promoting.

Of course Nozick's objection is not the end of the story. One interesting issue at stake is whether receipt of a benefit really does have to be voluntary, as Nozick suggests, in order

---

☆ KEY POINTS

- Hart argues that we have a duty of fairness to obey the law in return for the benefits that we have received from the state, made possible by our fellow citizens' obedience to the law.
- Nozick rejects the appeal to fairness, arguing that people should not be forced to participate in joint projects, when they may prefer to use their time and resources in other ways.
- Klosko argues that people can be bound to a duty of fair play by the non-voluntary receipt of something that is 'presumptively beneficial'.

to bind the recipient to a duty of fair play. Klosko (1992, 2005), for example, argues that people can be bound to such a duty by the non-voluntary receipt of something which is 'presumptively beneficial' or 'indispensible for satisfactory lives' (2005: 6), such as physical security and protection from a hostile environment.

Community

Perhaps, reading the arguments so far about why we should obey the law, you have been thinking that this whole debate about political authority and obligation is all rather bizarre. The preceding arguments seem to present us as atomized individuals with no immediate moral connection to each other that exists independently of our consent or our receipt of benefits from others. But the bottom line, you might think, is that we are all members of the same society and, as such, it is inconceivable that we do not all obey the law and uphold the authority of the state which binds us together.

If you have been thinking something like this, then you would not be alone. A number of theorists have claimed that political obligation is something that we are bound by simply because we are members of political communities. It is not important, they argue, whether or not we chose to be members of these communities. The mere fact that we are members of these communities means that we are obliged to obey their rules. This obligation is bound up with the very notion of membership; it is not an optional add-on. One theorist who has defended such an argument is Ronald Dworkin (a similar view, something of a hybrid between consent theory and the community-based justification, is suggested by Gilbert, 1993). Dworkin (1986) compares political association to other forms of association like family and friendship. The mere fact that another person is family or is a friend entails that you owe certain duties to him or her. If he or she is sick in hospital, for example, you might feel a sense of duty to visit. Likewise, argues Dworkin, the mere fact that you are a part of a political community entails that you owe certain duties to members of your community. Foremost amongst these duties, he argues, is a duty to obey the laws by which the community regulates itself.

Three main types of objection have been raised against community-based justifications for political authority and obligation (e.g. Wellman, 1997). First, it has been argued that the bonds of political community are not analogous to the bonds of family and friendship. Nation states are large diverse entities whose members lack the intimate relationships present between family and friends. As such, members of nation states cannot be held to be under the same duties of association that families and friends are under. Second, it has been argued that even though members of a political community may *feel* an obligation towards each other, this does not show that they really have such obligations. Thirdly, it has been reasoned that membership-based arguments would require us to obey the rules of any groups that we happen to be members of, regardless of what those rules require us to do. Not only would citizens of rights-respecting democracies be required to obey the law on this account, so too would citizens of oppressive states like Nazi Germany and present-day Burma (Myanmar). For all three of these reasons, then, it is doubtful whether our mere membership of a political community is sufficient to place us under an obligation to obey the law. Nevertheless, it remains possible that advocates of the view can respond to these objections. Horton (2006, 2007) has recently made a powerful attempt to do so.

☆ KEY POINTS

- Some theorists argue that mere membership of a political community can give rise to a duty to obey the law, whether or not we chose to be members of that community. Dworkin compares this duty to the associative duties which we owe to family and friends.

- One objection to this argument claims that political communities, which are much larger and more diverse than families and friendships, cannot give rise to the same kinds of associative duties as those present among families and friends.

- A second objection notes that just because members of a community may feel obligations towards each other, this does not show that they in fact have such obligations.

- If the community-based argument for political authority and obligation were correct, then it looks as though we would have to obey the law no matter how morally repugnant the laws of our country were.

Morality

Think about the law for a moment and about some of the things that it requires us to do. The law forbids us to steal, to murder, to rape, and to do a number of other things that most of us would not dream of doing anyway, even if the law were not to exist. So it looks as though much of the law simply tells us to do, or not to do, things that we already think we should or should not do out of an independent sense of right and wrong. Perhaps, then, our duty to obey the law amounts to nothing more than a duty to obey the rules of morality, which distinguish right from wrong. We do not need to consent to these rules in order to be bound by them, because we cannot opt in or out of the demands of morality.

One thing that will be immediately apparent is that this argument requires obedience only to just laws. The citizens of Nazi Germany or present-day Burma (Myanmar), for example, would not be required to obey the oppressive laws imposed by their governments. But even liberal democracies tend to do a lot more than only enforce rules that are obviously basic to morality. They also, for example, tend to tax people, tell people on what side of the road to drive, steer the economy in favour of particular outcomes, and require us to do a number of other things that are prima facie unrelated to morality. Quite which of these activities do fall beyond the remit of morality depends on what the rules of morality *are*. For example, disagreements about the roles of justice and equality in morality have implications for the permissibility of redistributive taxation. But however wide or narrow one's conception of morality, many theorists have tended to argue that morality alone cannot justify the authority that existing states claim for themselves. There is, however, one very influential and recently popular exception to this rule. According to the so-called 'natural duty' view, we have a basic moral duty— which neither requires our consent nor need be derived from some other moral starting point or our membership of a particular community— to 'support and to comply with just institutions that exist and apply to us' (Rawls, 1999: 99). If this is right, then the mere fact that just states already exist, combined with the putative duty, may seem to provide sufficient reason to obey them. One difficulty with this view, that has been widely discussed (e.g. Simmons, 1979), is whether the putative duty can justify the claim that people are especially obligated to their own states, rather than merely to support just states in general, without any particular regard to the country of their birth or residence.

The minimal state

One theorist who has famously argued for a particularly narrow conception of morality—a **libertarian** conception of morality—is Robert Nozick. In common with other libertarian theorists, but in conflict with other schools of political theory, Nozick (1974) argues that justice prohibits redistributive taxation that is aimed at promoting equality. Any government that enforces such taxation does so unjustly and illegitimately. According to Nozick, all that morality permits the state to do is to enforce basic property rights and rights against harm. A state that restricted itself to enforcing only these rights would be legitimate, but quite different from the states that currently exist. Nozick calls his imagined state a **minimal state**.

 KEY THINKERS

Robert Nozick (1938–2002)

Nozick's first and best-known work, *Anarchy, State, and Utopia* (1974), offers a rigorous defence of the justice of the free market. Written in response to his Harvard colleague John Rawls' *A Theory of Justice* (1971), Nozick's tightly argued book earned him the respect of theorists across the political spectrum, although his conclusions were vigorously contested nevertheless. He became known as a reluctant ideologue of the right, a reputation he kept even after distancing himself from his earlier views, in *The Examined Life* (1989). After completing *Anarchy, State, and Utopia*, Nozick moved away from political theory to explore other areas of philosophy, covering themes as diverse as epistemology and metaphysics, rationality, animal rights, and the meaning of life.

A Nozickean minimal state may legitimately enforce rights. But states do not only claim for themselves the authority to enforce rights; they also claim for themselves the authority, uniquely, to enforce rights and to arbitrate in disputed cases. States do not permit private police forces to run parallel systems of enforcement, with private courts and private prisons that are outside of the state's control. Can morality justify this authority— the authority of states not only to enforce rights but, uniquely, to enforce rights? In

Part 1 of *Anarchy, State, and Utopia* (1974), Nozick argues that the state may indeed act as the unique enforcer of rights, prohibiting would-be private enforcers from setting up their own independent systems of enforcement. His argument hinges on the risk that is involved in enforcing rights. Because law courts will sometimes make the wrong decision and convict innocent people, enforcement is an inherently risky business. The state, Nozick argues, is entitled to stop would-be private enforcers from taking this risk with other people's lives, provided that the state itself enforces the rights of those who are disadvantaged by this prohibition.

Nozick's argument is ingenious and persuasive. But even if it succeeds, Nozick's argument shows only that people should obey the law in so far as the law matches morality, and that the state may, uniquely, enforce the law in so far as, by doing so, it enforces morality. Nozick's argument cannot show that the state has any particular reason to expect its citizens to obey the law by virtue of the fact that the state made the law, rather than by virtue of the content of the laws. That is, Nozick's argument may be an argument for obedience to the law, but that obedience depends on the authority of morality, rather than the authority of the state to issue directives that ought to be obeyed simply because they issue from the state. See also Box 1.3.

☆ **KEY POINTS**

- Many laws tell us to do that which the basic rules of morality demand that we do anyway, independently of the law.

- States may legitimately enforce obedience to the basic rules of morality. Most theorists agree that all existing states enforce at least some laws that go beyond the basic rules of morality.

- Nozick and other libertarians argue that states may enforce only property rights and rights against harm. Nozick calls a state that performs only these functions a 'minimal state'.

- Nozick argues that states are permitted, uniquely, to enforce morality by appealing to the risk involved in enforcing rights.

BOX 1.3 PROUDHON: AN ANARCHIST VIEW OF THE STATE

To be GOVERNED is to be kept in sight, inspected, spied upon, directed, law-driven, numbered, enrolled, indoctrinated, preached at, controlled, estimated, valued, censured, commanded, by creatures who have neither the right, nor the wisdom, nor the virtue to do so . . . To be GOVERNED is to be at every operation, at every transaction, noted, registered, enrolled, taxed, stamped, measured, numbered, assessed, licensed, authorized, admonished, forbidden, reformed, corrected, punished. It is, under the pretext of public utility, and in the name of the general interest, to be placed under contribution, trained, ransomed, exploited, monopolized, extorted, squeezed, mystified, robbed; then, at the slightest resistance, the first word of complaint, to be repressed, fined, despised, harassed, tracked, abused, clubbed, disarmed, choked, imprisoned, judged, condemned, shot, deported, sacrificed, sold, betrayed; and, to crown all, mocked, ridiculed, outraged, dishonored. That is government; that is its justice; that is its morality.

(Proudhon, 1851; 1923: 293–4)

Philosophical anarchism

Some thinkers who do not accept any of the arguments canvassed earlier argue, instead, that we are not bound by a duty to obey the law. Such thinkers do not necessarily believe that we should abolish the state, because some accept that there are good prudential reasons to maintain the current order—at least for the time being. In A. J. Simmons's terms (1999), the failure of the arguments canvassed means that no states are 'legitimate', even though we might nevertheless say that some states are in a sense 'justified' by the good things that they do. This position is known as **philosophical anarchism** and was first proposed by William Godwin (1793; 1976). Of the positive arguments for philosophical anarchism—those built on reasons not to obey the law, rather than merely the absence of reasons to obey it—the most widely discussed in recent times has been the claim of R. P. Wolff (1970) that we should not obey the law because obedience to the law requires us to neglect our primary obligation to act autonomously. This obligation requires us to act on the basis of our own moral judgements about situations, and not to let the state decide right and wrong on our behalf. In order to fulfil this obligation, we must refuse to surrender any part of our autonomy to the state. Yet Wolff does not defend his claim that our primary obligation is to act autonomously, and a number of theorists have rejected the claim. So even if Wolff is right that a duty to act autonomously is incompatible with a duty to obey the law, it nevertheless remains an open question whether we should, therefore, choose autonomy over obedience to the law.

 KEY TEXTS

Wolff, *In Defense of Anarchism* (1970)

In one of the boldest and most widely read statements of philosophical anarchism, Robert Paul Wolff argues that submission to political authority is incompatible with the duty that we are all under to maintain our **moral autonomy** to the maximum degree possible. Wolff argues that unanimous direct democracy—within which everyone participates in decision making and decisions are all made by unanimous consensus—would allow us to cooperate while retaining our autonomy. He suggests, however, that such a system will be impractical, given that just one vote against a decision can defeat consensus. In the final part of his book, Wolff explores how a society that does not rely on state **coercion** could function.

Not all anarchists, of course, are as reluctant as the philosophical anarchists to put their anarchy into practice. The anarchist vision of a world that is free from state coercion has attracted revolutionaries from the nineteenth century—when the great anarchist theorists Stirner, Proudhon, Bakunin, and Kropotkin held sway—to the present day. While anarchy is often portrayed as a chaotic, violent form of society, anarchists themselves have argued that an anarchist society could be more peaceful and harmonious than a **statist society**—a society governed by a state—can ever be. The modern anarchist theorist Colin Ward (1996) goes as far as to claim that '*war is the expression of the state in its most perfect* *form: it is its finest hour'*. Anarchists have tried to lend plausibility to their vision by pointing to anarchist experiments that have been tried in various localities, such as the Paris Commune of 1871 (see Box 1.4) and the Spanish Revolution of 1936, and to ways in which many of the modes of organization that structure our lives are already largely anarchic.

 KEY CONCEPTS

Anarchy

Anarchy—literally 'without rulers'—is a society in which the state has been abolished or, more widely, in which all forms of hierarchy or oppression have been abolished. Some people associate anarchy with a utopian vision of society in which everyone lives in blissful harmony, realizing their full potential as human beings. Others associate anarchy with a dystopian vision of society, in which order breaks down, warlords come to dominate, and each person is left to fight for his or her own survival. Most anarchists adopt a more pragmatic approach, arguing that an anarchic society could work better or worse depending on how well we cope with the problems that it throws up. Either way, they argue, anarchy is a necessary prerequisite to ending the exploitation and injustice that is intrinsic to the current order.

BOX 1.4 THE PARIS COMMUNE

The Paris Commune of 1871 was a short-lived council that ran Paris in the aftermath of the Franco-Prussian war. The delegates to the council could be recalled by the electorate at any time, thereby ensuring that ultimate control over the city remained with the people of Paris. Many of the delegates were political activists steeped in anarchism or communism. The delegates quickly enacted a number of radical changes, including the right of women to vote, the separation of church and state, the postponement of debts and the abolition of interest on debts, the right of employees to take over deserted firms, and the abolition of night work in the bakeries. The Paris Commune was brought to a bloody end, just two months after its formation, with the invasion of the city by the National Army.

☆ KEY POINTS

- Philosophical anarchists argue that existing states are not legitimate, but that, for prudential reasons, we should not actually abolish the state—at least for the time being.
- Negative arguments for philosophical anarchism claim that there are no good justifications for political authority and obligation.
- Positive arguments for philosophical anarchism point to reasons not to obey the law. R. P. Wolff argues that we should not obey the law because we have a primary duty to act autonomously.
- Anarchism as a vision for society has attracted followers since the nineteenth century. Anarchists point to successful experiments with anarchy throughout history and to the role of anarchic modes of organization in everyday life.

Conclusion

We began with the question, why should we obey the law? We have looked at a range of different answers to this question, each appealing to different moral principles. Each answer tries, with varying degrees of success, to show that we should (or should not) obey the law in order to fulfil a moral principle, to do what we have consented to do, to fulfil communal obligations, or to honour duties of fairness, etc. At a minimum—whatever the merits of the other arguments canvassed, and other arguments for political authority and obligation—it seems clear that the state is justified at least in so far as it seeks to enforce morality. Such reasoning may actually serve to justify a state rather more extensive than Nozick's minimum state if, for example, one thinks that morality requires us not only to respect rights to property and bodily integrity, but also to maintain certain patterns of distribution, such as an equal opportunity for welfare. The maintenance of such a distribution seems to require the oversight of some higher authority, such as the state.

Even amongst those theorists who think that a relatively extensive state can be justified, very few would maintain that states may act however they want without overstepping the bounds of their legitimate authority. As such, we should support the state when it acts within its authority, but not be afraid to hold it to account when it goes beyond that point. This raises the question of when and how we may disobey the law when we disagree with it on moral grounds. The case study that follows looks at one particularly salient example: the case of conscientious objection to military service. **➜ See Chapter 10.**

CASE STUDY

Conscription—by Jeremy Williams

Keith Hyams' chapter introduces us to what is often referred to as the 'problem of political obligation'— the problem, that is, of explaining whether, on what grounds, and to what extent, we are under a moral duty to obey the commands of the state. That problem, however philosophically arresting, would not be of great practical significance if what the state required of us were always undemanding, and in conformity with what we want to do anyway. However, in some cases, what the state demands of us is extremely arduous, or we have strong principled objections to doing as we are told. Consider, as a prime example, compulsory military service. Even in peacetime, military service is physically and psychologically taxing, and involves loss of personal freedom and privacy. But in wartime, the burdens are heavier still, as conscripts may then be called upon to risk life and limb in the theatre of conflict, and to engage in the killing of other human beings— an activity fraught with serious moral danger, and which some people believe to be categorically morally prohibited. On what grounds, then, can states claim the right to order their citizens to serve in the military? And how should it treat those who refuse to serve on conscientious grounds? This case study examines these theoretical questions. But first, to help make them more vivid, let us examine some of the details of an existing system of compulsory military service, and the sources of resistance to it.

A large number of countries have, or have had in recent history, a system of conscription, but perhaps the best-known and most discussed contemporary example is that of Israel. (Another well-known scheme was that of Germany, but this was finally wound down in 2011, after fifty-five years.) Compulsory military service in the Israeli Defense Force is provided for by the Defense Service Law, passed in 1949, and updated in 1959 and 1986. Under this law, both men and women are eligible for conscription from the age of 18, with men typically serving three years and women, two. Women are exempt from service if married, pregnant, or mothers. In addition, and intriguingly, the law allows women, but not men, an exemption on grounds of religious observance. Further exemptions can also be granted at the discretion of the Ministry of Defense, and students enrolled in yeshivas (Jewish seminaries) benefited from such an exemption from 1948. This arrangement, later codified in the so-called *Tal Law* of 2002, was originally justified on grounds that the yeshiva students were, like those undertaking military service, making an important contribution to the survival of the Jewish people (in their case, by rebuilding Jewish religious heritage after the Holocaust). But the exemption was widely resented as unfair, subject to legal challenges, and finally overturned by the High Court of Justice in 2012, on grounds of incompatibility with the principle of equality enshrined in Israel's Basic Law (Ettinger and Cohen, 2012). At the time of writing this, a new law to resolve the issue is under discussion, but has yet to be adopted.

Unauthorized conscientious refusal is a perennially controversial issue in Israel, and is often punished with court marshals and imprisonment. There are two kinds of 'refuseniks'— those who refuse military service altogether, and those who enrol, but selectively refuse to follow particular orders, or to fight in particular wars. Among the latter group are two prominent movements— 'Yesh Gvul' (meaning 'there is a limit'), which was founded in 1982 by soldiers who refused to participate in the Israeli invasion of Lebanon, and 'Courage to Refuse', formed in 2002 by soldiers refusing to serve in the occupied Palestinian territories. Among those who advocate wholesale refusal to serve, meanwhile, are the 'Shministim' (literally 'twelfth graders'), a group comprised of high-school students and leavers. Perhaps the most high-profile case of conscientious refusal involving this group was that of Yoni Ben Artzi, nephew of current Israeli Prime Minister Binyamin Netanyahu. Ben Artzi declared a belief in pacifism when called up, but was informed he had already been conscripted and subjected to a court marshal. Between 2002 and 2004, he served a total of 18 months in a military prison (a record for a conscientious refuser). Astonishingly, when his case was heard by a 'conscience committee' composed of military officers, he was told that he could not be a real pacifist because his dogged determination not to serve was evidence of his promise as a soldier (McGreal, 2009).

We shall return to the question of how states ought to respond to conscientious objectors later on. But first, let us consider on what grounds citizens might be thought to be obligated to perform military service if required by their government to do so.

The case for compulsory military service

The most straightforward argument in favour of a moral obligation to accept the draft appeals to the necessity of each citizen's contribution towards defending the nation against urgent threats to its survival or freedom. In a survey of the justifications adduced by states themselves in favour of their imposition of a legal duty of military service upon their citizens, George Klosko (2005: 169–78) has observed that this rationale has played an important recurring role in various decisions concerning conscription handed down by the Israeli Supreme Court. In justifying the obligation to serve, and rejecting rights of conscientious refusal, the Court's reasoning has often relied on what one justice quoted by Klosko (2005: 173) calls 'the hard security situation of the state of Israel', which 'does not resemble the security situation of other countries living in peace within their borders.' Israel, as the Court has seen it, is small and exposed to constant threats; thus, whereas other countries might be adequately protected by an all-volunteer military, Israel's security would be unacceptably compromised in the absence of conscription.

These are contested claims, and it falls outside the scope of this case study to consider whether the descriptive claim that Israeli national security could not be maintained in the absence of conscription is true. Even if it is, the same cannot be said of many other countries. In their case, then, any argument for a moral duty to perform military service would have to rest on other grounds. Consider, therefore, in that light, the *principle of fairness* which, according to Klosko (2005: 141–80), has underpinned judicial decisions regarding conscription in Germany and the United States (as well as, increasingly, in Israel). As we have seen in this chapter, the principle of fairness holds that, when our fellow citizens make sacrifices to provide important public goods, from which we derive benefit, we are under an obligation, in turn, to make similar sacrifices, thereby contributing fairly to the maintenance of these goods. Now, supposing the pre-eminent public good which citizens in well-run states enjoy is security. The principle of fairness might accordingly be taken to imply that, having benefited from the good of security, as provided by those who have already undertaken, or are currently engaged in, military service, each citizen is obligated to make a reciprocal contribution to the national defence. Notice that the fairness-based argument for compulsory military service does not rest on the claim that the provision of the good of national security cannot be continued if some refuse to help. Rather, it holds that, irrespective of whether future provision of the good would be jeopardized, 'free-riding' on others' efforts is wrong.

The foregoing arguments, based on national security and fairness, probably represent the most frequently invoked justifications for the moral obligation to undertake military service, though they are not the only ones. Rather than surveying other available arguments, however, the remainder of this case study addresses a different though closely related issue—namely that of the moral and legal status of conscientious refusal.

Conscientious objection

Although the focus of this case study is conscription, countries must obviously grapple with the issue of conscientious objection, whether they organize their militaries on a compulsory or a voluntary basis. The difference is that, whereas regimes with all-volunteer forces face only selective conscientious refusals by soldiers to obey particular orders, regimes with conscription also face conscientious refusals to enlist in the first place. Now, one might think that, if there is indeed a moral duty to perform military service— whether justified on grounds of the urgency of a country's security needs, fairness in the distribution of the burdens of providing the good of national security, or, in the case of volunteers, contractual agreement to serve— then conscientious objectors must lack a moral right to disobey, and ought indeed to be punished for doing so. But that would be too quick. For even if a duty to serve can be justified on one or other of the aforementioned grounds, that is compatible with saying that the duty is qualified or overridden in some cases, as well as with saying that disobedience should be legally tolerated.

There in fact exist certain cases in which, as a matter of international humanitarian law, soldiers have not only a right but a legal obligation to refuse to obey orders. These are cases in which the order is 'manifestly unlawful', such as, paradigmatically, the order to open fire on unarmed civilians. Not all orders that might be opposed as morally wrong are unlawful, however. Thus, the question is whether these legal provisions go far enough. A powerful argument to the effect that they do not comes from the just war theorist Jeff McMahan (2009, 2013). As we will see in more detail in Chapter 10, McMahan is part of a growing group within the literature on the ethics of war who believe (as do many conscientious objectors) that, when a country goes to war unjustly, those who should be considered to have acted wrongly include not only the political leaders who authorized the war, but also the individual soldiers who followed the order to fight in it. McMahan does not contend that it would be feasible or desirable to make fighting in an unjust war illegal. He does argue, however, that enlistees have an urgent moral responsibility to evaluate for themselves whether the war in which they are being called upon to fight is just, rather than simply deferring to the moral judgement of the state. Owing to McMahan's emphasis on the individual moral responsibility of soldiers for the wars in which they fight, he is a strong advocate of legal protections for conscientious refusers. However, as he acknowledges, difficult problems arise when it comes to the question of the precise shape which those protections should take.

At the heart of these problems is the following dilemma. On the one hand, McMahan's concern is to ensure that the costs of disobeying orders are not so severe that the path of least resistance is blind, unreflective obedience to the state. But on the other hand, if disobedience is made too easy, we are at risk of enabling not only well-considered conscientious refusals, but also disobedience on insincere, self-interested grounds. In the worst-case scenario, such disobedience may even jeopardize our ability to prosecute a just war (for instance, the humanitarian rescue of a distant people whom citizens lack a strong motivation to save). As a way of striking a balance between these competing considerations, McMahan proposes a legal right of conscientious refusal that is qualified in two ways. First, it will be granted only to those whose objections can be seen to meet a certain threshold of plausibility and good reasoning. And second, it will have some (non-punitive) penalty attached, as a test of the objector's sincerity, such as an obligation to perform an undesirable public service unrelated to the war effort, or to repay some of the investment made in his or her training by taxpayers.

McMahan's defence of a qualified right of conscientious refusal will no doubt fail to please everyone. For instance, some people believe that the values of human dignity or autonomy require that people have very wide rights to abide by the determinations of their consciences, irrespective of what we might make of the plausibility of their convictions. Such people are likely to think that rights of refusal should be extended to all soldiers with sincere objections, and not only those who can be judged to have reasoned well. Others, conversely, will predictably argue that McMahan's suggestion still gives too much discretion to soldiers, and that the right and responsibility for deciding whether a war is just, or ought be fought, lies not with individual combatants, consulting their private ethical standards, but with the community as a whole, acting through their democratic institutions (see e.g., Dunlap, 2013). Even on McMahan's own assessment, his proposal involves a morally regrettable trade-off, since the penalties imposed for refusing to obey would be an injustice to those whose objections to fighting in some war are well-founded.

Leaving the specific details of McMahan's position on conscientious refusal to one side, however, the wider point on which to conclude is that balancing the need for military discipline and cohesion with the need to encourage moral reflectiveness and vigilance about the ethical use of military force is no easy task, even for those who are genuinely concerned (as many states of course are not) with getting that balance right.

? QUESTIONS

1. How can we most usefully interpret the consent theorist's distinction between 'express consent' and 'tacit consent'?

2. Why did Hume disagree with Locke's claim that residence in a country counts as consent to obey its laws? Do you find Hume's objection convincing?

3. Why might we doubt whether voting in a democratic election counts as consent to obey the law?

4. What are the arguments for and against a 'duty of fairness' to obey the law? Who do you think is right in this debate?

5. In what ways are the bonds of political community akin to the bonds of friendship and family, and in what ways are they different? To what extent do you think these descriptive similarities and/or differences ground normative similarities and/or differences in the nature of our associative duties in each case?

6. What is a Nozickean 'minimal state'? Do you think that Nozick is right to assert that any state more expansive than a minimal state is illegitimate?

7. What is 'philosophical anarchism' and what arguments have been given for it?

8. How should the state treat those who conscientiously object to military service?

9. Should captured enemy conscripts be punished if they have fought on the wrong side in an unjust war?

FURTHER READING

■ Knowles, D. (2010) *Political Obligation: A Critical Introduction*, New York: Routledge A clear and helpful introduction to the key arguments for and against political obligation which provides more details on many of the arguments discussed in this chapter.

■ Locke, J. (1690; 1924) *Two Treatises of Government*, London: Dent and Sons The second treatise contains one of the most important classical statements of consent theory in which Locke introduces the notion of tacit consent.

■ Rawls, J. (1964) 'Legal obligation and the duty of fair play', in S. Hook (ed.) *Law and Philosophy*, New York: New York University Press, pp. 3–18 In this article, Rawls develops the fairness argument for legal obligation, first proposed by Hart (1955). Rawls later rejected this position in *A Theory of Justice* (1971).

■ Simmons, A. J. (1979) *Moral Principles and Political Obligations*, Princeton, NJ: Princeton University Press A comprehensive review and rejection by a philosophical anarchist of all of the historical arguments for political obligation.

■ Ward, C. (1996) *Anarchy in Action*, London: Freedom Press A thought-provoking exploration of the anarchy that surrounds us in our daily lives.

⊕ WEB LINKS

● http://www.freewestpapua.org The website of the UK campaign for a Free West Papua, supported by a network of international parliamentarians, which includes information about the 'Act of Free Choice' and alleged human rights abuses in West Papua.

- http://plato.stanford.edu/entries/political-obligation and http://plato.stanford.edu/entries/legitimacy *The Stanford Encyclopedia of Philosophy* entries on political obligation and legitimacy, which provide helpful summaries of the main arguments for political obligation and legitimacy in more depth than the present chapter.

- http://www.infoshop.org An anarchist information source, including the 'Anarchist FAQ Webpage', which will tell you everything you ever wanted to know about anarchism, and more.

- http://www.refusersolidarity.net The website of the Israeli Refuser Solidarity Network, which provides more information about the various refusnik organizations in Israel and the motivations of the conscientious objectors.

 Visit the Online Resource Centre that accompanies this book to access more learning resources: http://www.oxfordtextbooks.co.uk/orc/mckinnon3e/

2

Liberty

JONATHAN RILEY

Reader's guide

Liberty is a central moral and political ideal in advanced societies. Purely descriptive concepts of liberty must be distinguished from normative concepts. Hobbes provided a valid descriptive concept of liberty as doing as one wishes. A normative ideal of liberty must specify the areas of conduct in which an individual has rights to do as he or she wishes as a member of a given civil society. Civil liberty consists, in the abstract, of a set of civil rights, yet ethical disagreement persists over the specific content of the rights and their relative weights in cases of conflict, with important implications for other values. Mill argued that civil liberty or security must always include a basic right to do whatever one wishes, in relation to a natural domain of 'purely self-regarding' conduct. Civil libertarians should take seriously the Millian ideal of a constitutional democracy that recognizes the basic right of the individual to absolute self-regarding liberty.

Introduction

Individual **liberty**—that is, freedom of action, in some sense—is a central moral and political ideal in advanced societies such as the USA and the UK. But it means different things to different people and even to the same person. Distinct concepts need to be distinguished so as to avoid needless confusion. A distinction of particular importance is that between purely **descriptive** concepts, which purport only to describe or explain what individual liberty *is*, and **normative** concepts of individual liberty, which imply answers to normative or ethical questions such as:

- How much liberty, in a descriptive sense, *ought* to be permitted to members of a **civil society** by its code of laws?
- *Should* each member be permitted a like amount of liberty, in a descriptive sense?
- In relation to which acts and omissions *ought* an individual to have such liberty?

A purely descriptive concept of liberty cannot be of any normative significance on its own. But a normative concept must, at least implicitly, build on a valid descriptive concept by combining it with a normative theory of the importance, or value, of liberty in any given social situation. Hobbes (1651; 1994) provided a valid descriptive concept of liberty: doing as one wishes in relation to any given set of acts and omissions that are feasible for one to perform. As he puts it in Chapter 21 of *Leviathan*: '*A free man, is he, that in those things, which by his strength and wit he is able to do, is not hindered to do what he has a will to.*'

By itself, this Hobbesian concept has no normative appeal. It does not presuppose that the individual is rational in any sense, although Hobbes takes for granted that any living creature has an instinct for self-preservation. It does not presuppose that the individual has any right to perform the acts or omissions that he or she chooses to perform. It does not presuppose that the individual observes any moral or legal rules in interactions with other members of society. Threats and coercive offers are compatible with liberty in this sense, provided that the individual does what he or she wants to do (perhaps foolishly) under the circumstances. Laws backed up with credible threats of punishment are compatible with

---

✍ KEY TEXTS

Thomas Hobbes, *Leviathan* (1651)

This provocative work maintains that absolute monarchy is justified in terms of **social contract** theory. Although his idea of liberty, as doing as one wishes without any ethical limitations on the goals pursued, is a valid descriptive concept, Hobbes effectively has no normative concept of **civil liberty**, because he argues that the individual subject has no **claim rights** against the legal sovereign—that legal body or 'artificial person' (whether a king, council, or assembly) that has been established by national consent to rule the commonwealth. The sovereign's **authority** is absolute, indivisible, and permanent. This power, although supposed to be used to promote the **security** of the commonwealth, may be abused with impunity by those actual humans who occupy the office of the sovereign.

it, although the individual will choose to comply with the law (and recognize no liberty to break it) only if he or she foresees, and wishes to avoid, the punishment, which may include imprisonment and fines, each of which would significantly diminish the liberty to do what he or she wishes in the future. Moreover, an individual can have liberty in Hobbes' sense even when living under despotism, as long as the despot does not forcibly prevent that individual from doing as he or she desires, despite the fact that the desires and judgements may have adapted to the conditions of despotism and even to direct threats by the despot.

This chapter will explore the normative dimensions of liberty by relating the descriptive concept to normative theories of civil and **political liberty**, as well as security, defended by key thinkers in historical and contemporary debates.

Liberty and rights

To address normative issues of where, when, why, how much, and to whom liberty *should* be assigned, it is essential to talk about moral and legal rights. I am committed to a distinctive version of the interest theory of rights, according to which rights are moral or legal claims on society to protect or secure the individual's vital interests, including a vital interest in liberty and **individuality** as well as a vital interest in fulfilling the special duties of any political office or social role that he or she occupies. Rights thus conceived imply correlative duties for other people to respect the claims, although individuals also have duties that do not correlate to rights. Moreover, these claims may be combined with privileges, powers, and/or immunities and, thereby, appear as complex entitlements. Such an interest theory subsumes a suitably restricted version of the choice theory of rights, according to which any right must be a claim combined with powers to enforce or waive the correlative duties. The rights and duties that are recognized and distributed to an individual by his or her society may be said to constitute his or her civil liberty—that is, freedom of action in accord with a code of justice—within that society.

An individual's civil liberty consists, in the abstract, of a set of recognized rights and duties. This idea of liberty is normative, because it implicitly relies on a legal or moral theory of rights and duties. But disagreement persists over the most appealing legal or moral theory, with important implications for the content of rights and duties, relative priorities among them in cases of conflict, and, thus, the legitimate scope of liberty in the descriptive sense. Despite such disagreement, civil **libertarians** have long agreed that civil liberty involves obedience to social rules of justice that distribute rights and duties, including certain basic rights—**human rights** or **natural rights**—which are held to be virtually sacred and due equally to all human beings.

Locke, for example, extolled civil liberty in his *Second Treatise of Government* (1690; 1980), which itself reflected what was already received wisdom among lovers of liberty in seventeenth-century England. As he explains:

> [W]here there is no law, there is no freedom . . . freedom is not, as we are told [by Filmer and Hobbes], a liberty for every man to do what he lists . . . but a liberty to dispose, and

KEY CONCEPTS

Rights

As US legal scholar Wesley Hohfeld pointed out (1919), the term 'rights' is commonly used to refer to four distinct types of legal (and, by analogy, moral) position.

- **Claim rights** are claims on society to protect vital individual interests and imply correlative duties for other people.
- **Liberty rights**, or privileges, are permissions to do something, in so far as the individual has no duty to refrain from doing it.
- **Power rights** are abilities to create, exercise, or alter claims or any other types of right.
- **Immunity rights** protect existing claims and other rights, and imply that others have no powers to abolish, exercise, or alter the individual's rights.

Legal (and moral) codes may combine the simple rights into more or less complex rights.

As Hohfeld also suggested, it would be convenient to restrict the term 'rights' to claims and complex entitlements that include claims. But a satisfactory version of the interest theory must, I believe, reject Hohfeld's thesis that duties are always correlative with claims. Even ignoring duties of charity, there are so-called absolute duties (such as the duty to pay one's fair share of taxes) that do not correlate with any individual's claims. I also reject Matthew Kramer's view (1998) that Hohfeld's 'correlativity thesis' can be rescued by introducing the claims of irreducible groups such as society as a whole. Moreover, unlike Hillel Steiner (1998), I agree with H. L. A. Hart (1982) that the choice theory is, properly, of restricted scope.

order as he lists, his person, actions, possessions, and his whole property, within the allowance of those laws under which he is, and therein not to be subject to the arbitrary will of another, but freely follow his own.

(Locke, 1690: para. 57)

He makes clear, in paragraphs 6 and 22, that civil liberty under government is no different in this respect from natural liberty in a **state of nature**: civil liberty depends on positive laws that distribute legal rights and duties enacted with the consent of the citizens, whereas natural liberty depends on laws of nature that distribute basic rights and duties, which can apparently be discerned in outline (although not in concrete detail) by any individual capable of reflection. According to Locke's **contract theory**, civil liberty must harmonize with natural liberty: legal rights must help to clarify basic natural rights by declaring their concrete meaning within that particular community. Government is required to enact and enforce laws that distribute such legal rights, so as better to preserve and secure basic rights. Otherwise, reasonable individuals would never consent to live in a civil society under government.

Locke's moral and political theory, which grounds civil rights on natural rights that any rational person can apprehend, is not incontestable. Various alternative theories are available, including Mill's **utilitarianism** (1861; 1969; civil rights ought to be grounded on the general welfare), for example, or Berlin's **ethical pluralism** (1969; civil rights must be based on plural irreducible values that may conflict), or Rawls' political liberalism (2005; civil rights ought to be based on a liberal theory of justice that can be discerned by rational persons willing to cooperate in a fair process of deliberation). These, too, are open to objections. But these various theories do agree that civil liberty consists, in the abstract, of a set of rights and duties, some of which are viewed as morally basic in so far as any society that does not recognize and enforce them is classified as indecent and unfit for human beings. Moreover, it is worth emphasizing that, for any given theory of rights and duties, civil liberty is equivalent to the restriction of liberty, in the purely descriptive Hobbesian sense, to a suitable domain of conduct that the given theory regards as rightful or permissible. Civil liberty is choosing as one likes among whatever acts and omissions are permitted by one's rights and duties. If society recognizes property rights, for example, then any owners can use their property as they wish, in accord with their rights, provided that they fulfil their duties to others. Given that an individual is said to be fully reasonable if, and only if, he or she complies with standing rules of justice, civil liberty is doing only as such a rational and fair cooperator would wish. As Locke puts it:

> The freedom then of man, and liberty of acting according to his own will, is grounded on his having reason, which is able to instruct him in that law he is to govern himself by, and make him know how far he is left to the freedom of his own will.

(Locke, 1690: para. 63)

Such a reasonable individual obeys reasonable rules and values a like liberty—at least some more or less sacred core of liberty associated with basic rights—for his or her fellow citizens.

 KEY TEXTS

Locke, *Second Treatise of Government* (1690)

Locke's great treatise presents a social contract theory that, among other things, justifies people's moral right to revolt actively against 'despotical' and unjust government. This Lockean social contract theory had clearly been in the air throughout the civil wars. Americans appealed frequently to the *Second Treatise* to justify their revolutionary War of Independence from Britain, declared in 1776. James Madison, perhaps the most brilliant defender of the US Constitution of 1787, argued late in life that the American federal union should ultimately be understood as a federal version of Locke's contract theory (Madison, 1981).

☆ KEY POINTS

- The Hobbesian idea of liberty, by itself, has no normative significance, but rather must be situated within a moral and political theory of rights and duties to take on any normative value.
- Civil libertarians generally agree that civil liberty consists, in the abstract, of a set of rights and duties, including basic rights that are due equally to all human beings.
- There are many competing moral and political theories, including that of Locke.

Negative and positive liberty

Isaiah Berlin (1969: xxxvii–lxiii, 118–72) has drawn an influential—but ultimately unpersuasive—distinction between two concepts of liberty that he calls, respectively, negative liberty and positive liberty (see Box 2.1).

- Negative liberty is freedom from coercive interference by others in relation to some area or domain of personal conduct. Others must not deny the individual, either directly or by means of institutional practices, opportunities to choose acts or omissions within the relevant domain.

- Positive liberty is freedom to be one's own master. It involves '*a wish to be the instrument of my own, not of other men's, acts of will*' (Berlin, 1969: 131). The individual must exercise his or her will to choose acts and omissions in personal life and in the public arena, in which self-government means '*to have a voice in the laws and practices of the society in which one lives*' (Berlin, 1969: lx).

Remarkably, Berlin initially depicted the purely descriptive Hobbesian idea as negative liberty, and attributed it to Bentham and Mill, as well as to Hobbes. Yet the Hobbesian idea of a man doing '*what he has a will to*' seems to correspond to positive liberty. Moreover, positive liberty evidently implies negative liberty in the Hobbesian sense: if an individual does as he or she wishes, then that implies that others are not preventing that individual from choosing acts and omissions as he or she wishes in relation to some domain of conduct, however limited.

 KEY THINKERS

Isaiah Berlin (1909–97)

Berlin was a renowned historian of political thought, who was a professor at Oxford University for most of his life and is perhaps best known for his doctrine of value pluralism, according to which there are plural and (at times) incommensurable basic values, which may conflict in ways that do not admit of any universal rational resolution. He suggested that liberty is extremely valuable, because it enables the individual to choose among the plural conflicting values, although controversy exists as to whether value pluralism can consistently privilege liberty over other values. Even Berlin expressed doubts that his pluralism and liberalism were logically connected.

Berlin subsequently admitted that the Hobbesian idea was not really what he meant by negative liberty. He altered negative liberty so that it no longer depends on whether the individual wishes to do anything: '*For if to be free—negatively—is simply not to be prevented by other persons from doing whatever one wishes, then one of the ways of attaining such freedom is by extinguishing one's wishes*' (Berlin, 1969: xxxviii). Negative liberty, in Berlin's sense, is to be free from coercive interference with respect to a field of actions, so that one can potentially choose any of them, independently of whether one wishes to act at the moment or would rather do nothing.

But Berlin's revisionist move is not persuasive. It is false that one attains freedom to do an act as one wishes by extinguishing one's wish to do the act. Instead, one attains freedom to do something else as one wishes, which may merely be to forbear from acting rather than to choose another act. Moreover, a descriptive concept does not involve any evaluation of the individual's wishes. Perhaps one ought to wish to perform a given act or omission, and perhaps one ought not to eliminate or alter that wish, according to this or that normative theory. But this is irrelevant to the issue of whether one does, in fact, have liberty in the Hobbesian sense with respect to the given act or omission.

Some may insist that an individual might have negative liberty if he or she has no will-power to do anything and lacks even a wish to avoid being the instrument of '*other men's acts of will*'. As Hobbes suggests, however, it seems nonsensical to predicate liberty of anything that lacks any power to do anything. It is only because the river has the power to overflow its banks that the banks are said to constrain its liberty: if it were to lack the power, the banks could not be said to interfere with its freedom. Similarly, others could not properly be said to interfere with the liberty of an individual if he or she had no wish to choose any acts or omissions. There would be no need for others to prevent the individual from doing anything if he or she already lacked the will to do anything. Further, others could never *force* the individual to do anything against his or her will, because there is nothing that he or she wishes to do.

The odd implication of Berlin's revised notion of negative liberty—namely, that an individual who, like a stone, has no vitality to do anything, might still be said to possess such liberty—can be removed by insisting that an individual's wish to overcome coercive interference by others is a constituent element of negative freedom. Even Berlin admits that negative liberty presupposes that one '*wants to remove the yoke*' (1969: xliii, note). He also emphasizes that one may not wish to perform any further acts once the interference is removed. This merely implies, however, that one wishes to omit these further acts. But, then, negative liberty and positive liberty would be the same thing, given that coercive interference by others is a necessary condition for any loss of positive freedom through, say, fraud or brainwashing. A wish to determine one's own actions is a wish for others not to prevent one from choosing as one wants with respect to some domain of acts and omissions. An individual attains freedom if, and only if, he or she does as he or she wishes. If the individual does as he or she wishes, then it follows that others are not preventing that individual from doing as he or she wants.

By combining Berlin's two concepts into a single descriptive concept of liberty in this way, we have arrived back at the Hobbesian idea of liberty. The Hobbesian idea is not properly characterized as 'pure negative freedom' because, even if others are not hindering the individual from doing '*what he has a will to*', that individual is not properly said to be free unless he or she is an **agent**—that is, the sort of being who has a will (although not necessarily a rational will) to do something. Liberty, in Hobbes' sense, is simultaneously positive and negative in Berlin's senses.

Berlin is highly critical of certain normative concepts of liberty, such as those of Locke, Rousseau, and Kant, and even suggests that they illustrate the way in which positive liberty can be abused: a higher 'rational' and 'moral' self dictates to the lower 'empirical' self that 'true freedom' consists in obedience to certain universal 'rational laws' that alone are held to promote '*a man's "proper interests" or "general good"*' (Berlin, 1969: 147). Yet Berlin also adopts an idea of civil liberty, making reference to rights when discussing where and to whom liberty has *value*. His main complaint against Locke, Rousseau, Kant, and other so-called rationalists (including even Mill) seems to be that they failed to appreciate

BOX 2.1   ARE BERLIN'S TWO CONCEPTS NORMATIVE?

Berlin may have intended his two concepts to be normative rather than purely descriptive concepts of liberty, although his various ambiguities and inconsistencies make it impossible to be sure. He insisted that '*both are ends in themselves*' (Berlin, 1969: xlix). Moreover, in recorded conversations late in his life, he emphasized that both are 'political' ideas that presuppose a 'basic sense' of freedom as the capacity to make choices, said to be essential to humanity because its absence would reduce us to robots to whom the political concepts are inapplicable. Awareness of one's basic capacity to choose might serve as a third (purely descriptive) concept of liberty in Berlin's thought.

Consistent with this, he seems, at times, to depict negative liberty in terms of rights not to be obstructed by others with respect to some personal sphere of conduct, such as the sphere carved out by one's property rights. Thus, he asserts that 'basic human rights' are '*always a "negative" notion: a wall against oppressors*' (Berlin, 1969: xlv), and explains that '*If, although I enjoy the right to walk through open doors, I prefer not to do so, but to sit still and vegetate, I am not thereby rendered less free*' (Berlin, 1969: xlii). Negative liberty in this sense may amount to no more than a claim to be left alone, with correlative duties for others not to invade the individual's protected sphere. But it presupposes and builds upon the basic capacity to make choices. Given such a capacity, the individual or a proxy, logically, must choose whether to act or to refrain from acting within the protected sphere, and he or she also must choose whether to enforce or waive others' correlative duties.

Similarly, perhaps positive liberty is properly understood in terms of rights to make one's own choices without any essential reference to a personal sphere of conduct. Such rights can be spelled out in various ways: for example, rights to be given the resources needed to do as one wishes, or rights to be autonomous in accord with certain social norms of rationality and/or morality built into the rights, or rights to participate with others in democratic public decision-making procedures that establish general laws. Berlin appears unsympathetic to the first and second kinds of rights, but he seems to accept the third kind as a conception of positive liberty.

This normative interpretation allows that the distinct rights associated with Berlin's two concepts may come into conflict. Moreover, it is compatible with his thesis that positive liberty was historically perverted into its opposite: the individual's right to self-government was ultimately transferred, via the rationalistic fiction of an ideal moral self, to an oppressive state that claimed authority, in the name of this higher self, to force actual individuals to be truly free. Indeed, as Berlin admits, negative liberty might also be perverted into its opposite, even if (as he thinks) this has not yet happened: the individual's right to be left alone might be unduly extended to protect too much conduct, so that an elite is empowered to accumulate vast wealth and oppress the impoverished masses.

that universal 'rational laws' are fictitious, given the truth of his own normative theory—namely, value pluralism. But he does not dispute that any civil society must establish a code of justice, perhaps unique to the particular society, which most citizens comply with even if only out of fear of punishment. He agrees that an idea of civil liberty must be spelled out in terms of rights and duties distributed by the code, as long as the idea of freedom does not incorporate what he considers fake or rationalistic claims about the power of reason to produce singular solutions to all conflicts of values (Berlin, 1969: 153–4, n. 1). Indeed, he even insists—along with Locke and the others—that some core set of basic rights must be recognized and enforced within any society before that society can be viewed as decent for human beings. The core set of rights is a central component of a common moral horizon: a '*minimum of common moral ground*' that may gradually evolve to some extent over time, but which is essential to enable human beings to '*communicate across great distances in space and time and culture*' (Berlin, 1969: xxxii). Berlin is fairly vague about the nature of the basic human rights in the common core. Moreover, he does not maintain that this common core of liberty is '*inviolable . . . in some absolute sense*': even basic human rights '*may have to be disregarded*' to avert some terrible outcomes in 'wholly abnormal' situations, '*emergencies so critical that the choice is between great evils*' (Berlin, 1969: lx–lxi). But, in normal circumstances, the core rights are regarded as 'sacred' by decent human beings (Berlin, 1969: lxi).[1] ➡ **See Chapter 8**.

If liberty in the Hobbesian sense is a valid descriptive concept, then Berlin's emphasis on intractable conflicts between negative and positive liberty does not reflect any fundamental division in the idea of what liberty is. Rather, his emphasis flows from his contestable normative theory, which assigns plural and, at times, incommensurable values to liberty—doing as one wishes—in different situations. Different values are embodied in different rights, and incommensurability implies that a universal rational resolution cannot be expected if the relevant rights come into conflict. But the conflicts have nothing to do with two different descriptive concepts of liberty.

⭐ **KEY POINTS**

- Hobbes' descriptive concept of liberty remains valid, in spite of Berlin's distinction between negative and positive liberty.
- Despite his ethical pluralism, Berlin agrees with Locke and others that civil liberty consists of rights and duties, including a 'sacred' core of basic rights, which are distributed by rules of justice.
- Given the validity of the Hobbesian idea of liberty, conflicts of rights—however difficult to resolve—do not involve clashes of negative and positive liberty in any descriptive sense.

Civil liberty and political liberty

An individual's civil liberty depends on his or her social and legal status. Those who have the status of equal citizen possess the full complement of rights, comprising full civil liberty within the society of which they are members. In an egalitarian democratic society, almost all adults may be equal citizens, but in hierarchical societies, there may be different grades of citizenship and some people may even be treated as slaves, lacking civil liberty altogether. Moreover, in every society, an individual may forfeit even his or her basic rights as punishment for violating those of others. In any case, an individual exercises his or her civil liberty by complying with laws and conventions of justice that distribute the rights and correlative obligations to the members of society. The individual is not free to do as he or she wishes independently of society's code of justice—freedom in that sense is condemned as 'licence'. Rather, the individual is free to do only what the code permits him or her to do, and nobody in a constitutional state has what Locke calls 'absolute, arbitrary' power to dictate the laws and conventions of the code (1690: Chap. 15). ➡ **See Chapter 1.**

This immediately raises the question: who should have the authority to make the rules of justice for society? Aside from a few mad anarchists, no thinkers deny that leaders must be entrusted with political power to enact, interpret, and enforce general laws for regulating the affairs of the community. But what is political power and how is it reasonably distinguished from 'absolute, arbitrary' power? Locke's justly celebrated answer is that political power is power that is conveyed to leaders by the rational consent of fellow citizens, for the limited purpose of securing the basic rights of everyone in the community—that is, for the purpose of preserving their property, in Locke's broad sense. Any reflective person is supposed to be able to discern these basic rights in the abstract (although not in concrete detail), independently of government. Political power is the power to create and sanction public laws that, by distributing *legal* rights, help to clarify how the underlying basic moral rights are understood in concrete detail, to confirm which rights take priority in cases of conflict, and to establish how claims are combined with liberties, powers, and immunities to give effect to complex rights, etc. in that particular community. This helps to secure the basic rights of the citizens and thereby promotes a fundamentally important aspect of their common good. In contrast, 'absolute, arbitrary' power is power that ignores and violates basic rights, and this 'despotical' power cannot be conveyed by rational consent. Absolute, arbitrary power is thus an abuse of genuine political power, and the despot cannot be a genuine political leader.

Political power, although limited, includes power to compel any recalcitrant individual to comply with laws of justice, as well as power to inflict duly severe punishment on anyone for breaking those laws and thereby violating another's rights. Nobody's civil liberty includes a right to violate others' rights. The recalcitrant individual is legitimately forced to conform to laws of justice so that fellow citizens and resident aliens might be secure in the enjoyment of their respective rights. Such enforcement of the laws is deemed reasonable in the name of civil freedom itself, given that the laws impartially distribute rights and duties, and are grounded in rational consent. Rights' violators may well forfeit their own rights as punishment. ➡ **See Chapter 4.**

Berlin says little about what he considers to be reasonable forms of political processes. Given his endorsement of basic human rights, however, he cannot reasonably reject Locke's view of political power: no civil libertarian can. Like Locke, Berlin does not require **democracy** for a decent society: the full array of political rights needed for democracy is not included among the basic human rights of the common moral minimum. The basic rights do include the rights of free speech and association that are essential to democratic politics, but non-democratic forms of government can also recognize these basic rights. Civil libertarians generally agree that democracy, although perhaps the best form of government under certain conditions, is non-basic—that is, not required for a decent society.

To secure basic rights that protect vital interests of the individual, civil libertarians also generally accept that suitable constitutional checks and balances should harness even democratic procedures, and Berlin is no exception. He makes clear that a system of checks and balances is needed to prevent a great concentration of political power in the same hands (Berlin, 1969: lxii).

Without further argument, it may be taken for granted that some form of constitutional democracy effectively channels and reveals genuine political power in contrast with 'absolute, arbitrary' power. Any of myriad different systems of checks might be combined with democratic procedures to yield a constitutional democracy. Indeed, many different checking systems have historically been tried, including those of ancient Athens, modern Britain, the USA, and France. In any case, civil libertarians can turn to a long tradition of constitutionalism for insights into the design of a liberal democratic political procedure that may effectively secure basic rights (Gordon, 1999).

Some commentators—notably Philip Pettit (1997) and Quentin Skinner (1998)—suggest that 'liberals', and especially utilitarian liberals, have failed to appreciate a 'neo-Roman' or 'republican' conception of freedom as non-domination, according to which the mere presence of 'absolute, arbitrary' power is sufficient for unfreedom, even if the despot never actually employs coercive interference or threatens to do so. Unless liberals are defined oddly so as to exclude leading civil libertarians such as Locke, Madison, Mill, Rawls, and Berlin, however, the argument is unpersuasive. In the first place, given that 'absolute, arbitrary' power is defined as power to ignore or violate basic rights, its mere presence is incompatible with civil liberty, whether or not the despot desires, at this or that moment, to exercise it. The despot does not need actually to threaten unjust coercive interference against others' rights on any particular occasion, because the power itself *means* that such a threat to civil liberty is in play.

In the second place, neither Locke nor the others traditionally viewed as liberals accept the normative claim that civil liberty is compatible with despotism as long as the despot does not actually use force to prevent the individual from doing as he or she wishes in Hobbes' purely descriptive sense. Unlike Hobbes, these liberals conceive of civil liberty in terms of basic rights that correlate to duties for others, including government leaders. Civil liberty is lost if these rights are violated or credibly threatened with violation. Thus, an individual is deprived of his or her civil liberty if others, either directly or by means of institutions such as despotic institutions, credibly threaten arbitrarily to use physical force, financial penalties, social stigma, or any other form of **coercion** to prevent or impede the actual or potential choices that the individual has a right to make.

☆ KEY POINTS

- Civil libertarians cannot reasonably reject Locke's distinction between genuine political power and absolute arbitrary power.
- Genuine political power secures basic rights and civil liberty.
- Genuine political power and civil liberty may reasonably be expected in a well-designed constitutional liberal democracy.
- The neo-Roman or republican idea of liberty is implicit in any leading modern liberal theory of civil and political liberty.

Justice, security, and liberty

Civil libertarians agree that it is of fundamental importance to live under reasonable rules of justice that distribute rights and duties to the citizenry. The rules include higher order rules for enacting, interpreting, and enforcing the rules. Although democracy may not be essential for a decent outcome, the feasible higher order rules include liberal democratic political procedures that hold lawmakers responsible to the popular majority and also divide political power in such a way that the leaders of different parts of government have authority and incentives to make mutual checks on one another, to some extent, thereby tending to prevent abuses of power and render secure the rights distributed to the people. The higher order rules may also include rules for amending the political procedures.

A semantic issue arises as to whether living more or less peaceably with one's fellows under such a complex system of rules should be described as 'civil liberty' or as 'security'—that is, the enjoyment of civil rights effectively protected by a constitutional government. The **classical utilitarians**, including Bentham and Mill, tend to use 'security'. As Mill puts it, 'the interest involved' in living under rules of justice that distribute rights and duties '*is that of security, to every one's feelings the most vital of all interests*' (1969: 251). This is merely a terminological shift that implies no substantive disagreement with civil libertarians; indeed, Mill continues to speak regularly of 'civil liberty'. The terminological shift is defensible, however, because it throws light on the fact that others must cooperate with the individual, by fulfilling their correlative duties, before any individual can implement his or her rights. The individual is not striking out independently of his or her fellows, but rather is complying with a code of justice so as to coordinate his or her legitimate activities and expectations with those of the others, and thereby provide security for each person's vital interests. The code specifies *permissible* patterns of *interactions*. It assures each individual of his or her permissible choices by delineating the acts and omissions that anyone in a similar position has rights or duties to perform in given situations.

Constitutional democracy can be seen as a political procedure designed to provide higher order security for basic rights—that is, protection for the claims to protect certain

 KEY THINKERS

John Stuart Mill (1806–73)

Mill was the most brilliant political economist and utilitarian liberal philosopher of Victorian Britain. In *Utilitarianism* (1861; 1969), he suggests that the pleasure of the moral sentiment of justice is a higher kind of pleasure that is intrinsically more valuable than any other kinds of pleasure that come into conflict with it. This higher pleasure is a feeling that one's vital interests are secure because they are recognized and protected by right in one's society. Security is promoted for all if they are citizens of a constitutional democracy, living under a code of justice that distributes equal rights and correlative duties. In *On Liberty* (1859; 1977), Mill argues that every civil society's code of justice should recognize and enforce a basic right to absolute liberty of purely self-regarding conduct.

vital interests. The procedure achieves this higher order security by giving the citizens power to vote against elected officials who violate the basic rights of citizens, or who credibly threaten such violations, and by giving different groups of leaders power and incentive to make mutual checks on each other's abuses of power. In contrast, the presence of absolute, arbitrary power renders rights insecure. Even though benevolent despotism is conceivable, a great concentration of power in the same hands is reasonably expected to lead to injustice—that is, violations of basic rights. The fear of despotism is reasonable precisely because there is, by definition, no countervailing power to check the despot's refusal to respect the individual's rightful claims. Despotism includes a majoritarian democracy unrestrained by constitutional checks.

The sorts of consideration adduced by Skinner and Pettit to support their notion of political freedom provide at least as much support for this classical idea of security. Skinner (1998: 84–99) argues, for example, that the individual who lives under despotism is plagued by uncertainty about whether the despot will actually exercise absolute, arbitrary power against him or her. The individual has no incentives to be productive or creative, and is instead encouraged to be subservient and servile to the despot's whims. Such an individual lives as a de facto slave. Even if he or she possesses legal rights, such rights are what Madison *et al.* (1788; 1987) called mere 'parchment barriers' that cannot, by themselves, deter the despot's abuses in practice. Only a suitable system of constitutional checks and balances could effectively do that. Yet such a system is incompatible with despotism.

Mill's radical liberal doctrine of security, or civil and political liberty, is truly distinctive, because he argues that a mature individual member of any civil society has a *basic claim right* to absolute liberty in the descriptive Hobbesian sense, in relation to conduct that is 'purely self-regarding'—that is, conduct that does not directly and immediately affect other people without their consent. (An individual is mature only if he or she is generally capable of forming minimally competent intentions. This excludes children and mentally impaired, delirious, or insane adults.) By combining the Hobbesian idea with the notion of a basic claim in this way, Mill endorses society's protection of the mature individual's liberty to do whatever he or she wishes in relation to all feasible self-regarding acts and omissions. Other people have correlative duties to refrain from any sort of coercive interference, including credible threats or coercive offers, within the agent's self-regarding domain. This authorizes the minimally competent individual to display **autonomy** or individuality—that is, a disposition to choose acts and omissions in accordance with one's own judgement and desires—in relation to his or her entire feasible set of self-regarding acts and omissions. The individual can choose spontaneously in accord with his or her own judgement and inclinations, without any constraints imposed by others within his or her self-regarding field. (Strictly speaking, the individual also holds a power to exercise or waive the claim, as well as an immunity that disables others from abrogating or modifying the claim.)

Mill endorses constitutional democracy and a code of justice that distributes equal rights, including a right to absolute liberty of **self-regarding conduct**, as instruments for promoting the security of every member of a civil society—instruments that are so valuable for this purpose that they may come to be inseparably associated with the very meaning of general security or civil liberty for all, as a key ingredient of the general good.

KEY CONCEPTS

Individuality

Individuality requires a disposition to choose acts and omissions in accord with one's own judgement and inclinations. It may be 'miserable' or 'noble' in content, depending on what the individual is disposed to do. According to Mill, the only unfailing source of it is liberty—that is, actually doing as one wishes. By learning more about the consequences of his or her choices, a mature individual undergoes self development, and thus improves his or her intellectual and moral capacities to make rational and moral choices. The individual lacks individuality altogether if he or she lacks even a minimal capacity to form competent judgements about the probable consequences of his or her acts or omissions, or if, despite having such a capacity, that individual nevertheless blindly follows others rather than makes a choice in light of his or her own judgement and desires.

☆ KEY POINTS

- The term 'security', as used by utilitarian liberals such as Bentham and Mill, is another name for civil and political liberty.

- Constitutional democracy can be viewed as a political mechanism designed to provide higher order security for civil rights, which themselves secure vital individual interests.

- Mill's liberalism is distinctive, because he prescribes a form of constitutional democracy designed to secure a basic right to absolute liberty, in Hobbes' descriptive sense, in relation to a purely self-regarding sphere of conduct.

A right to absolute self-regarding liberty?

Mill says that an individual's self-regarding domain consists of conduct that '*directly, and in the first instance affects only himself, or if it also affects others, only with their free, voluntary, and undeceived consent and participation*' (1859; 1977: 225). He subsequently qualifies that statement by emphasizing that self-regarding conduct can, and should, affect others' feelings, including their likes and dislikes (1859; 1977: 277–8). But such conduct does not alter their personal circumstances in the sense of causing them direct and immediate perceptible injuries or benefits without their consent and participation. The boundaries of this self-regarding domain are not simply a matter for society to 'artificially carve out', even in a society that is committed to a liberal democratic form of lawmaking procedure. Rather, the self-regarding domain has natural boundaries that are open to scientific discovery independently of the majority's likes and dislikes in the matter.

Society has no legitimate authority, Mill insists, to regulate self-regarding acts or omissions. Its authority to compel obedience to rules is properly restricted to what he calls a 'social' domain of conduct. Properly defined, an individual's social conduct—or what some commentators (although not Mill) call 'other-regarding' conduct—includes any act or omission that directly and immediately causes others to experience perceptible changes in their personal circumstances, without their own consent and participation.

To understand the self–other distinction that is at work in *On Liberty* (Mill, 1859; 1977), it is necessary to dispel any confusions about what Mill means when he says that self-regarding conduct does not directly and immediately 'affect' other people unless they consent and participate. On the one hand, he says that *self-regarding* conduct 'affects' others if, and only if, they consent; on the other hand, he tells us that *social* conduct 'affects' others when they do not consent to be affected. Clearly, 'affects' must be referring here to something besides effects on others' judgements and inclinations—or, more generally, their feelings—which determine whether they consent or refuse to consent. Changes in their feelings will transform their consent into refusal to consent (and vice versa). Yet they must be 'affected' independently of whether they consent or refuse. 'Affect' refers here not only to effects on their feelings, I suggest, but also to effects on their personal circumstances which can be defined broadly to include one's body, reputation, finances, contractual relationships, informal engagements, and so forth.

If this is correct, self-regarding conduct does not affect others in the sense that it has no perceptible effects on their personal circumstances thus conceived, or, if it does affect others in this way, it does so only with their genuine consent and participation. If they prefer not to participate, then they can veto the conduct and its effects on their circumstances. If Bob does not wish to have a sexual relationship with Ted, for example, then Bob can refuse Ted's offer and veto the liaison. Self-regarding conduct typically will, and should, affect others in the distinct sense of merely having an impact on their feelings, including their convictions and likes or dislikes in relation to the agent of the self-regarding conduct. Bob may feel that homosexuality is disgusting and seek to avoid Ted as a result. Indeed, Mill emphasizes that certain 'natural penalties' are inseparable from self-regarding liberty, because people have equal rights to avoid freely the company of any adult whose self-regarding conduct displeases them:

> We have a right . . . to act upon our unfavourable opinion of any one, not to the oppression of his individuality, but in the exercise of ours . . . [A] person may suffer very severe penalties at the hands of others, for faults which directly concern only himself.

(Mill, 1859; 1977: 278)

But others' mere dislike never justifies coercive interference with an individual's self-regarding liberty. Those who are merely upset by the self-regarding conduct have equal rights freely to avoid the agent and to warn their acquaintances against him or her. Their acting on their aversion does not injure them without their consent, although it may result in harm to the agent of the self-regarding conduct. But the agent also, in effect, consents to the natural penalties so long as he or she persists in the upsetting self-regarding conduct. Thus, there is no need for society to employ coercive interference in this context to protect anyone from being forced by others to endure harm or perceptible damage.

But what about the objection that no scientific notion of harm is available that is applicable across different moral viewpoints? In this regard, any mature individual—whatever his or her moral viewpoint or social context—divides perceptible effects on personal circumstances (excluding feelings) into improvements and setbacks, or benefits and harms.

It is true that reasonable people may not classify all of the possible effects in the same way: one may view some effects as benefits, but another may view them as harms. Perhaps a clitoridectomy is viewed as beneficial in some cultures, for example, whereas it is viewed as harmful in others. Moreover, reasonable people may disagree over the relative weights that should be assigned to the effects that all of them view as harms or benefits. Nevertheless, self-regarding conduct is not touched by these difficulties, because such conduct has no perceptible effects at all on others' circumstances unless they consent. Which effects are classified as harms and which as benefits does not matter, because all such effects either do not occur (at least '*directly, and in the first instance*') or are consensual. Whatever classification is adopted, self-regarding conduct does not directly benefit or harm others, or, if it does so, it does so only with their genuine consent and participation.

This response assumes that harms can only reasonably be defined as perceptible effects on personal circumstances (apart from feelings). Harm cannot be reduced to mere dislike or distress, just as benefit cannot be reduced to mere like or satisfaction. An external element enters into the phenomena, which can, in principle, be perceived by anybody who, whatever his or her preferences or moral perspective, is capable of appreciating empirical evidence of effects on personal circumstances. That does not mean that these effects can be perceived without reference to any values or norms whatsoever. But the relevant norms of correct observation and inference are supplied by the phenomena themselves, and are invariant across different moral viewpoints or criteria of human good. What counts as an accurate description of the phenomenon called 'clitoridectomy' is inferred from observation of particular surgical removals of the clitoris, independently of whether the phenomenon is classified as harmful or beneficial.

Moreover, it cannot be overemphasized that self-regarding conduct can directly and immediately harm others in this descriptive sense, as long as they consent to the damage, whatever conceptions they may have of their vital interests as human beings. Strictly speaking, Mill's concern is not to prevent perceptible damage to others, but rather to prevent harm being inflicted on them without their consent. As he indicates, society does have legitimate authority to check, in non-coercive ways, whether people are genuinely consenting to participate in activities that directly and immediately cause setbacks to their personal circumstances (apart from their feelings). This is so even when others are not involved but the individual is inclined to engage in self-injurious behaviour. Thus, public officials may take a number of expedient steps, including: discussing with any individual whether he or she really knows what he or she is doing, and even attempting to persuade that individual to abandon potentially self-injurious courses of conduct; posting signs, product labels, and other warnings of potential injuries; and even demanding that the individual provides formal evidence of consent before allowing him or her to venture on some highly dangerous course of action. Once society has assured itself that an agent is genuinely consenting to self-harm, however, that is the end of the matter: society has no proper authority to interfere coercively with the self-regarding conduct that is the source of the consensual harm.

Evidently, the distress and even harm that any competent individual experiences as a direct result of his or her own, or anyone else's, self-regarding conduct *does* count in Mill's liberal philosophy. But such pains are accommodated within the individual's liberty to shape one's character in one's own way. Allowing a competent person to experience the distress and harm does not force that person to endure anything: one can avoid these painful effects by changing one's conduct if so wished. The freedom to do as one pleases in one's self-regarding affairs, and bear the consequences, improves the individual's personal circumstances. It increases one's knowledge of one's own, and others', feelings about one's self-regarding conduct, thereby encouraging further reflection and self-development in the direction that the individual wants, without impinging on anyone else's individuality.

KEY CONCEPTS

Purely self-regarding conduct

An individual's conduct is 'purely self-regarding' in Mill's sense if, and only if, it does not directly and immediately 'affect' other people or, if it does so, it does so only with their unforced and undeceived consent and participation. The term 'to affect' means to alter their personal circumstances, broadly conceived to include their bodies, reputations, finances, contractual agreements, and so on, but excluding their feelings per se. The relevant changes of circumstances may be classified as harms or benefits, depending on moral outlook, but this issue is irrelevant to the definition of self-regarding conduct. According to Mill, any mature individual member of a civil society has a basic right to absolute liberty of self-regarding conduct.

Society's authority to scrutinize whether consent to self-injury is genuine shows that the self-regarding sphere is not properly a matter of social *indifference*. Moreover, if society determines that an individual's consent is not really '*free, voluntary and undeceived*' (Mill, 1859; 1977: 225), then it may resort to coercive interference, if necessary. If others are misleading the individual, for example, then society has a right to employ coercion to prevent these other people from inflicting grave harm on that individual without his or her consent. Similarly, if an individual is found to be a child or otherwise incompetent, then society can rightfully interfere with that individual's own behaviour to prevent him or her from unintentional self-harm. Strictly speaking, the interference with self-injurious behaviour is not coercive in these cases, because the behaviour is not truly intended by the individual; rather, the individual is being forced by others, or by his or her own incompetence, to engage in unintentional behaviour that carries a definite risk of harm to self. The individual does not genuinely consent to engage in such behaviour.

Society may also reasonably decide that some self-inflicted injuries, although intentional, are incompatible with the individual's vital interest in liberty and individuality. Even if it is possible to consent genuinely to slavery contracts, homicide contracts, and marriage contracts in perpetuity, for example, a liberal society may enact into law its disapproval of such contracts, its refusal to enforce them, and its guarantee that one party will not be permitted to force another to keep to the terms of such contracts. These measures do not imply, however, that society has authority to employ coercion or punishment to prevent practices such as voluntary slavery, suicide, and marriage without possibility of divorce. Such practices may well persist, despite society's disapproval, until all individuals learn that they have better ways in which to manage their self-regarding affairs.

> ☆ KEY POINTS
>
> - Mill's distinction between purely self-regarding conduct and social conduct is workable if, and only if, it remains applicable across different moral viewpoints.
> - This, in turn, requires a scientific notion of harm that applies across moral viewpoints.
> - Harm cannot mean mere dislike or distress, but rather requires a perceptible change of personal circumstances.
> - Even though harm, thus defined, may refer to different perceptible changes, depending on moral viewpoint, harm never means mere dislike in any context.
> - The contextual variation in the meaning of harm does not affect Mill's distinction, which ultimately turns on whether any given perceptible changes are consensual or not.
> - Absolute liberty in relation to a natural domain of self-regarding conduct is thus a coherent ethical principle.

Conclusion

Civil libertarians should take seriously Mill's moral and political doctrine that the members of a society are not fully free until they jointly establish a constitutional democracy under which they have assurance that political leaders are unable to abuse basic rights, including a basic right of absolute self-regarding liberty, distributed by a social code of justice. In this respect, the striking defence of *absolute* liberty for any mature individual within his or her self-regarding domain must not be taken to imply that the individual is also forbidden *ever* to do as he or she wishes within his or her social domain. It is true that society has moral authority, Mill says, to consider regulating social conduct, because such conduct poses a risk of direct and immediate harm to others without their consent. But that does not mean that society should always decide to employ coercive measures to prevent social acts and omissions of every description. Rather, society properly establishes rules of justice that distribute rights to perform some social acts and omissions, as well as duties to perform others. Moreover, consistently with such rules, society may also decide to adopt general policies of *laissez-faire* in relation to some general classes of social conduct, including speech and market transactions, because letting individuals alone is estimated to yield net social benefits in these cases, despite any harms suffered by others without their consent. A general policy of *laissez-faire* admits of exceptions: some types of speech or trade may yield net social harm in some situations, for example, and thus might properly be regulated in the relevant circumstances.

The upshot is that a civil society legitimately decides to distribute legal rights that authorize individuals and groups (such as business firms) to do as they wish *to a limited extent* even in relation to social conduct. This legal authority, delegated by society, enables the relevant agents to choose as they please among limited sets of social acts and omissions—sets that society 'artificially' defines and carves out entirely by means of the distribution of rights itself. Unlike the basic right to absolute liberty of self-regarding conduct, these rights to limited liberty of social conduct are entirely contingent on ethical calculations of social benefits and harms, which may vary across different social contexts. Moreover, these rights are properly qualified, so that the holder of the rights is entitled to do as he or she wishes only to the extent that he or she obeys society's code of justice. Sellers are entitled to compete with others freely in the market if, and only if, they obey reasonable laws that forbid fraudulent dealing, for example, just as speakers are permitted to say what they please provided that they obey laws that forbid malicious libel or incitement to violence. Nobody has a moral right to *absolute* liberty in relation to social conduct.

Wisely, Mill never tried to mark out in detail an optimal boundary between individual liberty and social regulation—a boundary that must vary with the particular society under consideration. Rather, in *On Liberty*, he concentrates on making the case that *every* civil society should recognize and protect a natural self-regarding domain of conduct as a *minimum* domain of *absolute liberty* for any mature individual. But he is clear that any society may properly carve out artificial regions of liberty within an individual's domain of social conduct as well—and he joins a long line of civil libertarians in that respect. His radical step is to argue for a basic right to absolute self-regarding liberty as an essential component of civil and political liberty.

CASE STUDY

The USA Patriot Act of 2001 and the war on terror

The USA Patriot (an acronym standing for Uniting and Strengthening America by Providing Appropriate Tools Required to Intercept and Obstruct Terrorism) Act was hastily enacted on 26 October 2001, six weeks after the terrorist attacks that destroyed the World Trade Center towers in Manhattan on 11 September (9/11). This federal statute considerably expands the power of the President and his appointed advisers to conduct secretly the 'war on terror' at their discretion. Eighteen provisions relating to surveillance were originally set to expire at the end of 2005, but Congress made all except two of them permanent when it reauthorized the Patriot Act in March 2006. Although civil rights organizations such as the American Civil Liberties Union (ACLU) continue to agitate for wholescale reform, it seems highly likely that the Patriot Act will remain in force, essentially unchanged, for the duration of the 'war on terror'.

Many of the Patriot Act's provisions are controversial and arguably unconstitutional. One such provision, for example, allows, in any criminal investigation by the Federal Bureau of Investigation (FBI) that (according to the Attorney General) has foreign intelligence as 'a significant purpose', surveillance of any suspect whom a special court—established under the Foreign Intelligence Surveillance Act (FISA) of 1978—agrees in a secret hearing may be a foreign agent, even if there is no clear evidence that the suspect has engaged in criminal activity or is likely to do so. Another controversial provision makes it a deportable offence for immigrants to provide 'material support' (including weapons, personnel, services, expert advice, training, and money, among other things, but excluding medicine and religious materials) to any foreign group that the Secretary of State designates as a 'terrorist organization', even if the individual can show that his or her support was intended and used only for lawful purposes, rather than any violent activities. Still another controversial provision enables the Attorney General to detain indefinitely, and without a hearing, any foreigner—even a person who has been granted asylum and does not pose a current flight risk or danger to the community—whom he suspects of being a terrorist or of supporting a terrorist organization. As a final illustration, another provision authorizes secret 'sneak and peek' searches in the investigation of any federal crime, such as possession of illicit drugs and not limited to terrorism, and permits the government to delay notifying the suspects for as long as ninety days.[2]

It deserves emphasis that the Patriot Act is only one important component of a complex evolving web of federal anti-terrorist legislation. For example, the provision of material support to a designated terrorist group was already a federal crime under the Antiterrorism and Effective Death Penalty Act of 1996. The Patriot Act, in addition to expanding the definition of materal support to include expert advice or assistance, made the crime a deportable offence for immigrants. The Intelligence Reform and Terrorist Prevention Act (IRTPA) of 2004 further expands and clarifies the definition of 'material support', and also introduces various other key changes. In particular, the IRTPA states that violation of the material-support prohibition does not require an intent to advance the group's terrorist aims (knowledge of the group's designated status is sufficient), but that individuals who act entirely independently of the foreign terrorist organization to advance its goals shall not be considered personnel of the group.

The impact of the Patriot Act and, more generally, anti-terrorist legislation on civil and political liberty cannot be assessed without an understanding of the basic rights set out in the US Constitution, as interpreted by the courts—in particular, First Amendment rights (freedoms of speech, of association, and of religious opinion and practice), Fourth Amendment rights (freedom from unreasonable searches and seizures), and Fifth Amendment rights (various rights of due process in a criminal trial, including the right to confront one's accusers and to attempt to rebut their accusations). These constitutional rights are not confined to US citizens, but extend to all human beings who come within the jurisdiction of the USA.

The 'war on terror' is, in many ways, an extension of the 'war on drugs' initiated by the Reagan administration in the name of national security. For nearly thirty-five years, the drug war has given Congress and the President an excuse to carve out more and more exceptions to the Posse Comitatus Act of 1878, which generally bars the military from participating in civilian law enforcement activities. As a result of a series of measures beginning with the Military Cooperation with Law Enforcement Act of 1981, the military now plays a significant role in domestic policing efforts by providing National Guard troops, training, and massive supplies of assault weapons and equipment, including aircraft, drones, armoured personnel carriers, grenade launchers, and the like, either free of charge or at sharply discounted rates. Troops may be used not only to help to deal with emergency situations, such as a nuclear attack or a natural disaster, but also to assist in large-scale sweeps against drug dealers, and to search for crops of marijuana and opium, etc. At the same time, civilian law enforcement agencies have increasingly established their own special weapons and tactics (SWAT) teams to make use of the training, weapons, and equipment provided by the military. These paramilitary SWAT teams are now commonly deployed for routine drug raids even in small communities, whereas, prior to the 'war on drugs', they were generally confined to large cities and used only in highly dangerous contexts, such as bank robberies or hostage situations. Dressed in camouflage and often wearing masks, the SWAT teams typically conduct their drug raids by breaking into residences very early in the morning with little, if any, notice given to the suspects, provoking fear and violence, and raising serious Fourth Amendment concerns.[3]

In general, these 'wars' on drugs and terror elicit many civil rights concerns. A Millian doctrine of civil liberty or security arguably endorses the basic rights and political procedures outlined in the US Constitution, without necessarily holding them to be the best possible. However, it also prescribes a basic right to absolute self-regarding liberty, which is not mentioned in the Constitution and has never been properly recognized by any observed societies. If consuming narcotic drugs is a purely self-regarding act under certain conditions, for example, then mature individuals should be given a legal right to take narcotics as they please under the relevant conditions. Society can legitimately regulate the sellers and marketers of the drugs, but any regulatory scheme must not amount to a ban on consumption, because such a ban violates the individual's basic right to self-regarding liberty. Evidently, a 'war' to eradicate drug consumption is incompatible with this Millian doctrine—but what about a 'war' to eradicate terrorism?

Mill recognizes that society has legitimate power to prevent gravely harmful social conduct before it occurs: '*if a public authority, or even a private person, sees anyone evidently preparing to commit a crime, they are not bound to look on inactive until the crime is committed, but may interfere to prevent it*' (Mill, 1859; 1977: 294). Harmful social conduct includes inciting others to commit crimes (Mill, 1859; 1977: 260). So society can legitimately suppress speech if there is evidence that the speaker is attempting to incite others and that criminal activity is likely to be the more or less immediate result, because, for example, the speaker and his or her associates have been observed to be assembling weapons and other materials with which to carry out violent terrorist acts. But Mill also recognizes the considerable danger that the government's 'preventive function' will be '*abused, to the prejudice of liberty*' (Mill, 1859; 1977: 294). Uncertainty about people's intentions makes it easy to become suspicious of innocent conduct, especially in climates of anxiety such as that whipped up by the US government itself in the 'war on terror'. Thus, he emphasizes the need for evidence of current or impending criminal activity to justify any form of coercive interference, with the caveat that 'special legal restrictions' can properly be placed on anyone after he or she has been convicted of a crime. An individual with a record of terrorist violence might be specially forbidden, as a condition of his or her release from prison, to associate with other known terrorists or to make speeches advocating the aims of violent groups, for example, and be subjected to unusually severe punishment if he or she nevertheless does so.

Similarly, the US courts have generally settled that an individual's constitutional rights protect him or her from government interference if there is no evidence that he or she is engaging in criminal activity, or is about to do so. The Fourth Amendment requires that a search warrant must be denied if there is not probable cause to believe that criminal activity will be uncovered, for example, and the First Amendment requires that political speech—whatever its content—must be protected unless there is evidence that the speaker intends to incite 'imminent lawless action' and that such lawless action is likely to occur. The Patriot Act and, more generally, the 'war on terror' override, in the name of national security, constitutional rights thus understood. Searches and seizures may be warranted by the FISA court merely because there is evidence that the suspect is connected to a foreign nation or organization, the objectives of which are at odds with US foreign policy in the estimation of some official in the State Department, for example, and speech may be proscribed or punished on the basis of its political content, even though there is no probable cause to believe that the speaker intends to incite violence or that imminent lawless action is likely to be produced.

Unfortunately, there is no guarantee that the US courts will continue to reject oppressive ideas of national security that conflict with long-standing interpretations of constitutional rights. As the extensive leaks by Edward Snowden revealed in 2013, for example, the FISA court in 2006 secretly authorized the National Security Agency (itself so secretive that it is sometimes referred to as NSA: 'No Such Agency') to collect and search telephone metadata records of every resident of the US. The government argued that this sweeping surveillance program is 'relevant' to a terrorist investigation because currently unknown terrorist suspects might, in future, be identified by searching those records. In January 2014, however, the Privacy and Civil Liberties Board, an independent agency created by Congress and appointed by the President, recommended that the NSA telephone metadata program should be terminated because it was not authorized under the Patriot Act (Section 215 authorized the FBI, not the NSA, to conduct targeted searches with a FISA court warrant) and had produced insignificant national security benefits in any case.[4] The constitutionality of the metadata program is highly dubious: it is now being examined by plural federal courts of appeal and is likely to reach the Supreme Court.

As Snowden's leaks revealed, the NSA has also conducted various other surveillance programs, including surveillance of phone calls and emails of citizens and leaders of foreign countries, under the FISA Amendments Act of 2008. In December 2013, an expert panel, appointed by the President, assessed almost all of the known NSA programs and, after expressing serious concerns, proposed forty-six reforms, including removal of the phone metadata records from the NSA and storage of them at some unspecified private entity, as well as a requirement that the NSA obtain a court order for any specific search.[5] President Obama has accepted the latter two reforms, among others, but has so far remained silent about the many other NSA programs, including the program relating to foreigners' phone calls and emails. Although the President's response is disappointing, Congress is considering multiple reform bills to deal with the issues of privacy, freedom of speech and of association, and so on. In the meantime, a totalitarian world without privacy, of the sort depicted by George Orwell in *1984*, is looming on the horizon in this information age.

Just as it should never be made a crime to engage in purely self-regarding conduct, it should not be made a crime simply to be a foreign national or a member of an ethnic, racial, or religious minority. An individual's nationality, ethnicity, race, or religious belief per se does not imply any direct and immediate harm to others without their consent. Coercive interference with the conduct of that individual cannot properly be based on such characteristics. Indeed, merely by classifying and identifying people in terms of such properties, society and government may endanger individuality: any such classification tends to submerge the individual within this or that particular group and to assign an importance to the group identity that he or she does not choose, relative to other elements of his or her life and character (Sen, 2006). Coercive measures based on group identity are often defended as essential for national security—but security is properly only civil liberty by another name. Such measures as ethnic profiling, targeting immigrants, and searches and seizures predicated on group identity, rather than on probable cause of criminal activity, violate traditional understandings of basic rights and thereby detract from security no less than from civil liberty.

Technological advances in weapons of mass destruction have no doubt opened up the possibility of terrorist crimes—nuclear bomb explosions, chemical and biological attacks, etc.—so devastating as to endanger the very survival of the USA or the UK as civil societies. Moreover, there may be probable cause to believe that some such terrorist act is imminent and that basic rights must be sacrificed to deal with the crisis. In an emergency situation of this sort, in which some evils cannot be avoided, it might even make sense to suspend the Constitution temporarily so that the President can be transformed into something akin to an ancient Roman dictator. But the 'war on terror' apparently seeks to make this sort of dictatorship an ordinary feature of American political life, even prior to the acquisition of any evidence that some devastating terrorist crime is imminent. Coercive measures based on group identity must not be allowed to supplant constitutional rights, especially when there is no evidence of a current or impending terrorist disaster: to do so only helps the terrorists to achieve their aim of destroying civil liberty without a fight. Such measures as ethnic profiling, and unwarranted searches and seizures, are generally not effective ways of fighting crime, in any event. Discriminating against innocents on the basis of their ethnic identity or immigrant status typically alienates the very people who may be best placed to assist in the discovery of criminal activity, for example, whereas 'fishing expedition' searches and blanket seizures of assets without probable cause typically divert the police from more efficient uses of their scarce resources.

QUESTIONS

1. How does a purely descriptive concept of individual liberty differ from a normative concept of individual liberty, such as civil liberty? Are these two types of concept logically unrelated?

2. How are Berlin's concepts of negative and positive liberty related to Hobbes' descriptive concept of liberty?

3. What are the similarities and differences between Hobbes' and Locke's ideas of liberty?

4. According to Locke, how does genuine political power differ from absolute, arbitrary power? How is genuine political power related to civil liberty?

5. Does it make sense to use the term 'security' as a synonym for civil and political liberty?

6. In Mill's idea of a basic right to absolute liberty of purely self-regarding conduct, what are the meanings of the key terms 'liberty' and 'purely self-regarding conduct'?

7. How can the individual be given a right to *absolute* liberty of self-regarding conduct in light of the disgust and harm experienced by others as a result?

8. Are the objections to Mill's idea of a natural domain of purely self-regarding conduct compelling?

9. What liberties, if any, does Mill think people ought to have in the domain of social conduct?

10. Explain why the argument that civil rights must be sacrificed in the name of national security is problematic. In what exceptional situations, if any, does the argument have validity?

FURTHER READING

■ Berlin, I. (1969) *Four Essays on Liberty*, Oxford: Oxford University Press. Reprinted in H. Hardy (ed.) *Isaiah Berlin: Liberty,* Oxford: Oxford University Press, 2002, pp. 1–251. Includes his essay on the two concepts of liberty and an essay setting out a pluralistic critique of Mill's liberalism.

■ Carter, I., Kramer, M. H., and Steiner, H. (2006) *Freedom: A Philosophical Anthology,* Oxford: Blackwell Selections from key historical and contemporary texts, covering a wide range of political and philosophical issues.

■ Ivison, D. (1997) *The Self at Liberty*, Ithaca, NY: Cornell University Press An account of liberty in terms of enabling conditions that opposes Berlin by drawing on the ideas of Locke (among others).

■ Kramer, M. H., Simmonds, N. E., and Steiner, H. (1998) *A Debate Over Rights*, Oxford: Oxford University Press Critical discussions of interest theories versus choice theories of rights.

■ Mill, J. S. (1859; 1977) 'On liberty', in J. M. Robson (ed.) *Collected Works of J. S. Mill, vol. 18,* London/Toronto: Routledge/University of Toronto Press, pp. 203–310 This 'great short book' is a wonderful defence of the rights of liberty and individuality, although it is much misunderstood and commonly dismissed as vacuous.

■ Miller, D. (2006) *The Liberty Reader*, Edinburgh: Edinburgh University Press Twelve essays written in the twentieth century, covering key developments in debates about the nature and significance of liberty.

■ Riley, J. (2014) *Mill: On Liberty*, 2nd edn, London: Routledge Summarizes Mill's textual argument in considerable detail and discusses some of the leading objections raised against it in the literature.

■ Riley, J. (2014) *Mill's Radical Liberalism*, London: Routledge A companion to *Mill: On Liberty*, this volume offers interpretation of Mill's utilitarian theory of liberalism and situates the principle of absolute self-regarding liberty within his broader theory.

■ Swift, A. (2001) 'Part 2: Liberty', in *Political Philosophy*, Cambridge: Polity Press, pp. 51–90 Criticizes and revises Berlin's approach by identifying various conceptions of negative and positive liberty, including 'moralized' and 'non-moralized' conceptions, but tends to reinforce the common misimpression that Berlin rejects all notions of positive liberty.

 WEB LINKS

● http://berlin.wolf.ox.ac.uk The Isaiah Berlin Virtual Library is run by Berlin's Literary Estate and offers a comprehensive guide to Berlin's writing, intellectual activities, and life.

● http://www.aclu.org Founded in 1920, the American Civil Liberties Union is a large and storied non-profit organization that is dedicated to the preservation of constitutional principles and civil rights, with offices in every US state. It has successfully challenged various provisions of the Patriot Act in the courts and continues to work for wholescale reform. See ACLU (2009), a three-page appendix that usefully summarizes the main provisions of the Patriot Act.

● http://www.liberty-human-rights.org.uk Founded in 1934, Liberty is a cross-party, non-party membership organization that is at the heart of the movement for fundamental rights and freedoms in England and Wales.

● http://oll.libertyfund.org The Online Library of Liberty is run by the non-profit Liberty Fund and makes freely available, in digital form, the works of many great defenders of liberty, including John Locke and John Stuart Mill.

 Visit the Online Resource Centre that accompanies this book to access more learning resources: http://www.oxfordtextbooks.co.uk/orc/mckinnon3e/

 ENDNOTES

[1] John Gray (2013) has made an influential argument that, for Berlin, value pluralism reaches into justice and right such that even basic human rights can clash in ways that admit of no universal rational resolution. But Berlin seems to insist that a certain minimum of human rights must be respected for a society to be decent. Thus, for him, decency requires that value pluralism must be constrained to give moral priority to certain basic rights (Riley, 2013, 2014).

[2] For further analysis of these and other controversial aspects of the USA Patriot Act of 2001 and the 'war on terror', see Cole (2003: 57–71), Cole and Dempsey (2006: 195–218), and Cole and Lobel (2009).

[3] For further discussion of the 'war on drugs' and the increasing militarization of civilian law enforcement within the USA, see Baum (1996) and Balko (2006).

[4] Privacy and Civil Liberties Board (2014).

[5] President's Review Group on Intelligence and Communications Technologies (2013).

3

Toleration

ANNA ELISABETTA GALEOTTI

Reader's guide

Toleration has returned to the front line of philosophy and political theory in the last three decades or so. Although toleration is valued, it is a problematic virtue, because it is not clear that permitting some practices that are held to be wrong is a good thing. Toleration is much needed in contemporary pluralistic democracies because of the many divisive differences present in our globalized world. Two views of toleration are proposed in contemporary debate: the negative view of toleration as non-interference (which is continuous with the traditional doctrine); and the positive view of toleration as recognition (which is an expansion of the traditional doctrine). In both cases, toleration must be limited if the democratic society is to be preserved, and the tracing of such limits defines the practices of toleration in our society. The specific difficulty of setting limits for particular cases involves striking a balance between liberty rights, without which liberal society dissolves, and security measures for the defence of democracy from disruptive forces.

Introduction

In general terms, toleration enables the peaceful coexistence of conflicting views and ways of life within the same society. A tolerant person leaves other people free to behave as they think best, even when their behaviour looks objectionable and might otherwise be checked. Conflicting differences are the first circumstance for issues of toleration to arise: were there no differences, or only harmoniously combining differences, between people, there would be nothing about which to be tolerant. Furthermore, a tolerant person should also have the power to repress or interfere with disliked differences; otherwise, in not interfering, he or she merely acquiesces to them. Toleration properly consists in not exercising the power to interfere with disliked differences, for various kinds of reasons: prudential—that is, those relating to social peace; moral—that is, those relating to a respect for others' **liberty**; and political—that is, those relating to the maximization of liberty and equal respect for all.

From this very general definition, toleration appears to be a problematic virtue from the start. In so far as it helps to build a free and open society, it is certainly valuable—yet it also carries negative connotations. Being tolerant means accepting—or at least putting up with—practices and conducts that one finds objectionable, and it is not immediately clear why permitting practices that are contrary to one's morality and convictions is a good thing rather than a form of hypocrisy. Toleration is also problematic from the viewpoint of the tolerated person: people like to be accepted, rather than merely tolerated. Thus, toleration seems a demanding virtue for the tolerator, but also a limited blessing for the tolerated person. Nevertheless, there is a general agreement about its indispensability (McKinnon and Castiglione, 2003). Our pluralistic democratic world—in which conflicting differences are non-contingently present and are highly divisive, and in which people cherish liberal ideals and abhor paternalistic rule—needs more toleration, and of a more demanding kind, for the equal liberty of all to be possible despite persisting disagreement about world views and ways of life.

Such general considerations have made political thinkers ask which kind of toleration is the most appropriate to address the problems of peaceful coexistence in a contemporary pluralistic **democracy**. Some scholars consider toleration to be crucial for social peace and political stability, but only as a form of *modus vivendi*—that is, a contingent accommodation between two conflicting parties to supersede their conflicts, at least temporarily, for prudential and pragmatic reasons. Others adopt a more positive view of toleration as acceptance, which avoids the tone of moral condescension that characterizes the purely negative view of toleration as non-interference.

Toleration presents both philosophical and political problems. The philosophical problems relate to its nature and its justification: is toleration a necessity or a virtue and, in the latter case, is it only prudential, or is it also moral? Is it to be interpreted only in negative terms, as non-interference, or also in positive ones, as **recognition**? Is it justified only as an instrument for peace and coexistence, or is it required by principles of justice? Whenever issues of toleration arise in our society, the discussion becomes political and relates to tracing the limits to toleration—that is, discussion turns to whether contemporary democracy can or cannot afford to tolerate this or that practice, and, more specifically, whether a worse danger for liberal society and liberal values is represented by toleration (which might risk the stability of liberal democracy) or intolerance (which might involve oppression and the curtailment of **liberty rights** in a democratic society).

 KEY CONCEPTS

Modus vivendi

The Latin expression *modus vivendi* means 'a way of coexisting': an extemporary and contingent accommodation between two conflicting parties to supersede their contrasts, at least temporarily, for prudential and pragmatic reasons. The expression became part of the technical language of political theory after its use by John Rawls in *Political Liberalism* (1993: 147). He rejects *modus vivendi* as a basis of the political legitimacy of just and stable democracy. Being the result of self-interest, the equilibrium of *modus vivendi* is unstable and unprincipled, and is always open to a new phase of conflict, if the interest of one of the two parties changes.

The traditional doctrine of toleration

The origin

The concept of toleration emerged as a solution to the religious wars that erupted in sixteenth-century Europe as a consequence of the Protestant Reformation. The conflict among different creeds appeared intractable and non-negotiable, and no contending party succeeded in winning the contest and imposing itself as representative of the true religion, suppressing all others as the Catholic Church suppressed 'heretics' during the Middle Ages.

The first step towards toleration was represented by the doctrine of **territorialism**, stating that the religion in a given country should conform to that of the sovereign. Territorialism allowed religious pluralism in Europe, breaking the monopoly of the Church of Rome over matters of faith. But it also compelled religious minorities to emigrate into countries where the official Church corresponded to their faith. This solution could work only as a first compromise because it could not secure internal stability in contexts containing religious minorities, and it could not provide reasons why the religious beliefs of the King were the right ones to secure the salvation of one's own soul.

Toleration was thus, timidly at first, advanced as the alternative political solution to stop the killings for the sake of eternal salvation. Arguments in favour of toleration and against persecution varied, and comprised reasons of different kinds: political (emphasizing a preference for peace over conflict); epistemological (emphasizing the difficulty, or even impossibility, of humans gaining definitive access to truth, making the imposition of beliefs groundless); and moral (emphasizing prohibition of the use of **coercion** in matters of faith).

KEY THINKERS

John Milton (1608–74)

John Milton was a celebrated English poet, prose polemicist, and civil servant. His works include the epic poem *Paradise Lost* (1667), for which he is most well known, and the essay *Areopagitica* (1644), which is particularly relevant for the development of the doctrine of toleration and of the modern concept of liberty. The pamphlet offers an argument against censorship, grounded on (a) human fallibility, (b) the fact that truth can emerge only if tested through errors and that only in this way does coming to know truth have value, and (c) doubts about whether censors can be trusted, given their own human fallibility.

Pierre Bayle (1647–1706)

Pierre Bayle was a French philosopher, best known as a forerunner of the Encyclopaedists by his *Historical and Critical Dictionary* (1695). As a French Protestant, he was also known for his argument for the separation between faith and reason (*fideism*) and for his arguments for toleration, as presented in his *Philosophical Commentary* (1686–88) as well as in his *Dictionary*. His key argument in defence of toleration was epistemological: given the plurality of Churches, each claiming to be the right one, and given the absence of an independent and superior viewpoint to adjudicate among them, how could one be sure that the persecution of heretics was being performed by the true Church rather than by an heretical one?

However sustained, toleration was supposed to work for peace on the basis of a model of common civil coexistence. This basically consisted of giving primacy to a strict demarcation between matters pertaining to the political order and public affairs, on the one hand, and matters unrelated to the political order, on the other. This demarcation divided society into two areas. The first, built around matters that were relevant to order and peace, constituted the **political sphere**, a domain subject to the political authorities and public regulation. The second, concerned with issues that were irrelevant to order and peace, defined the private realm as one in which the state had no business and hence no reason to intervene through coercive action. This protected area, within which political interference had to be suspended, constituted the proper object of toleration. In this way, the original arguments for toleration, despite their variety, converged on the negative conception of toleration as non-interference. In the private area of conscience, errors in matters of faith can, and ought to be permitted by the political **authority**, given that not only do they not threaten political stability, but they also actually contribute to its preservation. By contrast, the righteous attempts by pious political authorities to save erring souls from eternal damnation engender endless conflict and civil disruption. Toleration recommends itself because it is politically more convenient than persecution and also because the latter is, anyway, useless in producing salvation: beliefs cannot be forced, outward conformity is not the same as faith, and only faith can save souls.

Consequently, seventeenth-century and eighteenth-century monarchies, granting toleration to some dissenting creeds within their kingdoms' territories, acted out of grace and **reasonableness**, not out of justice, in order to neutralize the disruptive effects of religious zeal. As the US philosopher Thomas Paine commented in relation to the 1791 French

KEY THINKERS

Voltaire (1694–1778)

François-Marie Arouet, known as Voltaire, was one of the main spokesmen of the French Enlightenment. Among his philosophical works related to toleration are *Philosophical Letters* (1734), *The Philosophical Dictionary* (1764), and *Treatise on Tolerance* (1767). His argument for toleration is based on natural law, which must orient civil law. There is no natural imperative of persecution for dissenting ideas and opinions. Religious intolerance was unknown in the ancient world—at least, when law and order were not threatened. Religious persecutions for the sake of eternal salvation were introduced by the Church of Rome and then by other Christian denominations. Voltaire strenuously opposed the obscurantism and bigotry exemplified by churches.

Constitution (Paine, 1791; 1969), toleration was a matter of the sovereign's discretion and the practice of toleration was intrinsically linked with absolute power, under which the will of the sovereign, rather than law, ruled people. By contrast, when the rule of law was established and the **bill of rights** declared, as in the liberal democratic French Constitution of 1791, toleration was displaced by the equal right to religious freedom.

Liberal toleration and neutrality

Pace Paine, though, liberalism did not do away with toleration but, rather, transformed it from an act of grace of an enlightened king into the universal right to free conscience of all citizens. At this point, toleration as a political principle and toleration (or tolerance) as a social virtue parted ways. Consider toleration first from a political perspective. While, before liberalism, the political authority had good reasons for non-interference with dissenting religious creeds, within liberal politics, the state has a duty of toleration that corresponds to the right of religious freedom. As a consequence, the meaning of toleration expands: if everyone is granted an equal right to free conscience, then the state is not only under the duty of non-interference with every citizen's conscience, but also under a duty of not favouring or disfavouring any religious conviction, because that would mean giving more weight to the choices of some citizens over others. Becoming embodied in universal rights, toleration enlarges its scope, because it implies more than freedom from persecution for dissenters: it now implies equal religious liberty. In order to grant equality in religious freedom, the state should become neutral in relation to its citizens' religious (and non-religious) convictions. **Neutrality** is not simply the suspension of political interference with an individual's religious and moral views; rather, it is the bracketing of religious and personal convictions in the political sphere, so as to avoid discrimination in relation to religious and moral beliefs. From a political perspective, then, liberal toleration implies no disapproval, but simply disregard, of conflicting differences, and equal rights to **freedom of expression**, association, and personal liberty.

From the Acts of Toleration of the absolute monarchies to liberal neutrality, the road was long and winding and paralleled the establishment of liberalism (see Box 3.1). The first instantiation of the principle of neutrality was the doctrine of the separation of Church and state, meant to establish a reciprocal non-interference of the two domains. This doctrine of Lockean ascent was clearly stated by Thomas Jefferson, first enacted in the Virginia Statute for Religious Freedom (1786) and then embodied in the First Amendment of the American Constitution. The separation doctrine became a flag for European liberals as well, but its implementation in constitutional charters had to take into account different historical heritage so that in a few countries, such as Great Britain and the Scandinavian countries, the established Church has survived up to the twenty-first century in the context of a wholly secularized society.

BOX 3.1 TOLERATION IN THE SEVENTEENTH AND EIGHTEENTH CENTURIES

The most widely known defenders of tolerance were Milton (1608–74), Bayle (1647–1706), Spinoza (1634–77), and Locke (1632–1704). The New World writings of Thomas Paine (1737–1809) and Thomas Jefferson (1743–1826) spelled out a theory of toleration that was directly tied to political practice. Paine's and Jefferson's ideas followed those of Locke. Not only were they critical of unrestrained political power, but they were also committed to an ecumenical approach to religious belief, known as deism, that was shared by the French defender of toleration, Voltaire (1694–1778). Tolerant ideas are embodied in practice in the US Constitution's Bill of Rights and the first ten Amendments to the Constitution (ratified in 1791). For example, the First Amendment states that there can be no law that prohibits freedom of religion, freedom of speech, freedom of the press, freedom of assembly, and freedom to petition to the government. The French Constitution of 1791, of which Paine approved, stated instead the universal right to free conscience. ➡ See Chapter 8.

 KEY CONCEPTS

Neutrality

While toleration grants citizens freedom of conscience, neutrality grants them the right not to be discriminated against because of that conscience. Contemporary political liberalism has generalized the ideal of neutrality into a constitutional argument for political legitimacy. Liberal legitimacy should constitute a neutral basis among the various and contrasting conceptions of the good that are held in society. While the idea that public treatment of citizens should disregard their religious, ethnic affiliation and personal differences is widely shared among liberals, the idea that liberalism is characterized by neutrality with respect to its legitimacy is controversial (Raz, 1986).

However, liberalism has not miraculously produced a social harmony of all differences in terms of religion, morality, and ways of life, etc. Liberal societies are still divided as to the nature of the good life and any path to salvation. Freedom of expression and association tend to nurture pluralism, rather than uniformity—and pluralism, at least within limits, is seen by liberals as a value, because it offers individuals real options from which to choose what best suits them. Nevertheless, if political conditions grant individual liberty, social conformism may put pressure on individuals and curtail their effective freedom to choose for themselves. In his well-known essay *On Liberty* (1859; 1972), John Stuart Mill stated that, by the mid nineteenth century, the danger of political oppression had receded (at least in some European and North American countries), only to be replaced by the danger of social oppression by the moral majority. Thus, the cause of liberty requires a fight against the tyranny of the majority in order to preserve free thinking and human development. For this reason, toleration of differing, disliked, and disapproved of views and ways of life has become a crucial social virtue, enabling individual liberty to prosper. In this case, toleration keeps its original character, because:

- its circumstances are disliked or disapproved differences;
- the potential tolerator has some power of interference;
- the potential tolerator refrains from using it for the sake of more important values than imposing his or her convictions on others.

For toleration as a social virtue, the power of interference consists in social pressure and disapproving judgement, rather than in coercion and repression: moral majorities enjoy a significant capacity to influence behaviour by various social sanctions.

A final consideration is in order. From its origin, all scholars have agreed that toleration is valuable only within limits, beyond which it turns into culpable indulgence. The limits of toleration have been traced in this way from the very beginning. More precisely, John Locke (1685; 1991) firmly stated that toleration should stop short of intolerants who, to his mind, were represented by Catholics. More generally, in his view, toleration should not be extended to whoever would undermine the basis of toleration itself: atheists, for example, should not be tolerated, because their oath could not be trusted. In other words, in his *A Letter Concerning Toleration* (1685: 1991), Locke traced the limit of toleration in the principle of self-defence of the liberal order against potential disruptive forces. That is to say, unrestrained toleration can turn against the tolerant society. Beside the self-defence principle, toleration should be limited by considerations of harm to others. Actions that cause harm to a third party do not qualify for toleration. It was John Stuart Mill (1859; 1972) who theorized the harm principle as a necessary limit to toleration if it is to stand as a liberal value.

While there is a shared agreement about these two principles as limits of toleration, their application is a controversial matter.

KEY TEXTS

Mill, *On Liberty* (1859)

In this text, Mill develops his argument so that the protection of individual liberty depends on a pluralism of opinions and lifestyles—hence, on the toleration of disagreement. Toleration is thus a fundamental ingredient of the individual flourishing against social conformism. Freedom of expression, coupled with a robust plurality of opinions and options, are the landmarks of a free society—yet they cannot be absolute, their limit being the harm principle. Harm constitutes a necessary, but not sufficient, reason not to tolerate an act or practice causing it. Harm to self is, in general, not a reason for intolerance. Mill takes a clear stand against paternalism: nobody is a better judge of his or her own good than his or her self.

- How far can self-defence trump the freedom of other individuals or groups, and vice versa? For example, can self-defence be invoked in defence of prohibiting forms of offensive speech and practice?
- What counts as harm (only bodily and material, or also psychological and symbolic)?
- Should toleration extend to self-harm?
- What is to be considered an actual threat for democratic order?

These are only a sample of the questions characterizing the contemporary political debate over toleration and defining the practices of toleration in different contexts. Think, for example, of the various regulations against terrorism following the 9/11 attacks on the World Trade Center in New York. Are the subsequent restrictions on the freedom of passengers justified by **security**? Are the search and scrutiny of the activities of Muslim groups, and of Muslim teachings, which interfere with religious and personal freedom of Muslims, acceptable for the sake of preserving liberal institutions? Even if the answer to these questions is 'yes, in principle', it does not follow that all actual police acts, searches, checks, are justified.

The contemporary debate

Toleration has returned to the front line of political theory in the last three decades or so. This renewed interest is the consequence of the growing political awareness that pluralism—not only of points of views, but also of traditions and of cultural groups—has become one of the key problems of our globalized world, both within and across democratic and non-democratic countries. Recent work on toleration can be grouped in three areas:

- philosophical works that explore the concept of toleration—its conditions, definitions, justifications, and limits—making use of the sophisticated analytical tools of contemporary moral theory;
- the area of liberal political analysis, which addresses toleration as the proper instrument for dealing with pluralism from a political point of view and explores toleration as the political principle allowing for a liberal society to exist; and
- a strand of political studies that advocates an extension of the meaning of toleration in positive terms, as recognition.

The first two areas revisit the traditional concept of toleration, both in its moral dimension of interpersonal virtue, and in its political dimension as a solution of religious and moral disagreement. Backed by different kinds of argument, they both share the negative view of toleration as non-interference. The third approach, however, rejects the negative conception as insufficient for addressing the issues of toleration that are raised in contemporary pluralism and proposes to go beyond non-interference. If toleration is required to face the divisive issues of contemporary pluralism, a new conception is called for, which overcomes the pitfalls of liberal toleration, while fulfilling its promises.

☆ KEY POINTS

- Toleration originally emerged as the political solution to the religious wars that devastated Europe after the Reformation. Toleration, as the suspension of political interference in the religious creeds of people was affirmed as the only way in which to stop the killings for the sake of eternal salvation.

- At its origin, toleration was patterned on a model of civil coexistence that implied a divide between political affairs (all that is relevant for peace and order) and private matters (a realm in which the state had no business).

- The original conceptions of toleration and the various acts of toleration, granted by the absolute monarchies of the seventeenth and eighteenth centuries, were discretionary acts of grace and reasonableness by enlightened sovereigns.

- In the liberal state, toleration was transformed into the universal right to free conscience of all citizens and its meaning was expanded accordingly. Here, toleration implies neutrality—the bracketing of religious and personal convictions, opinions, and corresponding practices in the political sphere—so as to avoid discrimination relating to religious and moral beliefs.

- The contemporary debate consists of three approaches: moral, liberal, and critical.

- The moral analysis of toleration is mainly concerned with the definition and justification of toleration as a moral virtue; the liberal analysis is focused on toleration as a political principle; and critical political theory proposes toleration as recognition.

The moral analysis of toleration

The contemporary philosophical analysis of toleration elaborates on the original meaning of tolerance as refraining from interference with disliked behaviour, and aims at providing firm moral grounds for both the social and political practices of toleration by showing that the negative connotation of putting up with something that is disliked ought to be replaced by positive moral reasons of respect for others. Circumstances for toleration are differences that are considered important both by the tolerator and by the tolerated (Galeotti, 2001; Heyd, 1996; Horton, 1996; Horton and Nicholson, 1992; Mendus, 1988; 1989; 1999; Mendus and Edwards, 1987; Mendus and Horton, 1985). It is, then, an open question whether the proper differences to be tolerated are only moral or also those that are non-moral (Warnock, 1987) and, in the latter case, only chosen or also non-choosable (King, 1976).

The issue is not merely academic, because the scope of toleration varies according to the approach adopted. If only disapproved differences are held to be conditions for toleration, this limits the scope of toleration to behaviour, practices, and traits that are open to moral assessment. If disliked differences are also included as conditions for toleration, then the scope of toleration will also encompass tastes and personal preferences, as well as ascriptive—that is, received and unchosen—differences. Moral disapproval emphasizes the specific *moral* quality of toleration. It is because the tolerator morally disapproves of something that his or her effort to overcome his or her feelings (by appealing to a stronger moral reason) is a virtue. For only disliked behaviour, the moral effort of toleration would be less remarkable, coming closer to indifference. However, if only morally disapproved of differences count for toleration, these differences must not form part of universally condemned practices—such as racism, slavery, or torture—that ought not to be tolerated at all (Horton, 1996); rather, such differences must be related to morally controversial practices, such as contraception, abortion, and sexual promiscuity. In any case, disapproval, and perhaps dislike, should be supported by some reasons, otherwise it is unjustified in the first place. And respect for others requires one to stop unjustified disapproval altogether, rather than merely to refrain from acting on it (Williams, 1996). In this sense, it becomes clear that unchosen differences—such as race, nationality, and sex—cannot be the appropriate circumstances for the virtue of toleration, given that it is morally wrong to disapprove of or dislike these differences. There is no merit in refraining from racist attack, because it is wrong to have racist attitudes in the first place.

The differences that can be the proper candidates for the virtue of tolerance are, then:

- disliked or disapproved;
- important;
- choosable or revisable;
- not clearly and universally morally condemned.

In turn, disapproval or dislike should be sustained by some reasons, otherwise respect for others requires abandoning these negative judgements.

Once the proper circumstances for toleration have been defined, the moral analysis has to face the matter of justifying tolerance—but this is problematical. Why, in fact, should

KEY CONCEPTS

Difference

Alternative conceptions of differences correspond to distinct views of toleration. The conception of toleration as moral virtue, for example, considers, as proper circumstances of toleration, differences that are disliked, important, and chosen or revisable. According to the political conception of toleration, the relevant aspect is the potential or actual conflict of differences that, consequently, should be judged in terms of compatibility with the laws of the country and the persistence of democracy. Toleration as recognition acknowledges the importance of the collective dimension of differences and takes into account the asymmetry of power among differences; it aims at reversing the symbolic and social exclusion that is linked to differences between minority groups.

one allow something of which one morally disapproves and which one thinks there are good reasons to prevent (Raphael, 1988: 147)? Put this way, toleration looks paradoxical (Cohen, 1967; Harrison, 1979), but the paradox of toleration can, in fact, be shown to be merely apparent. Briefly, the conflict between the two contradictory duties—one requiring the tolerator to intervene in order to prevent some wrongdoing; and the other, to let others do as they see fit—can be solved if tolerance is acknowledged to follow from a principle of a higher order than the first-order moral judgements from which requirements to interfere with perceived wrongdoing issue. Such a higher order principle is found, for example, in respect for other people (Mendus, 1988): one ought to tolerate a disapproved practice because of the respect due to the **agent,** and to his or her **autonomy** and integrity, despite moral disapproval of what he or she does. Alternative justifications, showing tolerance as either a rational ideal or as the prudential alternative to repression, are less convincing, because they do not account for the special moral quality of tolerance (Waldron, 1988: 61–86). By contrast, respect provides strong moral reasons for accepting what is disliked or disapproved of. The moral value of the agent, beyond his or her acts, is what the virtue of toleration is supposed to recognize. The moral quality of the agent lies in the capacity for free choice, which is the real ground for respect, even when the chosen actions, attitudes, and beliefs may be objectionable. The value of free choice, independent of what is chosen, is autonomy: so, as much as the differences to be tolerated are the result of choices, autonomy turns out to be the ultimate value on which to ground tolerance.

KEY CONCEPTS

The ethical paradox of toleration

The paradox lies in the fact that the demands of toleration can be opposed to the demands of one's ethical code. If I believe that a certain kind of conduct is wrong, it should follow that I have a duty to prevent the wrongdoing, if I am able to do so. But toleration asks that I suspend my power of interference with the wrong conduct and let the other person act as he or she wants. The apparent paradox is solved if toleration is justified by means of a principle that is more important than the principles of one's morality, such as respect for others.

Does the philosophical interpretation of tolerance provide the basis for the crucial corresponding social and political practice? It is doubtful, because the moral virtue of tolerance turns out to be rather narrow in its meaning and scope. On the one hand, it encompasses only the negative conception of toleration as 'putting up with' and non-interference; on the other hand, it leaves out much of the most relevant and divisive differences of contemporary pluralism, which have to do with ascriptive traits, such as race, sex, nationality, and collective identities. What happens, then, to the differences that cannot be ascribed to the autonomous choices of individuals? Can they be rightfully suppressed, despised, or in any way penalized? Despite these possible limitations, the philosophical analysis provides a set of analytical definitions and distinctions that can help to clarify practical cases.

☆ KEY POINTS

- The moral analysis aims to provide a highly detailed conception of toleration to be used as a foundation for the corresponding social and political practice.

- Toleration is thus accounted as a distinct moral attitude, not to be confused with indifference and acquiescence, and justified by the higher principle of respect for other persons, which prevents the tolerator from curbing the disapproved conduct.

- The resulting moral virtue of tolerance is rather narrow in its meaning and scope. It implies only the negative meaning of non-interference, and leaves out much of the most relevant and divisive differences of contemporary pluralism, such as race, sex, and nationality. This limits the possible application of tolerance at the social and political levels.

The contemporary liberal theory of toleration

An alternative conception of toleration is as the political principle allowing for the coexistence of conflicting differences in the same society. The relevant circumstance for this political principle of toleration is pluralism of contrasting views, traditions, and culture (Rawls, 1993). In line with the liberal tradition, political toleration does not require the suspension of the power of interference with disliked differences, but rather the adoption of a neutral stance vis-à-vis conflictual social differences that have been acknowledged as irrelevant for political matters. Once the rule of law is established, and the universal rights of religious liberty, freedom of expression, and freedom of association are granted, opinions, conducts, and practices that do not harm any third party and which do not threaten social order belong to the area of personal and social freedom. The disapproving judgement constituting a crucial condition for the moral virtue of tolerance cannot be reconciled with the political disregard that is required by neutrality. The reasons for political toleration are thus independent of the content of the difference, deriving instead from principles of justice (Rawls, 1971).

The political conception of toleration proposed by **neutralist liberalism** overcomes the tone of moral condescension characterizing the moral virtue. Neutralist liberalism is a strand of contemporary liberal theory for which neutrality is not only a guideline for the public treatment of citizens, but also the central feature of liberal institutions, which ought to be designed independently of any substantive moral outlook, so as to be recognized as legitimate by people who widely disagree about values and morals (Ackerman, 1980; Dworkin, 1978; Larmore, 1987; Nagel, 1991; Rawls, 1993). The judgemental gaze implied by tolerance is substituted by neutrality and this makes the political principle truly universal, aimed at the openness, inclusion, and impartiality of anyone within the boundary of liberal institutions. The meaning of political toleration, though, is still negative: toleration is translated as individual freedom from political or social obstacles to pursue one's ideals of the good life. Individual freedom from obstacles requires negative liberty, as opposed to positive liberty—that is, the capacity to be the real author of one's choices (Berlin, 1969; 2002). In sum, the political principle of liberal toleration unites the universal ideal of equal liberty and respect with the negative meaning of liberty as non-interference.

But liberal neutrality has perverse effects by virtue of two basic problems. The first lies in the liberal consideration of pluralism in terms of potentially conflicting conceptions of the good (Rawls, 1988). Conceptions of the good, whether shared or not, are individualistic: individuals hold them and can change or revise them. This makes the collective dimension of differences disappear. But contemporary pluralism is characterized by collective identities that are linked to different cultures and traditions, which have a different dimension and weight from those of personal opinions and beliefs. The latter can easily be ignored in the public arena and be practised in the **private sphere**, well away from public sight. By contrast, differences linked to collective identities—whether cultural, religious, or sexually oriented—are less fit to be pursued in private spaces and hidden from public areas. Liberal toleration keeps the original divide between public and private areas, but while equal freedom is certainly granted in the private space, it is not clear that it can extend to the public exhibition of differences.

The second problem relates to a basic insensitivity towards issues of power. ➔ See Chapter 14. From the neutral viewpoint of liberal politics, all differences appear equally irrelevant, but this disguises the fact that some are more relevant than others: differences linked to race, ethnicity, sexual orientation, and culture are markers of oppressed or excluded collective identities to which various kinds of disadvantages are assigned and to which non-membership, or second-class membership, in the polity often attaches. Disregarding these differences in the **public sphere** means that the issue of inclusion is simply conceived as the extension of rights to individuals despite their identity. The resulting difference-blind attitude, far from neutralizing the exclusionary effect of certain differences, actually reinforces it. Liberal toleration opens liberal citizenship to anyone, at least in principle, but only as individuals. This approach does not help bearers of different identities to become members on an equal footing with the majority, whose collective identity is settled, taken for granted, and deposited and protected in societal standards. In order to become citizens in the full sense, bearers of different identities are implicitly asked to bracket those identities and the related differences in public, and to acquire political membership only as 'naked' individuals. If they claim that toleration of their differences becomes both public and positive, they are seen as trespassing on the public sphere and on the required public blindness to differences. Yet the neutral public sphere, which is strenuously defended against invasion, is in fact already inhabited by the particular and partial identities of the majority, and so the rigorous exclusion of different identities now appears unfair. Thus the anti-discriminatory aim of neutrality turns out, perversely, to imply unequal and unfair consequences for members of oppressed or excluded groups.

☆ KEY POINTS

- Contemporary liberal theory construes toleration as the political principle allowing for the coexistence of conflicting differences in the same society.
- The relevant circumstance for political toleration is pluralism and its nature requires the adoption of a neutral stance vis-à-vis conflictual social differences.
- The liberal approach overcomes the tone of moral condescension that characterizes the moral virtue. Toleration is grounded on justice, and is aimed at the openness, impartiality, and inclusion of anyone in liberal politics, independently of his or her origin, views, and culture.
- The liberal disregard of social differences, which aims at avoiding discrimination, produces perverse effects because it disguises the unequal standing of some social differences in relation to others. Members of oppressed 'different' groups are tolerated as such in the private sphere, but enjoy less than the equal respect and liberty that is promised by liberal institutions.

Toleration as recognition

Toleration as recognition is meant to overcome these shortcomings and to fulfil toleration's original aims of equal liberty, equal respect, and openness. The argument for toleration as recognition starts with a reconsideration of the problems giving rise to issues of toleration. ➡ **See Chapter 7.** In contemporary democracy, freedom from persecution and non-interference with religious conscience are taken for granted; toleration is therefore directed at something beyond this. In order to grasp what is at stake, pluralism needs to be reconsidered. Behind apparently individualistic conceptions of the good, there are, in fact, groups in marginal and subordinate positions, demanding to be recognized on an equal footing with societal majorities and conflicting over the public acceptance of their different identities. Thus, the present-day conflict does not primarily concern incompatible differences of values and cultures—which are mostly taken care of by toleration as non-interference embodied in civil rights—but, rather, the unequal public standing of those professing minority views who therefore demand toleration as a fair access for their differences in the public space (Leader, 1996).

Only if pluralism is seen to include groups, cultures, and identities that are excluded or unequally included in democratic citizenship can the conflict underlying issues of toleration be seen as going beyond the disagreement about values, beliefs, and practices (Phillips, 1993). The fight over the public acceptance of differences can then be understood not simply as an issue of compatibility with the ideal, and the practice, of liberal values and principles, but rather as a contested attempt to reverse marginality and exclusion, and to gain fair access to public spaces and the benefits that this brings. Because marginality or exclusion come to individuals as the consequence of membership of minority groups, recognition—that is, the positive assertion of differences in the public space—is seen as the first symbolic step towards full inclusion.

In this framework, sources of contemporary problems of toleration are, in general, collective or group differences, disliked by the majority of society. These problems erupt when different groups resist the confinement of their differences outside the mainstream of liberal society, in the various real, or ideal, ghettos composing contemporary pluralism. When group members stop being quietly separated, or refuse to be obediently assimilated or conveniently masked to gain a fragile inclusion, the boundaries of liberal toleration are questioned and a double extension is demanded: first, a spatial extension from the private to the public domain; second, a semantic extension from the negative meaning of non-interference to the positive sense of acceptance and recognition (Apel, 1997).

When these extensions are demanded, contests over the public toleration of differences develop, because some groups' practice in public space is perceived to be loud and provocative, and hence as an invasion of particular identities into the political domain and as a plea for special consideration, which infringes neutrality. In these cases, toleration of differences in the public sphere can be defended on the grounds of justice. Public exclusion of differences is unfair, first, because it treats members of minorities differently from members of the majority, whose identity and practices are openly visible everywhere in the political domain, and second, because the invisibility of differences contrives to keep minorities in a marginal position of second-class citizenship. Toleration can meet these questions of justice relating to minorities' unequal social standing if it is conceived of as the public recognition of excluded, marginalized, and oppressed identities (Galeotti, 2002). Thus, the argument for toleration as recognition can be shown to be grounded on principles of liberal justice—namely, non-discrimination, equality of respect, and inclusion.

Yet some may object that toleration as recognition nevertheless implies a conflict with liberal principles—that is, with neutrality, universality, and impartiality. Recognition seems to suggest that differences should be considered in their content in order to be valued; in doing so, the state and its officials have to refer to some ideal of the good as the criterion of value. In this way, the liberal state must give up its neutralist stance if it is to practise toleration as recognition. Moreover, public recognition of differences cannot be granted universally, but only always specifically and only for those differences that have been acknowledged as valuable. Thus, impartiality, too, would be sacrificed in the name of identity politics.

This objection, however, depends on a questionable conception of recognition. Recognition is interpreted here as acknowledging, or even endorsing, the intrinsic value of the difference in question (Taylor, 1993). In this strong interpretation, recognition cannot apply to democratic institutions. But public recognition of differences admits of another, less problematic meaning (Fraser, 2003; Galeotti, 2002). Differences can be recognized not for their intrinsic value (which it is not the function of the political authorities to appreciate), but instrumentally, for the value that they represent to their bearers. In other words, the public recognition of differences has nothing to do with the public appreciation of a difference and of its value, not to say its public

KEY CONCEPTS

Recognition

In Charles Taylor's (1993) sense, recognition means that minorities that have suffered oppression or exclusion do not simply want equal rights and **assimilation**; they also want to have their full-blown identities recognized as valuable by democratic politics. The claim can be supported by various reasons, but, so stated, cannot be fully met, given that some identities appear to be incompatible with democratic principles and values, and incompatible among each other. However, recognition admits of other less stringent interpretations than Taylor's (see Fraser, 2003; Galeotti, 2002).

endorsement. This more modest notion requires the acceptance, and hence the inclusion, of a different trait, practice, or identity in the range of the legitimate, viable, 'normal' options of an open society. In this respect, the public recognition of differences, being independent from their content, is in fact compatible with public neutrality, although under a revised interpretation. It neither means the equal banning of all differences and particularities from the public sphere, nor the disregard of all differences in public action.

Although recognition works only if granted to single identities, this does not mean singling out and favouring any group in particular, hence giving up the principle of universal justice. Symbolic recognition, which is implied in toleration, is not exclusive—that is, it is not a scarce commodity, posing problems of distribution. Provided that the difference in question does not infringe any right, public recognition, although it must be granted to each difference separately, can be generalized to all claimants.

A final point: toleration as recognition implies reasons for toleration that differ from those of the liberal approach, and this makes toleration symbolically significant in a different way. From a literal point of view, toleration always means granting freedom of expression to some practice or conduct—but the change of attitude from the negative view of non-interference to the positive view of recognizing the difference as legitimate is crucial. The supporters of toleration as recognition think that this change of reasons to support the same political act helps to build a superior-quality coexistence of differences within pluralism.

☆ KEY POINTS

- Toleration as recognition proposes a double extension of liberal toleration: a spatial extension, from the private to the public domain, and a semantic extension, from the negative meaning of non-interference to the positive sense of acceptance and recognition.

- Toleration as recognition is grounded on justice and aims at reversing the unfair public exclusion of collective differences, which unjustly reinforces oppression and marginality.

- Toleration can address the problem of unequal social standing of minority groups if it implies a symbolic acceptance of their different practices in the range of legitimate social alternatives; toleration as recognition achieves this symbolic acceptance.

Conclusion

Historically, the theory of toleration emerged as the solution to the challenge posed by the religious wars that devastated early modern Europe after the Reformation, and it constituted a first step for liberal politics. Theoretically, toleration has provided a strategy for making the liberty of each individual in matters of beliefs, values, and ways of life compatible with the liberty of everybody else, and for minimizing state coercion. In the last few decades, toleration has been called anew to the front line of philosophy and political theory to meet the challenges of democratic pluralism in a globalized world. Despite general agreement on the need for more toleration in the present political and social circumstances, its nature, scope, and justification are matters of theoretical contention among philosophers and political thinkers.

The contemporary debate is characterized by three approaches, which deliver two distinctive views.

1. The moral analysis of toleration addresses the problem of a proper definition of the concept and justification of toleration, with the sophisticated tools of contemporary moral theory.

2. The liberal political analysis sees toleration as the political principle for dealing with pluralism in a liberal fashion.

3. A different, critical strand of political analysis revises the traditional concept of toleration so as to make it better suited to face pluralistic conflicts.

The first two approaches revisit the traditional concept, with their own different tools, and propose the view of toleration as non-interference with the different behaviour and practices of others, no matter whether and how much these are disliked, as long as rights are not infringed. The third approach finds the negative conception of toleration as non-interference insufficient for facing contemporary problems and proposes a double extension from the traditional concept: a spatial extension, from the private to the public, and a semantic extension, from non-interference to recognition.

Toleration as recognition consists in a change of attitude towards the difference under scrutiny and, indirectly, towards the bearers of the difference. When dealing with actual cases, supporters of the negative conception usually ask questions of compatibility, such as:

- Does this practice infringe any liberal values and principles?
- If it does, does it constitute a threat to the liberal order?
- Is that a sufficient reason not to tolerate it, even if no harm is caused?

By contrast, supporters of toleration as recognition ask questions of justice, such as:

- Is it fair to prohibit this practice?
- Does it harm anyone?
- Does it represent a real danger for public security?
- Is the alleged contrast of this practice with liberal values well grounded, or is it loaded with biases and prejudices and double standards?

In other words, the reasons for toleration should be acceptable for the tolerated as well as for the tolerator. So conceived, toleration is not only on firmer ground but also constitutes a crucial step for the inclusion of those identified with the different and contested practice.

 CASE STUDY

The contest over purpose-built mosques in Europe

In recent decades, Muslim communities coming from many different African and Asian countries have steadily been growing throughout Europe. In all European countries, religious freedom is acknowledged to be a fundamental right, usually embodied in Constitutions. Thus, the building of appropriate places of worship for Muslims would be expected as the obvious consequence of their residency in European countries. But this is not the case. While the so-called 'garage or backyard mosques' multiply, the resistance over the construction of purpose-built mosques, with or without the minaret, is widespread and has produced intense political conflicts in many cities including Cologne, Copenhagen, and Milan, often becoming an issue in national politics (Allievi, 2010).

The controversy over mosque building raises two questions of toleration. First, is the mosque issue truly a problem of toleration? Second, does it raise issues of *religious* toleration? The first question arises because those who oppose mosque building deny that their position infringes Muslims' religious freedom, and thus deny that their opposition is intolerant. Instead, they maintain that Muslims are free to pray to Allah but within the boundary of our laws and customary practices, without creating problems of public order and security. In other words, building mosques in the public squares of European cities is alleged to violate the limits of toleration on the grounds that (a) it is an invasion of religion into the secular space, (b) it constitutes a threat to public order as secluded places for Islamic propaganda and, possibly, terrorism nurturing; (c) it represents a sign of Muslim unwillingness to integrate into European society; and (d) it is an unacceptable Islamization of the traditional landscape of European cities. On the opposite side, Muslims, and people who favour mosque building, maintain that these arguments are intolerant and curtail Muslims' right to religious freedom.

This controversy represents a typical instance of issues of toleration in the context of contemporary pluralism within a framework of democratic politics, where both parties accuse each other of intolerance (Newey, 2013). In our times, the issue is no more the persecution, suppression, and forced conversion of the infidels, but rather, the public visibility and hence, ultimately, the social legitimation, of their different practices of worship. Muslims' rights to freedom of religious belief and worship are not questioned in general, but it is claimed that purpose-built mosques exceed the limits of toleration in a pluralist, democratic society. Here, the distance between traditional and contemporary issues of toleration can be appreciated: the focal point of the argument around toleration in advanced democracies has shifted from the reasons in favour of toleration and against persecution to *the pros and cons of placing the limits of toleration at a certain point*. In this way, we can explain why, for some actors and commentators, the conflict over mosque building does not raise questions of toleration and freedom of religion, but rather, activates concerns about public order, architectural fitness, the risk of nurturing terrorism, and so on (Galeotti, 2014). I turn, then, to an examination of the problem of the justifiable limits of toleration regarding mosques.

Those who oppose mosque building refer to the Lockean divide between the private area of conscience, representing the proper object of toleration, and the public arena, wherein liberty may legitimately be restricted. Using the private/public distinction, the building of a proper mosque could represent a trespass in the public secularized sphere. This view, however, is heavily vitiated by double standards: no majority religion is totally confined in private and hidden from public sight. Furthermore, this approach fails to register that 'public' may mean either 'political' or 'non-personal': the claim to public visibility need not be understood in terms of the desire to trespass in the political and secular space, but rather, in terms of the desire to be openly present in civil society instead of hidden in ghettos, in the closet of garage mosques.

In connection with this is the argument that Islam is incompatible with liberal and democratic principles, which also suggests limiting toleration of it to strictly private areas. The claim that mosques constitute a real risk to law and order can take two forms. First, a literal concern for 'public order', such as petty crime, traffic, and parking problems. These are the legitimate, if narrow, worries of neighbours who are afraid of the worsening of their daily life, of the circulation of people and parking in the area surrounding the new mosque. Such worries are, however, similar to those raised by new shopping malls, cinemas, or clubs, and, as such, do not bring up issues of toleration. Second, the putative risk to law and order may be understood in terms of a concern for state security and the survival of democracy. Here, the reference is to Islamic fundamentalism and terrorism, which has indeed been a real threat to citizens' security in the last decades. While few would underestimate the potential for terrorism to stem from fundamentalism, just how strong the connection is between terrorism, fundamentalism, and Islam, as such, is far from settled—for all the vehemence with which this is insisted upon by mosque objectors such as Ralph Giordano, in the Cologne case (Giordano, 2007), or politicians of the Lega Nord for Milano (Allievi, 2010).

According to this extreme view, moderate Islam is just a kind of cover-up—a vehicle for gaining easy tolerance from our overly indulgent democracies. This view, fuelling Islamophobia throughout Europe, is clearly against all evidence, and can be maintained only thanks to an underlying conspiracy theory which discounts the beliefs and actions of the wide majority of moderate and secular Muslims as mere pretence (Allievi and Nielsen, 2003).[1] The main points of this position are that: (a) Islam nurtures fundamentalism and thus (indirectly) terrorism; (b) because of the lack of distinction between religious and political authority, Islam threatens the very foundation of liberalism, grounded on the separation between State and Church, civil law, and moral codes; and (c) Islam essentially embodies a degrading view of women and their oppression within the family and in society. According to this view, a moderate Islam and a secular Muslim are intrinsically contradictory. This position is clearly implausible for it does not reflect facts about Muslims in Europe that are well supported by data, showing that the majority of Muslims in Europe are either secular or moderately religious and willing to integrate (EUMC, 2006). Concerning the mosque issue, in all cases considered, Muslim representatives have been very open to negotiations about the location, size (height and minaret), and architectural features of the proposed building; in real circumstances of controversy, Muslims played the role of the 'reasonable side', while their opponents voiced stereotypes and prejudices as 'non-negotiable Western values' (Allievi, 2010).

But even granting the risk of fundamentalism, the opposition to mosque building does not follow. The fact is that anti-Islamic intellectuals and politicians do not yet dare to add a call either for the direct expulsion of the Muslim population from European countries, or for the forced conversion of Muslims to Christianity. Such measures, though hardly legitimate, would actually be the consistent consequence of holding Islam as intrinsically intolerable—and yet they are clearly out of the question in liberal democracies. But then, if Muslims are to live in European democracies, and not be expelled or forcibly converted, why should the establishment of mosques constitute a *special* danger? Why should purpose-built mosques, as opposed to their backyard alternatives, pose a special terrorist risk? For if it is the gathering of people which is regarded as dangerous (perhaps because of how it enables proselytism and propaganda), then backyard mosques are all the more dangerous, being less visible and so more fit for secret goals.

Another, less serious, threat to law and order sometimes claimed to be associated with mosques is that they enable Muslim self-seclusion, signalling a symbolic rejection of integration. Here, the claim is that proper mosques ensure that Muslim people remain an alien culture, characterized by suspicion towards the Western democratic city (Calder and Zuolo, 2014). Those who oppose mosque building sometimes interpret the Muslim desire for a proper place of worship as a clear rejection of our culture and of integration. This argument may strike emotional chords among the majority, but it hardly makes sense. The underlying idea here seems to be that if a religious group wants to gather and pray in such an exotic and alien building, totally unfit for 'our' urban landscape, they are perversely attached to a culture which is, by analogy, similarly unfit to be accommodated in our culture. This reasoning ignores the fact that a place of worship is, by definition, reserved for the community of believers, and that religious rituals and prayers are necessarily specific to that faith. Thus, all believers in all religions, when engaged in practices of worship, gather together and temporarily 'segregate' themselves from other activities and other aspects of public life. Should we infer that all believers are not properly integrated? Either we hold religion *as such* as an encouragement to non-integration, or we must acknowledge that Muslims have the same right to a proper place of worship as any other congregation. As to the exotic and alien look of a mosque, compared to a church, there is no difference here between mosques and any architectural innovation in our cities. Thus, the argument of self-segregation leading to a risk for law and order is unsuccessful.

In the end, what is left of the claim that mosques are a threat for public order is the claim that their establishment upsets societal standards and the established identity of public space. The majority's uneasiness about different and strange customs and practices upsetting societal standards and established conventions, should be granted and taken seriously, yet it cannot constitute a sufficient reason to stop toleration of the public presence of immigrants' expressions of difference, such as through the establishment of a purpose-built mosque. In conclusion, the arguments advanced for constructing proper mosques in European cities beyond the limits of toleration do not stand, and refer to a minimal conception of toleration confined to private space only. Public visibility is, instead, a condition for toleration as recognition, understood as a requirement of equal respect for minorities, and issuing in their full inclusion in society.

Returning now to the second question raised at the start of this case study: is the controversy over mosque building one of *religious* toleration? Mosques are no doubt places of worship and of meeting for Muslim believers, and hence they are symbols of faith. Yet the resistance to the building of proper mosques is not based on specifically religious reasons: the worry is not that a heresy may take hold among Christians, nor that miscreants are encouraged to proliferate. And there is no desire to eradicate the 'wrong' religion in order to save the souls of the erring people. These were the reasons motivating the religious wars in sixteenth- and seventeenth-century Europe. In the case of mosques, that is clearly *not* what is at stake. Religious disagreement is not the real point—which also explains why many commentators maintain that religious freedom is protected for Muslims even if they are prohibited from building mosques. The real point is the contest over the control of societal standards and the identity of public space—control felt, by the majority, to be threatened by the visible presence of symbols, practices, customs which are unfamiliar and upset the orderly stability of public life. Islam provides a ready-to-use label, unifying immigrants from many and different cultures, so different to those of Eastern Europe, and hence more threatening, and allegedly more dangerous, for the societal standards. In order to lump a variety of groups and communities together, Islam comes in handy, for it provides a means of articulating the diffidence and hostility towards alien customs and darker, usually poor people that can appear in public discourse.

In summary, the essence of the fight over mosques, as well as over the public display of other religious and cultural symbols, is not related to religious disagreement. On the contrary, the demonization of Islam serves as a kind of cover for the cultural distaste for newcomers with a darker skin and unfamiliar customs and rituals 'invading' our cities and countries. Such intolerant feelings cannot be licensed by democratic principles (i.e. equal respect and equal rights), while the appropriate type of toleration here must imply the recognition both of the legitimate presence of different identities and wider and more diverse social standards.

? QUESTIONS

1. What is 'toleration'? Why is it a problematic virtue?
2. What, and how, does toleration contribute to peace and order?
3. Why are social differences necessary for toleration to be possible?
4. What is the origin of the doctrine of toleration?
5. How can toleration, as a political principle, and tolerance, as a social virtue, be distinguished?
6. What is the link between toleration and neutrality?
7. What is the link between toleration and pluralism?
8. 'Different conceptions of toleration presuppose different kinds of differences.' Can you illustrate this statement?
9. What are the limits of toleration?
10. What is the paradox of toleration? Can it be solved?
11. What are the negative and positive conceptions of toleration, respectively?
12. Why is the mosque case an issue of toleration?
13. What is the focus of the mosque controversy: expulsion or forced conversion of Muslims living in Europe, or placing rigid limits on their religious liberty?

FURTHER READING

■ Brown, W. (2008) *Regulating Aversion: Tolerance in the Age of Identity and Empire*, Princeton, NJ: Princeton University Press This book examines the dark side of tolerance from the perspective of the tolerated instead of that of the tolerator. It argues, against liberals, that tolerance is an expression of power and condescension, rather than a virtue. Moreover, that tolerance is instrumental in tracing the difference between the 'civilized' West and 'barbaric' Islam and, in that respect, is not a tool for peace, but rather of empire.

■ Castiglione, D. and McKinnon, C. (2003) *Toleration, Neutrality and Democracy*, Dordrecht: Kluwer Academic and McKinnon, C. and Castiglione, D. (2003) *The Culture of Toleration in Diverse Societies*, Manchester/New York: Manchester University Press Two collections of essays providing the reader with a wide range of perspectives, approaches, theoretical analyses, and political issues surrounding toleration in contemporary democracy. The essays are all written by well-known subject scholars. The result is a well-informed, up-to-date, and rich map of toleration.

■ Forst, R. (2013) *Toleration in Conflict. Past and Present,* Cambridge: Cambridge University Press A vast study on the concept and the conceptions of toleration, as they have been expressed in the history of political thought from antiquity to the modern era, and as they are debated today in philosophy and politics. Toleration is portrayed as an intrinsically contentious notion that philosophy helps to clarify.

■ Galeotti, A. E. (2002) *Toleration as Recognition,* Cambridge: Cambridge University Press Develops an argument in favour of a positive view of toleration as recognition, starting from the criticism of the traditional negative view of tolerance as non-interference.

■ Leiter, B. (2013) *Why Tolerate Religion,* Princeton: Princeton University Press Questions the special status of religious convictions as objects of toleration compared with other claims of conscience.

■ McKinnon, C. (2006) *Toleration: A Critical Introduction,* London: Routledge Presents a useful overview of the theoretical and political aspects of toleration. The author examines various theoretical accounts of toleration, the main authors who contributed to the doctrine, and possible application to contemporary issues, such as the 'headscarves affair' in French schools, female circumcision, pornography, and Holocaust denial.

■ Newey, G. (2013) *Toleration in Political Conflict,* Cambridge: Cambridge University Press Argues for a concept of toleration which is intrinsically political and bound up in political disputes and partisan advocacy. Criticizing the liberal conception of toleration, Newey indicates the mechanisms of power which remain invisible in a purely conceptual or normative approach.

■ Tyler, A. (2008) *Islam, the West and Tolerance: Conceiving Coexistence,* London: Palgrave Macmillan This work draws original insights from the history of thought, religions, and cultures on the possibility of the coexistence of different cultures. The concept and the practice of tolerance are the crucial intercultural bridge for coexistence to prosper.

■ Williams, M. and Waldron, J. (eds) (2008) *Toleration and Its Limits,* Nomos XVIII, New York: New York University Press This collection of essays comprises four sections: the first on classical thinkers of toleration (Hobbes, Spinoza, Bayle, Locke, and Mill); the second on toleration as a political virtue; the third on liberal toleration; and the fourth and last on toleration and identity.

■ Zuolo, F. (ed) *European Journal of Political Theory,* 12, July 2013, special issue on *Frontiers of Toleration and Respect: Non Moral Approaches and Group Relations* Contains five articles and an introduction exploring the concept of toleration in relation to that of equal respect.

 WEB LINKS

● http://www.iep.utm.edu/tolerate Entry on 'Toleration', authored by Andrew Fiala, in *The Internet Encyclopedia of Philosophy.*

● http://plato.stanford.edu/archives/sum2012/entries/toleration/ Entry on 'Toleration', authored by Rainer Forst (2012).

● http://www.pluralism.org In 1991, the Pluralism Project at Harvard University began a pioneering study of the USA's changing religious landscape. Through an expanding network of affiliates, it documents the contours of US multi-religious society, explores new forms of interfaith engagement, and studies the impact of religious diversity in civic life.

- http://www.tolerance.ca A French webzine on tolerance that claims to be independent and neutral in relation to all political and religious orientations. Tolerance.ca® aims to promote awareness of the major democratic principles on which tolerance is based.

- http://www.tolerance.org Teaching Tolerance is introduced by its creators as *'a principal online destination for people interested in dismantling bigotry and creating, in hate's stead, communities that value diversity'*.

- http://www.yale.edu/lawweb/avalon/avalon.htm A complete web collection of documents in law, history, and diplomacy, hosted by the University of Yale. All of the most important documents relating to the right of religious freedom and toleration can be accessed via this website.

 Visit the Online Resource Centre that accompanies this book to access more learning resources: http://www.oxfordtextbooks.co.uk/orc/mckinnon3e/

 ENDNOTE

1 And yet, the Islamophobic position is shared throughout Europe by many anti-immigrant/right-wing parties such as Vlaams Belang, FPÖ (The Freedom Party of Austria), the BNP (British National Party), and Lega Nord, to mention but a few.

4

Democracy

THOMAS CHRISTIANO

Chapter contents

- Introduction
- Instrumentalism
- Does democracy have non-instrumental value?
- The problem of democratic citizenship
- Democratic institutions
- Conclusion

Reader's guide

Democracy is perhaps the most successful and, for many, the most normatively compelling form of political organization in history. For many, democratic institutions are the zenith of political development—but not everyone agrees with this assessment. Some reject them as key mechanisms for the colonization of less-developed nations by powerful industrialized interests. In this chapter, we will discuss some of the different conceptions of the normative grounds of democracy. After some preliminaries, we will review instrumental considerations that favour and disfavour democracy, before exploring some arguments for the intrinsic value of democracy. We will then discuss one of the most fundamental challenges that a theory of democracy must face: the problem of citizenship. After elaborating a conception of citizenship, we will discuss some of the institutional prerequisites of democratic institutions if they are to meet the challenge of citizenship. Finally, we will discuss deliberative polling as a way of realizing democratic ideals.

Introduction

Although many assert that something similar to **democracy** existed in pre-agricultural societies, it makes its first formal appearance in the Greek city states of the classical period—most notably, in Athens in the sixth and fifth centuries bc. This was a highly attenuated form of democracy, because women could not participate and a large proportion of the population were slaves. Nevertheless, it was a remarkable and hard-won achievement in the ancient world. After the demise of ancient Greek democracies, 'democracy' was essentially a term of abuse until the end of the nineteenth century, although popular (free, male) participation did exist in the Roman Republic and the Italian city states between the twelfth and sixteenth centuries. Democracy makes its appearance in the form as we know it, of representative democracy, at the end of the eighteenth century, with the French and American Revolutions. Even these did not describe themselves as democratic and only the French Revolution included women—and even then, only for a very short period, before pulling back from political equality for women. Representative democracy comes into its own with universal manhood suffrage at the end of the nineteenth century and women's suffrage in the mid twentieth century. Much of the current debate in political theory concerns whether and how representative democracy can live up to the ideals that underpin democracy. This chapter will attempt to navigate some of the main issues in this debate.

The term 'democracy', as I will use it in this chapter, refers very generally to a method of group decision making that is characterized by a kind of equality among the participants at an essential stage. The task of **normative** democratic theory is not to settle questions of definition, but to determine which, if any, of the forms that democracy may take are morally desirable, and when and how. To evaluate the arguments of democratic theorists, we must decide on the merits of the different principles, and conceptions, of humanity and society from which they proceed.

We can evaluate democracy along at least two different dimensions:

- instrumentally, by reference to the outcomes of using it compared with other methods of political decision making;
- intrinsically, by reference to qualities that are inherent in the method—for example, whether there is something inherently fair about making democratic decisions about matters on which people disagree.

Instrumentalism

Instrumental arguments in favour of democracy

Two kinds of instrumental benefit are commonly attributed to democracy: relatively good laws, and policies and improvements in the characters of the participants. John Stuart Mill (1861; 1991) argued that a democratic method of making legislation is better than non-democratic methods in three ways: strategically, epistemically, and via the improvement of the characters of democratic citizens.

 KEY TEXTS

Mill, *Considerations on Representative Government* (1861)

John Stuart Mill's *Considerations on Representative Government* is one of the seminal works—along with John Locke's *Second Treatise on Civil Government* (1690) and Jean-Jacques Rousseau's *Of the Social Contract* (1762)—in the history of democratic theory. In *Considerations on Representative Government*, Mill defends universal popular participation in government and a kind of proportional representation, on the bases that these forms of rule are likely to enhance the quality of legislation and to improve the characters of individual citizens. Mill also defends the justifiability, in principle, of plural voting, which aimed to give more votes to the better educated sections of the citizenry.

 KEY CONCEPTS

Instrumentalism

Instrumentalists contend that instrumental arguments for and against the democratic process are the only bases on which to evaluate democracy or to compare it with other forms of political decision making. Three types of argument support instrumentalism. One proceeds from moral theories, such as **utilitarianism**, in which only the well-being of individuals is valuable. A second argues that, because political power is exercised by some over others, it can only be justified by reference to the interests of the subjects (Arneson, 2002). A third questions the coherence of the idea of intrinsically fair collective decision-making processes. Social choice theory is thought by some to support this conclusion (Riker, 1980).

Strategically, democracy has an advantage, because it forces decision makers to take into account the interests, rights, and opinions of most people in society. Because democracy gives some political power to each, more people are taken into account than under aristocracy or monarchy. One forceful contemporary statement of this instrumental argument is provided by Amartya Sen, who states, for example, that '*no substantial famine has ever occurred in any independent country with a democratic form of government and a relatively free press*' (1999: 152). The basis of this argument is that politicians in a multi-party democracy, with free elections and a free press, have incentives to respond to the expressions of needs of the poor.

Epistemologically, democracy is thought to be the best decision-making method, on the grounds that it is generally more reliable in helping participants to discover the right decisions. Because democracy brings a lot of people into the process of decision making, it can take advantage of many sources of information, and of the critical assessment of laws and policies. Democratic decision making tends to be more informed than other methods about the interests of citizens and the causal mechanisms that are necessary to advance those interests. Furthermore, the broad-based discussion that is typical of democracy enhances the critical assessment of the different moral ideas that guide decision makers (Estlund, 2007).

 KEY THINKERS

Jean-Jacques Rousseau (1712–78)

Rousseau's career as an intellectual started with a very influential essay, *Discourse on the Arts and Sciences* (1750; 1997), which questioned the predominant view that humanity is progressing. He wrote a highly influential novel and a major treatise on education. His key works are the *Second Discourse on the Origin of Inequality among Men* (1755; 1997) and *Of the Social Contract, Principles of Political Right* (1762; 1947; 1968). The latter is the most important work of political philosophy of the modern period. In these works, the concept of the person, and the secular ideals of freedom and equality that have dominated moral and political thought, are fully developed.

Many have endorsed democracy on the basis of the proposition that it has beneficial effects on character. Many have noted, with Mill and Rousseau, that democracy, more so than other forms of rule, tends to make people stand up for themselves because its collective decisions depend more upon the will of the people than do those made under monarchy or aristocracy. Hence, in democratic societies, individuals are encouraged to be more autonomous. In addition, democracy, in contrast to other forms of rule, tends to encourage people to think carefully and rationally, since whether they do so or not makes a difference. Finally, some have argued that democracy tends to enhance the moral qualities of citizens: when they participate in making decisions, they have to listen to others, they are called upon to justify themselves to others, and they are forced to think partly in terms of the interests of others. Some would claim that, when people find themselves in this kind of circumstance, they genuinely come to think in terms of the common good and justice and that, hence, democratic processes tend to enhance the **autonomy**, rationality, and morality of participants. Because these beneficial effects are thought to be worthwhile in themselves, they count in favour of democracy and against other forms of rule (Mill, 1861; 1991; Elster, 2002).

Instrumental challenges to democracy

Not all instrumental arguments favour democracy. Plato (360 BC; 1974) argued that democracy is inferior to various forms of monarchy, aristocracy, and even oligarchy, on the grounds that it tends to undermine the expertise that is necessary for properly governed societies. In a democracy, he argued, those who are effective at winning elections and nothing else will dominate politics. Most people do not have the kinds of knowledge that enable them to think well about the difficult issues that politics involves. But to win office or get a piece of legislation passed, politicians must discern and appeal to the majority's sense of what is right or not right. Hence, genuine expertise on law and policy is ignored and the state is guided by poorly worked out ideas that politicians have used to help themselves into office.

Hobbes (1651; 1968) argued that democracy is inferior to monarchy because democracy fosters destabilizing dissension among subjects. The main idea is that since there are many voters, no voter has a decisive influence on the outcome of the vote. It does not make much difference how an individual votes. As a result, no one feels much responsibility for the outcome of collective decision making—so citizens do not think much about politics or the common good. Even politicians, in a large assembly, do not have very much power—so they do not worry about the common good either, Hobbes argued. As a consequence, politicians simply concern themselves with gaining more power by mobilizing citizens. The only way in which to do this is by appealing to emotionally charged and highly divisive issues. Hence, they sow the seeds of conflict among irresponsible citizens.

☆ KEY POINTS

- Instrumental arguments for democracy ground it in the benefits that arise as a consequence of democratic decision making.

- Two kinds of instrumental benefit are often attributed to democratic decision making: that it produces good legislation and policy, and that it has a positive effect on the characters of democratic citizens.

- Some have argued that democracy actually has detrimental consequences for law and policy, and for the characters of citizens. Plato argued that democracy undermines expertise necessary for the proper exercise of political power. Hobbes argued that democracy creates destabilizing divisions in society.

- Some argue for instrumentalism on the grounds that political decision making involves the exercise of power of some over others. Others argue that there is no coherent way of describing how a political system can satisfy non-instrumental values.

Does democracy have non-instrumental value?

Some argue that, in addition to the instrumental values mentioned, some forms of decision making are independent of the consequences of having those beliefs. I will focus attention here on two different conceptions of the intrinsic worth of democracy: the deliberative conception of democracy and the egalitarian conception.

Deliberative democracy

The idea behind **deliberative democracy** is that laws and policies are legitimate to the extent that they are publicly justified to the citizens of the community. Public justification is justification to each citizen as a result of free and reasoned debate among equals. Citizens justify laws and policies to each other on the basis of mutually acceptable reasons. Democracy, properly understood, is the context in which individuals freely engage in a process of reasoned discussion and deliberation on an equal footing. The ideas of freedom and equality provide guidelines for structuring democratic institutions.

The basis of public justification is reasonable consensus among citizens. But because political societies are characterized by extensive disagreement, it has been urged that forms of consensus that are weaker than full consensus are sufficient for public justification, and that the weaker varieties are achievable in many societies. For example, there may be consensus on the list of publicly acceptable reasons, but disagreement on the weight of the different reasons. And there may be agreement on general reasons abstractly understood, but disagreement about particular interpretations of those reasons. Furthermore, it has been urged that the consensus on general reasons need only be partial. Reasons on which there is disagreement can be excluded from public justification; only those reasons that are part of an **overlapping consensus** of reasons—that is, when individuals agree only on a proper subset of their moral and political ideas, while disagreeing on other elements—are necessary for public justification. Finally, the consensus that is aimed at is reasonable consensus among reasonable persons.

Reasonableness

The basic principle behind most conceptions of deliberative democracy seems to be the principle of **reasonableness**, according to which reasonable persons will offer only principles for the regulation of their society that other reasonable persons can reasonably accept. The notion of the 'reasonable' is meant to be fairly weak on this account. One can reasonably reject a doctrine to the extent that it is incompatible with one's own doctrine, as long as one's own doctrine does not require its imposition on others and it is a doctrine that has survived sustained critical reflection. This is a principle of reciprocity, because one only offers principles that others, who restrain themselves in the same way, can accept. Reasonable persons restrain themselves from proposing laws and policies on the basis of controversial principles for the regulation of society. When individuals offer proposals for the regulation of their society, they ought not to appeal to the whole truth as they see it, but only to that part of the whole truth that others can reasonably accept (Cohen, 2009).

There are three key arguments for this principle of reasonableness:

- **Epistemological**

  There is no justification independent of what people, or at least reasonable people, believe. Hence, if one cannot provide a justification for principles that others can accept given their reasonable beliefs, then those principles are not justified for those persons.

- **Moral**

  One fails to respect the reason of the other members of society if one imposes terms of association on them that they cannot accept, given their reasonable views. This failure defeats the value of the principles that one is proposing for the society.

- **Democratic**

  One does not genuinely treat others as equals if one insists on imposing principles on them that they cannot reasonably accept, even if this imposition takes place against the background of egalitarian decision-making processes.

But each of these three arguments can be questioned. Within the democratic argument, it is not clear why it is necessary to **democratic equality** to justify one's views on terms that others can accept. If each person has robust rights to participate in debate and decision making, and each person's views are given a hearing, it is not clear why equality requires more. My rejection of another person's beliefs does not, in any way, imply that I think that person is inferior to me in capacity or in moral worth, or in the rights to have a say in society. The epistemological argument, meanwhile, seems to presuppose a conception of justification that is far too restrictive to be plausible. Many beliefs are justified for me, even if they are not compatible with the political beliefs that I currently hold, as long as those beliefs can be vindicated by the use of procedures and methods of thinking that I use to evaluate beliefs. The conception of respect for reason, in the moral argument, seems not to favour, obviously, the principle of reasonableness. It may require that I do as much as I can to make sure that the society in which I live conforms to what I take to be rationally defensible norms. Of course, I may also believe that such a society must be democratically organized, in which case, I will attempt to advance these principles through the democratic process.

Moreover, it is hard to see how this approach avoids the need for a complete consensus, which is highly unlikely to occur in any, even moderately diverse, society: it is not clear why it is any less of an imposition on me that I must restrict myself to considerations that other reasonable people accept, when I propose legislation or policies for society, than it is an imposition on others when I attempt to pass legislation on the basis of reasons that they reasonably reject. If I do restrain myself in this way, then the society in which I live will not meet the standards that I believe are essential to evaluating the society. I must then live in, and support, a society that does not accord with my conception of how it ought to be organized. It is not clear why this is any less of a loss of control over society than for those who must live in a society that is partly regulated by principles that they do not accept (Christiano, 2008b).

Egalitarian conceptions of democracy

Many democratic theorists have argued that democracy is a way of treating persons as equals when there is good reason to impose some kind of organization on their shared lives, but they disagree about how best to do it. On these views, democracy can be non-instrumentally justified because it realizes the ideal of political equality (Dahl, 1989). On the one hand, as defended by Peter Singer (1973), when people insist on different ways of arranging matters properly, each person, in a sense, claims a right to be dictator over their shared lives. But these claims to dictatorship cannot all hold up. Democracy embodies a kind of peaceful and fair compromise among these conflicting claims to rule. Each compromises equally on what he or she claims, as long as the others do the same, resulting in each having an equal say over decision making. In effect, democratic decision making respects each person's point of view on matters of common concern by giving each an equal say about what to do in cases of disagreement (Waldron, 1999a).

The trouble with this view is that if people disagree on the democratic method or on the particular form that democracy is to take, we must decide these latter questions by means of a higher order procedure. And if there is disagreement on the higher order procedure, must we also democratically decide that question? The view seems to lead to an infinite regress.

Another egalitarian defence of democracy asserts that it publicly embodies the equal advancement of the interests of the citizens of a society when there is disagreement about how best to organize their shared life. The idea is that a society ought to be structured to advance the interests of the members of the society equally; this ought to be done in such a way that each can see that he or she is being treated as equal. It requires equal advancement of interests in accordance with a public measure of those interests. Hence, justice requires the publicly equal advancement of the interests of the members of society or **public equality**—that is, a kind of equality that is realized in society in such a way that everyone can see that he or she is being treated as an equal.

The idea of public equality requires some explanation. Does it imply equality of well-being, or equality of opportunity for well-being, or **equality of resources**? The problem with this kind of account is that it cannot be realized in such a way that every conscientious and informed person can know them to be in place. There is too much disagreement on what well-being consists of, or how to compare the well-being of different people, or the importance of opportunity. So, even if one of these principles is implemented, many will think that they are not being treated equally. **➜ See Chapter 5.**

The publicly equal advancement of interests requires that individuals' judgements be taken into account equally when there is disagreement—and this is the argument for the transition from equal concern for interests to equal concern for judgement. Respect for each citizen's judgement is grounded in the principle of public equality, combined with a number of basic facts and fundamental interests that attend social life in typical societies. The basic facts are that individuals are very diverse in terms of their interests; they have different natural talents; they are raised in different sectors of society; and they are raised in diverse cultural milieus. Furthermore, people are likely to have deep cognitive biases when they attempt to understand other people's interests and how they compare to their own. Those biases will tend to assimilate other people's interests to their own in some circumstances, or to downplay them when there is a wide divergence between the two. Hence, people also have deep cognitive biases towards their own interests. The facts of diversity and of cognitive bias ensure that individuals are highly fallible in their understanding of their own and others' interests, and that there will be considerable disagreement among them. And they are likely to be highly fallible in their efforts to compare the importance of other people's interests to their own. So, they are highly fallible in their efforts to realize the equal advancement of interests in society. And, of course, there will be a lot of substantial disagreement about how best to advance each person's interests equally.

🔑 KEY CONCEPTS

Publicity

The importance of publicity itself is grounded in equality. Given the facts of diversity, cognitive bias, fallibility, and disagreement, each will have reason to think that if he or she is ruled in accordance with some specific notion of equality that has been advanced by some particular group, his or her interests are likely to be set back in some way. Only a conception of equality that can be shared by the members of society can give each good reason to think that this will not happen. Within the context set by public equality, people can argue for more specific implementations of equality among citizens in law and policy, all the while knowing that there will be substantial and conscientious disagreement on them.

Against the background of these facts, each person has interests that stand out as especially important in a pluralistic society. They have interests in correcting for the cognitive biases of others when it comes to the creation or revision of common economic, legal, and political institutions. Each person has interests in living in a world that makes some sense to them—a world that accords, within limits, to their sense of how that social world ought to be structured. The basic facts just described, and the principle of equality, suggest that each person ought to have an equal say in determining the common legal, economic, and political institutions under which they live. In the light of these interests, each citizen would have good reason to think that his or her interests were not being given the same weight as those of others if he or she were to have less decision-making power than others. And so each person who is deprived of a right to an equal say will have reason to believe that he or she is being treated, publicly, as an inferior. Furthermore, because each person has an interest in being recognized as an equal member of the community and because having less than an equal say suggests that he or she is being treated as inferior, only equality in decision-making power is compatible with the public equal advancement of interests.

☆ **KEY POINTS**

- Some have argued that democracy has non-instrumental value in addition to whatever instrumental value it has.

- The deliberative conception of democracy realizes the value of citizens engaging in free and reasoned discussion among equals, and making decisions only to the extent that these decisions are grounded in commonly accepted values.

- The key normative principle at work in many conceptions of deliberative democracy is the principle of reasonableness, which asserts that citizens will propose only terms of political association that other reasonable citizens can reasonably accept.

- The egalitarian conception of democracy realizes equality among citizens in the context of irresolvable disagreement on basic matters of political value.

- The key normative notion behind the egalitarian conception is the idea of public equality, which holds that, despite the many disagreements among persons about law and policy, and their grounds, democracy is a way of publicly treating each person as an equal.

The problem of democratic citizenship

A vexing problem of democracy, pointed out long ago by Plato and Hobbes, is whether ordinary citizens are up to the task of governing a large society. Because individuals have so little impact on the outcomes of political decision making in large societies, they have little sense of responsibility for the outcomes. The expected value of voting is so small, and the consequent value of informing oneself about how best to vote is so small, that almost all of those who do vote have little reason to become informed about how best to vote. If we think that citizens reason and behave on their narrowly defined self-interests, either the society must, in fact, be run by a relatively small group of people with minimal input from the rest, or it will be very poorly run. But, as we will see after the discussion of the problem from the standpoint of some prominent contemporary political theories, the problem remains even after we give up the self-interest postulate.

Some solutions offered for the problem of democratic citizenship

Elite theory of democracy

Some modern theorists of democracy, called elite theorists, have argued against any robustly egalitarian or deliberative forms of democracy. They argue that high levels of citizen participation tend to produce bad legislation that is designed by demagogues to appeal to poorly informed and overly emotional citizens. They look upon the alleged uninformedness of citizens, as evidenced in many empirical studies in the 1950s and 1960s, as perfectly reasonable and predictable. Indeed, elite theorists regard the alleged apathy of citizens in modern states as a highly desirable social phenomenon. The alternative, they believe, is a highly motivated population of persons who know nothing, and who are more likely than not to pursue irrational and emotionally appealing aims.

The view expressed by Joseph Schumpeter (1956) emphasizes responsible political leadership. Political leaders are to avoid divisive and emotionally charged issues, and make policy and law with little regard for the fickle and diffuse demands made by ordinary citizens. Citizens participate in the process of competition by voting, but because they know very little, they are not, effectively, the ruling part of the society. The process of election is usually only a peaceful way of maintaining or changing those who rule.

 KEY THINKERS

Joseph Schumpeter (1883–1950)

Joseph Schumpeter was one of the foremost economists of the twentieth century, because of his contributions to the explanation of economic development and his history of economic analysis. Schumpeter's principal contribution to economic theory was in the advancement of the concept of the entrepreneur as the driving force behind economic development. At the same time, he argued that capitalism would be replaced in the long run by social democracy. He was also an important political thinker, because of his arguments predicting the decline of capitalism, and his powerful, sceptical attacks on the theory of democracy, that were defended by Mill and Rousseau.

From the Schumpeterian perspective, however, citizens do have a role to play in avoiding serious disasters: when politicians act in ways that almost all can see are problematic, the citizens can throw them out. So democracy, even in this stripped-down version, plays some role in protecting society from the worst politicians.

In terms of the deliberative and equality arguments, the **elite theory** simply rejects the possibility that citizens can participate as equals: the society must be ruled by elites, and the role of citizens is merely to ensure the smooth and peaceful circulation of elites.

 KEY TEXTS

Downs, *An Economic Theory of Democracy* (1957)

Anthony Downs' text is the seminal work in the economic analysis of democracy. It is also a highly accessible read. Most other treatments of politics among economists depend, in various ways, on the ideas in this work. Two central ideas play a key role in Downs' book: first, the median voter theorem states that politicians tend to adopt the position of the median voter on issues in order to win elections; second, Downs defends the thesis of rational ignorance, which asserts that voters have little or no reason to become informed about politics. All of the other theses in the book depend on these two central claims.

In terms of the deliberative view, ordinary citizens cannot be expected to participate in public deliberation, and the views of elites ought not to be fundamentally transformed by general public deliberation.

Interest group pluralism

One approach that is partly motivated by the problem of democratic citizenship, but which attempts to preserve some elements of equality against the elitist criticism, is the **interest group pluralism** account of politics. Robert Dahl's early statement of the view is very powerful:

> In a rough sense, the essence of all competitive politics is bribery of the electorate by politicians . . . The farmer . . . supports a candidate committed to high price supports, the businessman . . . supports an advocate of low corporation taxes . . . the consumer . . . votes for candidates opposed to a sale tax.

(Dahl, 1956; 1959: 69)

In this conception of the democratic process, each citizen is a member of an interest group with narrowly defined interests that are closely connected to their everyday lives. On these subjects, citizens are supposed to be quite well informed and interested in having an influence. Or at least, elites from each of the interest groups that are relatively close in perspective to the ordinary members are the principal **agents** in the process. On this account, democracy is not rule by the majority, but rather, rule by coalitions of minorities. Policy and law in a democratic society are decided by means of bargaining among the different groups.

This approach is conceivably compatible with the more egalitarian approach to democracy. This is because it attempts to reconcile equality with collective decision making by limiting the tasks of citizens to those that they are able to perform reasonably well—and it attempts to do this in a way that gives citizens a key role in decision making. The account ensures that individuals can participate roughly as equals, to the extent that it narrowly confines the issues with which each individual is concerned. It is not particularly compatible with the deliberative public justification approach, because it eschews deliberation about the common good or about justice. It also takes the democratic process to be concerned essentially with bargaining among the different interest groups, where the preferences to be advanced by each group are not subject to further debate in the society as a whole. There may, indeed, be some deliberation within interest groups, but it will not be society-wide.

 KEY THINKERS

Robert Dahl (1915–)

Robert Dahl is probably the most important democratic theorist of the second half of the twentieth century. His work is a model of combining abstract considerations of political theory with a firm and thorough grasp of the empirical knowledge of democracy. His *A Preface to Democratic Theory* (1956;1959) was a seminal work in the area of democratic theory. He is the author of many influential works on the theoretical and empirical analysis of democracy. His most recent, highly influential book, *Democracy and its Critics* (1989), is a wide-ranging treatment of abstract theoretical considerations, empirical knowledge, and the history of democracy.

Neoliberalism

A third approach inspired by the problem of citizenship may be called **neoliberalism**: an approach to politics favoured by public choice theorists such as James Buchanan and Gordon Tullock (1965). In criticism of elite theories, they contend that elites and their allies will tend to expand the powers of government and bureaucracy for their own interests, and that this expansion will occur at the expense of a largely inattentive public. For this reason, they argue for severe restrictions on the powers of elites. They argue against the interest group pluralist theorists that the problem of participation occurs within interest groups more or less as much as among the citizenry at large. As a consequence, interest groups will not form very easily. Only those interest groups that are guided by powerful economic interests are likely to succeed in organizing to influence the government. Hence, only some interest groups will succeed in influencing government, and they will do so largely for the benefit of the powerful economic elites that fund and guide them. Furthermore, they argue that such interest groups will tend to produce highly inefficient government, because they will attempt to advance their interests in politics, while spreading the costs to others. The consequence of this is that policies will be created that tend to be more costly (because they are imposed on everyone in society) than they are beneficial (because they benefit only the elites in the interest group).

Neoliberals argue that any way of organizing a large and powerful democratic state is likely to produce serious inefficiencies. They infer that one ought to transfer many of the current functions of the state to the market, and limit the state to the enforcement of basic property rights and liberties. These can be more easily understood and brought under the control of ordinary citizens.

But the neoliberal account of democracy must answer to two large worries. First, citizens in modern societies have more ambitious conceptions of social justice and the common

KEY THINKERS

James Buchanan (1919–2013) and Gordon Tullock (1922–)

James Buchanan and Gordon Tullock are the seminal thinkers in the extremely important and expanding field of public choice theory. Their book *The Calculus of Consent: Logical Foundations of Constitutional Democracy* (1965) laid the framework for the public-choice analysis of institutions (which is also heavily indebted to Anthony Downs). The theory of public choice is the application of economic theory—in the sense of economic models that are centred around utility-maximizing individuals—to political processes. It has both an explanatory and a normative dimension. Buchanan and Tullock have continued to play leading roles in this young branch of economics. James Buchanan received the Nobel Prize for his work in 1986.

good than are realizable by the **minimal state**. The neoliberal account thus implies a very serious curtailment of democracy of its own. More evidence is needed to support the contention that these aspirations cannot be achieved by the modern state. Second, the neoliberal approach ignores the problem of large private concentrations of wealth and power that are capable of pushing small states around for their own benefit, and of imposing their wills on populations without their consent. The assumptions that lead neoliberals to be sceptical about the large modern state imply equally disturbing problems for the large private concentrations of wealth in a neoliberal society.

The self-interest assumption

A considerable amount of the literature in political science and the economic theory of the state is grounded in the assumption that individuals act primarily—and perhaps even exclusively—in their self-interest, as narrowly construed. The problem of participation and the accounts of the democratic process described earlier are largely dependent on this assumption. While these ideas have generated interesting results and have become ever more sophisticated, there has been a growing chorus of opponents.

In criticism of the self-interest axiom, defenders of deliberative democracy and others claim that citizens are capable of being motivated by a concern for the common good and justice. And, they claim—along with Mill and Rousseau—such concerns are not merely given prior to politics, but they can evolve and improve through the process of discussion and debate in politics. They assert that much debate and discussion in politics would not be intelligible were it not for the fact that citizens are willing to engage in open-minded discussion with those who have distinct morally informed points of view. Empirical evidence suggests that individuals are motivated by moral considerations in politics, in addition to their interests. Accordingly, many propose that democratic institutions be designed to support the inclination to engage in moral and open-minded discussion with others (Mansbridge, 1990).

The role of citizens as choosers of aims

The problem of citizenship can now be understood as a result of the central fact of modern life: the necessity of a division of labour. The modern state is simply too complex in its activities for it to be grasped by any particular person. Ordinary citizens have important time-consuming jobs and social lives. They cannot fruitfully regulate government in all of its complexity or even the process of making legislation. This is the central reason for rejecting direct democracy and embracing representative institutions. The question arises then: is there an appropriate role for a citizen in a democracy that reconciles the need for a division of labour with the importance of equality and deliberation?

One proposal asserts that citizens must think about at what ends the society ought to aim and leave the question of how to achieve those aims to experts (Christiano, 1996). This kind of view needs to answer the problem of how to ensure that politicians, administrators, and experts actually do attempt to realize the aims set by citizens—and it must show how institutions can be designed, so as to establish the division of labour while preserving equality among citizens. But if citizens genuinely do choose the aims, and others faithfully pursue the means of achieving those aims, then citizens are in the driver's seat in society.

☆ **KEY POINTS**

- The basic problem of citizenship in a democracy is that, because political decisions are invariably about complex and difficult issues, and citizens only have limited time and resources with which to come to an understanding of those issues, citizens are likely to be very ill informed about the issues on which they are supposed to govern.

- Elite theories of democracy resolve the above problem by limiting the citizen to voting, while putting all of the responsibility of the political system on the shoulders of political leaders who are voted into office.

- Interest group pluralist views of citizenship resolve the problem by getting citizens to focus on how to advance their own narrow interests in the system and then on bargaining with the representatives of other narrow interests.

- Neoliberalism resolves the problem by minimizing the scope of the authority of the state and turning most decisions over to the market or voluntary organizations.

- All of these approaches suffer from defects that result, ultimately, from the illegitimate assumption that people act in their narrow self-interests.

- That citizens can be the choosers of the aims of society, while the rest of the state and **civil society** participate in realizing the means, satisfies the basic desiderata of a democratic system. Citizens can have an appreciation of what aims they want to achieve and, if the system works in this way, the citizens are the main rulers of the society.

Democratic institutions

An account of citizenship that assigns citizens a limited role must say how the institutions of the society ensure that:

- citizens are able to play that role;
- the other complementary parts of the democratic state do their parts.

The first function is the 'citizen enabling' function of a democratic society; the second is the 'agency' function of the democratic state and society.

In modern representative democracies, it is the function of the system of legislative representation, along with a robust and broad-based civil society—that is, the collection of voluntary associations in political societies that help to mediate between the state and the citizens—to enable citizens to perform their limited roles as choosers of aims for the society.

A system of proportional representation is likely to ensure voices for the many different sectors and groups in society (see Box 4.1). It will give rise to a multiparty system, within which each party attempts to articulate the important interests and concerns of particular groups of citizens. The consequence of this is that, in the process of electoral competition, citizens will have access to a broader array of ideas about how society should be organized and they will have a wider perspective on all of the interests that must be reconciled within the society.

The formal political institutions enable citizens to perform their roles only if civil society is composed of associations and parties that represent all of the main interests within the society. Political parties and interest groups, which together represent the broad array of interests in society, enable citizens to play their role. These groups sift through all of the issues and problems that might arise for a society, and present these issues and alternative responses to them so that citizens can make reasonable choices of aims for the society. Without political parties and interest associations, citizens would be at sea in the huge amount of information available about their society: they would not be able to perform their role.

Because parties and associations play such significant roles in enabling citizens to perform their roles, the system of political parties and interest group associations must represent the interests and concerns of all of the relevant different groups in society. Otherwise, only those whose interests and concerns are represented will have a serious say in how the society is to be organized and this will imply deep inequalities of control over the society. Some system of financing a broad array of parties and associations will be necessary to ensure this broad-based representation in civil society.

The agency function of a democratic society must be performed by the legislative and executive branches of government, in conjunction with the oversight function of associations in civil society. To the extent that the citizens of a democratic society focus on the choice of aims and not on the issue of how to achieve those aims, they will not be able to determine, on their own, whether the executive, legislative, or administrative branches of government are doing their jobs properly. To expect citizens to have properly informed opinions on the functioning of these branches is to expect too much. As a consequence, a modern democratic state faces a very large principal–agent problem, which occurs when one person has discretion to act for another and that person has distinct interests.

There are two basic ways in which this principal–agent problem can be solved. One is that we must rely, in part, on morally disposed persons to occupy positions within these branches of government. The second is that we must rely on the associations in civil society to monitor and evaluate the activities of these branches of government. Political parties and interest associations are capable of developing and cultivating the expertise to engage in oversight of the executive and administrative branches of government. In this way, they can act as agents of citizens in this process, ensuring that these branches of government do as they are supposed to do: namely, to find the best means to implement the aims that the citizens have chosen. In order for this function to be carried out in an egalitarian way, it must be the case that the associations and parties are representative of the broad spectrum of interests and concerns in society. Otherwise, there will be associations that ensure that certain interests and aims are pursued, while others are left dormant. So, just as in the case of the enabling function, the agency function of associations and parties requires a broad-based system of associations that is representative of the manifold interests in the society.

Overall, we can see that the system of civil society must have the properties of breadth, depth, and trustworthiness in order to carry out its function in sustaining an egalitarian democratic society. We can see that a democratic society cannot be egalitarian unless there is a broad array of associations and parties that are concerned with advancing the interests and concerns of citizens. These parties and associations must have significant depth, in that they must cultivate the expertise and experience that is necessary for carrying out the roles of monitoring the government and enabling citizens to develop their conceptions of the appropriate aims for society to pursue. Furthermore, these parties and associations must develop a relation of trust with citizens in order to carry out their roles: only if citizens properly trust them can citizens make use of these associations in the development of their conception of aims.

BOX 4.1 PERSISTENT MINORITIES

The problem of persistent minorities is a vexing problem of democratic theory. There is a persistent minority in a democratic society when that minority always loses in the voting. This is always a possibility in democracies, because majority rule is the principal decision rule in a democratic legislature. If the society is divided into two or more highly unified voting blocks, in which the members of the groups tend to vote in the same ways as all of the other members, then the group in the minority will find itself always on the losing end of the votes. This problem has plagued some societies—particularly those in which indigenous peoples live within developed societies.

☆   KEY POINTS

- The conception of citizens as choosers of aims requires that we have a conception of democratic institutions that complements the role of citizens in crucial ways.
- Institutions can enable citizens to develop their conception of aims for the society. Political parties and interest group associations serve this citizen-enabling function.
- Institutions must also serve as the agents of citizens, to the extent that they genuinely attempt to realize the aims of citizens. A bureaucratic state monitored by competing political parties and interest group associations can serve this function.
- One difficulty that democratic institutions have faced is the problem of persistent minorities. This difficulty arises when a minority finds itself consistently outvoted on all issues by the other groups in society.

Conclusion

We have now surveyed some main issues of normative democratic theory and examined a variety of accounts of the justification of democracy, from instrumental to intrinsic. We have explored some of the chief challenges that democracy in the modern world faces, such as the problems of citizenship and questions concerning what kind of institutional system can enable citizens to perform their roles. Finally, we have outlined the problem of persistent minorities in democracy. Overall, thinking about democratic ideals and values has direct and obvious practical salience: these ideals are supposed to inform the design of democratic institutions, the focus of democratic processes, and, indeed, the self-conceptions of democratic citizens. In the case study, we examine a radical suggestion for realizing some key democratic ideals: deliberative polling.

 CASE STUDY

Deliberative polling—by Jeremy Williams

As we have seen in this chapter, for many political philosophers, the ideal of democracy requires more than merely that citizens turn out to vote in elections. Rather, it requires that they do so after having informed themselves about the issues relevant to their vote, having weighed them up in private, and having deliberated about them with their fellow citizens in public. However, as we have also seen, any philosophical view that emphasizes the importance of citizens engaging in these activities must address the problem that, as things stand, they often have little incentive to do so. Indeed, they have an incentive *not* to do so, insofar as informing oneself about politics, and debating it with others, is time-consuming (as well as, for many, tedious), and perhaps also pointless, given that there is little prospect that a single ballot, whether or not it is cast in an informed, reflective fashion, will sway the outcome.

Contemporary democracy, it is often observed, suffers from the twin defects of 'rational ignorance', whereby citizens have insufficient reason to seek out information about the political decisions facing them in elections and referendums, and 'civic privatism', whereby citizens vote on the basis of their own narrow self-interest, without considering the common good, or the perspectives of others. How, then, to address these problems? One proposal, to be examined in this case study, imagines a nationwide extension of a distinctive method of opinion polling, called '**deliberative polling**', developed by political scientist James Fishkin.

Deliberative polling involves giving a group of citizens the opportunity to hear information about some policy issue, debate with one another, and question experts, before coming to a verdict. One of the most striking things about deliberative polling experiments is the changes recorded in the views of the participants at the conclusion of the process. In this case study, we shall examine in more detail what deliberative polling consists of, and consider the idea of a national 'Deliberation Day', as envisaged by Fishkin and his co-author Bruce Ackerman. Deliberation Day might seem an attractive proposition, not only to deliberative democrats in the technical sense described by Christiano earlier (who hold there to be intrinsic value in citizens publicly justifying their favoured policies to each other, on the basis of a set of shared reasons and values, with the aim of reaching consensus) but also, more generally, to those who believe that democracy would benefit in some way from greater citizen engagement and dialogue. As we shall see, however, there are significant reasons to be sceptical of the idea.

How deliberative polling works

Consider the conventional opinion poll, which aims to uncover how much support a given policy or political position has among the public. These polls record the views of an electorate who will often not have considered the issue about which they are being quizzed at all, or will have come to a view based mainly on snatches of television reporting, newspaper headlines, and politicians' sound bites. In many cases, they are likely to have thought only about how the issue affects *them*, rather than others, or the country (or world) as a whole. Of course, for some purposes, conventional opinion polls are invaluable—notably to politicians, who want to know which stance to adopt to maximize their support, and who arguably just have to take the voting public as they find it. However, we may often want to know what the electorate would think about some matter if citizens were more reflective and informed. This is what deliberative polling is designed to find out.

The technique works as follows. First, a scientifically-chosen random sample of voters is surveyed on some contemporary issue facing their country—whether to join the European single currency, say (as in the case of a Danish deliberative poll from 2000). The group is then invited to a location in which briefing materials (chosen for their informativeness and balance) are handed out, and spends two or three days deliberating. Deliberative events are of two kinds—small group discussions, led by a moderator, and plenary sessions, in which the participants come together to quiz experts representing different points of view. At the end of the event, the participants are given a survey, including the same questions they answered before the process started. In many cases, the difference of opinion recorded after the deliberative process has been marked. To give just a couple of examples,[1] a deliberative poll on crime conducted in the UK in 1994 saw the proportion of participants who agreed that imprisoning more offenders is 'an effective way of fighting crime' reduce from more than half, 57%, to only 38% after deliberation. The same poll found the percentage who disagreed with the idea that a 16- year-old first-time burglar should be sent to an ordinary prison increase from 33% to 50%. Meanwhile, a deliberative poll conducted in Australia in 1999, and coinciding with the referendum of that year on whether the country ought to replace the Queen as Head of State and become a republic, found that, after deliberation, 73% favoured a republic—an increase of 20% (the proposal to replace the monarchy was defeated in the referendum itself).

Deliberative polls have now been held in a significant number of countries around the world, including not only the United Kingdom and Australia, but also, for instance, the US, Canada, Brazil, Italy, Hungary, and Bulgaria. In some cases, the proceedings and results have been shown to the wider electorate on television. There has been Europe-wide deliberative polling, beginning with 2007's *Tomorrow's Europe* poll which canvassed the views of European citizens on the future of the European Union (EU), the merits of further EU expansion, and the role of the EU in the world (see http://cdd.stanford.edu/polls/eu/2007/). And surprisingly, deliberative polling has even been conducted in China, allowing some of the local residents of Zeguo township, Wenling City, to have their say over the local government's allocation of funding for infrastructure projects.

As Robert Goodin (2008: 38–63) notes, deliberative polls—and the use of what he calls 'mini-publics' in general—have a number of potentially beneficial applications in a democracy, even when only relatively small numbers of citizens are able to take part. These include, for instance, leading or informing wider public debates (in cases where the process is televised, or the results disseminated), market testing prospective policies, and providing citizen oversight for policies in the process of being implemented. On the other hand, as Goodin also argues (2003: 174ff), precisely because deliberative polls and other mini-publics can include only a small subset of the population at a time, they represent a rather 'ersatz' (to use his word) substitute for the ideal of mass deliberation among the citizenry at large. Is there, then, a case for rolling out the deliberative polling model on a grander scale, so that all citizens have an opportunity to participate?

Deliberation Day

In a well-known paper co-authored with Bruce Ackerman (2002; see also Ackerman and Fishkin, 2004), Fishkin has imagined deliberative polling on a large scale: a nationwide 'Deliberation Day', to be held in the run-up to major elections, during which each citizen participates in one of numerous deliberative polls taking place simultaneously around the country. The authors summarize their proposal as follows:

> Deliberation Day—a new national holiday. It will be held one week before major national elections. Registered voters will be called together in neighbourhood meeting places, in small groups of 15, and larger groups of 500, to discuss the central issues raised by the campaign. Each deliberator will be paid $150 for the day's work of citizenship, on condition that he or she shows up at the polls the next week. All other work, except the most essential, will be prohibited by law.
> (Ackerman and Fishkin, 2002: 129).

As described by Ackerman and Fishkin, citizens, on Deliberation Day, will have the opportunity to read specially-produced briefing materials, and ask questions of the candidates seeking their vote (or their representatives) in moderated debates. The aim is to ensure that not only are citizens better informed about the issues at stake, but that the competing parties and candidates treat them as such, and accordingly rely less on pre-packaged soundbites and opportunistic attacks on their opponents, and more on carefully and informatively articulating their own policy agenda, in a way that is more likely to withstand sustained critical scrutiny. According to Ackerman and Fishkin, then, Deliberation Day has the potential to transform our elections. Their proposal is certainly arresting. But does it deserve our 'vote'?

In evaluating Ackerman and Fishkin's blueprint for Deliberation Day, it is worth noting that it has been put together in such a way as to arguably allow it to meet some of the principal objections that beset deliberative exercises generally. For instance, some people are sceptical of the value of deliberation on grounds that some demographics will inevitably be over-represented—namely, those with enough free time to attend, or enough money to afford a day off work. This concern would not apply to Deliberation Day, however, because it is a compulsory national public holiday, for which everyone is paid for their time.

Another reason for concern about deliberative exercises in general stems from empirical evidence suggesting that deliberation under certain realistic conditions will not increase social welfare, and may in fact decrease it (that is, lead to participants making decisions that serve their common interests less well than if they had not deliberated at all). Evidence to this effect comes from experiments conducted by Matthew D. McCubbins and Daniel B. Rodriguez (2006). The problem, as these authors see it, arises in deliberative models that are egalitarian, in the sense that distinctions are not made between participants on the basis of knowledge or expertise, and each is expected to listen to and learn from all others. Deliberative democrats often advocate deliberation that is egalitarian in these ways. But in such settings, McCubbins and Rodriguez's experiments indicate that participants will find it difficult to discern who has knowledge that is worth paying attention to and will consequently (given that speaking and listening are not cost-free) have little incentive either to listen to others or to share their own relevant expertise (expecting that it will fall on deaf ears). McCubbins and Rodriguez also note, however (2006: 38–9), that the design of Deliberation Day, rather than being fully egalitarian, has elements of what they call an 'expertise system', whereby participants have opportunities to draw on expert input (by reading the briefing materials, for instance, or questioning the candidates). Thus, Deliberation Day might escape the particular difficulty exposed in these authors' findings.

Yet another concern expressed about deliberative exercises is that they often involve like-minded people coming together (think of, for instance, neighbourhood watch meetings or parent–teacher associations), in which cases the deliberation tends to result only in the corroboration and intensification of the group's existing beliefs, rather than their being re-evaluated. Cass Sunstein (2002) calls this the phenomenon of 'group polarization'. But Sunstein also suggests (2002: 193–5) that the set-up of a deliberative poll—involving representative sampling of the population, the provision of balanced information, moderated discussion to ensure fair participation, and so on—mitigates against group polarization. On that basis, if the discussions held on Deliberation Day were adequately modelled on a deliberative poll, they might also be able to avoid this tendency. Note, however, that this might require, among other things, splitting up local communities who form enclaves with similar political outlooks, making the logistics of Deliberation Day yet more complex.

Supposing Deliberation Day manages to successfully evade the foregoing objections, it does so at a hefty price. On Ackerman and Fishkin's own estimation, the cost of implementing Deliberation Day in the US would be some $15 billion a year. It is reasonable to wonder not only whether there are better ways of spending that money, but also whether there are more effective ways of enriching democracy, such as providing subsidies to minor political parties to help them compete (Shapiro, 2003: 25). Goodin (2003) has argued that, given the huge financial and practical obstacles to mass deliberation in modern large-scale democracies, we should shift more of our attention towards finding ways to encourage what he calls 'deliberation within' (i.e. the sort of reflection on the perspectives and interests of others that we are capable of inside our heads, even when our fellow citizens are not present). Goodin (2008: 38–63) provides evidence suggesting that the 'deliberation within' that participants in deliberative exercises conduct before taking part in face-to-face discussion may be just as important in changing attitudes as the discussion itself, if not more so. If he is correct, we may be able to reap many of the benefits envisaged from Deliberation Day without incurring all the costs, by taking more economical steps towards enabling and incentivizing a more internally-reflective citizenry.

Finally, even if money were no object in implementing a Deliberation Day, time still would be. This fact gives rise to concerns about the sidelining of certain minority perspectives, which connect in turn to further concerns about how the agendas of the various local events that make up Deliberation Day would be determined, and by whom. Given limited time, what points of view are to be explored in the debating sessions, and how are moderators to judge how long to allocate to each? If a great many candidates all run for one elected office, and they cannot all be invited to speak, how are we to decide who will or will not be given a platform? Concerns about exclusion from the deliberative process have been notably expressed by Iris Marion Young (2001). In her view, deliberative exercises of the kind pioneered by Fishkin are problematic insofar as they will tend to sideline proponents of more radical politics, and operate only within the narrow confines of the debate set by the mainstream media, politicians, and powerful interest groups. The terms of conventional political debate, Young argues, assume, as unchangeable, a status quo that radical political activists oppose, and that includes numerous profoundly unjust inequalities. If Young is right, then ironically enough, as radical as the Deliberation Day proposal appears, it might only serve to further entrench the status quo.

? QUESTIONS

1. Plato and Hobbes think that democratic institutions corrupt citizens, while Rousseau and Mill argue that democratic institutions enhance the virtues of citizens. How would you evaluate the overall effect of democracy on citizens?

2. Some, such as Hobbes and Mill, think that all political institutions must be evaluated entirely in terms of their effects on society and never in terms of their intrinsic procedural fairness or justice. Is there room for an intrinsic defence of democracy?

3. Are deliberative democrats right to argue that it is very important that citizens advance proposals for legislation on the basis of principles that others can reasonably accept? Why should one not advance proposals on the basis of what one takes to be the whole truth about the right principles for society?

4. Can there be genuinely public equality in modern societies within which people seem to disagree about everything?

5. Can the modern state, with its complex division of labour and the complexity of the problems that it solves, be genuinely ruled by equal citizens, or must it be ruled primarily by elites?

6. Is it possible for citizens to engage in rational deliberation as equals in modern political societies, given the immense complexity of the modern state?

7. Under what conditions, if any, can the bureaucratic institutions of modern democracies be trusted to carry out the instructions they receive from democratic legislatures?

8. Would a Deliberation Day benefit democracy?

9. What are the virtues of democratic citizenship?

10. With what political ideals (if any) does the ideal of democracy conflict?

FURTHER READING

■ Archibugi, D., Keonig-Archibugi, M., and Marchetti, R. (2011) (eds) *Global Democracy: Empirical and Normative Perspectives*, Cambridge: Cambridge University Press A collection of new essays representing the broad array of theoretical and normative approaches to global democracy.

■ Beitz, C. (1989) *Political Equality: An Essay on Democratic Theory*, Princeton, NJ: Princeton University Press A very well-reasoned contractualist account of the grounds of democracy, which includes chapters on some key institutions in modern democracies.

■ Buchanan, J. and Tullock, G. (1965) *The Calculus of Consent: Logical Foundations of Constitutional Democracy*, Ann Arbor, MI: University of Michigan Press The seminal work on democratic theory from the perspective of public choice theory.

■ Christiano, T. (1996) *The Rule of the Many: Fundamental Issues in Democratic Theory*, Boulder, CO: Westview Press A systematic defence of the egalitarian conception of democracy, along with a discussion of the major challenges posed by modern democratic states to political equality among citizens. It also includes guidelines for the design of legislative institutions and the institutions of civil society.

■ Christiano, T. (2002) (ed.) *Philosophy and Democracy*, Oxford: Oxford University Press A collection of some of the most important work of philosophers, political scientists, and economists during the last half-century on the nature and normative basis of democracy.

■ Christiano, T. (2008b) *The Constitution of Equality: Democratic Authority and its Limits*, Oxford: Oxford University Press A foundational justification of democracy starting from an argument for equality, and resulting in an account of the authority and limits of democracy.

■ Cohen, J. (2009) *Philosophy, Politics, Democracy: Selected Essays*, Cambridge, MA: Harvard University Press Some clear and concise essays on the theory of deliberative democracy by its leading philosophical exponent.

■ Estlund, D. (2007) *Democratic Authority: A Philosophical Framework*, Princeton, NJ: Princeton University Press The leading contemporary development of the idea that democracy is justified on epistemic grounds.

■ Held, D. (1995) *Democracy and the Global Order: From the Modern State to Cosmopolitan Governance*, Stanford, CA: Stanford University Press Probably the leading treatment of the normative foundations and nature of democracy on a global scale.

■ Riker, W. (1980) *Liberalism versus Populism*, San Francisco, CA: W. H. Freeman The leading effort to apply the modern theory of social choice to the analysis of democratic institutions.

■ Waldron, J. (1999a) *Law and Disagreement*, Oxford: Oxford University Press A powerful defence of democracy, and a critique of the theory and practice of judicial review.

■ Young, I. M. (1993) *Justice and the Politics of Difference*, Princeton, NJ: Princeton University Press A very clear and concise critical exposition of some of the leading postmodern approaches to democracy, applied to particular social and political problems.

 ## WEB LINKS

● http://www.demos.co.uk Demos describes itself as a *'think tank for everyday democracy'*.

● http://www.ifes.org/home.html The International Foundation for Election Systems (IFES) is an international non-profit organization that supports the building of democratic societies.

● http://www.opendemocracy.net/home/index.jsp The website of the e-zine openDemocracy, which promotes dialogue and debate on issues of global importance, linking citizens from around the world, and which is committed to human rights and democracy.

● http://www.sfgd.org Students for Global Democracy is a non-partisan student group that promotes global democracy and stands against dictatorship.

● http://www.unlockdemocracy.org.uk Unlock Democracy is a UK-based movement for constitutional reform in Britain, aimed at 'unlocking' democracy for all.

 Visit the Online Resource Centre that accompanies this book to access more learning resources: http://www.oxfordtextbooks.co.uk/orc/mckinnon3e/

 ## ENDNOTE

[1] These examples are taken from the website of the Centre for Deliberative Democracy at Stanford University, of which Fishkin is the director, and which is devoted to research into deliberative polling. See http://cdd.stanford.edu/polls/docs/summary/archive/ (last accessed 16/01/14).

5

Equality and social justice

JONATHAN WOLFF

✔ **Reader's guide**

It is common for politicians and commentators to assess particular social and political arrangements in terms of social justice. Yet the demands of social justice are not always clear. Does it condemn all inequalities, or is its concern, the provision of equal opportunity or the elimination of extreme poverty? Furthermore, does social justice focus only on the distribution of resources and opportunities within society, or does it also require the creation of a particular type of society? Naturally, a socially just society opposes distinctions that are based on race, gender, or social class, but does it also mandate movement towards a world in which everyone regards each other as an equal? → **See chapter 12**. There is great theoretical disagreement on these issues and, hence, often no agreed answer on what it would mean for a society to achieve social justice.

Introduction: the history of social justice

For centuries, many societies have made provision for the support of their vulnerable members through institutions such as parish relief or the Poor Law. In previous eras, however, these measures were normally regarded as a matter of charity, or religious duty. Not until the twentieth century was it widely argued that provision for those unable to support themselves was a requirement of justice and that individuals had the right to social support if they were unable to support themselves. The term 'social justice' has been used to mark the idea that distribution of resources and opportunities in a society, as well as its conditions of work, and the patterns of wages and profits, can be evaluated in terms of how well they meet principles of justice.

 KEY CONCEPTS

Justice and charity

Do the poor have a moral right to assistance? If so, then the duty of the rich is one of justice, otherwise any duties to the poor are those of charity. Duties of justice are generally taken to be enforceable by the state, whereas duties of charity are private and a matter of individual discretion. The distinction also reflects a difference in the understanding of the status of the recipient: insisting that other people observe their duties of justice seems very different from asking them for charity, which can often seem demeaning.

 KEY CONCEPTS

The Poor Law

The Poor Law was set up in the early seventeenth century in England and Wales to provide assistance to the sick, the old, and those in poverty. Initially, a duty fell on each parish to provide support for those in need. In the eighteenth century, workhouses were established, and parishes were entitled to decline support if the poor refused to enter the workhouse. The motivations for the Poor Law were complex, including an element of religious or charitable duty to support the needy and an element of self-protection, in that no parish could afford to have a significant number of people who may have needed to resort to crime to survive.

Ideas of social justice became a common reference point in political debates in the UK after World War II. The social services had been a refuge for all social classes during the Blitz and the experience of an efficient, centralized war economy was a welcome contrast to pre-war *laissez-faire* capitalism, which had led to the General Strike and economic depression (Lowe, 1993: 12). Furthermore, the experience of working together to fight a common enemy brought together people of different classes and backgrounds who would not otherwise have met and mixed, and who developed greater sympathy and a sense of justice towards each other. The Beveridge Report of 1942, the foundation of the British welfare state, remarked that '*the war is abolishing landmarks of every kind*' and set out to slay the 'five giants': want, disease, ignorance, squalor, and idleness (that is, unemployment). In the USA, related ideas had underpinned Roosevelt's 'New Deal', Truman's 'Fair Deal', and Johnson's 'Great Society' (Barry, 2005: 6).

These ideas resonated with the British socialist tradition of Richard Tawney (1931), George Orwell (2000), and, later on, Richard Titmuss (1971), who argued against the class division and selfishness of acquisitive market societies. The Beveridge Report led to the foundation of the British National Health Service (NHS), systematic unemployment benefit, and the idea that citizens were to be protected 'from the cradle to the grave'. Although such changes were not an attempt to implement a particular theory of justice, nevertheless, it was argued, at least on the political left, that such changes were moving society in the direction of social justice.

The attempt to articulate **principles of social justice** in political philosophy arguably reached its high point in 1971 with the publication of *A Theory of Justice*, written by the Harvard philosopher John Rawls. Rawls argues for a complex theory of justice, which comprises the following principles.

1. Each person is to have an equal right to the most extensive basic liberty compatible with a similar liberty for all.
2. Social and economic equalities are to be arranged so that they are both: (a) to the greatest benefit of the least advantaged; and (b) attached to offices and positions open to all under conditions of fair equality of opportunity.

   (Rawls, 1971; 1999: 71)

Rawls also argues that the **first principle**—the **basic liberty principle**—has what he calls 'lexical priority' (meaning that it has priority in cases of conflict) over the second principle, and that the second half of the second principle—the **principle of fair equality of opportunity**—has similar priority over the first half (famously known as the **difference principle**).

Rawls' theory contrasts with the influential theory of utilitarianism, devised by Jeremy Bentham and John Stuart Mill, which instructs governments to maximize the sum total of happiness in the world. While intended as an enlightened, humane theory, utilitarianism has the defect that, strictly, it may require the sacrifice of some people for the benefit of the great majority, for example, by forcing some people into brutal and ill-paid labour that benefits society as a whole. Rawls' principles, by contrast, protect the rights of every individual, by means of the liberty and fair opportunity principles, and promote the economic well-being even of the least advantaged, by means of the difference principle.

Rawls argues for these principles by imagining how you would want your society to be if you stood behind a '**veil of ignorance**', not knowing such things as your talents, race, sex, age, or social position. What principles would you wish to govern your society if you did not know your place in it? By basing the choice of principles of justice on decision under imagined ignorance, Rawls' theory turns out to generate an account of justice which is impartial between all interests. If you do not know your role in society, it is in your interests to try to make all roles as attractive as possible. You have to consider yourself as potentially occupying every position in society. This explains the particular concern for the worst off.

The political rejection of social justice and its revival

The rejection of social justice

At around the time that Rawls published *A Theory of Justice* (Rawls, 1971; 1999), concern in the UK was growing over the economic consequences of the policies of a succession of socialist governments, which, in addition to pursuing Beveridge's goals, had also nationalized many key industries, both as part of post-war reconstruction and in pursuit of the socialist idea of the common ownership of the means of production. By the 1970s, high taxation, the inefficiency of nationalized industries, the strength of trade unions, the disruption of labour disputes, and the unintended side-effects of progressive legislation designed to increase job and housing **security** all led to resentment among a considerable portion of the electorate (Lowe, 1993). Such political discontent went hand in hand with an intellectual and political onslaught against ideas of social justice, and paved the way for the policies of the Conservative government of Margaret Thatcher that were designed to break union power, to privatize nationalized industries, and to reduce entitlement to welfare benefits. In the USA, in parallel, Ronald Reagan inaugurated policies of 'Reagonomics', in which concerns of social justice took second place to goals of economic efficiency.

 KEY TEXTS

Rawls, *A Theory of Justice* (1971; 1999)

An influential text, *A Theory of Justice* revives the themes of classical '**social contract**' thinking—especially that of Immanuel Kant—in justification of liberal egalitarian principles of justice guaranteeing equal liberties to all, equal opportunity for all, and a distribution of economic goods that makes the least advantaged as well off as possible. Rawls argues that these principles would be the rational choice of people placed behind a veil of ignorance, denying to them knowledge of characteristics—for example, sex, race, and class—that can be (dis)advantaging in the real world, but which ought not to be (dis)advantaging in a just society.

The governments of Ronald Reagan and Margaret Thatcher became convinced that the pursuit of social justice was harming economic growth, to the detriment of all members of society. The intellectual strand of this reaction was developed by Frederich von Hayek (1944; 1960; 1973; 1978; 1979), Milton Friedman (1962), and Robert Nozick (1974), who argued that government action to enforce a theory of social justice interfered with the **liberty** of individuals to govern their own lives and property. ➡ **See Chapter 2**. But, more fundamentally, Hayek and Nozick both argued that society, as a whole, cannot be assessed as just or unjust. Hayek (1973; 1978; 1979) famously asserted that social justice was a 'mirage', while Nozick (1974) argued that if individuals have acquired their property through just transactions, then whatever results is just. During this era, both philosophy and politics focused less on society and much more on individuals, not only as rights' holders, but also as having the duty to take primary responsibility for their own fates. Individuals should not automatically expect the state to 'bail them out', but should look to themselves, and their families, first.

 KEY THINKERS

Friedrich von Hayek (1899–1992)

An Austrian, Nobel Prize-winning economist and political thinker, Hayek spent most of his professional life at the London School of Economics and the University of Chicago. He argued for the indispensability of the economic market in the face of limited knowledge and against the possibility of rational central economic planning. His major works, which have had a great influence on the development of neo-conservative thought, include *The Road to Serfdom* (1944), *The Constitution of Liberty* (1944; 1960), and *Law, Legislation and Liberty* (three volumes, 1973; 1979), the second volume of which is subtitled *The Mirage of Social Justice*.

The revival of social justice

During the Thatcher and Reagan years, few, if any, government policies were defended in terms of social justice. Indeed, justice was conceived of primarily in terms of the protection of individual rights—especially rights to private property.

In the USA, it remains difficult to argue for policies in the name of social justice, as distinct from economic growth, security, and defence. In the UK, under the New Labour government from 1997–2010, things changed and social justice was high up on the political agenda. Since the economic recession and the coalition government, however, austerity and the need to grow the economy has meant that the goal of social justice has retreated, and is more often used as a critique of government policy rather than a policy aim. However, for New Labour, the first step to the political rehabilitation of the idea of social justice was to disentangle it from more traditional ideas of socialism. The project of government running industry on behalf of the people fell out of favour throughout the world, largely on grounds of inefficiency, and after Thatcherite privatization, there seemed to be no going back. The struggle to assert the people's ownership of the means of production had failed.

To reawaken serious political interest in social justice, it was necessary to isolate it from the Labour Party's project of common ownership, enshrined in the notorious Clause IV of its Constitution, which called for '*the common ownership of the means of production, distribution, and exchange*'.

This wording makes clear the radical socialist roots of Labour Party politics in that common ownership is also the cornerstone of much communist theory. By contrast, Rawls (1971; 1999) had argued that the question of the nature of the economy—the degree to which the means of production were to be individually or collectively owned—was not the most fundamental issue; rather, what matters, instrumentally, is creating a society in which the least advantaged are as well off as possible, subject to respect for their basic liberties and opportunities (see Box 5.1).

KEY TEXTS

Nozick, *Anarchy, State, and Utopia* (1974)

This text is the leading philosophical statement of a **libertarian** approach to social justice, in which Nozick argues for the 'entitlement theory' of justice, comprising three principles.

- A principle of justice in initial acquisition explains the circumstances under which property can be appropriated from nature.
- A principle of justice in transfer explains how property can justly be transferred from one person to another.
- A principle of justice in rectification deals with violations of the first two principles.

According to Nozick, as long as a distribution of property comes about in accordance with these principles, it will be just, whatever 'pattern' of holdings results.

The British Labour Party began to take a similar view and, while still in opposition, the then leader, John Smith, set up the Commission on Social Justice to attempt to state a new agenda for the Party. The Commission included several leading academics: A. B. Atkinson, Ruth Lister, David Marquand, and Bernard Williams. Their report, published in 1994, abandoned several aspects of traditional socialist thought, including the commitment to national ownership, and paved the way for the next Labour leader, Tony Blair, to drop common ownership from a revised Clause IV of the Party Constitution in 1995. At the same time, the existence of the Commission made apparent that it was acceptable, once more, to use the term 'social justice' in political debate.

Despite this, the question remains: what is it that politicians think they are talking about when they use the term 'social justice'? The leading principles of the Commission of Social Justice are surprisingly vague, setting out the following:

1. The foundation of a free society is the equal worth of all citizens.
2. All citizens are entitled, as a right of citizenship, to be able to meet their basic needs for income, food, shelter, education and health.
3. Self-respect and personal autonomy are inherent in the idea of equal worth, but their fulfilment depends upon the widest possible access to opportunities and life chances.
4. Inequalities are not necessarily unjust—but those which are should be reduced and, where possible, eliminated.

   (**Commission on Social Justice, 1994: 17–18**)

The first three principles are unexceptional within the egalitarian tradition, but the fourth came under contemptuous attack for its triviality. As G. A. Cohen puts it (1994: 11), '*Those who are eager to declare their support for unjust inequalities will oppose the fourth core idea*'. Barry (2005: 7) remarks of the same principle: '*Well, it would be hard to disagree with that—in fact logically impossible on the assumption that injustice is bad thing*'. The real issue is to identify unjust inequalities and to set out the reasoning that shows that they are unjust. On this, the Report is evasive. However, arguably, the rehabilitation at least of the term 'social justice' was completed in the foundation of the Centre for Social Justice think tank in 2004, headed by Iain Duncan Smith (past leader of the Conservative Party).

 KEY THINKERS

Brian Barry (1936–2009)

Brian Barry was an English political philosopher who taught at Oxford University, the University of Chicago, the California Institute of Technology, the European University Institute in Florence, the London School of Economics, and Columbia University. He is known for his pioneering work combining analytical political philosophy, game theory, and theoretical and empirical social science. He was an uncompromising defender of liberal egalitarism, arguing that many of the economic and cultural policies that are accepted in contemporary Western democracies are not justifiable from the point of view of social justice. His final book was *Why Social Justice Matters* (2005).

BOX 5.1 RAWLS AND THE BRITISH LABOUR PARTY

The similarity between Rawls' theory and ideas implicit in politics of social justice were well expressed by the British philosopher Stuart Hampshire, who wrote, in his 1972 review of *A Theory of Justice*, that it provided:

> a noble, coherent, highly abstract picture of the fair society, as social democrats see it. In England, books about the Labour Party's aims . . . needed just such a theory of justice as this, stated in its full philosophical generality. This is certainly the model of social justice that has governed the advocacy of R. H. Tawney and Richard Titmuss and that holds the Labour Party together. Society must repair the cruelties of nature, and it exists not only to preserve law and order but also to correct the natural differentials between the strong and the weak, and to give institutional support to self-respect, which is for Rawls a primary value.

(Hampshire, 1972: 3)

 KEY POINTS

- In the 1980s and 1990s, the goal of social justice was challenged both on political and philosophical grounds, and was largely supplanted by an emphasis on economic growth and individual responsibility.

- Although still given little emphasis in the USA, considerations of social justice came back onto the political agenda in the UK following the election of the new Labour government in 1997.

- To rehabilitate social justice, it was necessary to decouple it from traditional socialist ideas of common ownership of the means of production.

Equality

The general difficulties in specifying a determinate account of social justice can be seen by exploring three questions:

1. Are all inequalities unjust— in other words, does social justice require equality?
2. Should social justice focus on distributions of income and wealth, of happiness, of standard of living, or something else again? This is the question of the 'currency' of justice.
3. Finally, what is the connection between social justice and individual responsibility?

To start with the first, we noted that the Commission on Social Justice explicitly denied that all inequalities are unjust. One argument for this denial derives from Rawls and is known as the **levelling down objection**: sometimes, inequalities are to the benefit of everyone. If so, then to insist on equality would be to endorse 'levelling down', making everyone worse off, simply for the sake of equality. Rawls instead proposes that the justice of a society is to be measured in terms of how the worst off fare, and therefore an unequal society can be just so long as inequalities are to the benefit of the worst off (for example, by creating a vibrant economy).

Rawls' view is now often called a 'prioritarian theory' in that it gives priority to the worst off in society. **Prioritarianism** can, as Rawls' theory of justice does, give absolute priority to the worst off. Alternatively, it can give a very high degree of priority to the worst off, falling short of absolute, sometimes allowing the claims of the worst off to be outweighed by the claims of those who are already better off. Typically, this could arise when it is very expensive to improve the position of the worst off and any improvement would be marginal. Under such circumstances, it can seem just to be prepared to use scarce resources in other ways. This latter view can be called 'weighted priority' in that it gives extra, but not absolute, weight to the least advantaged (Parfit, 1998).

So far, then, we have contrasted 'equality', 'absolute priority', and 'weighted priority'. A fourth view also jostles for consideration: what has been called 'sufficiency' theory. According to this view, what matters are simply **sufficiency principles**: whether everyone has enough to lead a flourishing life (Frankfurt, 1987). If so, then justice does not call for further redistribution.

Each of these theories provides a different account of social justice. At a theoretical level, it is very hard to know how to settle this disagreement, which is one reason why there is no agreement among philosophers as to the correct theory of social justice. However, at a practical level, some agreement is possible. Under all of these theories, the claims of the worst off will normally have a special urgency in the circumstances of the real world.

The second of the three questions set out previously is the question of the 'currency' of justice: equality, priority, or sufficiency of what, exactly? As Ronald Dworkin (1981a,b) and Amartya Sen (1999) have both pointed out, different currencies of justice can have very different distributive effects. If one person has more expensive needs or desires than another, then to equalize income and wealth could lead to inequalities in 'welfare'—understood as a subjective measure of well-being, such as happiness or preference satisfaction. Should governments concentrate on income and wealth, and not worry about the effects of this on happiness, or should their main concern be happiness and should they, therefore, take steps to bring people out of misery, as distinct from poverty?

We will return to this central issue but, in the meantime, it is necessary to say something about the third question: that of individual responsibility. In some ways, this has been, politically, the most important of the debates in that egalitarian theorists' apparent difficulties with the topic of individual responsibility opened the door to the libertarian challenge of Nozick, Friedman, and Hayek, and was part of the perceived weakness that led to the discrediting of the idea of social justice.

To illustrate the problem, consider once more Rawls' theory of justice, which says that society should maximize the wealth and income of those who have least. Now, the critic asks: is it not relevant to consider how it is that people came to have the least wealth and income? In a famous example, we are asked to imagine those who decide to spend their days surfing in Malibu rather than working for a living. If you can surf, most likely you can work—but does society have any duty of justice to help you? Strictly, Rawls' theory entails that society does have this duty, but, like many critics, Rawls (1988) attempts to avoid the implication. Many will feel it unjust for the hard-working to be taxed for the benefit of those who are not in any sort of real misfortune, but simply have decided not to work.

Some egalitarian theorists have risen to this challenge to defend the claims of people such as Malibu surfers. One argument is that all human beings are joint owners of the earth and those who are not making use of raw materials are owed 'rent' from those who are (Steiner, 1994). Another argument is that the sort of unconditional benefits that would allow surfers an income have other highly desirable consequences, such as making economic exploitation much less likely, and thus are beneficial (Van Parijs and van der Veen, 1986). A third argument is that the surfers are no different from very high earners under capitalism: neither can justify their income in terms of desert, but why pick on the surfers if the high earners are allowed to keep their ill-gotten gains (Van Parijs, 1995)? But these arguments notwithstanding, theories of equality seem to be in difficulties, at least from the point of view of practical political debate, if they are unable to distinguish between those in some sort of objective difficulty—people who are unable to find a job, for example—and those whose difficulties are of their own making and who could help themselves.

For this reason, Dworkin (1981b) introduced a refinement into egalitarian thinking to show how it is possible to incorporate ideas of responsibility into a commitment to social equality. Dworkin argues that while justice requires an equalization of people's background circumstances, it should also make people responsible for the consequences of their freely made choices. To put this another way, while justice should insulate people from the good and bad effects of what he terms '**brute luck**', it should not subsidize people's choices. If someone wishes to surf all day off Malibu, that is their choice—but they should not expect others to pay to allow them to exercise that choice. However, if a person has a disability that prevents him or her from working, then he or she is in a completely different position—and suffers from bad brute luck—and they do have a right to call on society for assistance. Hence Dworkin's theory accommodates issues of personal responsibility even within an egalitarian theory and provides a model for how it could be incorporated into other theories of social justice.

⭐ **KEY POINTS**

- The nature of social justice is contested.
- Key debates concern theories of equality, priority, and sufficiency, and how inequality should be defined and measured.
- Of particular concern has been the place of personal responsibility for disadvantages causing inequalities.

Equality of opportunity

It is sometimes thought that these detailed debates can, nevertheless, be cut short by defining equality or social justice in terms of equality of opportunity. From such a perspective, the government's task is to create equal opportunities for its citizens, but what an individual does with those opportunities—that is, whether he or she makes use of them or neglects them—is a matter for each citizen, not the government. This theory also has the apparent virtue of balancing social and individual responsibility: society must create opportunities and it is for each individual to make the best of the opportunities that are available.

The great advantage of this approach is that it appears to be able to draw on a wide consensus. Few would argue that, in general, they oppose equality of opportunity; indeed, there appears to be great convergence on the idea. Yet, once again, an agreement on the use of a phrase is not necessarily an agreement on any underlying idea. Cohen (1999), for example, usefully contrasts three notions of equality of opportunity:

- 'Bourgeois' equality of opportunity removes barriers based on prejudice and deliberate discrimination.
- 'Left liberal' equality of opportunity tries to compensate for differential family and social circumstances, creating a world in which those with the greatest talent get the best jobs.
- 'Socialist' equality of opportunity aims even to cancel out differential rewards due to differential talent, leaving differential outcomes a matter of pure taste or preference.

Unfortunately, the problem is even more complex than this. Janet Radcliffe Richards (1998) makes the distinction between two conceptions of equality of opportunity by considering the analogy of the distribution of shoes. Suppose that ten athletes are running a race, but, before they start, five find that their running shoes are lost or stolen. There seems good reason here to 'level down' and insist that all athletes run barefoot, because otherwise the race will be unfair. Consider now a similar situation, in which five of the ten have lost not their running shoes, but their warm winter boots. Here, there seems to be no case at all for levelling down—for making everyone equally uncomfortable by taking away their boots. In one case, the shoes are instruments that help in a competition and, in order to make the competition fair, it is necessary to equalize access to the instruments; in the other situation, there is no competition and the goods are valued in a non-competitive way.

Now, if life is a race, there is an argument for strict equality of opportunity. In a running race, other factors should be controlled so that outcomes are determined by running ability; in university selection, by academic potential, and so on. Equality of opportunity can be needed in order to make a competition fair. We can call this 'competitive opportunity'—that is, levelling the playing field. But to imagine that society is like a running race might seem very unattractive to those who believe in social justice. To continue with the analogy, if—as many believers in social justice propose—all are to get prizes and no one cares who comes first or last, then it really does not matter whether everyone has the same running shoes, or even whether they all start in the same place. Paradoxically, then, the more unequal society is in its rewards, the more important competitive equality of opportunity becomes.

Opportunity need not, however, be understood in competitive terms. Access to opportunity might be considered to be part of a flourishing life, rather than a mere means to another good. Consider, for example, what it is to bring up one's children with wide opportunities. Perhaps this means giving them access to a variety of cultural and social goods—art, music, sport, outdoor pursuits—so that they can experiment and each find what suits them best. Opportunity, in this sense, is not access to a scarce good awarded in a competition, but rather the provision of access to goods that any number of other people can also enjoy.

We find ourselves with what may seem to be a surprising conclusion: equality of competitive opportunity should be considered to be a rather minor issue by those who believe in trying to fashion society as some sort of community of equals. Equality of competitive opportunity makes sense only in an anti-egalitarian meritocratic conception of society, in which some rare social positions are prized. By contrast, equality of non-competitive opportunity suffers from the defects of any view that advocates strict equality in distribution—that it entails that society should level down, or destroy all of the winter boots if not everyone can have them. In the context of the discussion so far, equality of non-competitive opportunity should be replaced with a prioritarian view: governments have a special responsibility to improve the opportunities of those with the fewest opportunities and inequalities can be tolerated if they are genuinely to the benefit of the worst off.

In response to these arguments, however, it can still be argued that competitive equality of opportunity remains highly important in the actual world. Like it or not, market societies contain some jobs with high salaries and many with low salaries; some people are able to find ways in which to start their own businesses or to work independently, while others lack access to the means to do this. Similarly, some people find themselves in positions of great power, while many others do not. We live in a world in which some positions are analogous to prizes in a race. Theorists and activists of social justice may protest and work towards a world in which such differences are minimized, but, in the meantime, there is also every reason to level the playing field to make the race fair, so that all can compete on equal terms. This would mean, for example, not only that the most suitably qualified person should get the job, but that all should have the background opportunity to develop their talents and to obtain qualifications.

☆ **KEY POINTS**

- It is sometimes proposed that social justice should be conceived of in terms of equality of opportunity.
- Opportunity can be understood both in competitive and non-competitive terms.
- While theorists of social equality may wish to work towards a world in which competition is less important, in the meantime, social justice requires equality of competitive opportunity.

Social justice and social relations

Many approaches to social justice concentrate on devising principles for the distribution of scarce goods—that is, goods that are 'rival', in the economists' sense that if something is possessed or enjoyed by one person, it cannot be possessed or enjoyed by another—and hence social justice essentially provides rules to settle competition over desirable scarce goods. However, not all goods have this rival or competitive structure. Consider, for example, goods arising out of companionship, community, friendship, or belonging. It is not the case that there is a fixed pot of friendship and that if one person enjoys greater friendship, others must have less. Of course, it might happen that making friends with one person means losing another friend, but equally it is possible that, within a group, all will increasingly enjoy the goods of friendship without anyone suffering a loss.

Some theorists of social justice argue that the most important goods fall into this category, within which, in Tawney's words, '*to divide is not to take away*' (1931: 291). This goes hand in hand with the view that there is something very odd in focusing so heavily on material goods as the keystone of social justice. Of course, gross material inequality can undermine social justice: avoidable poverty should not exist in a just society. Nevertheless, the socialist roots of the theory of social justice encourage a view of the human good that plays down the importance of the acquisition and consumption of material goods, and replaces it with an emphasis on the enjoyment of what can be shared, rather than privately consumed—art, culture, conversation, and companionship, as well as the development of a many-sided human potential. These remarks, of course, tie in with the discussion of non-competitive opportunity in the previous section.

From this perspective, the goal of social justice is not so much to achieve an equal distribution of material goods, but to create a society in which each individual can think of themselves as valued as an equal. Although, as noted, gross material inequality can be an important obstacle to social justice (as powerfully argued recently by Wilkinson and Pickett, 2009), perhaps more important still is the way in which people in society view themselves and each other. For Tawney (1931), for example, the enemies of equality are snobbery and servility. In contemporary theory, David Miller (1994) suggests that an equal society is one that avoids hierarchy, while Richard Norman (1998) points out that a society might decline to follow a path of economic growth if it suspects that high economic development might lead to the alienation of people from each other.

KEY THINKERS

Richard Henry Tawney (1880–1962)

An English historian and political philosopher who taught primarily at the London School of Economics, Tawney was also a theorist and champion of adult education, especially for those traditionally denied educational opportunities. His writings combined socialist and Christian views to argue against material acquisitiveness, and to break the entrenchment and reinforcement of privilege that he observed in contemporary society. His defence of equality proved influential in the development of the ideas of the British Labour Party. His books include *The Acquisitive Society* (1920), *Religion and the Rise of Capitalism* (1926), and *Equality* (1931).

A systematic and more radical form of the anti-distributional framework has been set out in the work of Iris Marion Young. Starting from the idea that radical social movements often seek what they think of as **emancipation**—that is, the freeing of an individual or group from slavery or bondage—rather than **distributive justice**, she has argued that social justice should not be understood primarily in the terms of the distribution of material goods. Rather, it needs to pay much more attention to the way in which social structures empower some people and oppress others. Young (1990) has suggested that there are '*five faces of oppression*'—that is, that there are five quite distinct ways in which people can be oppressed in modern society.

- Exploitation draws on the Marxist class analysis of the labour process, suggesting that capitalist profit is ultimately based on the worker's lack of access to the means of production and his or her subsequent need to work on whatever terms are offered.

- Marginalization is to be excluded from the workforce—that is, to be in a position in which one cannot even be exploited.

- Powerlessness is again particularly related by Young to the workplace and concerns the lack of **autonomy** that many workers have in their daily lives. ➡ **See Chapter 14.**

- Cultural imperialism is the consequence of the emergence and domination of a majority cultural norm, and hence the exclusion of other ways of life. ➡ **See Chapter 3.**

- Violence is a more overt expression of the power of the majority over minorities, in that members of many groups must live with the constant threat of violence.

Young's approach to social justice, which brings sociological factors alongside those of political philosophy, greatly enriches the analysis, while at the same time showing the complexity of the problems.

Young adds that '*Distributive injustices may contribute to or result from these forms of oppression, but none is reducible to distribution and all involve social structures and relations beyond distribution*' (1990: 9). The emphasis here on the way in which people can be disadvantaged by facts of social structure—of laws, **cultural norms** and expectations, and social traditions—is worth counterposing to the essentially distributive concerns on which we have largely focused so far. ➡ **See Chapter 7.**

KEY THINKERS

Iris Marion Young (1949–2006)

An American political philosopher who taught at the University of Pittsburgh, the University of Chicago, and elsewhere, Young became famous for her book *Justice and the Politics of Difference* (1990). She argued that liberal egalitarian theory had tended to conceive of social justice purely in distributive terms, and thereby had ignored group-based oppression and the ways in which people can be adversely affected by the social structures within which they live. Her other writings include *Intersecting Voices: Dilemmas of Gender, Political Philosophy and Policy* (1997), *Inclusion and Democracy* (2000), *On Female Body Experience* (2004), and *Responsibility for Justice* (2011).

Picking up on Young's theme—and explicitly applying it to thinkers such as Ronald Dworkin (1981b) and G. A. Cohen (1989), who appear to suggest that the point of equality is to equalize life fortunes and thereby insulate individuals from the effects of bad luck—Elizabeth Anderson suggests that:

> The proper negative aim of egalitarian justice is not to eliminate the effect of brute luck from human affairs, but to end oppression which by definition is socially imposed. Its proper positive aim is not to ensure that everyone gets what they morally deserve, but to create a community in which people stand in relations of equality to others.

> **(Anderson, 1999: 288–9)**

Yet there remains something of a nagging question: can a just society really ignore questions of distribution? Should it not also matter whether or not people do get what they morally deserve? Anderson and Young do not overlook questions of distributive justice, but see them as largely instrumental to ending oppression. Other thinkers—most notably, Nancy Fraser—feel that this is not the right picture. Fraser (1995, 2000) presents a 'dualist' view, in which overcoming oppression and achieving distributive justice are both essential parts of a socially just society, neither subservient to the other.

Attractive though this picture may be, questions remain about how the pieces fit together, especially if there could be conflict between the goals. Consider, for example, the theory of distributive justice, according to which justice requires people to pay the full costs of their freely made choices. From this perspective, a claimant of welfare benefits must show that he or she is unemployed not through choice, but through lack of opportunity. It has been argued, however, that revealing that one cannot find a job at a time when others have little difficulty can be humiliating and, thereby, undercut one's standing as an equal in society (Wolff, 1998). Similarly, redistribution—especially when offered as compensation for 'natural misfortune', such as lack of talent—can carry humiliating messages of pity (Anderson, 1999). More generally, attempts to achieve precise distributive fairness can be experienced as oppressive. Work therefore needs to be done to show how issues of fair distribution can be reconciled with non-oppressive social relations.

> ☆ KEY POINTS
>
> - Although discussions of distributive justice often focus on 'rival' goods, which if used by one person cannot be used by another, there are also 'non-rival' goods, for which *to divide is not to take away'*.
> - Non-rival goods can include such things as friendship and a feeling of belonging, which can be incorporated into theories of social equality.
> - Social equality needs also to focus on the ways in which oppression constitutes a form of injustice.
> - Attempts to render society fair can, at the same time, undermine social equality by humiliating those who benefit from redistributive policies.

Advantage and disadvantage

Those who feel that distributional equality alone is inadequate as a theory of social justice, and that issues of oppression must also be incorporated, must then set out a view that provides a viable alternative. Many have been attracted to the **capability approach**—initially proposed by Amartya Sen (1992, 1999), and developed by Martha Nussbaum (2000) and others—as providing at least part of the conceptual repertoire needed to set out a positive view.

Sen argues that the theories of equality discussed earlier are in error regarding the second question that we identified: that of the 'currency' of justice. What matters, he argues, is not what resources you have or what level of subjective welfare you can achieve, but rather what your resources and other opportunities allow you to 'do and be'—and this he calls your 'capability to function'. Different individuals might need different packages of resources to function to the same degree, dependent on their particular needs.

In Sen's account, a functioning is an 'achieved' being or doing—being healthy, having control over your environment, and so on—whereas a capability is, in effect, one's opportunity to achieve a functioning. If, to use an example from Sen, a rich person decides to fast, he or she may lack the functioning of nutrition, but he or she still has the capability. The person could nourish him or herself, if they were to choose to do so. Sen argues that governments should be concerned with ensuring capabilities rather than functionings.

Frustratingly, Sen always resists setting out a list of capabilities, supposing that different societies may have different priorities. Martha Nussbaum (2000), however, goes further and does produce a provisional list, which she claims has universal validity.

- Life: Being able to live to the end of a human life of normal length.
- Bodily health: Being able to have good health, including reproductive health; to be adequately nourished; to have adequate shelter.
- Bodily integrity: Being able to move freely from place to place; being able to be secure against assault, including sexual assault, child sexual abuse, and domestic violence; having opportunities for sexual satisfaction and for choice in matters of reproduction.

- Sense, imagination and thought: Being able to imagine, think, and reason—and to do these things in a way informed and cultivated by an adequate education. Freedom of expression, speech, and religion.

- Emotions: Being able to have attachments to things and people outside ourselves; to love those who love and care for us.

- Practical reason: Being able to engage in critical reflection about the planning of one's life.

- Affiliation: Being able to live with and towards others; to recognize and show concern for other human beings; to engage in various forms of social interaction. Having the social bases of self-respect and non-humiliation. Not being discriminated against on the basis of gender, religion, race, ethnicity, and the like. ➜ **See Chapters 3 and 7.**

- Other species: Being able to live with concern for and in relation to animals, plants, and the world of nature. ➜ **See Chapter 11.**

- Play: Being able to laugh, to play, to enjoy recreational activities.

- Control over one's environment: Being able to participate effectively in political choices that govern one's life. ➜ **See Chapter 4**. Being able to have real opportunity to hold property. Having the right to seek employment on an equal basis with others.

The capability view has been extremely influential in at least two ways: first, it has been applied to development economics; second, it has helped to move forward the debate on equality and social justice. Other theorists continue to modify the view by arguing, for example, that it also matters whether people can sustain their functionings, and that therefore risk and vulnerability need also to be taken into account (Wolff and de-Shalit, 2007). In general, the combination of a pluralistic view of well-being—that is, that there are many different things that go to make up a good life—and the definition of a 'good life' in Aristotelian or Marxist terms of human development or functioning is its great attraction.

The strength of the view—its realistic pluralism—is, unfortunately, also its weakness: something that afflicts all pluralist views. If social justice tells us to direct our attention to the worst off, but there are many dimensions of well-being, how are we to tell who is the worst off in society? Is it those with the poorest health? Is it those with the weakest social networks and sense of belonging? The least educated? How can we decide?

In practice, however, this problem is not as difficult as it looks. Typically, those people who do badly in one respect, do badly in others, and so, whatever we think most important,

---

☆ KEY POINTS

- One way in which to reconcile distributive and social justice is to appeal to the capability view in which 'affiliation' and 'control over the environment' are part of the individual good.

- Pluralist views, such as the capability view, face a difficulty in 'indexing disadvantage' in order to determine which group of society is worst off overall.

- In practical terms, because some people do badly on a variety of criteria, indexing disadvantage is less problematic.

such people will turn out to be among the least advantaged. In this sense, then, it is very likely that, in the actual world, disadvantage 'clusters'. Following this line of thought, the government's responsibility in the attempt to achieve social justice should be to pay special attention to those who do badly on a range of capabilities (Wolff and de-Shalit, 2007).

Conclusion: prospects for achieving social justice

We began with a certain amount of puzzlement about the requirements of social justice: many people use the term, but what social justice itself requires is disputed. In this chapter, we have explored some of these disputes, including disputes between theories of equality, priority, and sufficiency, and between different theories of the currency of justice, differ- ent views about the place of responsibility, and different views about the importance of distributional fairness and of social equality. We have also noted some promising recent theoretical developments that may help to resolve some of these issues.

But what are the prospects that such philosophical accounts of social justice might have any influence on actual, practical policy? To approach this question, it will help to make a distinction between two ways of thinking about the relationship between political philoso- phy and public policy. One model suggests that the task of the political philosopher is to come to an understanding of what would be an ideally just set of institutions, which is then handed over to the policymaker, who has the responsibility of trying to move the world in the direction of justice. In a way, this is the traditional understanding of the task of the political philosopher: a legislator for an ideal kingdom. An alternative view is that the task for the political philosopher is not to design the best possible world, but to design the best possible world *starting from here*. Therefore, the political philosopher needs to understand a great deal of actual policy, as well as history, sociology, and economics, before making any recommendation. Without such knowledge, the philosopher risks irrelevance or, even worse, proposing schemes that, while attractive in theory, would do a great deal of harm if attempts were made to implement them.

CASE STUDY

Social justice and disability

The question of what is owed to people with disabilities is a severe test for any theory of social justice. The history of the way in which societies have treated people with disabilities has not, in general, been a happy one. According to some commentators, a great deal of social policy in this area has been concerned to isolate disabled people and to keep them out of sight of mainstream society, by placing disabled people—especially those who suffer from mental disabilities—in large institutions in rural settings, away from towns and cities. In the later part of the twentieth century, however, a growing movement of activists argued for the **integration** of disabled people into broader society, forcing the question of what it is that social justice owes to people with disabilities.

Political philosophers have taken some time to face up to the challenges set by this question. In *A Theory of Justice* (1971; 1999), John Rawls deliberately chose to put the question to one side, suggesting that the first task for a theory of justice is to work out principles for those who are able to enter into cooperative productive relations with each other over a whole life. This is not to say that he regarded the question as unimportant, but rather that it needs to be settled at another level. It is, indeed, easy to see the difficulty of applying Rawls' difference principle to people with disabilities or special health needs. For Rawls, well-being is measured in terms of possession of **primary goods**, and the difference principle distributes income and wealth; those with the lowest income are therefore the worst off. But people with special needs might possibly find that even an above-average income is insufficient to pay all of their necessary expenses and, thus, find themselves unable to cope even if, in Rawlsian terms, they are not among the worst off.

Although it may well be possible to modify Rawls' theory so that it can apply to people with disabilities, Rawls did not attempt this in detail. Ronald Dworkin (1981b) offers a different type of solution. Dworkin asks us to imagine, first of all, that resources have been distributed equally in society. He then suggests that we should imagine ourselves not knowing what our disability status is, yet knowing how common various disabilities are and the further consequences of disability for living a normal life. With these facts in mind, yet coupled with ignorance about our own disability status, Dworkin asks us to consider what level of insurance we would take out against finding ourselves disabled in various ways. It is tempting to think that we would take out very expensive forms of insurance, so that if we do find ourselves disabled, we receive very generous support. Yet Dworkin argues that we also have to consider the situation of finding ourselves without disability and therefore paying out a very large insurance premium. Both sides of the uncertain situation therefore have to be considered: what my life would be like with disability and what would it be like without it? A balance needs to be struck and a suitable 'hypothetical insurance policy' purchased.

The beauty of this idea is that hypothetical insurance decisions can be used to model social tax and transfer policies. The average hypothetical insurance policy can be used to calibrate the amounts to be transferred with tax, represented by the insurance premium, and welfare payments, represented by the hypothetical insurance payout. At a theoretical level, this is a very elegant solution.

At a more practical level, however, when we explore the actual policies pursued by governments on behalf of people with disabilities, we see that they are rarely restricted to 'tax and transfer'. Most developed societies now have legislation to protect the position of people with disabilities: in the USA, the Americans with Disabilities Act of 1990; in Australia, the Disability Discrimination Act of 1992; in the UK, the Disability Discrimination Acts of 1995 and 2005, and the Equality Act of 2010. Although the details of these Acts differ, law and social policy is now dominated by the idea that disabled people do not so much need 'compensation' for their disabilities as they do adjustments to society, so that they can overcome prejudice and discrimination and take their place as equal members of society, through access to work, leisure, politics, and all facilities and amenities that are available to other members of society.

This approach to policy has been heavily influenced by the social model of disability. Traditionally, disability had been conceived of in terms of a physical or mental impairment—a falling short of typical human norms of healthy functioning—which, in turn, leads to difficulties in living a 'normal life'. Against such assumptions, it seems appropriate that disability should be the concern of the medical profession—that the disabled person needs surgery, drugs, or other forms of medical assistance in order to achieve something closer to 'normal' physical or mental functioning. But some disability activists have objected to this way of conceiving disability, rejecting the idea that disabled people somehow fall short of a natural norm. Rather, they suggest, the notion of the 'normal' is a social construct, not a natural fact, and ideas of normality have been constructed in ways that disadvantage people who are different in particular ways. Just as the laws and attitudes of the societies in which they live have discriminated against women and people of minority races, people with disabilities suffer similar discrimination.

The social model of disability suggests that the way in which the problems of disabled people are to be addressed is not through financial compensation, as Dworkin's theory suggests, or through medical means, as the medical model implies, but through social change. Such social change can take many forms. One, importantly, will be change to the material and social environment—especially that related to the workplace and public buildings—so that people with mobility difficulties can, nevertheless, gain access. Such changes to building codes are a key part of that disability discrimination legislation already referred to, involving making buildings accessible by means of ramps and lifts, the better placing of handles and light switches, etc. Related changes involve ensuring that new technologies are used in inclusive ways, so that, for example, websites can be read by screen readers for the benefit of the visually impaired.

Changes to laws are relatively easy to introduce; ensuring that they are implemented is more of a challenge. Even more difficult, however, is cultural change, to alter attitudes commonly held towards people with disabilities. In some cases, this has meant reconsidering names of groups and organizations. For example, in the UK, a support group for children with cerebral palsy was known, for many years, as The National Spastic Society, named after the spasticity of limbs commonly associated with the condition. But the word 'spastic' became a common term of abuse and the name of the charity therefore reinforced negative stereotypes. Consequently, the charity renamed itself 'Scope', in an attempt to create a more positive image of children with cerebral palsy. Numerous small steps such as this can help to bring about a general change in social attitudes.

Defenders of the social model sometimes give the impression that the only difficulty that people with disabilities suffer is discrimination—'disablism'—and that changing laws and social attitudes is the route to bringing about liberation for people with disabilities. This is reasonably plausible in the case of physical disabilities—especially for mobility impairment—for which technical change, and sensitive architecture and design can overcome many of the effects of physical impairment, and which seems clearly required from the standpoint of social justice. It is unclear, however, how far the social model of disability generalizes.

Consider, for example, an argument made by some people who identify as members of the deaf community. Without doubt, given the way in which society is currently organized, life is more difficult for people who cannot hear. But a great deal of thought is now being given to the question of how better planning and design can be used so that deaf people no longer suffer such significant exclusion. Examples include such things as ensuring that information at stations and airports announced over public address systems is also easily available in visual form, ensuring that television programmes are adequately subtitled, and ensuring that sign language is provided at public lectures. The question remains, however, as to whether, once all of this has been done, there remains any disadvantage to being deaf. A profoundly deaf person cannot appreciate music, or the rhythms of the spoken word, or the laughter of their children. The question, then, is whether this is where the social model runs out and we find ourselves with a brute physical impairment, for which medical means, such as cochlear implants, are the only possible solution.

One response is that defenders of the social model do not deny that there are natural differences between human beings that enable some to enjoy pleasures that are closed off to others. Some people have a discerning palate; others, try as they might, cannot taste the difference between the finest wine and the supermarket special offer. Even among the hearing, there is great difference in the capacity to enjoy and, especially, to perform music. Many people are tone deaf and cannot sing—yet this has never seemed a matter of political concern. The difference between deafness and being tone deaf seems to be that the latter does not currently affect one's ability to function socially. According to some advocates of the social model, if the world were to be adequately reformed, deafness would no longer be of any political concern. Granted, to be deaf may well cut people off from a range of pleasures, but not having access to all forms of pleasure is simply part of the human condition.

Indeed, members of the deaf community have pushed the argument even further, arguing that the deaf have access to the culture and imagery embodied in sign language, which provides for them something that those who do not know sign language lack. For this reason, some deaf people have refused to accept cochlear implants, which would give them some hearing, preferring to be a fully functioning member of the deaf community rather than to become a 'substandard' member of the hearing community. It is, however, one thing for adults to make such decisions for themselves; it is another when children are involved. The primary ethical question is whether deaf parents should have the right to decide that their deaf child should not be given an implant, even when the evidence suggests that it would allow him or her close-to-normal hearing. One side of the argument draws an analogy with racism: would it be a reasonable response to racism to encourage the changing of the colour of the skin of newborn babies if that were possible? Obviously, this seems to be the wrong way in which to address the discrimination of racism. In response, it is said that the colour of one's skin is not an impairment, while deafness is, and that this is the reason why we should try to give babies the ability to hear, but not try to change the colour of their skin. The matter is, of course, further complicated by disputes about the state's right or duty to interfere with parental decisions.

If there are difficulties in applying the social model to all aspects of deafness, it is harder still, however, to imagine how the social model can deal with other forms of disablement. Cognitive disability, such as forms of learning impairment, cannot be addressed merely by designing buildings in different ways or by changing forms of communication—although without doubt, this could do some real good. It has taken philosophy and social policy a long time to come to understand what is owed, by way of social justice, to people with physical disabilities, although there has been progress. In the case of mental disability and learning difficulties, however, we remain at an even earlier stage. What it is to treat a person with learning difficulties as an equal is not a simple matter. For a long time, such people have been treated as perpetual children, unable to make decisions about their own lives and needing to be looked after by others. But one promising suggestion is that everyone, including people with learning disabilities, should be given the background help and resources so that they can exercise a good deal of autonomy in their own lives, and play a part in making important decisions. But while there are important experiments taking place, such as the In Control movement, there remains much to be done at both the theoretical and practical levels.

? QUESTIONS

1. What is John Rawls' theory of social justice?
2. What is the basis of Nozick and Hayek's opposition to the idea of social justice?
3. How did the British Labour Party rehabilitate social justice?
4. What are the main issues that need to be resolved in constructing a theory of equality?
5. What is 'equality of opportunity'?
6. Is equality of opportunity a sufficient basis for social justice?
7. What is the difference between distributive equality and social equality? Is there any conflict between them?
8. What is 'oppression'?
9. How can we understand human well-being?
10. Does the capability approach provide an objective account of the human good?
11. How should political philosophy aim to influence social policy?
12. How can the needs or claims of people with disabilities be addressed from the point of view of social justice?

FURTHER READING

■ Barry, B. (2005) *Why Social Justice Matters*, Cambridge: Polity Press An argument for the importance of social justice from a leading contributor to contemporary debates, drawing both on philosophical argument and on many empirical sources.

■ Nozick, R. (1974) *Anarchy, State and Utopia*, New York/Oxford: Basic Books/Blackwell The leading philosophical statement of libertarianism, arguing against conceptions of social justice in favour of individual rights to property.

■ Nussbaum, M. (2000) *Women and Human Development: The Capabilities Approach*, Cambridge: Cambridge University Press An influential statement of the capability view, with particular application to the condition of women in the developing world.

■ Rawls, J. (1971; 1999) *A Theory of Justice*, revd edn, Cambridge, MA: Harvard University Press Arguably the most important work of political philosophy written in English in the twentieth century, setting out and arguing for a detailed conception of social justice.

■ Sen, A. (1999) *Development as Freedom*, New York/Oxford: Knopf/Oxford University Press Building on the analysis of much of his earlier work, arguing that human deprivation should be understood not in terms of income and wealth, but rather those of freedom to achieve valuable functionings (the capability view).

■ Von Hayek, F. (1973; 1978; 1979) *Law, Legislation and Liberty*, three vols, Chicago, IL: University of Chicago Press Combines philosophical and economic reasoning to argue against government intervention in the economy.

■ Walzer, M. (1983) *Spheres of Justice*, New York: Basic Books Argues that it is wrong to conceive of equality in terms of satisfying a single principle, but that rather each 'sphere of justice' has its own principle for distributing the goods characteristic of that sphere.

■ Wolff, J. and de-Shalit, A. (2007) *Disadvantage*, Oxford: Oxford University Press A modified account of capability approach, emphasizing the importance of risk and vulnerability in understanding disadvantage, and the tendency for someone suffering from one disadvantage to find themselves facing others.

■ Young, I. M. (1990) *Justice and the Politics of Difference*, Princeton, NJ: Princeton University Press A highly influential argument against the 'distributive paradigm', which is the view that equality concerns only the distribution of goods. By contrast, Young argues that social justice must combat oppression.

 WEB LINKS

● https://hd-ca.org The Human Development and Capability Association is '*a global community of academics and practitioners focused on people-centred development and the capability approach.*'

● http://www.centreforsocialjustice.org.uk The Centre for Social Justice is a 'centre-right think tank', established by Iain Duncan Smith in 2004.

● http://www.fordham.edu/halsall/mod/1942beveridge.html The Modern History Sourcebook provides extracts from the Beveridge Report (1942).

● http://www.in-control.org.uk In Control is an organization that aims to enable people with disabilities to take control of their own support.

● http://www.parliament.uk/about/living-heritage/transformingsociety/ livinglearning/19thcentury/overview/poorlaw/ Gives some history and analysis of the Poor Law.

 Visit the Online Resource Centre that accompanies this book to access more learning resources: http://www.oxfordtextbooks.co.uk/orc/mckinnon3e/

6

Crime and punishment

MASSIMO RENZO

 Chapter contents

- Introduction
- Consequentialist justifications of punishment
- Retributivist justifications of punishment
- Mixed approaches to the justification of punishment
- Conclusion: punishment and beyond

 Reader's guide

The institution of criminal punishment is morally problematic for a number of reasons. To begin with, it treats people in ways that would otherwise be morally impermissible, by depriving them of their liberty, of important financial resources, and sometimes even of their life. But criminal punishment is also problematic because of the costs it imposes on non-criminals. Given the enormous annual budget that countries like the UK and the USA devote to sustaining the criminal justice system, we might wonder whether other ways of spending the same money would be more efficient in reducing suffering and enabling people to live better lives. What might be the justification for an institution whose costs are so significant? In this chapter we will consider the most prominent answers that have been offered to this question.

Introduction

That states have the right to punish those who break the law seems to be one of the very few uncontroversial ideas in common sense political morality. People with different moral views and inclinations will radically disagree as to which conduct states should punish (should the consumption of drugs be punished? Should prostitution?) and which form should punishment take (is capital punishment ever an option? Can criminals be deprived of specific civil rights?). But that states are permitted, indeed required, to punish those who break the law is normally taken for granted.

This consensus is striking, given the many respects in which criminal punishment seems highly problematic. Even if we restrict our attention to imprisonment, leaving aside more controversial forms of punishment such as capital punishment and corporal sanctions, criminal punishment is problematic in at least three respects (Tadros, 2013). First, because of the harm it imposes on those who are punished. It is worth noticing that this harm is not limited to the deprivation of liberty and of other important rights.[1] ➔ See Chapter 2. Given the conditions of prisons in many countries, prisoners are also regularly exposed to the risk of severe psychological as well as physical harm. Moreover, their jobs and their personal relationships are often endangered, and the stigma attached to punishment is such that it can be hard to get them back once the sentence has been served.

Second, and relatedly, there are the costs that the punishment of criminals imposes on their families and friends. Here, in addition to psychological distress and the harm created by the disruption of personal relationships, we should notice the harm produced by the fact that imprisoning someone may deprive his or her family members, including vulnerable ones, of important resources and opportunities they would otherwise have had access to. These family members will have rarely done anything to become liable to bearing these costs.

Finally, there are the costs that punishment institutions impose on other innocent parties, who are in no way connected to the criminals. One of these costs is the risk of being wrongfully convicted; another one is the financial cost of maintaining the criminal justice system. The former has traditionally received more attention in the philosophical debate, but the second is no less important. The resources that are used to maintain the criminal justice system are huge and could be used to address other pressing issues such as medical research, natural disasters, or poverty relief (Husak, 2008).

In light of these considerations, the question of what justifies the alleged right of states to punish their citizens becomes a pressing one. ➔ See Chapter 1. Without a convincing answer to this question, the radical conclusion that the criminal justice system should be abolished ought to be seriously considered (Christie, 1977; Bianchi, 2010). In this chapter, we will examine some of the most important answers offered thus far in the philosophical debate.

To begin with, let us elucidate what we mean by 'punishment'. Most philosophers agree that punishment typically involves the imposition of hardship or suffering on a supposed offender for a supposed crime, by a person or body who claims the authority to do so. Moreover, it is commonly agreed that the harm inflicted by punishment is intended to communicate censure or moral condemnation, and that this is the feature that distinguishes punishment from mere penalties such as taxes or compensatory damages (Feinberg, 1970b). This characterization will be sufficient for our purposes. Our question is: *what can justify the infliction of this sort of suffering?*

Two strategies are available: one is instrumental, in that it starts by acknowledging that the suffering imposed through punishment is bad in itself, but then goes on to justify it by pointing at the good consequences that inflicting such suffering will produce (Bentham, 1789; 1970; 1996). If these consequences are sufficiently good as to outweigh the disvalue of inflicting the suffering, and if there is no way of achieving those goods at lower cost, doing so will be justified according to the instrumental view.

KEY TEXTS

Bentham, *An Introduction to the Principles of Morals and Legislation* (1789; 1970; 1996)

Jeremy Bentham is considered the father of utilitarianism. He was the first thinker to provide a systematic formulation of the view that actions, practices, and institutions are to be approved when they promote good consequences and disapproved when they produce bad consequences. His most important work is *An Introduction to the Principles of Morals and Legislation*. Here, he argues that '*all punishment is mischief; all punishment is in itself evil. Upon the principle of utility, if it ought at all to be admitted, it ought only to be admitted in as far as it promises to exclude some greater evil*'. (1996: 158)

The alternative strategy consists in denying that suffering is bad in itself. Whether suffering is good or bad will, according to this strategy, depend on its character or meaning, and, in particular, on whether it is deserved. While undeserved suffering is bad, deserved suffering is good, and this is why the state can permissibly inflict it.

The way in which the instrumental strategy has been traditionally pursued is by endorsing some version of **consequentialism**, the moral theory according to which the rightness or wrongness of a given conduct, practice, or rule depends only on its consequences (or the consequences that it is likely to produce). Non-instrumental justifications, on the

---

⭐ KEY POINTS

- Punishment involves the imposition of hardship or suffering on a supposed offender for a supposed crime, by a person or body who claims the authority to do so. Many also believe that the harm inflicted by punishment is intended to communicate censure or moral condemnation.

- Criminal punishment is problematic in at least three respects: it harms those who are punished; it also harms, indirectly, their families and friends; it imposes significant costs (financial and otherwise) on the rest of the political community.

- Without a convincing justification for the practice of punishment, the radical conclusion that the criminal justice system might have to be abolished should be considered.

- Instrumental justifications suggest that while the suffering imposed through punishment is bad in itself, it can be nonetheless justified if the value of its consequences outweighs the disvalue of inflicting the suffering.

- Non-instrumental justifications suggest that whether suffering is good or bad depends on whether it is deserved. While undeserved suffering is bad, deserved suffering is good, and this is why the state can permissibly inflict it on wrongdoers.

other hand, have been traditionally defended by **retributivist theories**, according to which, wrongdoers deserve to suffer in proportion to the gravity of the wrong they have committed.

However, it would be a mistake to believe that consequentialism is the only way in which an instrumental approach to the justification of punishment can be defended. There can also be non-consequentialist theories that justify punishment instrumentally, i.e. theories that appeal to the fact that punishment will produce good consequences, while denying that in justifying punishment we should look exclusively at its consequences. We shall consider some of these theories after investigating the traditional consequentialist and retributivist approaches.

Consequentialist justifications of punishment

There are three types of good consequences that consequentialist theories normally appeal to in justifying punishment:

- *incapacitating* criminals by depriving them, at least temporarily, of the capacity to commit crimes (typically, by imprisoning them);[2]
- *deterring* criminals (and potential criminals) by providing them with prudential reasons not to commit crimes;
- *reforming* criminals by persuading them that they should obey the law and refrain from committing crimes.

It would be hard to deny that the justification of punishment has something to do with its capacity to produce such consequences. The problem with consequentialist theories, however, at least in their classic formulations, is that they tend to treat the production of these consequences as a necessary and sufficient condition for the justification of punishment. So, whenever inflicting a given punishment on someone will produce (or will be likely to produce) the relevant consequences, doing so will be permissible, even if the person in question is innocent or, assuming that he or she is not, even if the punishment at hand would be disproportionate for the crime committed. But intuitively, both punishing the innocent and inflicting disproportionate punishment seem wrong.

One way in which consequentialists have tried to rebut this objection is by pointing out that, although their view in principle does not rule out punishing the innocent or inflicting disproportionate punishment, it does so in practice, given the risks that, once these practices became known, the criminal justice system would lose its capacity to function effectively (Hare, 1989). This is because if we were to suspect that punishment was not inflicted only on those who are guilty and that its severity did not reflect the gravity of the crime, we would consider criminal justice institutions unjustified and stop complying with them. Obviously, the consequences of this would be disastrous.

However, this answer is unconvincing, for it is not clear that it would be impossible for cases of punishment of the innocent or disproportionate punishment to be kept secret; and if they could be kept secret, the idea that these practices, once known, would produce bad consequences cannot be employed to explain why they are not permissible. And yet, even if these practices could be kept secret, we would consider them wrong. Punishing an innocent, or inflicting disproportionate punishment, is wrong even if no one will ever find out about it. These practices are wrong because they involve treating the victim of punishment 'merely as a means' for our own good (Kant, 1998). Even if the good produced by inflicting these punishments outweighs the harm suffered by the person punished, doing so is wrong because people have rights that protect them against being used in this way. Unless someone has done something to lose these rights, they cannot be disregarded in order to benefit others.

> ☆ KEY POINTS
>
> - Consequentialist theories justify punishment by appealing exclusively to its consequences.
> - The good consequences produced by punishment are mainly of three kinds: incapacitation, deterrence, and moral reform.
> - Consequentialist theories struggle to account for the fact that it would be wrong to inflict disproportionate punishment and to punish the innocent.

Retributivist justifications of punishment

One way in which we might be tempted to put the objection to consequentialism just discussed is by saying that consequentialism cannot account for the idea that punishment should be inflicted only on those who *deserve* it. This view is known as 'negative retributivism' (Dolinko, 1991). As we will see, negative retributivism is indeed compatible with consequentialism (H. L. A. Hart's view, for example, combines both—Hart, 2008). However, many critics of consequentialism object not only that desert should be a *necessary* condition of punishment, but also that it should be a *sufficient* one. According to this view (known as 'positive retributivism'), it is a good thing that wrongdoers are punished, because it is a good thing that they 'get what they deserve'. This idea is very popular, and most people seem to share it. However, once we try to spell out exactly what the idea of desert consists in, things become more complicated. In this section, we will consider two of the most prominent ways in which the notion has been articulated in the contemporary debate.

Punishment and fair play

One influential strand of retributivism starts by locating the justification of punishment against the backdrop of a picture of society as a joint enterprise in which citizens accept the burden of having to obey the laws of their state in exchange for the benefits that their state provides them with, most notably, security and the rule of law. ➔ See Chapter 1. Within this picture, the sense in which criminals deserve to be punished can be explained by appealing to the idea that punishment removes the unfair advantage that criminals acquire over their fellow citizens by their crimes. Since security can be guaranteed only to the extent that a sufficient number of individuals exercise self-restraint and obey the law, those who break the law enjoy this benefit without sharing in the burdens that citizens are required to bear as a matter of fairness. The function of the suffering imposed through punishment is to restore the right balance of benefits and burdens (Morris, 1968; Murphy, 1973; Sher, 1987).

At first sight, this seems like a plausible way of explaining what it means that wrongdoers deserve to be punished. Think about tax evasion. Wouldn't it be great if everyone were to pay their taxes *except* you? The services that you would receive from the state would remain the same (since the difference that your taxes make to the provision of those services is negligible, as long as most people pay their taxes), but you would not have to give up a significant portion of your income to receive them. Doing so, however, would involve gaining an unfair advantage over your fellow citizens, who do give up a significant portion of their income in order to contribute to the production of those services. It is unfair that they do their part while you do not. The idea that you deserve to be punished because punishing you will remove this unfair advantage, in this case seems to have some plausibility.

The same idea, however, is less plausible once we try to use it to justify the punishment of crimes like murder or rape. Claiming that the punishment of these crimes aims at removing the unfair advantage that their perpetrators have gained over their fellow citizens mistakenly represents refraining from murder and rape as a burden. But this is not how we think about these crimes. Most people do not think of murder and rape as conducts in which they would like to engage, were it not for the fact that this would be unfair towards those who refrain from doing so (Duff, 2001).

The very idea that offenders gain an unfair advantage over law-abiding citizens mistakenly presupposes that not offending constitutes a burden for the latter, for if there was no burden to begin with, in what sense would offenders have an unfair advantage? But, while this might be true in the case of *mala prohibita* (conduct that, like tax evasion, is wrongful in virtue of its being legally prohibited), the same does not seem to be true for *mala in se* (conduct that, like murder or rape, is wrongful, independently of its being legally regulated).

 KEY CONCEPTS

Malum in se and *malum prohibitum*

Malum in se refers to conduct that is wrongful, independently of having been criminalized or legally prohibited. Murder, assault, and rape are classic examples. *Malum prohibitum*, by contrast, refers to conduct that is wrongful only in virtue of its being criminalized, or at least legally prohibited. For example, driving without insurance is morally wrong only insofar as there is a law that requires drivers to be insured. If no such law were in place, there would be nothing wrong with driving without insurance (although it would be wrong not to compensate the victims of accidents we might cause).

Defenders of fair play could reply here that the burden they are talking about is not the one involved in obeying particular laws, such as those prohibiting murder or rape but, more generally, the one involved in obeying *the* law, i.e. the system of prohibitions that states lay down for their citizens (Dagger, 2008). It is failing to comply with this system of restrictions that triggers punishment. But even so, we might wonder about the theory's plausibility. For it would still be the case, according to this view, that the reason why murderers and rapists can be permissibly punished is, ultimately, that they took an unfair advantage over law-abiding citizens. Is this the best way to understand the reasons why we punish murderers and rapists? Can we adequately account for the justification of their punishment by simply appealing to the idea of free riding?

Notice that if that were the case, there would be no principled reason why the balance of benefits and burdens within society should be restored by punishing those who broke the law. Why not do so by providing those who did not break the law with extra benefits instead? Maybe such a policy would be hard to implement, but certainly the option would be worth exploring, given the enormous costs, both financial and non-financial, that punishment imposes on innocent parties as well as on wrongdoers. And yet, most people would object to this policy, even if it turned out that it *could* be successfully implemented. The thought that we could let murderers and rapists go unpunished, as long as law-abiding citizens receive a benefit which is roughly comparable to the (alleged) one that these offenders gained in disobeying the law, is one we would find repulsive. But nothing in the logic of the fair play argument seems to rule out this possibility, at least in principle.

Deserving to suffer

We have seen that fair-play theories encounter problems accounting for the central idea of retributivism, namely that punishment should be inflicted on those who deserve it. Better equipped, in this respect, seems to be another variant of retributivism, which explains the idea of desert by appealing to the thought that it is good that wrongdoers suffer (Murphy and Hampton, 1990; Moore, 1997). Those who take this view simply deny that if we are to justify the infliction of suffering on wrongdoers by way of punishment, we need to show that doing so is instrumental to achieving valuable states of affairs such as deterrence or rehabilitation. We do not need to do that because certain forms of suffering are good in themselves, and as such we should welcome them. Whether suffering is good or bad will, according to this view, depend on whether it is deserved. Undeserved suffering is bad, and thus can be inflicted only to the extent that doing so will produce valuable consequences; deserved suffering is good, and this is why the state can permissibly inflict it, without any further justification needed.

The idea that deserved suffering is good will perhaps be intuitive to some, but it is certainly in need of an argument. Why should we want wrongdoers to suffer? In what respect is their suffering good? A possible answer is that we want wrongdoers to recognize that what they did was wrong, and we might think that, psychologically, it would be impossible to do so without feeling bad about their crime. Surely realizing that what they did was wrong will come with a certain amount of remorse, and remorse is a painful emotion. But none of this suggests that suffering is good. What is good is the recognition that a given conduct was wrong, not the suffering per se (Scanlon, 2003). In other words, what we value is not suffering, but a particular kind of suffering, namely the sort of suffering that goes with recognizing the wrongfulness of certain conduct; and we value this suffering only to the extent that it signals the presence of such recognition (Tadros, 2013).

Suppose that it was possible for wrongdoers to recognize that their conduct was wrong without suffering. Shouldn't we want them to do so? According to retributivists, we should not. Retributivists will argue that there is independent value in wrongdoers' suffering, and that it is good when wrongdoers suffer, even if their suffering does not come from the recognition of the wrongfulness of their conduct. For example, imagine that Carl is a killer who is paid to place a bomb in a shopping mall that kills dozens of innocent people. Carl is never apprehended after completing his crime and never comes to repent or recognize that what he did was wrong. He lives happily enjoying his money. However, one day, while hiking, Carl falls into a crack and breaks his legs, losing his capacity to walk. Some retributivists will argue that there is value in the suffering that Carl goes through when he breaks his legs. A world in which he suffers after his terrible crime is better than a world in which he lives happily. It is 'fitting' or 'appropriate' that he suffers, and it is unfitting that he does not. Carl does not deserve to live a happy life and we should welcome the fact that he does not, even if the suffering that makes his life unhappy is in no way related to the recognition of the wrongfulness of his conduct.

Thus, according to this view, saying that someone deserves to be punished is saying that there is a fitting or appropriate relationship between the moral value of our conduct and the level of happiness or well-being that we enjoy, and that it is good that this relationship exists. The state can permissibly punish offenders in order to pursue the good of bringing about this relationship.

One way to challenge this view consists in granting that it would be good if fitting relationships between moral value and happiness or well-being were realized, while rejecting the idea that states have the right to do so by punishing wrongdoers. As Joel Feinberg puts it: '*a person's desert of X is always a reason for giving X to him, but not always a conclusive reason*,' for '*considerations irrelevant to his desert can have overriding cogency in establishing how he ought to be treated on balance*.' (Feinberg, 1970a: p. 60)

 KEY THINKERS

Joel Feinberg (1926–2004)

Joel Feinberg is one of the most influential legal and political philosophers of the twentieth century. His work spans a wide range of issues, including the nature of rights, the justification of the criminal law, and questions of bioethics. His most important contribution is *The Moral Limits of the Criminal Law* (1984–88), a four-volume treaty in which he carefully examines four possible justifications for criminalization. In this work, Feinberg argues that the state can permissibly criminalize conduct that harms or offends others, but cannot criminalize conduct on the grounds that it harms the agent him or herself or on the grounds that it is inherently immoral.

What could these considerations be? To begin with, wrongdoers might retain a right not to be punished by the state (Dolinko, 1991). Many things are good—eating more healthily, exercising, reading poetry—but we normally think that we have a right against being forced to achieve these goods. Similarly, it might be argued that even if it is good that we suffer for acting wrongfully, we might have a right against being made to suffer what we deserve. Thus, even if retributivists are correct in pointing at the importance of desert, this is not enough to show that the state is permitted to punish those who deserve it. We must also show that the latter have lost their right not to be punished by it (Wellman, 2012).

A second consideration has to do with the very idea that state resources may be employed to promote a particular good, such as giving wrongdoers what they deserve. Some will object to this idea because they believe that states should not be involved in pursuing particular conceptions of the good (Rawls, 2005). But suppose that it was permissible for the state to give wrongdoers what they deserve (either because the idea that states should not pursue specific conceptions of the good is mistaken or because giving people what they deserve is something about which holders of different conceptions of the good could not reasonably disagree). Would that be enough to give the state the right to punish wrongdoers? Not necessarily. We might still wonder whether the best way to employ the limited resources of the state is by pursuing the good of giving wrongdoers what they deserve, rather than addressing other pressing problems, such as improving access to health and education, reducing poverty, or ameliorating job conditions. ➡ **See Chapter 5.**

And even if pursuing the good of giving people what they deserve was indeed so valuable as to take precedence over these other ends, we might still wonder why states should spend so much money to give wrongdoers what they deserve, rather than using that money to ensure that those who act in morally praiseworthy ways get the happiness they deserve (Tadros, 2013: p. 69). For if what matters is that states pursue the realization of the appropriate relationship between the moral worth of our conduct and the level of happiness or well-being that we enjoy, there is no reason to focus on the conduct of those who do bad things, rather than focus on the conduct of those who do good things.

A number of further problems arise here. Retributivists presumably will agree that given that happiness rarely tracks moral goodness, agents who act in morally praiseworthy ways are often unhappier than they deserve. They might also agree that states should indeed intervene to remedy this situation. An obvious way to do that is for states to reward these agents in appropriate ways. But notice that if what we are interested in is that happiness and moral goodness are aligned, there is no principled reason not to pursue this end in a different way, namely by encouraging good-doers to act wrongly. At least when we cannot increase their happiness, or doing so would be too costly, it looks as if we might have reason to try to bring down the value of their conduct, so as to realize the right balance between the happiness they deserve and the happiness they enjoy (Tadros, 2013). This implication, however, seems morally repugnant, and even committed retributivists will be uneasy about having to embrace it.

☆ **KEY POINTS**

- Retributivism justifies punishment by appealing to the idea that wrongdoers deserve to be punished.

- One way to explain the sense in which wrongdoers deserve to be punished is by appealing to the thought that punishment removes an unfair advantage that criminals obtain over law-abiding citizens. However, this view seems to misrepresent the nature of crimes like murder and rape.

- Another way to articulate the idea of desert is by appealing to the thought that it is good when wrongdoers suffer. But should we value their suffering per se, or should we value it because it signals the presence of true repentance?

Mixed approaches to the justification of punishment

We have seen that traditional consequentialist and retributivist approaches encounter a number of problems in accounting for the justification of the state's right to punish. Consequentialist theories successfully capture the idea that given the significant costs of maintaining punishment institutions, doing so will be justified only if punishing wrongdoers will produce significant goods. These theories, however, seem unacceptable to the extent that they ignore the fact that there are restrictions on how these goods can be pursued. Most notably, they fail to acknowledge that it is impermissible to punish the innocent or to inflict disproportionate punishment whenever doing so would produce good consequences.

Retributivist accounts seem better suited to capture the 'backward-looking' dimension of punishment (Hart, 2008), i.e. the idea that punishment can be permissibly inflicted only upon those who acted in certain ways. This is the role that the notion of desert is (at the very least) supposed to play within these accounts. However, they seem to struggle in clearly articulating what it means to say that someone deserves to be punished. Moreover, some of them fail to acknowledge that the justification of punishment should also have a 'forward-looking' dimension. Although punishment cannot be justified by looking exclusively at its consequences, it seems plausible that these consequences should play a role within its justification. If the suffering of punishment served no further good, we might doubt that its infliction would be justified. Thus, it looks as if a plausible justification of punishment will have to pay attention to the forward-looking as well as to the backward-looking dimension of punishment.

The Hartian model

An influential model that combines forward-looking and backward-looking elements is the one defended by H. L. A. Hart. After distinguishing between the question of what constitutes the 'general justifying aim' of punishment (*why* we punish) and the question of how punishment should be distributed (*who* we may punish), Hart argues that the general justifying aim of punishment lies in the valuable consequences that punishment produces, particularly in terms of deterrence, but that there are non-consequentialist constraints on how these valuable consequences can be pursued. These constraints rule out the permissibility of punishing the innocent and inflicting disproportionate punishment (Hart, 2008).

This view might seem to nicely capture what is attractive about both consequentialism and retributivism. However, its plausibility will ultimately depend on how the constraints in questions are justified. Why is it permissible to punish offenders, but not the innocent, in order to produce the desired deterrence? We might be tempted to answer by appealing to the idea that offenders deserve to be punished, but then we would be left with the question that retributivists struggle to answer: what does it mean exactly that someone deserves to be punished? Hart's strategy is different, and appeals to the value of individual choice. Adopting a system of punishment in which only those who break the law can be punished enables individuals to control what is going to happen to them, insofar as they

> ### KEY TEXTS
>
> **H. L. A. Hart, *Punishment and Responsibility* (1968; 2008)**
>
> H. L. A. Hart's *Punishment and Responsibility* is one of the most influential books on the philosophy of the criminal law. It consists of nine essays that cover a wide range of problems, including the justification of the death penalty and the relevance of free will for responsibility. In the most famous essay of the book ('Prolegomenon to the Principles of Punishment'), Hart defends the view that punishment institutions aim at deterring future crimes, but they can permissibly do so only within certain constraints, the most important of which are the prohibition on punishing the innocent and the prohibition on inflicting disproportionate punishment.

can decide whether to break the law, thereby running the risk of being punished, or obey the law and steer clear of punishment. In this sense, punishment institutions aim at:

> maximizing within the framework of coercive criminal law the efficacy of the individual's informed and considered choice in determining the future and also his power to predict that future.
>
> (Hart, 2008: p. 46)

This, according to Hart, is the best way of treating others 'as ends', rather than 'merely as means'. By creating a system of sanctions, we treat those who are subject to the criminal justice system as ends because, while we provide them with reasons to act in certain ways, we leave to them the choice as to whether to act according to those reasons or to refrain from doing so and suffer the consequences. But is this enough to treat someone as an end? We might think that it is not. After all, the gunman who threatens us with his gun is giving us the same option. He gives us reasons to hand over the wallet and lets us choose whether to do so or to suffer the consequences. But surely we would not say that the gunman is treating us as ends when he offers us this choice (Duff, 1986).

Thus, if we are to be treated as ends in ourselves i.e. autonomous moral agents, by the criminal law, more is needed than being offered a system of incentives and deterrents (though one mitigated by the presence of side constraints introduced by Hart). If the state is to treat us as autonomous moral agents, it must not use the threat of punishment to provide us with coercive reasons to obey the law. Rather, the state should justify its demands to us and seek our allegiance by using punishment as a way of pointing out the reasons we already have to obey the law:

> the proper aim of a system of law which addresses its citizens as rational agents is to bring them not merely to obey its requirements, but to accept those requirements as being appropriately justified; and the proper aim of a criminal conviction is to communicate and to justify to the defendant an appropriate judgment on his past conduct, and thus to bring him to recognize and accept his duty to obey the law.
>
> (Duff, 1986: p. 185)

If we take this view, it looks as if the main justification of punishment should be found in its capacity to communicate a message to wrongdoers.

The communicative model

The idea that punishment can be justified in communicative terms has received increasingly more attention in the contemporary debate and has been formulated in a number of different ways (Nozick, 1981; Hampton, 1984; Primoratz, 1989; Von Hirsch, 1995; Tasioulas, 2006; Bennett, 2010). The most sophisticated version of the theory is the one offered by Antony Duff, who argues that punishment communicates a message of censure of the conduct of wrongdoers. This message is communicated primarily to them, but also to the victims and to society at large. The aim is to persuade wrongdoers of the wrongfulness of their conduct and to give them an opportunity to repent and express their repentance to the other members of the political community, in order to regain their place within it (Duff, 1986, 2001).

 KEY THINKERS

R. A. Duff (1945–)

R. A. Duff is one of the most prominent philosophers of the criminal law. His works include *Intention, Agency, and Criminal Liability* (1990), *Trials and Punishments* (1986), *Criminal Attempts* (1996), *Punishment, Communication and Community* (2000), and *Answering for Crime* (2007). In his work, he has developed a sophisticated formulation of the view that the justification of punishment is grounded in its capacity to communicate a message of condemnation aimed at reintegrating wrongdoers into the political community.

This idea is promising in that it seems to reconcile the forward-looking and the backward-looking dimensions of punishment, while avoiding the problems encountered by the Hartian model. The forward-looking dimension of punishment is captured by the idea that the communicative process initiated by punishing the wrongdoer aims to redeem him or her and reintegrate him or her within the political community. These are valuable states of affairs that punishment aims to secure. At the same time, the backward-looking dimension is captured by the idea that we can successfully convince someone that their conduct was wrong only if he or she did indeed act wrongfully. For how could we hope to convince someone that what he or she did was wrong, if they did not act wrongly, or if the wrong they committed was less serious than the one we are imputing to him or her? The message communicated when we punish the innocent, or inflict disproportionate punishment, would literally be false.

Here, the difference between the communicative model and consequentialist approaches becomes apparent. Think about what happens when you are trying to convince someone of the validity of a certain view or a philosophical position. Your aim is not simply to get your interlocutor to take your view. What you are interested in is persuading him or her that your view is correct, and to the extent that this is your aim, you will refrain from using manipulative arguments. If your interlocutor were to agree with you, but simply because they like you, or are afraid of you, or are confused about what you are saying, you will have failed to convinced them of the validity of your position. The very idea of genuine communication rules out the possibility of deceiving or manipulating.

But while promising, the communicative view has its own problems. One is that even if we agree that punishment can communicate the sort of censure described by Duff, the same message could be communicated in other ways, which do not involve the infliction of suffering or hard treatment. If the justification of punishment is exhausted by its communicative function, then shouldn't we prefer ways of communicating the relevant message without inflicting unnecessary suffering (Hart, 1963)? As T. M. Scanlon puts it: '*Insofar as expression is our aim, we could just as well 'say it with flowers' or, perhaps more appropriately with weeds*' (Scanlon, 1986: p. 214).

The reason why the message of censure should be communicated by hard treatment, according to Duff, is that this message aims at eliciting a particular kind of response from the wrongdoer, namely a sort of 'secular penance' through which he or she can repent and formally apologize to those they have wronged, as well as to the rest of the community. The hard treatment typical of punishment serves the function of focusing the attention of the wrongdoer on the crime committed and making sure that he or she understands its seriousness. Less burdensome forms of communication might be ineffective, Duff argues, because given our fallible human nature, we might be keen to think that the process is over before its time:

> Repentance . . . cannot of its nature be something that is achieved and finished within a moment. It must go deep with the wrongdoer and must therefore occupy its attention, his thoughts, his emotions, for some considerable time. [The role of hard treatment is to facilitate this process by providing] a structure within which . . . [the wrongdoer] will be able to think about the nature of and implications of his crime, face up to it more adequately than he might otherwise (being human) do, and so arrive at a more authentic repentance.
>
> **(Duff, 2001: p. 108)**

However, we might agree with Duff that repentance requires time and prolonged reflection, but disagree with him about the role that hard treatment should play in this process. Why believe that only hard treatment can provide a suitable structure within which wrongdoers can think about the nature of their crime and repent? In fact, we might worry that, if anything, hard treatment will often be distracting, encouraging hostility and resentment in those whose repentance it seeks to secure.

Others have suggested that the reasons to choose hard treatment as the way to communicate the message of censure is that while punishment is to be understood primarily in communicative terms, its secondary function is to produce a deterrent effect. Such a deterrent effect is important because given our imperfect human nature, some of us would fail to pay due attention to the message of punishment if it was communicated in some other way (Von Hirsch, 1995; Matravers, 2011). This answer seems plausible, but whether or not we think that communicative theories of punishment should leave room for deterrence, a worry remains. We might wonder, once again, whether the value of censuring offenders and securing repentance is so important as to justify the significant costs that punishment institutions impose on us (Tadros, 2013).

To be sure, these goals are important, but are they sufficiently important to justify their costs, in light of the fact that other pressing issues could be addressed with the financial resources currently spent on punishment institutions, and in light of the non-financial costs that, as we have seen, these institutions impose on innocent people? We might think that these costs are so high that something more significant than the mere communication of censure should be at stake in punishment, if punishment is to be justified. What could this be?

The idea that punishment is necessary in order to deter crime and prevent future suffering seems a plausible candidate, but we have seen that once we decline this idea in its traditional consequentialist terms, we end up with a view that allows punishing the innocent or inflicting disproportionate punishments. However, there are other ways in which a deterrence-based account can be declined. An intriguing solution has been recently advanced by Victor Tadros.

The duty view

Tadros argues that the justification of punishment is to be found in its deterrent effects but, like Hart, he acknowledges that there are limits on who can be punished in order to produce these effects. The key move Tadros makes consists in focusing on the idea that offenders incur certain duties when they wrongfully harm others with their crimes. One of these duties, as stressed by Duff, is the duty to acknowledge that what they did was wrong and repent their conduct, but an even more important duty offenders incur is the duty to provide a remedy to their victims for the wrongful harm they have caused; and the best way to discharge this duty, Tadros argues, is by protecting the victims against future harm. One way in which offenders can provide this sort of protection is by being punished in order to deter potential offenders. Thus, what explains the fact that offenders can be permissibly punished, whereas non-offenders cannot, is that the former, but not the latter, have a remedial protective duty. It is the presence of this duty that ultimately justifies the permissibility of inflicting punishment.

Tadros' view is instrumentalist, in that punishment is for him justified by the valuable consequences that punishing wrongdoers has in terms of deterrence (this is the forward-looking dimension of the theory), but is non-consequentialist because consequences are not the only considerations at play in his view. Tadros operates within a non-consequentialist framework in that he acknowledges that there are limits on treating others as a means for the sake of deterrence. Only offenders can be treated in this way, because only offenders have incurred the relevant protective duties (this is the backward-looking dimension of the theory). In punishing them, the state is simply enforcing these duties.

This way of combining the forward-looking and the backward-looking dimension of punishment is ingenious, but in order to have a full justification up and running, a number of details of this picture need to be filled. To begin with, even if we accept that when I commit a crime against you, I incur a protective duty to you, we still need to explain why the best way for me to discharge this duty is by being punished. Why cannot I discharge my protective duty in some other way, say by temporarily being your bodyguard? Indeed, we might wonder why I should pay compensation specifically by protecting you. Why cannot I compensate you in some other way, say financially, or by providing you with other services you might need? Why can the state permissibly punish me instead of leaving you free to choose how to be compensated in the way that would suit you best?

Tadros' answer is that the state is justified in assisting you in harming me as a means to avert future threats that I, as well as other potential wrongdoers, might pose not only to you, but also to your fellow citizens. Why? Because in addition to having an interest in not being harmed yourself, you also have a duty to protect others, at least when you can do so at a reasonable cost. One way in which you can discharge this duty is precisely by using my punishment as a way to deter other criminals from committing similar crimes. This is why you are not free to be compensated in some other way. If you were, you would not be fulfilling your protective duty towards your fellow citizens. You fulfil this duty by having me punished in order to protect them from similar crimes.

But we might think of cases in which you could fulfil your protective duties towards your fellow citizens in some way other than by having me punished. For example, if you are wealthy, you could make a big donation to the local police and be privately compensated by me in some other way for the crime I committed. If the protective effects produced by your donation are at least as good as those that would have been produced by punishing me, why should that not be an option within Tadros' picture? In fact, it is not clear that what the victim wants should matter at all. What if the offender was wealthy and he could produce better results in terms of protecting the victim and others by making a big donation to the local police, rather than by being punished? And yet these ideas seem disturbing, and at odds with the way in which punishment is normally understood.

The more general worry here is that Tadros' account threatens to blur the distinction between punishment and compensation. These two practices, while similar in some ways and overlapping to some extent, ultimately respond to different logics. When they are assimilated too closely, the risk is that we lose sight of the distinctive features that characterize each of them.

☆ KEY POINTS

- Consequentialism justifies punishment in forward-looking terms. Retributivism justifies punishment in backward-looking terms. Mixed views incorporate both dimensions in their attempt to justify punishment.

- H. L. A. Hart argues that deterrence constitutes the general justifying aim of punishment, but that there are constraints on how this aim can be pursued. Disproportionate punishment and punishment of the innocent are not permissible ways of achieving the aim of deterrence.

- A popular view in the contemporary debate is that punishment can be justified in communicative terms. According to this view, the main purpose of punishment is to communicate a message of censure, with the aim of persuading wrongdoers of the wrongfulness of their conduct. But could the same message not be communicated in less burdensome ways?

- A third approach, that combines forward-looking and backward-looking considerations, is the one that grounds the justification of punishment in remedial duties incurred by criminals. According to this view, it is because criminals acquire a duty to protect their victims from future crimes that they can be punished for purposes of deterrence. One problem with this view is that it seems to blur the distinction between punishment and compensation.

Conclusion: punishment and beyond

This chapter has surveyed some of the most important answers offered to the question of the justification of punishment. As we have seen, this question is of fundamental importance, and traditionally, it has monopolized the attention of philosophers of the criminal law. But it should be noticed that this is not the only question we need to answer if we are to make sense of the demands that the criminal justice system places on us. An adequate account of these demands will require addressing a number of other important questions. To begin with, the question of criminalization (Husak, 2008; Duff et al., forthcoming): which sort of conduct should the state criminalize (i.e. regulate by using the criminal law) and how? Is it just conduct that threatens harm to others? What about conduct that, although not harmful, is offensive? Or conduct that threatens harm to the agent him or herself? Or conduct that is not harmful or offensive, but is morally wrong (Feinberg, 1984)?

 KEY CONCEPTS

Criminalization

What sort of conduct can be permissibly regulated by using the criminal law? This is the question of 'criminalization'. Four main answers have been offered:

- Harm principle: it is permissible to criminalize conduct in order to prevent harm to others.
- Offence principle: it is permissible to criminalize conduct in order to prevent offence to others.
- Paternalism: it is permissible to criminalize conduct in order to prevent individuals from harming themselves, or in order to make them better off.
- Moralism: it is permissible to criminalize conduct in order to ensure that wrongdoers receive the punishment they deserve.

In addressing these questions, we should pay attention to the relationships between criminal law and other modes of legal regulation, such as civil law and hybrid measures that do not formally count as 'criminal' but ultimately involve the use of sanctions (Ramsay, 2012). When is it appropriate to resort to these alternative modes of regulation and what is at stake in the choice between using them and using the criminal law instead?

Moreover, given the significant costs of punishment institutions, and the problems that most justificatory theories of punishment seem to encounter, we should also consider the possibility that punishment might have to be either abolished (Boonin, 2008; Zimmerman, 2011) or replaced by processes that rather aim at restoring the relationship between offenders and their victims through reconciliation programmes (Von Hirsch, 2003; Johnstone, 2012). According to this latter view, instead of punishing wrongdoers, the role of the state should be to bring together wrongdoers and those who have been affected by their crime, so that they can discuss the wrong perpetrated, as well as possible ways in which these wrongs can be repaired.

Finally, with the development of institutions of international criminal justice, it becomes increasingly more important to establish why certain crimes should be subject to international prosecution and punishment.

For reasons of space, we shall not consider the first three questions here. The fourth one will be the focus of our case study.

 CASE STUDY

International crimes

The Nuremberg Trials (see Box 6.1), held by the allied forces at the end of World War II, are unanimously recognized as the birth moment of international criminal law. While the emergence of a body of **customary international norms** attributing criminal responsibility for certain violations of the rules of war can be traced back at least to the mid eighteenth century, this body of law does not have much in common with international criminal law as it is currently understood. This is because its function was to govern relations between states (Ratner et al., 2009). Violations of its norms could only be prosecuted and punished by the authorities of the state where the violations had occurred. Failing that, the state of the victims could only demand that the state where the violation had occurred punish the wrongdoers (or alternatively, provide compensation).

BOX 6.1 THE INTERNATIONAL MILITARY TRIBUNAL

The International Military Tribunal was the first international tribunal to prosecute individuals for international crimes. The Tribunal was set up in Nuremberg by France, the UK, the US, and the USSR in order to punish the atrocities perpetrated in the course of World War II. The Tribunal's jurisdiction extended over three crimes: war crimes, genocide, and crimes against humanity.

Article 6 of the Charter of the Tribunal states that:

> The Tribunal established by the Agreement referred to in Article 1 hereof for the trial and punishment of the major war criminals of the European Axis countries shall have the power to try and punish persons who, acting in the interests of the European Axis countries, whether as individuals or as members of organizations, committed any of the following crimes.

The following acts, or any of them, are crimes coming within the jurisdiction of the Tribunal for which there shall be individual responsibility:

(a) **crimes against peace**: namely, planning, preparation, initiation or waging of a war of aggression, or a war in violation of international treaties, agreements or assurances, or participation in a common plan or conspiracy for the accomplishment of any of the foregoing;

(b) **war crimes**: namely, violations of the laws or customs of war. Such violations shall include, but not be limited to, murder, ill-treatment or deportation to slave labor or for any other purpose of civilian population of or in occupied territory, murder or ill-treatment of prisoners of war or persons on the seas, killing of hostages, plunder of public or private property, wanton destruction of cities, towns or villages, or devastation not justified by military necessity;

(c) **crimes against humanity**: namely, murder, extermination, enslavement, deportation, and other inhumane acts committed against any civilian population, before or during the war; or persecutions on political, racial or religious grounds in execution of or in connection with any crime within the jurisdiction of the Tribunal, whether or not in violation of the domestic law of the country where perpetrated.

Leaders, organizers, instigators and accomplices participating in the formulation or execution of a common plan or conspiracy to commit any of the foregoing crimes are responsible for all acts performed by any persons in execution of such plan.

Although judgement on the Tribunal has been generally favourable, a number of criticisms have been raised against it. To begin with, the Tribunal was criticized for trying exclusively political and military leaders of the Third Reich. War crimes perpetrated by members of the allied forces were not prosecuted. Secondly, there was objection that no German judges were sitting on the bench. The four chief prosecutors were taken from each of the four major allies (France, the UK, the US, and the USSR). Finally, since the legal categories of '*crimes against humanity*' and '*crimes against peace*' were newly introduced, the Tribunal was criticized for punishing defendants for conduct that was not criminal at the time of its perpetration. This led some to complain that the Tribunal constituted a form of 'victor's justice'.

Most importantly, crimes that only affected members of the same political community, no matter how serious, were considered domestic crimes, and thus outside the scope of international criminal law. Perpetrators of these crimes were liable to punishment only to the extent that they were domestically prosecuted, and any attempt to interfere with the state's decision as to which of these crimes should be prosecuted and punished would be considered an unjustified form of interference with its sovereignty.

The reason why the Nuremberg Trials represent such a momentous turning point in the history of international law is precisely because, for the first time, the principle was affirmed that certain crimes are so serious that their perpetrators are answerable for them to the international community, even when they are committed by members of a political community against their fellow citizens (as it was the case with the crimes perpetrated against Jewish citizens in Nazi Germany). Whether these crimes should be prosecuted and punished is not something over which the political community in question has discretion.

It is the idea that these crimes constitute wrongs for which we are answerable to the international community, no matter where they are committed and no matter who the victims and the perpetrators are, that eventually led to the creation of international tribunals such as the International Criminal Tribunal for the former Yugoslavia (whose aim was to punish serious violations of international humanitarian law perpetrated in the former Yugoslavia after 1991), the International Criminal Tribunal for Rwanda (whose aim was to prosecute crimes committed during the Rwandan genocide in 1994), and the International Criminal Court (the first permanent international court (see Box 6.2)). Moreover, this idea is what grounds the right of individual states to claim **universal jurisdiction** over these crimes and to punish them, regardless of where they have been committed or of their relationship with the victims or the perpetrators.

At least four crimes are of this kind—namely, crimes against humanity, genocide, war crimes, and aggression. The crucial question of course is *why* these crimes should trigger international prosecution. The Statute of the International Criminal Court states that these are '*the most serious crimes of concern to the international community as a whole.*' But why are these crimes so serious? And why should we think that they properly concern the international community, whereas other crimes are merely domestic?

BOX 6.2 THE INTERNATIONAL CRIMINAL COURT

The International Criminal Court is the first permanent international tribunal. The Court is regulated by the Rome Statute, which came into force on 1 July 2002, after having been ratified by sixty countries. The purpose of the Court is to prosecute four international crimes: genocide, crimes against humanity, war crimes, and the crime of aggression. Currently, 122 states are parties to the Statute, but it is worth noticing that influential states such as the United States, Russia, India, and China are not among them.

Preamble and Article 1 of the Rome Statute

Preamble

The States Parties to this Statute,

Conscious that all peoples are united by common bonds, their cultures pieced together in a shared heritage, and concerned that this delicate mosaic may be shattered at any time,

Mindful that during this century millions of children, women and men have been victims of unimaginable atrocities that deeply shock the conscience of humanity,

Recognizing that such grave crimes threaten the peace, security and well-being of the world,

Affirming that the most serious crimes of concern to the international community as a whole must not go unpunished and that their effective prosecution must be ensured by taking measures at the national level and by enhancing international cooperation,

Determined to put an end to impunity for the perpetrators of these crimes and thus to contribute to the prevention of such crimes,

Recalling that it is the duty of every State to exercise its criminal jurisdiction over those responsible for international crimes,

Reaffirming the Purposes and Principles of the Charter of the United Nations, and in particular that all States shall refrain from the threat or use of force against the territorial integrity or political independence of any State, or in any other manner inconsistent with the Purposes of the United Nations,

Emphasizing in this connection that nothing in this Statute shall be taken as authorizing any State Party to intervene in an armed conflict or in the internal affairs of any State,

Determined to these ends and for the sake of present and future generations, to establish an independent permanent International Criminal Court in relationship with the United Nations system, with jurisdiction over the most serious crimes of concern to the international community as a whole,

Emphasizing that the International Criminal Court established under this Statute shall be complementary to national criminal jurisdictions,

Resolved to guarantee lasting respect for and the enforcement of international justice,

Have agreed as follows:

Article 1: The Court

An International Criminal Court ("the Court") is hereby established. It shall be a permanent institution and shall have the power to exercise its jurisdiction over persons for the most serious crimes of international concern, as referred to in this Statute, and shall be complementary to national criminal jurisdictions. The jurisdiction and functioning of the Court shall be governed by the provisions of this Statute.

Let us start by clarifying what these crimes consist in exactly. **Aggression** covers the planning, preparation, and execution of an act of armed force by a state against the sovereignty, territorial integrity, or political independence of another state. **War crimes** are violations of the rules of war, i.e. the rules that regulate the way in which wars can be permissibly fought. They typically involve using unjustified violence against subjects who are not liable to be attacked, or employing prohibited methods and means of warfare. ➡ **See Chapter 10**. **Genocide** is the perpetration of crimes such as killing and causing serious harm, when committed with the intent to destroy a national, ethnical, racial, or religious group. Similarly, **crimes against humanity** are inhumane acts such as murder, torture, rape, or enslavement, when committed as part of a widespread or systematic attack against the members of a certain group (though not necessarily with the intent to destroy the group in question).

What is so special about these crimes? Aggression is in a class of its own, as it can only be committed by someone who is in a position to exercise control over the political or military actions of a state. The other three categories of crimes, however, can, in principle, be committed by anyone, which raises an interesting problem. These crimes refer to conduct that is already covered by domestic criminal law, but that becomes an international crime only when it is committed in a certain context. Murder or rape, for example, are standard domestic crimes, but can become war crimes when committed in the context of an armed conflict; or become crimes against humanity when committed as part of a systematic attack against members of a certain group; or genocidal acts when committed with the intent to destroy the group in question. But why should the same crime become a matter of international concern only when committed in one of these contexts? This is the key question we need to answer if we are to find a principled distinction between domestic and international crimes.

To some extent, doing so might be easier in relation to war crimes, as it is obviously in the interests of the international community that wars are fought within certain constraints. This might explain why crimes that involve blatant disregard for such constraints ought to be internationally prosecuted. But what about crimes against humanity and genocide? Larry May argues that crimes that have this group-based component are matters of international concern because they harm the international community in ways in which crimes that lack this component do not. First, they harm humanity because they are likely to spill over borders, thereby threatening international security. Since this is a risk that afflicts the international community, the international community has a right to prosecute and punish them. ➡ **See Chapter 9**. Second, these crimes harm humanity because, in singling out their victims solely because they belong to a specific group, they fail to treat the victims with the respect owed to them as human beings (May, 2005).

Both these views seem problematic. As for the first, crimes that target the members of certain groups do not seem to be the only ones that risk spilling over borders, thereby threatening international security. When committed on a large scale, crimes like torture, murder, and rape, will create this risk, even if the victims are not targeted simply by virtue of their membership of a particular group. So, for example, if a state cannot maintain the rule of law over its territory, violence might spread to neighbouring countries. And yet, in this case, no specific group is targeted. Should these crimes be internationally prosecuted? Perhaps they should, but if so we should reject the view that only crimes including the group-based component identified earlier can be internationally prosecuted. Or perhaps they should not, in which case the reason why crimes against humanity and genocide can be internationally prosecuted cannot simply be that these crimes threaten international security.

The second reason offered by May is that humanity is harmed when people are not treated as humans, and people are not treated as humans when, instead of treating them according to their individual features, we treat them according to features that they have simply as members of a certain group. Since these features are not chosen, in responding exclusively to them, wrongdoers respond to characteristics that are beyond our autonomous agency. If the distinctive feature of humanity is the capacity to act as autonomous moral agents, failing to treat individuals as autonomous moral agents is failing to treat them as human beings. It is in this sense that crimes that treat individuals in this way are *against humanity*.

This view is also problematic. To begin with, some crimes against humanity will target individuals who *did* choose to join a certain group. (For example, I might choose to join a certain religious community and then be tortured because of this membership.) More importantly, while we are not responsible for many of our group-based features (e.g. belonging to a specific ethnic group), we are not responsible for many of our individual features either (e.g. having a certain aspect). Thus, May's interpretation of the idea of 'harm to humanity' does not seem enough to explain why, say, rape can be internationally prosecuted only when committed against someone, qua member of a group. For victims of rape did not choose their group-based features any more than they chose their individual ones (Renzo, 2010).

This has led some philosophers to reject the idea that the group-based element is necessary in order for certain crimes to trigger international prosecution and punishment. For example, some argue that it is permissible to internationally prosecute and punish widespread or systematic violations of human rights, even when they do not target the members of a specific group (Altman and Wellman, 2011). ➡ **See Chapter 8**. If no principled rationale can be found to support the view that only group-based crimes can be internationally prosecuted, this conclusion seems hard to resist. But we might be tempted to take an even more radical stance. Why think that only widespread or systematic violations should trigger international prosecution and punishment?

There are obvious pragmatic reasons, of course, why states should not be subject to having their sovereignty pierced every time a murder or rape is committed within their territory. But we might think that, at least in principle, violations of human rights should concern the international community, whether or not they are widespread or systematic. Since human rights protect conditions required for a minimally decent life, prosecuting their violation is not something over which the political community in question should have discretion, even when they are not committed in a widespread or systematic way. Condoning or failing to prosecute these crimes falls outside the scope of states' right to self-determination (Geras, 2011; Renzo, 2012).

If we were to take this view, the practical implications need not be huge. For example, we might think that, since we have pragmatic reasons to minimize the number of interferences with state sovereignty, this should be permissible only in the case of widespread or systematic violations of human rights; and yet think that when courts punish ordinary cases of murder or rape, they should be seen as acting not only on behalf of their domestic political communities but also on behalf of the international community.

However, we might be also tempted to draw more radical implications. Consider the case in which a citizen of country A commits rape or murder in country B and then flees to country C.

The crime in question does not target the victim as a member of a specific group, nor is it part of a widespread or systematic series of human rights violations perpetrated in B. Suppose that neither A nor B prosecute the wrongdoer, nor do they request his extradition. Would it be morally objectionable if C were to punish him, provided that sufficient evidence could be collected and a fair trial could be guaranteed? And should we object to the possibility of giving C, or an international institution, a legal right to do so by claiming universal jurisdiction (Renzo, 2013)?

These are hard questions. Thinking about these questions, however, is essential, not only because developing an adequate philosophical understanding of international crimes and international criminal law is important in its own right, but also because the way in which we conceptualize these categories will inevitably affect the way in which we understand our current categories of domestic crimes and domestic criminal law. As with other classic problems of political philosophy, thinking about the challenges posed by the demands of international justice often leads us to revise the way in which these problems are understood when we look at them in the domestic context.

? QUESTIONS

1. Consequentialist theories aim to justify punishment by appealing exclusively to its consequences. What are the main problems with this approach?

2. What do we mean when we say that wrongdoers 'deserve to be punished'? Can this idea justify state punishment?

3. Is there a sense in which criminals obtain an unfair advantage over their fellow citizens by breaking the law?

4. Can the suffering imposed via punishment ever be good?

5. In what sense can punishment communicate a message? Is this idea sufficient to justify the existence of punishment institutions?

6. Can the forward-looking dimension typical of consequentialist theories be combined with the backward-looking dimension typical of retributive theories? If so, how?

7. Can the criminal law ever permissibly treat its subjects 'as means'? If so, under what conditions?

8. Are we committed to accepting some version of consequentialism if we believe that punishment is to be justified in instrumentalist terms?

9. Can punishment be justified by appealing to the idea that wrongdoers incur protective duties towards their victims?

10. Why should certain crimes be classified as international crimes?

FURTHER READING

■ Braithwaite, J. and Pettit, P. (1990) *Not Just Deserts*, Oxford: Oxford University Press Defends a consequentialist approach that grounds the justification of punishment on the maximization of republican dominion (i.e. assured individual liberty).

■ Duff, R. A. (2001) *Punishment, Communication, and Community,* New York: Oxford University Press Provides the most sophisticated formulation of the communicative theory of punishment.

■ Duff, R. A. and Garland, D. (1994) *A Reader on Punishment,* Oxford: Oxford University Press Helpful collection of classic papers, including some of the papers discussed in this chapter (by Feinberg, Morris, Von Hirsch, and Murphy).

■ Feinberg, J. (1984–88) *The Moral Limits of the Criminal Law (vols 1-4: Harm to Others; Offense to Others; Harm to Self; Harmless Wrongdoing),* New York: Oxford University Press Highly influential four-volume treatise on the question of which conduct should be criminalized. Each of the volumes can be read independently.

■ Fletcher G. (1978) *Rethinking Criminal Law,* Boston: Little, Brown Influential volume that critically examines some of the most important structures and notions employed in contemporary systems of criminal law. Particularly valuable in that it focuses not only on the Anglo-American tradition but also on the German one.

■ Hart, H. L. A. (1968; 2008) *Punishment and Responsibility: Essays in the Philosophy of Law,* Oxford: Oxford University Press Collection of seminal papers by H. L. A. Hart on the justification of punishment and on criminal responsibility. The second edition (2008) includes an excellent introduction by John Gardner, one of the leading contemporary philosophers of the criminal law.

■ May, L. (2005) *Crimes Against Humanity. A Normative Account,* New York: Cambridge University Press One of the first attempts to offer a philosophical account of international crimes.

■ Moore, M. S. (1997) *Placing Blame: A Theory of the Criminal Law,* Oxford: Oxford University Press A prominent formulation of retributivism. Defends the idea that wrongdoers deserve to suffer on the backdrop of a realist account of morality.

■ Murphy, J. G. and Hampton, J. (1988) *Forgiveness and Mercy,* Cambridge: Cambridge University Press Discusses the role that retributive emotions play in the justification of punishment and forgiveness.

■ Tadros, V. (2011) *The Ends of Harm. The Moral Foundations of Criminal Law,* Oxford: Oxford University Press Thoroughly criticizes retributivism and provides an innovative account that justifies punishment in instrumentalist terms within a non-consequentialist framework.

⊕ WEB LINKS

● https://www.gov.uk/government/topics/crime-and-policing Website of the British Government, dedicated to crime and policing. Among other things, you can find here the most recent prison population figures.

● http://www.cps.gov.uk/about/cjs.html Website of the Crown Prosecution Service, explaining the functioning of the British Criminal Justice System.

● http://www.justice.gov/cjs/ Website of the United States Department of Justice, devoted to the Criminal Justice System.

● http://www.amnestyusa.org/our-work/campaigns/abolish-the-death-penalty Website of an Amnesty International campaign to abolish the death penalty in the USA. In addition to providing information about cases, the website includes reports, petitions, and other tools to support the campaign.

● http://avalon.law.yale.edu/subject_menus/imt.asp Website of the Avalon Project (based at the Yale Law School), which contains a significant number of documents about the activities of the International Military Tribunal.

● http://www.icc-cpi.int/Pages/default.aspx Website of the International Criminal Court. Contains information about the Court and reports on its activities.

Visit the Online Resource Centre that accompanies this book to access more learning resources: http://www.oxfordtextbooks.co.uk/orc/mckinnon3e/

 ENDNOTES

1 In some countries, including the US and the UK, criminals can lose the right to vote or to apply for certain jobs.

2 Sadly, the goal of incapacitation can hardly ever be achieved, since imprisonment does not prevent criminals from committing crimes against other prisoners or prison officers.

7

Multiculturalism

MONICA MOOKHERJEE[1]

Chapter contents

Reader's guide

Many would defend the objective of promoting harmony between people of different cultural groups and react against inequalities suffered by their fellow citizens on account of culture, religion, or ethnicity. Multiculturalism, the policy and social ideal that addresses these inequalities, might be easy to defend as long as all groups conform to liberal values, such as free speech or sexual equality. However, thorny problems arise if cultural groups defend values that conflict with those of liberal democracy. Taking this concern seriously, this chapter engages with debates about multiculturalism in political theory. Themes of the chapter include: thick and thin multiculturalism; cultural rights; multiculturalism and oppression; and the politics of recognition.

Introduction

The end of colonialism in many parts of the world and consequent global migration patterns have entailed that most states today are made up of different cultures. In fact, very few countries are now monocultural: Iceland and Japan are among the few examples. The term 'multiculturalism' can refer to the fact of cultural diversity, as found in countries ranging from the former Yugoslavia to the UK, and may also describe the coexistence of different kinds of cultural group within a country. Such groups can include those that seek to become separate nations (for example, the Catalans in Spain may be called national minorities), indigenous groups (for example, the Inuit, who are among the original inhabitants of Canada), voluntary immigrants (such as British Asians), religious groups (for example, the Amish in the USA, who wish to remain separate from the rest of society), and involuntary migrants (such as political refugees) (Kymlicka, 2002: 348–65). The presence of such groups in modern societies highlights the importance of **cultural identity**—that is, the inherited beliefs and practices that give a person a sense of who he or she is and where he or she has come from. On grounds of cultural identity, the groups just mentioned campaign for special rights, **exemptions** (that is, entitlements not to comply with general laws), partial **secession** (that is, the voluntary decision of a group to break away from a larger nation, in order to rule itself), and other measures to preserve group members' dignity. Multiculturalism is thus not only a **descriptive** term, but also a moral and political one. Examples of multicultural policies include the UK law that exempts Sikh policemen from wearing helmets and secession from the Canadian government by the Québécois.

Most multicultural policies are the subject of heated controversy, because they depart from the notion of uniform citizenship. This form of citizenship usually involves members of a polity being literate in a national language and accepting common symbols, such as a national flag and a standard educational system. Defenders of multiculturalism claim that national belonging should not be made unduly difficult for some citizens on account of their cultural origin. Liberal societies may impose serious burdens on minority citizens by retaining customs and laws that privilege people of Christian descent. For example, some British schools do not provide time or facilities for Muslims to pray during Ramadan (the holy month in the Muslim year, during which Muslims usually fast strictly and pray more than usual—that is, five times a day). In these cases, it may therefore be more difficult for a Muslim than for a Christian schoolchild to profit fully from the country's educational system. Multicultural theory argues that it is unjust if the law of the land demands much greater sacrifices of minorities than it does of the majority.

In the 1990s, some argued that it was impossible not to be in favour of multiculturalism (Glazer, 1997). But recent events, such as, in 2012, the bomb attack at Burgas airport in Bulgaria and the shootings by a lone gunman in France, which claimed the lives of fourteen people, and the renewed controversies over immigration and asylum that followed these events, have led some to fear that supporting cultural diversity undermines a strong national identity. These critics have called vigorously for **assimilation**—a policy that encourages cultural minorities to lose their distinctive customs or norms, gradually or suddenly, in order to fit in more easily with a common national culture (Browne, 2007). Multicultural thinkers tend to find this idea problematic. They prefer the notion of **integration**—that is, the idea that different cultural groups may belong equally to the nation, while still retaining some distinctive social customs or rights. Whether integration can be achieved in a multicultural society depends on exactly how the nation responds to differences of belief and custom. In fact, the central question raised by multiculturalism is how to secure common belonging to a nation that may be divided, sometimes bitterly, by ethnic, cultural, and religious differences.

Multiculturalism: thick or thin?

Before the late twentieth century, the greatest social injustice was normally thought to be economic inequality. Even prominent campaigns for racial equality, such as the US Civil Rights movement of the 1950s, concentrated on economic redistribution. While key supporters of this cause promoted black cultural identity in the form of 'Black Pride', African Americans were taken to desire parity with whites in income expectation and quality of life (Morris, 1984). Equality was understood as non-differentiation—that is, the idea that race should not matter from the perspective of justice. This understanding may be aligned with the idea of uniform citizenship already explained. On this view, special policies, such as affirmative action, are permissible only in order to enable members of disadvantaged groups to attain equality with other citizens in goods such as income. As minority groups gradually increased in confidence in the USA, the UK, and other locations of post-war immigration, however, they began to give a voice to their experiences and highlighted the fact that inequality does not always involve a lack of tangible goods such as money, but may instead involve social marginalization or discrimination on grounds of beliefs or practices.

There are thus two types of inequality in modern societies, involving economics and status, respectively (Fraser, 1998). While these inequalities may overlap in practice, they are importantly different. Traditional English working-class men may enjoy high social status, while nonetheless suffering from economic inequalities (Kymlicka, 2002: 331–2). By contrast, Arab and Japanese immigrants in the USA tend to be well off financially, but they still suffer discrimination, such as taunts and stereotyping. Thus, if one suffers harassment or ridicule on account of one's inherited culture, one might have an interest in achieving respect for one's culture in society. While cultural diversity may also be important because of its aesthetic benefit, in that diverse forms of music, dance, or literature enrich everyone's lives, multicultural theories tend to focus on the predicament of status inequality. One problem with doing so, however, may be that it is too hasty to assume that minority cultures' struggles for justice differ from traditional claims for equality and social justice.

According to Brian Barry (2001: 13), while people from minority groups should not suffer disadvantage on account of their cultural origin, remedies for any injustice that they face should not focus on their culture as such. Not only can doing so deepen social conflict, he believes, but it would also sidestep the real problems, which are often social and economic. For example, statistics show that French citizens of Algerian origin suffer from poorer employment prospects and housing in comparison with white French citizens. If this is the case, the question is why one should focus on the cultural identity of immigrants rather than their economic conditions. We will return to this issue in the course of the chapter. For now, another problem with the notion of status inequality is that, if liberal democracies believe that its remedy lies in respecting different **cultural norms**, they also face the problem of how to react to illiberal beliefs and practices. An initial way of thinking about this problem involves asking whether multiculturalism is 'thick' or 'thin'.

'Thin' multiculturalism

Thin multiculturalism assumes that only weak disagreements over beliefs and values divide citizens in modern liberal states (Tamir, 1995). While cultural differences are taken to matter greatly to the parties involved, this approach takes into account only the views of groups that share liberal values and excludes those that are illiberal. So, for example, because the English-speaking and French-speaking communities in Canada already share a set of liberal beliefs, the problem of **cultural relativism**—or the idea that it is impossible to judge which cultural values are better and which worse—does not arise. The approach assumes that, while French Canadians understand the culture of English Canadians perfectly well, the two groups simply have different interests or objectives (Tamir, 1995: 162): one group wishes to speak French; the other, English. In this case, the Canadian government should accept that, because the Québécois perceive a greater threat to their language than do members of the wider Canadian society, it should support the Québécois in taking more explicit measures to protect their language than the wider society needs to do.

 KEY THINKERS

Yael Tamir (1954–)

Yael Tamir is an Israeli political philosopher who has written on liberalism, nationalism, feminism, and theories of rights. She was one of the founders of the Peace Now movement in Jerusalem and also chaired the Israeli Civil Rights Organization. She has been active in politics, served as Minister for Education, and is currently Minister for Science, Culture, and Sports in Israel. Her book, *Liberal Nationalism* (1993), argues that liberals should not surrender the concept of nationalism to conservative, chauvinist, or racist ideologies. In her view, liberalism, with its respect for personal autonomy, and nationalism, with its emphasis on loyalty and belonging, are reconcilable. Tamir sees nationalism as part of a quest for recognition and self-respect.

Because all groups are taken to be committed to liberal values in this approach, its advantage seems to be that disagreements between cultural groups would not produce too much political conflict. However, the disadvantages are twofold. First, thin multiculturalism assumes that, as long as a group has a fair opportunity to present its views publicly, if their interests are outvoted, this should not be regarded as unfair. In democratic systems, minority groups of many kinds, from communists to opera lovers, may find themselves outvoted on issues that are important to them. This approach does not explain why *cultural* interests should be regarded as special. Second, the approach faces a problem that affects interest-group politics generally—namely, that a group has no reason to consider the interests of others seriously unless it has strategic reasons to do so. Therefore, thin multiculturalism only seems workable if the government insists on educating all young people to accept liberal values, so that they show concern and respect for one another (Tamir, 1995: 165). In practice, however, many cultural groups—even those that are not authoritarian—are likely to find certain aspects of compulsory liberal education unfair and contrary to their inherited values. This issue indicates that thin multiculturalism underestimates the scope of conflicts between cultures in a liberal society.

'Thick' multiculturalism

Thick multiculturalism (Tamir, 1995: 166) recognizes deep disagreements between liberal and non-liberal groups regarding beliefs and practices. It thus recommends a *modus vivendi*—that is, a pragmatic compromise—in order to achieve peace and stability. Consider the controversy, in the 1980s, over the publication of Salman Rushdie's novel *The Satanic Verses*, which was inspired, in part, by the life of the Islamic prophet Mohammed. What liberals saw as a neutral law permitting freedom of artistic expression, some British Muslims viewed as a harmful disregard for their religious identity. Moreover, the dispute over Rushdie's novel may reflect a conflict between Western Christian societies, which maintain that religion is a private matter, and belief systems such as Islam, which contend that God's commands apply in all areas of personal and social life. In this case, a suitable *modus vivendi* solution might have been to withhold the sale of the novel from Muslim districts, or to encourage Rushdie to clarify in public that his intention was not to offend Muslims.

Thick multiculturalism holds, then, that if modern societies are ready to recognize the depth of cultural disagreements, they should avoid judging which culture is right or wrong and opt instead for a policy that accommodates both parties. The advantage of doing so is that liberals can then accept the claims of non-liberal cultures to some extent. *Modus vivendi* liberals concede that there are many advantages to be gained from living alongside non-liberal groups and that, by tolerating and accepting such communities, societies stand to expand their moral horizons (Feinberg, 1995: 203). But one difficulty with this perspective is that groups that do not share liberal values may not approach matters with the same spirit of tolerance. A religious fundamentalist would view toleration itself as a threat to his or her belief system. Therefore, for the strongly illiberal culture, the *modus vivendi* might be based on self-interest, rather than on the desire for moral growth. That culture would view the compromise merely as a necessary and, perhaps temporary, measure to keep its members from bitter conflict with others in society, until such a time that they gain greater social power and thus no longer need to compromise. ➡ See Chapter 3.

A different problem with thick multiculturalism is that it seems to draw too simple a distinction between liberal and illiberal cultures. This approach may alienate minority groups, by insisting that pragmatic compromise is the only solution to cultural disagreements and that principled accommodation of minorities is impossible. The underlying assumption of this approach is that non-liberal groups cannot be fully included as participating members of the society and must, thus, remain on its margins. Moreover, the trouble with drawing the distinction too sharply between liberal and illiberal cultures is that almost all societies contain illiberal elements. For example, despite laws against sex discrimination in liberal societies, women often still feel more pressure than men to assume domestic and childcare responsibilities. Conversely, Muslim communities, which are often thought 'illiberal', sometimes practice *zakat*—the principle that holds that the individual has a social responsibility to assist the most needy—which may be considered fairer, and more egalitarian, than many liberal societies which often defend equality as a central ideal.

☆ KEY POINTS

- Multiculturalism emphasizes status, as well as economic inequalities.
- Thin multiculturalism views all cultural differences as disagreements between groups that agree on liberal values. This view may underestimate the extent of conflict between cultures.
- Thick multiculturalism appreciates that some cultural differences occur between liberals and non-liberals.
- While the solution to cultural conflicts in thick multiculturalism is often a *modus vivendi*, the question is whether this solution treats non-liberal minority cultures fairly.

Liberalism and cultural rights

Let us leave aside for now the question of whether multiculturalism is thick or thin, and consider again Brian Barry's (2001: 320–33) contention that one should not think of inequalities arising from cultural membership as different from the economic inequalities—that is, disparities in income or wealth—that have traditionally concerned political theorists. Barry criticizes multicultural policies, first, on grounds that using the term 'culture' can be abused in justice claims. He argues that cultural divisiveness is inherently dangerous. Groups could use seemingly progressive philosophical notions in order to promote goals that multiculturalists themselves would not support. Also, the divisiveness involved in cultural claims would not only compromise national unity, but would also evoke world events, such as the 'ethnic separatist' wars in Kosovo. Barry is, in addition, sceptical about the usefulness of multicultural programmes in helping to secure real equality. He believes that multiculturalism could promote a 'divide-and-rule' ethos that would, as noted earlier, divert attention from the problems common to many cultural groups, such as poverty and poor housing. Finally, Barry worries about what he considers the naivety of multiculturalists: by rejecting the truth of Enlightenment ideals of universal freedom and equality, they unthinkingly question basic moral notions. To Barry's mind, it is clearly '*better to be alive than dead. It is better to be free than be a slave. It is better to be healthy than sick*' (2001: 285).

One way of responding to these challenging criticisms is to note that not all multicultural thinkers in fact reject Enlightenment ideals, and to focus on why some of them defend group-specific, or 'cultural', rights on the basis of these values. Notably, these thinkers claim that uniform citizenship—including rights to vote, to free speech, and to free movement—is not enough to achieve real equality and justice for members of minority cultures in a liberal society. They also require protection for ways of life that might be under threat. Examples of group-specific rights include the freedom of indigenous groups in North America to fish in their sacred waters, the British Muslim community's right to funding for religious schools, or entitlements to partial self-government for the Scots in the UK.

Will Kymlicka (1989) takes these rights to be an important aspect of 'differentiated citizenship'. This form of citizenship entails that, in order to treat people with fairness and equality, governments should recognize that their groups may have different needs and goals. While citizens must all enjoy basic **human rights**, the government should appreciate that groups with societal cultures—that is, those with a shared history, language, and sometimes a shared territory—require special protection. The way in which Kymlicka defines a 'societal culture' rules out gays, the disabled, or lifestyle groups (such as opera lovers) from having **cultural rights**. Holders of cultural rights are typically groups that either occupy an insecure place in their larger society (such as the Kurds in Turkey and Iraq, Christians in the Sudan, or Muslims in post-independence India) or those that have long been subjected to oppression (such as the former 'untouchables' in India). The requirement that cultural rights pertain only to struggling forms of life rules out granting them to powerful minorities, such as South African whites during the apartheid regime.

While liberals normally contend that only individuals, not groups, may have rights, Kymlicka ingeniously shows that group rights are consistent with liberalism. Building on the theories of Rawls (1971; 1999) and Dworkin (1981b), he argues that if liberals care about equality, they should recognize that members of minority cultures have to struggle harder than those of the dominant society to develop an equal amount of basic goods, such as self-respect. This is because they risk lacking a stable 'cultural structure'. A cultural structure is an inherited set of values and customs, and is necessary for developing personal **autonomy**—or the capacity to make meaningful choices (Kymlicka, 1989: 177). Kymlicka thus explains the importance of cultural identity and why justice and equality involve doing more for minorities than simply providing them with the same rights as those enjoyed by all other citizens.

 KEY THINKERS

Will Kymlicka (1962–)

Will Kymlicka is a Canadian political philosopher who has written extensively on multiculturalism. His most important early book is *Liberalism, Community and Culture* (1989), in which he argues that if liberals care about equality, then they should recognize the importance of cultural identity to individual autonomy. On this basis, Kymlicka contends, liberals should support group-specific rights. Kymlicka's later writings develop his early theories. For example, *Multicultural Citizenship* (1995) argues that, while collective rights may sometimes provide a just solution to multicultural conflicts, no single formula can be applied to all groups. The needs and aspirations of voluntary immigrants, for example, differ from those of indigenous peoples and national minorities.

Kymlicka's claim is supported by liberal thinkers such as Raz (1986), who argue that autonomy should not be understood as unlimited freedom, but as the ability to choose out of a range of *meaningful* options. In this account, a person's cultural structure is very important, because it provides them with conceptions of what is honourable and shameful, and thus illuminates the meaning and value of the choices that they confront in life. Without a stable moral background, a person may end up making unprincipled decisions and, thus, fail to be genuinely autonomous. For this reason, then, Amish communities might campaign to protect their culture in law—for example, by requesting exemptions from laws regarding education or jury duty. Muslim and Christian communities in India, similarly, claim group-specific rights in order to preserve their ways of life in a society with a strong Hindu majority.

Many questions arise, however, about the idea of group-specific rights. First, who possesses them? Is it the group as a whole, or individual members of that group? If the latter, what if individual members were to disagree about the group's most important practices? Would it not then be impossible to agree on the content of the group's entitlements? Additionally, the idea of a 'cultural structure' might be thought very unclear. In the case of a Muslim immigrant community, the concept might refer to the basic moral precepts of Islam, such as those in the Qu'ran, or it might mean every custom and practice in Muslim communities. If Kymlicka means the former, then it would be extremely hard to damage the Muslim cultural structure; if the latter, Muslim communities would never be allowed to evolve. Present-day Muslims would have the right to insist that absolutely every custom remained the same in the future, which is unrealistic. Finally, there is the question of which sort of cultural rights would be allowed. Should Hindu parents in the UK have a right to special funding for faith schools, so that their children can be brought up to accept the principles of Hinduism, even if this would be very expensive and the government would have to impose heavy taxes on all citizens to meet the cost? While it is likely that young people require a stable moral background in order to become fully functioning citizens, why should a second-generation immigrant Hindu need his or her *own* cultural structure for this purpose? He or she may need only *a* cultural structure (Tomasi, 1995; Walker, 1997). However, if this is the case, attending an ordinary state school might be equally suitable, even if it were not to teach Hinduism. Moreover, if we press this point further, we might ask why Hindu communities in a liberal society should not be encouraged to lose their cultural structure and assimilate to liberal society entirely, if this is less costly for all concerned, and if, according to this view, Hindus would develop autonomy anyway.

To answer the last question, we need to go back to the issue of status inequality and consider how undervaluing people's inherited identities can lead to injustice. One cannot simply transplant members of one community into another because '*respecting one's own cultural membership and facilitating their transition to another culture are not equally legitimate options*' (Kymlicka, 1989: 176). Similarly, converting all citizens to Christianity would not be an honest way of achieving religious equality. Finally, there is the issue of how past injustices create current inequalities between groups: for example, governments should be conscious of the brutal way in which minorities, such as the Australian Aboriginals, were treated by liberal democracies, which included policies of forcible 'resocialization' into white society between 1910 and 1970.

Yet even if these points are accepted, it might not seem fair to grant cultural groups unlimited rights. For one thing, doing so would risk supporting morally undesirable practices. Kymlicka thus distinguishes between **external protections** (that is, rights that protect a culture from the policies of the wider society in relation to issues such as education and health care) and **internal restrictions** (that is, group rights that limit individual liberties within a culture). An example of an internal restriction might be the denial by certain indigenous groups in North America of the inheritance rights of women who marry outside the group. Internal restrictions are not morally justified, according to Kymlicka, because 'differentiated citizenship' entails that all citizens must enjoy basic political rights to equality. Finally, the range of cultural rights may also have to be limited according to the *nature* of the cultural group. For example, Kymlicka assumes that immigrants wish to integrate with their wider society more than indigenous peoples and, thus, that the former have fewer cultural rights. This is because immigrants have made a conscious choice to live in their host countries, whereas indigenous groups usually only belong to modern political societies as a result of force and deception. This is a hotly contested point, however. If culture is a basic resource for living a good life, it is difficult to see how anyone, including an immigrant, could have abandoned their right to it any more than to their life or their **liberty** (Parekh, 2002: 103).

 KEY CONCEPTS

Cultural rights: external protection and internal restriction

Kymlicka (1989) argues that there are different forms of group rights: one involves a group's claim against its own members (an internal restriction); the other involves a claim of a group against the larger society (an external protection). Critics of cultural rights are usually concerned that internal restrictions might support coercion within patriarchal or otherwise conservative cultures, and that the human rights of women, children, or homosexuals might be denied. By contrast, an external protection aims to protect the group from the nation's policies regarding education, health care, or public funding that might affect the group's survival. Kymlicka sees the latter rights as morally necessary.

⭐ **KEY POINTS**

- Defenders of cultural rights hold that governments should recognize that all citizens deserve equal opportunities for developing self-respect and autonomy.

- Developing self-respect and autonomy is thought to require a stable cultural structure—that is, a basic set of inherited beliefs and customs.

- In order to protect this structure, the liberal state sometimes needs to grant group-specific rights.

- A group-specific right enables a minority to preserve its traditions and thus to protect itself from the policies of the wider society.

- Not all group rights are permitted in a liberal society. Kymlicka distinguishes between different types of right. Morally permissible rights are called external protections and morally illegitimate ones are called internal restrictions. The latter are problematic because they deny individual civil liberties.

Do cultural rights oppress the oppressed?

As Kymlicka is aware, an important aspect of the debate about multiculturalism is the concern that granting group-specific rights might support gender oppression within particular communities. The worry is that defending cultural diversity involves supporting injustices against those who traditionally lack power, and that those who lack power are often women. Okin (1999) thus argues that cultural minorities should not receive special support from their governments if doing so perpetuates harmful practices, such as child marriage or female circumcision. She argues that women of minority cultures should be encouraged to assimilate to—that is, lose their inherited cultural identity in order to fit in more easily with—the wider liberal society, in which the state at least protects the equal human rights of all.

KEY TEXTS

Okin, 'Is multiculturalism bad for women?' (1999)

Okin's important and provocative essay argues that a great number of cultural norms and practices are sex discriminatory. She seeks to show how the liberal feminist commitment to gender equality often entails rejecting claims for cultural independence. Okin cites polygamy, forced marriage, female genital mutilation, punishing women for being raped, and the differential access of women and men to education and health care as practices that routinely violate women's rights in many parts of the world. She forcefully contends that, for many women of non-Western origin, living in a liberal culture would better protect their human rights.

Of course, not all multicultural policies seem oppressive. For example, neither the Québécois' language rights, nor British Asians' requests for public funding to cremate deceased family members seem obviously harmful to group members. This is so, even though, as we have seen, such rights may involve imposing certain costs on the wider society, which some citizens could regard as unfair. Alternatively, these rights might protect particular practices with which individual group members might disagree. But even if not all cultural rights are clearly coercive or harmful, liberal feminists do not seem wholly mistaken: many demands for special rights are motivated by the desire of cultural groups to preserve their kinship networks—and, thus, rules concerning marriage and divorce—which they see as crucial to their collective survival. For some minorities, for instance, the liberal right to choose one's marriage partner freely appears threatening, because it could result in inter-mingling between groups and, thus, a loss of cultural identity. Moreover, it is often thought particularly threatening if women in particular marry outside the group. This is because of women's traditional role as reproducers of culture—not only in terms of their childbearing capacity, but also because they typically educate children and sustain the home.

Thus, pursuing multiculturalism may be bad for women in certain situations. We might consider, furthermore, that cultural norms—that is, rules within a group including how to behave in social situations—have occasionally been considered relevant in certain US criminal law cases. Courts have held that if the defendant was raised in a foreign culture, he or she should not be held fully liable for behaviour that violates basic criminal laws, if that behaviour would have been permissible in his or her native culture. On this basis, persons on trial for wife beating, or even honour killing, have received reduced sentences. (Honour killing typically involves the murder of women who are perceived to have disgraced their families, often because they choose partners of a different faith.) In addition, in India, the right to live according to one's religious law entails that Muslim men may practise the 'triple talaq', which enables them to divorce a wife with immediate effect. This situation raises serious human rights concerns for Muslim women in a society with no comprehensive welfare state. The problem, then, is that minority communities do often demand special rights, particularly in relation to marriage, divorce, or reproduction, in such a way that often limits female members' freedoms. This is why Okin (1999) claims that multiculturalism may often be harmful for women, and that minority women are thus faced with a choice between remaining in their cultures and securing their basic rights. ➔ **See Chapter 8.**

Anne Phillips also raises important concerns about the relationship between gender equality and multiculturalism. In *Multiculturalism without Culture* (2007), she argues that, while the general project of seeking equality between cultures is justifiable, assertions of 'cultural difference' carry considerable risks. Such assertions can, for example, perpetuate stereotypes and the belief that so-called 'Western' values are entirely different from those of other cultures, which is not always true. In particular, Phillips is worried about the danger that such stereotyping carries for minority women. She therefore defends a form of multiculturalism that is consistent with women's equality. Multiculturalism must be robust enough to address inequalities between different cultural groups whilst also attending to inequalities of power within them.

As we saw earlier, Kymlicka responds to the question of gender oppression within cultural groups by holding that a cultural right is not morally legitimate if it undermines the individual rights of group members. However, this approach may be inadequate, because it does not consider fully the subtle nature of gender inequality. Even if a culture does not openly deny women's rights, it might still socialize women to accept inferior roles. In contrast, a very different objection is that Kymlicka's approach is liable to be too paternalistic. Why should governments have the power to judge minority cultures at all? Moreover, should they worry unduly about gender oppression within them? Rather than granting cultural rights, a liberal society might simply ensure that citizens have the right to free association—or the liberty to belong to any groups they wish (Kukathas, 2003)—so long as they also have a **right to exit** (that is, the freedom to leave their culture if they are dissatisfied with it). While this approach has the advantage of not permitting the state to make paternalistic judgements about gender oppression in minority cultures, the problem with the right to exit is that it is likely to be extremely painful for a person to make a clean break with his or her culture of birth. The question here is whether those who have been treated unfairly by their communities should be expected to go through such a damaging experience. Surely cultural groups should be required to treat their members with humanity and respect?

A balanced view of this issue might recognize that oppression occurs in all cultures and one should not think of non-Western women as pure victims or as essentially unfree. Cultures are, after all, both positive and negative. Cultures can provide many benefits, such as a sense of belonging, while at the same time containing oppression (Nussbaum, 1999a). Because there is likely to be no simple response to the question 'is multiculturalism bad for women?' recent approaches to the problem of gender justice and multiculturalism (Deveaux, 2001; Shachar, 2001; Phillips, 2007) emphasize the unfairness of forcing women to choose between their culture and their basic rights. They insist that, because cultural rights protect important human interests as much as individual rights, the two types of right must not be taken to conflict. Rather, one should focus on the way in which women of minority cultures actively challenge injustice within their own communities without abandoning their cultural identities. Of course, hard questions then arise. For example, how can liberals judge from outside a culture whether women within it have the ability to challenge injustice? What might governments to do to encourage this ability? Finally, what are liberals to think about people who appear satisfied with (apparently) unjust cultural practices? These dilemmas seem acute because, if multicultural theories are correct, exiting entirely from one's culture is likely to be extremely difficult, if not impossible.

☆ KEY POINTS

- By respecting cultural rights, a government risks supporting injustice against individuals *within* groups.

- Because those who lack power within groups are often women, a significant problem is that multiculturalism may be harmful for women.

- One might argue here that women should have the right to accept life in an illiberal culture, if they wish. Everyone should have the right to associate freely, as long as they also have a right of exit.

- Alternatively, one might hold that group rights and individual human rights need not inevitably conflict, if one focuses on promoting women's capacities to contest cultural norms without renouncing their cultural identities.

The politics of recognition

While the debate about cultural rights is crucial to understanding the nature of the ideal of multiculturalism in political theory, it is also necessary to consider the **politics of recognition**. This term refers to policies and campaigns that are designed to create equal respect for marginalized groups in a multicultural society. The approach is related to the looser idea of a 'politics of difference' (Young, 1995). Involving a variety of methods for improving the status of minority groups, the politics of recognition holds that justice is not simply a question of granting rights, but also of overcoming informal social discrimination. Defenders of the politics of recognition often follow other multicultural thinkers in emphasizing a distinction between inequalities that require economic redistribution and those that are questions of social disrespect, and thus which sometimes require a more subtle solution. ➡ See Chapter 3.

Theories of **recognition**, such as that of Charles Taylor (1992), begin by assuming that human beings make sense of the world through 'frameworks', or broad networks, of values that are constructed between people within the same culture. Taylor attacks liberal theory's assumption that, when thinking about principles of justice, we should imagine that we do not know our group identities. On the contrary, our sense of morality derives from our frameworks and, thus, from our cultures. In accordance with Kymlicka's account, a person with no cultural framework would lack a sense of morality and would not be fully human.

Moreover, according to this view, a person suffers extreme harm if his or her cultural framework is badly regarded or ignored by others. Until comparatively recently, for

> ### KEY THINKERS
>
> ### Charles Taylor (1931–)
>
> Taylor's most famous texts are *Sources of the Self* (1992)—a sweeping study of the history of Western thought and civilization—and his groundbreaking essay, 'The politics of recognition' (1993), which has become core reading for anyone interested in multiculturalism. Taylor's multiculturalism is informed by the claim that a person always finds his or her identity in the context of frameworks or communities of meaning. He is particularly famous for explaining that the recognition of cultural difference is essentially related to a politics of equal dignity. Rather than understanding equality as 'sameness', he contends that treating people with equal dignity might involve recognizing their different needs, identities, symbols, and goals.

instance, non-Western cultures in the UK were largely ignored in education and the media. The rare portrayals of Asians and Afro-Caribbeans on television tended to involve significant stereotyping. While the situation is different today, the politics of recognition holds that, even in the present day, people are damaged if others do not acknowledge them or produce demeaning images of them. Positive recognition is a 'vital human need' (Taylor, 1992: 25–6). While political theorists normally assume that human beings share common attributes, such as autonomy or rationality, the politics of recognition focuses on people's different values, languages, and symbols. For example, it takes a Muslim woman's belief in the principle of modesty, or *hijab*, as equally fundamental to her humanity as the capacity for autonomy (see the case study at the end of this chapter). Taylor (1992: 39) shows how the politics of recognition grows out of the liberal politics of equality: '*We give due acknowledgement only to what is universally present—everyone has an identity—through recognizing what is peculiar to each.*'

The politics of recognition applies to many disadvantaged groups, including cultural minorities, women, gays, blacks, and the disabled. The theory is broader than that of Kymlicka, in that, while it accepts the importance of group rights, it maintains that rights are unlikely to be enough to bring about mutual recognition between groups. Taylor does support the group right of the Québécois to self-government (1992: 58), but he is also concerned that, for example, granting a right to Sikh policemen to wear turbans on their patrols means only that others must tolerate them: members of the wider society do not have to appreciate this Sikh convention as a valuable cultural practice. The politics of recognition is concerned to transform attitudes by ensuring, for example, greater professional role models or political representation for minority cultures. It echoes feminist claims that, while women now have many formal rights to equality, they will not gain real equality as long as they experience social discrimination. To encourage recognition, Taylor therefore also recommends that schools and universities expand the range of authors studied in literature classes to reflect students' diverse cultural backgrounds. This is a controversial claim. Some believe that education should encourage values such as toleration and a respect for rights, and that doing so does not involve altering the content of the curriculum.

The politics of recognition has been deemed especially appropriate in relation to the indigenous peoples of North America. This is partly because the approach seeks to accord positive value to non-liberal groups. James Tully (1995) highlights that, within the same

> **KEY TEXTS**
>
> James Tully, *Strange Multiplicity: Constitutionalism in an Age of Diversity* (1995)
>
> This text questions the received view in modern political theory of a unified nation state and a unified notion of **sovereignty**. It addresses six types of demand for cultural recognition that are particularly problematic: supranational associations, nationalism and federalism, linguistic and ethnic minorities, feminism, multiculturalism, and aboriginal self-government. The book rejects the idea of 'modern constitutionalism' and argues instead in favour of a 'post-imperial constitutionalism' that justifies different sources of law in a liberal state. Tully defends the traditional laws of North American indigenous peoples, arguing that they ought to be recognized alongside modern, Western laws in Canada.

nation, people can hold vastly different ideas of justice. The politics of recognition appreciates that the very idea of rights may be problematic for indigenous peoples. The view, central to the concept of a 'right', that individuals are the ultimate source of moral value appears to conflict with the cultural framework of some indigenous peoples, which concentrates on the community and the environment. For Tully, then, the politics of recognition enables liberals to recognize not only a set of rights, but also radically different communities' understandings of justice. Indeed, some forms of the politics of recognition might even question liberal conceptions of nationhood and sovereignty.

A difficult question raised by the politics of recognition, however, is whether all cultures should be deemed equally valuable. It is problematic to assume that all cultures have produced equally worthy works of art and literature, or that they have all contributed equally to the development of science. Moreover, the problem runs deep because, when we judge other cultures, we also confront serious *moral* issues: every culture has propositional content—that is, each world view contains a perspective on what is morally right. Logically, it is impossible to conclude that two cultures that disagree on basic moral precepts are both equally correct and, thus, deserve equal respect (Barry, 2001: 270). Recognizing this problem, Taylor makes the modest claim that all cultures at least deserve a '*presumption of equal respect*' (1992: 72). For example, even if one is not familiar with Indian music, one should assume that an Indian raga (song) has value, without assuming that its value, when discovered, will be the same as that found in Western classical music. This does not entail cultural relativism, but the awareness that only when we practise open-mindedness and recognize the limitations of our own outlook can we hope to understand others better and adopt a more respectful attitude towards different cultural value systems.

While recognition so understood may be a noble ideal, it is also a demanding one. Human beings may be too limited in their outlook to appreciate the value contained in non-Western art, for instance, quite apart from recognizing the worth of cultural practices that appear extremely unfamiliar. Can the politics of recognition avoid falling into the trap of valuing only those works of art and practices that conform to what the dominant community believes to be beautiful or worthy? Moreover, it could be problematic to think that giving public exposure to, for example, a culture's traditions of art or its marriage practices addresses cultural inequalities. Strangely, this may actually create injustice, because group members may feel that they must stick to those traditions and practices, or lose their claim to equality. Consider the recent debate about Muslim *hijab*. Do liberal societies risk associating Muslim groups so closely with this practice that Muslim women cannot reject veiling in the future? Would unveiled Muslim women be accused of cultural betrayal? (See the case study for further consideration of this debate.) Finally, does the politics of recognition sidestep the real source of minority cultures' problems, which may not lie in their devalued artistic traditions, but in **cultural racism**—that is, racial prejudice that is expressed by using 'cultural' insults (Modood, 2005)? The real problem thus might arise from prejudice against people's ethnicity, rather than from culture per se—and for these reasons, the debate about the politics of recognition continues vigorously.

☆   KEY POINTS

- Defending cultural diversity might involve supporting group-specific rights, as well as overcoming hostile attitudes towards minority cultures in society at large.

- To this end, the politics of recognition recommends greater political or media representation of minorities and expanding the curricula in schools, amongst other things, in order to represent the cultural backgrounds of all students.

- The dangers arising from the politics of recognition are similar to those affecting cultural rights in some ways. In particular, the politics of recognition may: (a) extend only to cultures that conform to liberal values; (b) associate the group's identity too closely with particular practices, making it harder for future generations to reject these practices; and (c) ignore the real basis of minority groups' inequality, which may be ethnic or racial.

Multiculturalism: open-minded dialogue and a common culture

One final understanding of multiculturalism remains to be discussed. This is Parekh's (2002) 'dialogical', or conversational, approach. The prospect of potential conversation between people of potentially very different world views certainly overlaps with both the cultural rights' perspective and the politics of recognition, as considered earlier. However, the dialogical approach goes further by specifying that cultural diversity is educational and the cause for celebration. According to this approach, the encounter with unfamiliar persons and customs is not merely a problem that must be controlled or overcome.

In Parekh's account, there are two equally important aspects to life in a multicultural society. Each must involve a conversation between different world views, such that neither the minority nor the majority culture remains unchanged. The first aspect—to which liberals pay much attention—is the issue of how conflicts should be resolved legally. The debate about cultural rights focuses on this aspect of multicultural life. This is understandable, because cultural diversity does present hard questions concerning the morality of, for example, polygamy, the refusal of certain communities such as the Roma to send their children to school, or requests by Hindus to cremate their deceased on open pyres. But no single principle can resolve all of these controversies. Solutions can emerge only by engaging in a dialogue using the society's **operative public values** (Parekh, 2002: 272)—that is, the principles that one finds if one studies a society closely enough, because they are embedded in its everyday practices. In the UK, for example, free movement and **sexual equality** are operative values. The dialogue between the majority and minority group about how a disputed practice conforms, or does not conform, to a society's operative values is likely to trigger a debate *within* the minority culture as well. This means that the critical conversation about a practice such as polygyny occurs at a variety of levels at once. The conversation helps a multicultural society to recognize that there are some liberal principles that should never be forsaken (such as tolerance and dignity) but that, equally, there are non-liberal principles (such as solidarity, humility, and selflessness) that can also find a place in a multicultural society.

 KEY THINKERS

Bhikhu Parekh (1935–)

Parekh is a professor of political philosophy and a Labour peer in the House of Lords. As well as writing extensively on multiculturalism, he acted for five years as deputy chair of the Commission for Racial Equality and the Commission on the Future of Multi-Ethnic Britain. The Parekh Report was published in 2000. Parekh's most famous book, *Rethinking Multiculturalism* (2002), puts forward an innovative theory of multiculturalism that seeks to retain certain truths contained in the liberal tradition—that is, its support for human dignity, tolerance, and procedural fairness—while enabling minority cultures to help liberalism to grow and expand its moral horizons in the encounter with new and different cultural identities.

The second important aspect of multicultural life—one that is seldom discussed by liberal theorists—is its common culture. Different cultures influence and illuminate the dominant society's music, dance, arts, literature, and lifestyle through their participation (Parekh, 2002: 220). The imaginative work of writers such as Hanif Kureishi and Chitra Divakaruni—whose stories recount young immigrants' search for identity, and have helped to shape the lives of new generations of multicultural citizens—have also reconstituted national identities. Thus, in the UK, Tariq Modood (2005) puts forward the idea of 'plural Britishness', because he believes that many cultures contribute to the public culture of that country as a multicultural society. This common culture is likely to be the precondition for open-minded conversation about justice.

Finally, the idea of what Parekh calls a *'dialogically constituted multicultural society'* suggests that while people are formed by their cultures, this does not mean that they are incapable of critically evaluating their way of life. People necessarily view the world from inside a culture, whether this is one that they have inherited and uncritically accepted, or one that they have reflectively revised. Different cultures represent alternative systems of meaning and visions of what is good in life. If, like Parekh, we accept that no culture contains the whole truth about the human good, but that each, only in a limited way, realizes a range of human capacities and emotions, it is possible to see that any culture—including liberalism—needs others to understand itself better and to expand its horizons.

⭐ **KEY POINTS**

- Cultures are produced through dialogue. In a multicultural society, this conversation occurs between cultures—that is, between majorities and minorities—as well as within them.
- Parekh's idea of a *'dialogically constituted multicultural society'* suggests two aspects to a multicultural society: one that is concerned with resolving conflicts; and another concerned with evolving a common life—composed of cuisine, dance, and literature.
- Conversation seems to be a mutually beneficial activity in a society divided by differences in belief and cultural identity.

Conclusion

The existence of cultural diversity within many nation states today leads political theorists to consider inequalities arising from cultural membership. Multiculturalism is not only a fact, but also a policy and an ideal. While some thinkers, such as Barry, argue that multiculturalist policies deny universalist ideals of the Enlightenment, liberal political theory contains resources for responding to cultural diversity in terms of cultural rights and a policy of cultural recognition, in the name of equality and freedom. Both of these approaches, however, confront the problem of *which* cultural differences to support. The debate about cultural identity is often thought to pose particularly hard questions in relation to women's human rights, and also in regards to sexual and other 'internal' minorities.

Of course, even with regard to the last approach to multiculturalism considered, many questions remain. One is whether Parekh's notion of a dialogue between cultures presupposes equality between cultures from the outset—because without such equality, any conversation would become a monologue. Additionally, the question might be whether, even in the most open-minded view of multiculturalism, it is possible to realise Parekh's hope to retain the truth of liberalism—cherishing the values of tolerance and dignity—and go beyond it. The pursuit of multiculturalism, then, while undoubtedly a worthy social goal and public ideal, remains full of complexities and challenges at the current time.

📌 **CASE STUDY**

The Muslim veil

One of the most problematic questions for multiculturalism is the debate over whether Muslim women should have the right to wear the veil in liberal societies. This debate dates back to the 1980s, to what is known as the 'headscarves affair' (*l'affaire du foulard*) in France. The controversy has recently resurfaced in relation to France's 2010 law against wearing full-face coverings in public. This case study analyses the initial French controversy, and the arguments for and against prohibiting the veil in schools.

The Muslim veil: clothing or concept?

The veil is a garment that is traditionally worn by Muslim women or older girls. It can take different forms: the *burqa* is a full-length garment that covers the whole body, including the face; some varieties of the veil cover only the head and shoulders, but not the face. All such garments exemplify the practice of *hijab* (veiling). The veil is not only a piece of clothing, but also expresses an important idea in the Muslim world view (Mernissi, 1991: 5). Traditionally, women wore the veil for reasons of modesty. The word *hijab* literally means 'curtain', and is thought to derive from verse 33 of the Qu'ran, in which the *hijab* is a cloth that the Prophet Mohammed draws between himself and an impostor who appears unexpectedly in his wedding chamber. The story of the '*descent of the hijab*' holds that the cloth appeared from heaven to enable the Prophet to preserve his privacy without resorting to aggression. Consequently, the word *hijab* in Arabic has three aspects to its meaning:

- it means 'to hide';
- it marks a border or threshold; and
- it conveys an ethical idea of the forbidden—that which is hidden by the veil should be protected from others.

Because the original story of the *hijab* describes the separation of a married couple (the Prophet and his wife) from others, the question is why veiling became only a female practice in Muslim societies. The answer lies in the way in which such societies separated the private world (the household) and the public world (the mosque and the wider society). Women were taken to symbolize the former.

 KEY TEXTS

Cécile Laborde, *Critical Republicanism: The Hijab Debate and Political Philosophy* (2008)

Cecile Laborde is a professor of political philosophy at University College London. Her recent book, *Critical Republicanism*, analyses the difficult issues raised by the Muslim veil (hijab) in France, and situates these questions within a significant reformulation of French republican theory, especially its official philosophy of state neutrality (*laïcité*). While republicanism is often relied upon to ground France's contentious legal prohibition, in 2004, of religious symbols, based on its three constituent principles (liberty, equality, and fraternity), Laborde reinterprets these ideals in order to criticize the ban. Her important claim is that such a policy fails to support Muslim women's struggles for integration and that a more generous form of immigrant integration is, in fact, consistent with the republican tradition.

Veiling has become contentious in European countries containing sizeable Muslim populations, such as France. In the 1980s, in a town near Paris, two Muslim schoolgirls were expelled from school for refusing to comply with a rule that stated that no one should wear religious symbols in class. The girls—backed by their parents—insisted that the veil was an important symbol of their identity and that they should thus be allowed to wear it. The incident gave rise to a controversy that spread throughout the country and continued for many years. The government led inquiries into the nature of republican neutrality, or what is called *laïcité*. Finally, in 2004, it voted in favour of a law that prohibits any visible religious symbols in public institutions, such as schools. While religious neutrality in France derives from the country's tradition of secular citizenship (which emphasizes the idea that all citizens belong equally to the nation), a special concern behind the 2004 law was that some Muslim girls were being pressurized by radical sections of their communities into wearing the veil.

 KEY CONCEPTS

Veiling issues in the UK

In 2012, a British Muslim woman, Maroon Rafique, was asked to leave a school's parents' evening in Manchester. The school authorities contended that her veil posed a security risk, even though she had suggested sitting in an area where her veil would not be so visible to the other parents. (See: http://www.manchestereveningnews.co.uk/news/greater-manchester-news/mum-maroon-rafique-banned-from-manchester-689978).

A spokesperson for the Muslim Council of Britain found the decision authoritarian: '*Wearing the veil is not obligatory, and is a freedom of choice issue . . .Children may have to follow a particular dress code, but for a parent to be stopped, it doesn't make sense.*' (http://rt.com/news/uk-veiled-woman-kicked-out-723/)

Veiling issues in the USA

Soon after a new rule was introduced, in 2009, that banned the veil and similar garments, the Massachusetts College of Pharmacy and Health Sciences (MCPHS) exempted the Muslim veil from the policy. While the college authorities initially justified the rule on grounds of safety, connections had been made to the earlier arrest of a Muslim former student suspected of terrorist activities. (See: http://edition.cnn.com/2010/US/01/08/massachusetts.security.policy/ and http://www.danielpipes.org/blog/2009/12/niqabs-or-burqas-banned-at-the-massachusetts) Although the incident did not escalate into a large controversy, because at this private institution only two of some four thousand students wore veils, it was one of the first significant issues regarding the Muslim veil to achieve widespread media attention in the USA since a woman in 2007, in Florida, sued the state for refusing to allow her to wear a veil in her driver's licence photo (http://news.bbc.co.uk/1/hi/world/americas/2970514.stm).

In this case study, each major argument for prohibiting the veil will be contrasted with counter-arguments that bring into play the issues considered earlier concerning identity and self-respect. The three main issues are:

- equality as neutrality;
- intolerance of sexual discrimination; and
- autonomous consent to a religious world view.

Equality as neutrality

The case for prohibition may rest on the idea that school is a place in which people of all backgrounds and beliefs should be treated equally. No student should be privileged or enjoy different treatment on account of his or her group identity. This thought lies at the root of the French state's concern about allowing Muslim girls to wear the veil. The French idea of *laïcité* does not translate simply as 'neutrality', but as 'secular neutrality' (Scaramuzzi, 2004). This means that it focuses on the injustice of privileging certain religious groups over other significant minorities — such as Jews—in France's history. The defence of secular neutrality in education also originates in the idea that everyone should have the same opportunities to pursue knowledge and that schools should not favour any one sectarian creed. Finally, education should encourage all citizens to belong to the nation—and signs of religious membership hinder young people in forming this sense of common belonging (Laborde, 2008).

Against this account, however, one might, in fact, use arguments from neutrality to support the right of Muslim girls to wear the veil: if schools wish to be even-handed, they may need to acknowledge that treating people of different religious groups equally does not necessarily mean treating them *in the same way*. This is partly because religious groups do not all enjoy equality in the first place. The marginalization of certain cultures and religions in European countries is such an everyday occurrence that one often has to think twice before noticing that the public sphere is not in some senses in fact neutral. For example, as we saw earlier, schools in the UK do not generally schedule time during the school routine for Muslim children to pray during Ramadan. Thus, it may be easier for a Christian child to comply with school rules than it is for a Muslim child. In the case of the French law against the veil, Christian children fare much better, because a typical symbol of Christianity—for example, a crucifix—goes unnoticed in French society, as would a person who wears grey trousers at a boardroom meeting. From this perspective, it is wholly unsurprising that small crucifixes are exempt from the 2004 ban. By contrast, because the veil is not the usual dress for French schoolchildren, it is immediately regarded as 'visible' (Galeotti, 2002). In addition, it is arguably easier for students of Christian origin than it is for Muslims to treat religion as a private matter. Whereas Christians in European societies have a long history of secularism (a policy of public neutrality on matters of religion), Muslim communities typically do not recognize the distinction between religion and the public world. Thus, if cultural identity is as important to developing self-respect as multicultural thinkers claim, equal, in the sense of genuinely neutral, treatment might involve allowing Muslim girls to wear the veil to school.

Intolerance of sexual discrimination

One might seek to prohibit the veil on grounds that it is harmful. The strongest argument on these grounds is put forward by Elisabeth Badinter (1989), who claimed that the veil symbolizes sexual oppression. According to Badinter, the veil should not be tolerated, because it harms women by supporting sexual discrimination. In defence of this argument, it is true that the veil is a sex-specific practice that may be hard to differentiate entirely from, for example, prohibiting women from going out to work. Accordingly, Fatima Mernissi (1991) argues that the veil is oppressive on account of the practices that it supports—such as the seclusion of women in the **private sphere** and their elimination from politics. According to others, the *burqa* is particularly harmful, because it is a cumbersome outfit that is designed to restrict women's movement. The *burqa* has also been thought to cause women health problems, ranging from respiratory complications to depression (Ellis, 2000: 62).

There are a number of responses to these claims. While they do not settle the matter, they appear to point to a case in *favour* of tolerating the veil. First, in response to the argument that the *hijab* is sexually discriminatory, one might reply that Islam requires men to dress modestly too, and that men are expected to conform to certain dress codes. In most Muslim communities, men are expected to cover themselves between the navel and the knees. (Moreover, to give an extreme example, in Afghanistan, the Taliban required men to grow beards; men whose beards were too short were beaten.) Furthermore, liberal practices such as pornography or wearing miniskirts might be thought to convey attitudes of sexual discrimination. Thus, Badinter would have to be as ready to ban, say, pornography as she would the veil. The view that encouraging norms of sexual restraint threatens women's equality more than supporting sexual freedom may be a biased view that sidesteps the positive value that some cultures attribute to modesty. Additionally, Badinter would have to distinguish between practices such as rape and other violent crimes against women, on the one hand, and on the other, the veil, which is not a violent practice. In fact, the veil might be seen to be a minor issue for women globally, when compared with issues such as domestic abuse and poverty.

Finally, let us turn to the argument that the *burqa* harms individual women by restricting their movement and causing health problems. Even if this were true in some cases, the *burqa* may not be *more* physically damaging than many Western practices, including dieting, cosmetic surgery, or wearing high heels. Yet there is no strong consensus on banning these practices. Therefore, if multicultural thinkers are correct about the significance of cultural identity to the development of self-respect, the arguments from sex discrimination may not suffice and thus, arguably, the veil should be tolerated.

Concern for autonomous consent to religious beliefs

A final argument for prohibiting the Muslim veil in schools arises on grounds of autonomy. No one, it may be argued, should adopt a belief system as a result of social pressure. Religion is so important that one should consent to it in a genuinely autonomous spirit, and young people of school age are not necessarily mature, or informed, enough to make an autonomous decision about religion. In school, they should have the luxury of keeping an open mind, and the opportunity to think deeply and take time to decide for themselves to which religion, if any, they wish to commit as adults. Allowing the veil in schools might mean that more and more people commit to religion as a result of family pressure or threats from radical sections of their communities.

While the concern about social pressure may be persuasive, the difficulty with this view is that religious or cultural identity is often significant exactly *because* it is not a matter of choice. Religion is *not* a mere lifestyle option, such as going to restaurants or being a football fan. People are born into religious and cultural groups, and even those who undergo religious conversions do not usually see their commitments simply as matters of personal choice. Second, the value of autonomy—or the capacity to control one's life—might not be rated highly by everyone: some cultures prioritize goods such as obedience and harmony with the community. Is it fair to demand that everyone believe autonomy to be all-important? Girls who undertake to wear the veil may gain significant benefits of solidarity with their communities and their families' support. Additionally, veiling and *purdah* (the seclusion of women inside the home) might provide women with the sense of stability that enables them to resist pressures from the wider society. In this sense, the practice may help them to be autonomous.

Finally, cultures are ever-changing, and the veil has been taken to hold a variety of meanings in the modern day. For some, it symbolizes modesty and chastity; for others, the transition to maturity; for others still, it represents resistance to pressures of 'Westernization'. Thus, the assumption that Muslim girls do not choose the veil autonomously is problematic. Young Muslim women seem to choose it for a variety of reasons: out of religious devotion; for community solidarity; in order to enter professional life; to avoid unwanted attention from men; or even as a fashion accessory. If the veil enables women to retain cultural identity *and* act freely, then prohibiting it would seem unjustified.

In conclusion, the veil has given rise to a thorny debate. The core issues are:

- the meaning of neutrality in a multicultural society;
- whether the veil is (or leads to) harmful discrimination; and
- whether Muslim women freely choose to wear it.

All of these questions are central to the controversy that persists vigorously in many European countries today. The wealth of arguments for and against recent French laws, in particular, suggests that fierce debate will continue in years to come.

QUESTIONS

1. How do you understand the term 'multiculturalism'?
2. What is the difference between 'thick' and 'thin' multiculturalism?
3. What are 'group-specific rights'?
4. Should groups such as British Asians and/or indigenous groups in Australia, the USA, and Canada have rights to preserve their cultures?
5. What is an 'internal restriction'? Why might this type of right be problematic?
6. Why do some feminists believe that multiculturalism is harmful for women?
7. What is the 'right of exit'?
8. Is the politics of recognition useful in supporting cultural diversity? If so, how?
9. Does the politics of recognition challenge liberal theory's idea of the self?
10. What, according to Parekh, are the two levels of intercultural dialogue?
11. Why is veiling such a controversial issue for defenders of multiculturalism?

FURTHER READING

- Barry, B. (2001) *Culture and Equality*, Oxford: Polity Press Criticizes theories that focus on cultural identity and argues instead for a strong politics of equality.

- Laborde, C. (2008) *Critical Republicanism: The Hijab Debate and Political Philosophy*, Oxford: Oxford University Press Argues that republican political theory responds positively to multicultural conflicts—particularly that concerning the veil—on account of the tradition's commitment to equality, autonomy, and non-domination.

- Lenard, P. T. (2012) *Trust, Democracy and Multicultural Challenges*, Pennsylvania: University of Pennsylvania Press One of the most thought-provoking recent contributions to multicultural theory, this book argues that minority claims in Western democracies may be best understood through the theoretical lenses of trust, distrust, and anti-trust.

- Modood, T. (2007; 2013) *Multiculturalism: A Civic Idea*, London: Polity Press Argues that multiculturalism should be conceptualized as a key aspect of citizenship and as contributing to the shared purposes of a democracy.

■ Mookherjee, M. (2009) *Women's Rights as Multicultural Claims: Reconfiguring Gender and Diversity in Political Philosophy*, Edinburgh: Edinburgh University Press Argues that women's rights need not be considered to conflict with cultural diversity, once the natures of two basic rights are clarified.

■ Okin, S. M. (1999) 'Is multiculturalism bad for women?', in S. Okin et al. (eds) *Is Multiculturalism Bad for Women?*, Princeton, NJ: Princeton University Press, pp. 7–24 Argues that feminist and multicultural objectives are likely to conflict.

■ Parekh, B. (2002; 2008) *Rethinking Multiculturalism: Cultural Diversity and Political Theory*, Basingstoke: Macmillan A clear defence of a 'dialogical' approach to multiculturalism.

■ Phillips, A. (2007) *Multiculturalism without Culture*, Princeton, NJ: Princeton University Press Rejects exaggerated ideas of cultural difference and defends a form of multiculturalism that focuses on gender justice.

■ Taylor, C. (1993) 'The politics of recognition', in A. Gutmann (ed.) *Multiculturalism and the Politics of Recognition*, Princeton, NJ: Princeton University Press, pp. 25–73 Defends equal recognition for a variety of cultural groups and explains why liberals should be committed to this ideal.

■ Tully, J. (1995) *Strange Multiplicity: Constitutionalism in an Age of Diversity*, Cambridge: Cambridge University Press Defends a variety of claims for recognition through the idea of a 'post-imperial constitutionalism'.

WEB LINKS

● http://www.bristol.ac.uk/sociology/ethnicitycitizenship The University of Bristol's Centre for the Study of Ethnicity and Citizenship is one of the most active research groups on multicultural citizenship in the UK, and regularly contains valuable links and information.

● http://www.cwis.org/index.php The Centre for World Indigenous Studies is a non-profit organization for research and education, giving access to indigenous people's knowledge.

● http://www.equalityhumanrights.com The Equality and Human Rights Commission deals with controversies surrounding race and cultural diversity. It was formed in October 2007, following the merging of the Disabilities Commission and the Equal Opportunities Commission.

● http://homepage.isomedia.com/~jmele/mcultlink.html This website contains particularly useful further links to information concerning multicultural education worldwide.

● http://www.minorityrights.org Minority Rights Group International is a non-governmental group, working to secure the rights of minorities and indigenous peoples worldwide.

● http://post.queensu.ca/~kymlicka The homepage of Will Kymlicka, the multicultural political theorist and Canada Research Chair in Political Philosophy at Queen's University, Ontario. The page contains valuable links to books, articles, and recent research projects in the field of citizenship and ethno-cultural diversity.

Visit the Online Resource Centre that accompanies this book to access more learning resources: http://www.oxfordtextbooks.co.uk/orc/mckinnon3e/

ENDNOTE

[1] I would like to thank Catriona McKinnon for her editorial support and advice.

8

Human rights

TOM CAMPBELL

Chapter contents

- Introduction
- Natural rights, the rights of man, and human rights
- Analytical issues
- Justifying theories
- Implementing human rights
- Conclusion

Reader's guide

The origin of the idea that human beings have certain fundamental rights that ought to be recognized in all societies may be traced to a variety of philosophical, legal, and religious sources, mainly in the Western tradition. Its main application has been in the sphere of politics, within which the concept of human (or 'natural') rights has been used to justify and to limit the authority of states in relation to their citizens and their dealings with other states. This chapter discusses issues arising from analyses and critiques of human rights (moral rights that belong to all human beings by virtue of their humanity, which override, or generally outweigh, other moral considerations). These issues include the nature and significance of rights in general, and the distinctive content, scope, and functions of human rights. Consideration is given to the philosophical and practical justifications for believing (or not believing) in human rights, to different theories concerning how we might determine their content and scope, to practical implications, and to how human rights should be implemented.

Introduction

Normative political theory is about justifying the distribution and deployment of the power that some human beings have over significant numbers of others. In recent times, these justifications have often been expressed in terms of **human rights**. This may be seen as the triumph of one form of political discourse (rights) over others (such as utility, well-being, traditional values, or contract). Approaching politics in terms of rights places an overriding emphasis on the intrinsic equal value of all human beings and the obligations relating to how they are to be treated to which that equal worth gives rise, rather than on more generalized social goals, such as maximizing human happiness or increasing gross national product.

Human rights are particularly associated with law, both in relation to domestic human rights law—including equal opportunity legislation and bills of rights—and international human rights law—including the International Covenant on Civil and Political Rights (ICCPR) of 1966 and the International Covenant on Economic, Social, and Cultural Rights (ICESCR) of 1966. But human rights are primarily part of the moral and political discourse that is used to justify the creation of human rights law and other social institutions. The discourse of human rights is utilized by a variety of political movements—including many non-government organizations (NGOs), such as Amnesty International—and is particularly associated with the United Nations and the 1948 Universal Declaration of Human Rights (UDHR), which constitutes the foundational document of current human rights thinking and practice. This document has led to many conventions and treaties committing participating states to a variety of human rights objectives, such as non-discrimination, children's rights, and the rights of indigenous peoples.

At the core of the moral and political concept of human rights is the idea that social and political arrangements should be based on the **recognition** of the equal worth of every human being. This recognition excludes such practices as torture, arbitrary and extreme punishments, and slavery; it requires political mechanisms that ensure membership of a democratic state and guarantees a minimum level of material well-being for all human beings. Much of this global political morality focuses on the plight of individuals who are victimized by governments, and the neglected interests of deprived and often despised minority groups, but it is also of direct relevance to the universal human interest in curbing and channelling the power that is exercised by governments, religious organizations, and economically powerful corporations.

Natural rights, the rights of man, and human rights

The idea of rights entered politics in the form of **natural rights**—that is, rights that exist in nature independently of any human laws or customs—when medieval European thought developed the idea that certain things are lawful, in so far as they promote or violate a person's 'rights', rather than, for example, going against the commands of God. This acquired its meaning largely within the context of law, particularly in circumstances in which people used the term 'right' to claim that others owed obligations to them. The basis of such claims was sometimes held to be a 'natural' order of things, or a **law of nature**—that is, a way of thinking about nature that is derived from ancient Greek thought and Roman law. This was, in part, based on religious belief about divine purposes in creating the universe, and partly derived from empirical observations as to the nature and needs of human beings, such as their desire to live, their capacity for moral choice, their need for physical **security**, and their social dependency.

📖 KEY TEXTS

Paine, *The Rights Of Man* (1791; 1969; 1989)

The writings and rhetoric of Thomas Paine (1737–1809), an Englishman of lowly origins, contributed to both the US Revolution of 1776 and the French Revolution of 1789. A radical democrat, Paine is best known for combining his secular liberalism and rampant republicanism with the pioneering idea of a natural right to welfare, including education, old-age pensions, and maternity allowances. In this text, Paine connects the equal right to self-governance to the right to equal treatment, including the equal distribution of the benefits of government through fair taxation and socially responsible government policies.

During the Enlightenment of the sixteenth to eighteenth centuries—when religious **authority**, hereditary monarchies, and the feudal system were being questioned—natural law was given a more rationalist foundation. At this time, rights came to be associated with the idea of a **social contract**, whereby individuals existing in the **state of nature**—that is, a condition of human life in which there is neither government nor positive laws—agree to form a society and/or a state to protect and promote their natural rights in a **civil society**, under a sovereign power to which they pledge their obedience for as long as the sovereign power does not infringe their natural rights. ➡ **See Chapter 1**. The precise content of the social contract varied in line with the postulated state of nature. Very dangerous and amoral states of nature led to social contracts in which individuals pledged almost unlimited allegiance to an individual sovereign power (as envisaged by Thomas Hobbes). Mildly dangerous and impoverished, but morally constrained, states of nature led to social contracts that both empowered and limited governments (as envisaged by John Locke). Pleasant, but underdeveloped and uncivilized, states of nature led to social contracts that sought to retain and develop the rights, particularly the freedoms, of the individual in the state of nature (as envisaged by Jean-Jacques Rousseau). In all cases, consent established the legitimacy of the constitutional arrangements established by the social contract (see Box 8.1).

Critics of natural rights came from a variety of political positions. Eighteenth-century conservatives, such as Edmund Burke (1729–97), saw natural rights as undermining the settled traditions on which genuine **liberty** is based in actual societies, and as licensing the anarchic destruction of legitimate authority and settled rights, resulting in insecurity and war. The founder of **utilitarianism**, Jeremy Bentham (1748–1832), ridiculed natural rights as a pernicious fiction used to obstruct the social reforms that were needed to promote

> ⚭ KEY THINKERS
>
> ### John Locke (1632–1704)
>
> Locke deployed the idea of a social contract agreed on by those living in the 'state of nature', prior to the existence of government, but subject to the moral requirements set down in God's law, to generate the thesis that all human beings have the right to life, liberty, and property. His belief that governments forfeit the right to obedience if they violate these 'natural rights' was influential in the formulation of the US Declaration of Independence (1776) and his ideas, in the form of self-evident 'rights of man'—along with those of Rousseau and Thomas Paine—feature in the French Revolution of 1789.

> ### BOX 8.1 THE US DECLARATION OF INDEPENDENCE
>
> In Congress, 4 July 1776:
> We hold these truths to be self-evident, that all men are created equal, that they are endowed by their creator with certain unalienable rights, that among these are life, liberty and the pursuit of happiness.—that to secure these rights, governments are instituted among men, deriving their just powers from the consent of the governed,—that whenever any form of government becomes destructive of these ends, it is the right of the people to alter or to abolish it, and to institute new government, laying its foundation on such principles and organizing its powers in such form as to them shall seem most likely to effect their safety and happiness.

human happiness. Karl Marx (1818–83) scorned universal natural rights as an ideological set of beliefs that promoted the competitive individualism of capitalist society to the detriment of freedom and prosperity of the vast majority of the population. The rhetoric of natural rights, so powerful in the overthrow of feudalism, lost much of its force in the nineteenth and early twentieth centuries, when politics focused more on ameliorating the inequities of industrial society, either through the competitive individualism of free markets and electoral **democracy**, or through more socialist and communitarian measures.

Human rights

The resurgence of rights discourse that followed the atrocities of World War II led to the foundation of the United Nations, the Charter of which linked the promulgation and protection of what are now called 'human rights' to the reduction of those evils that had led to war and inhumanity. Emphasis was placed on the freedom from oppression of minority groups, providing everyone with the basic necessities of life, fostering the **self-determination** of peoples, limiting the use of force in international relations, and promoting those economic freedoms on which peace and prosperity was held to depend. Despite the uneasy tensions between the more liberal and capitalist approach of Western democracies, and the more communitarian and socialist ideals of communist regimes, the resultant Universal Declaration of Human Rights (1948), the International Covenant on Civil and Political Rights (1966), and the more socially oriented approach of the International Covenant on Economic, Social and Cultural Rights (1966) endorsed a model of a democratic welfare state in which individuals, within their states, enjoy certain civil and political powers, and social and economic benefits 'by right'. (See Box 8.2.) At the same time, 'peoples' subject to colonial rule were regarded as having a human right to self-determination, and this collectivist aspect of human rights has been developed to safeguard the interests and **autonomy** of ethnic and indigenous minority groups.

Following the collapse of the Soviet Union in 1989 and the rapid growth of global capitalism, human rights became closely associated with the moral ingredients of liberal philosophy, with the emphasis on individual liberty and the rule of law as the basis for economic success. This coincided with the increasing 'constitutionalizing' of human rights on the US model and more emphasis on human rights within international law, including UN human rights treaties dealing with anti-discrimination, women, torture, and children. There are now several regional human rights regimes, based on the European Convention on Human Rights (1950), the US Convention on Human Rights (1969), and the African Charter on Human and Peoples' Rights (1981). Recently, there has been a willingness of states to use the discourse of human rights to license intervention in the affairs of other states and the promotion within civil society of global responsibility for the eradication of world poverty.

   KEY TEXTS

Dworkin, *Taking Rights Seriously* (1977)

In an essay that gives its title to this book, Ronald Dworkin, a US legal philosopher and constitutional lawyer, famously declared that 'rights are trumps'. By this, he meant that basic rights take moral and legal precedence over other norms, including the interests of the community as a whole. Rights are individual possessions that cannot be violated simply because this would bring benefits to people other than the right holder. The idea of 'rights as trumps' describes the status of those constitutional rights that are used by courts in some **jurisdictions** to override legislation, even if that legislation has been democratically endorsed and serves the public good.

BOX 8.2   UNIVERSAL DECLARATION OF HUMAN RIGHTS (1948)

Preamble

Whereas recognition of the inherent dignity and of the equal and inalienable rights of all members of the human family is the foundation of freedom, justice and peace in the world,

Whereas disregard and contempt for human rights have resulted in barbarous acts which have outraged the conscience of mankind, and the advent of a world in which human beings shall enjoy freedom of speech and belief and freedom from fear and want has been proclaimed as the highest aspiration of the common people,

Whereas it is essential, if man is not to be compelled to have recourse, as a last resort, to rebellion against tyranny and oppression, that human rights should be protected by the rule of law,

Whereas it is essential to promote the development of friendly relations between nations,

Whereas the peoples of the United Nations have in the Charter reaffirmed their faith in fundamental human rights, in the dignity and worth of the human person and in the equal rights of men and women and have determined to promote social progress and a better standards of life in larger freedom,

Whereas Member States have pledged themselves to achieve, in co-operation with the United Nations, the promotion of universal respect for and observance of human rights and fundamental freedoms,

Whereas a common understanding of these rights and freedoms is of the greatest importance for the full realization of this pledge,

Now, therefore,

The General Assembly,

Proclaims this Universal Declaration of Human Rights as a common standard of achievement for all peoples and all nations, to the end that every individual and every organ of society, keeping this Declaration constantly in mind, shall strive by teaching and education to promote respect for these rights and freedoms and by progressive measures, national and international, to secure their universal and effective recognition and observance, both among the peoples of Member States themselves and among the peoples and territories under their jurisdiction.

☆ KEY POINTS

- Human rights are derived historically from the idea of natural law as it developed on a strong religious basis in late medieval Europe and, later, in a more secularized form during the more rationalist period of the Enlightenment.

- The self-evident rights of man developed in the bourgeois revolution against feudalism in the eighteenth century have been criticized as being anarchic (Burke), fictional (Bentham), and excessively individualistic (Marx).

- The contemporary human rights movement stems from the aftermath of World War II. It is associated, domestically, with constitutional bills of rights and, internationally, with the work of the United Nations.

- Human rights may be defined as universal rights of great moral and political significance that belong to all human beings by virtue of their humanity. They are said to be overriding and absolute.

- Human rights may be divided into three overlapping groups: (1) civil and political rights; (2) economic, social, and **cultural rights**; (3) group or collective rights for development and self-determination.

Human rights are now viewed as rights of great moral importance that are universal, in that they belong to all human beings in virtue of their humanity, overriding, in that they ought to be given the highest priority in the organization of social and political life, and, perhaps, absolute, in that they can never be infringed or taken away from any person. But are human rights really rights, as distinct from values or goals? Are they really universal, as distinct from culturally, politically, and morally specific? Are they really overriding, as distinct from merely weighty or aspirational? Are they really absolute, as distinct from conditional and provisional? Failure to find convincing answers to such questions threatens to undermine the intellectual, moral, and political credibility of human rights.

Analytical issues

Controversies about what we mean by 'rights' and 'human rights' raise a number of important moral and political questions about their existence, their form, their content, and their implications.

What are rights?

Having a right is not the same thing as being either morally right or good. Rights identify legitimate expectations as to what their holders may have or do. Thus, if I have a right to speak, then I ought to be permitted to speak whether or not other people think, for some other reason, that it is right or good that I should not speak. Rights exclude, or trump, other considerations being brought to bear in determining entitlements. They are valuable **normative** features of institutional arrangements, because they can be used to settle disputes, to bring order to human relationships, and to protect the interests of those who have the rights in question.

We can identify types of right by how they relate to duties or obligations (Hohfeld, 1919):

- **Liberty rights** involve no more than the absence of a duty on the part of the right holder. The idea is that a person enjoys freedom in so far as he or she lacks duties.

- **Claim rights** exist when one person's right to do or have something correlates with other people's duties to allow, or enable, that person to have or do that to which he or she has the claim right. This correlative duty may be 'negative', as when the right to life correlates with other people's duty not to kill the right holder, or 'positive', as when the correlative duty is to actually do something to help the right holder to stay alive. These correlative duties are owed to the right holder and, usually, the right holder may normally either demand or waive the duties in question.

- **Power rights** enable their holders to change the rights and duties both of themselves and others, such as when two people enter into a contract.

- **Immunity rights** render their holders immune from having their rights and duties changed by another person.

Duties are expressed in terms of rules about what people must do. Legal rights derive from authorized rules that identify the protected interests. Social or 'societal' rights derive from the informal social rules that govern most human relationships. Legal and societal rights are called '**positive rights**'—that is, rights posited in law or social mores, which can be identified by empirical observation of the source of the rules in question, in that their existence in a legal or social system is a matter of fact that arises from human convention or decision making. These rights vary between different jurisdictions and societies.

It is not clear whether the analysis of rights in terms of rule-protected interests applies to what are called 'moral rights'. Clearly it does if, by moral rights, we mean the positive rights that ought to exist. These may be called 'manifesto rights' (Feinberg, 1973). This is the approach normally favoured by consequentialist theories that base morality, including the decision about what positive rights we ought to have, on the benefits that arise therefrom. But the term 'moral rights' may be taken to refer to rights that are said to be based on moral rules that exist independently of any rules made by human beings, such as natural law. Thus, **deontological** theories of morality hold that morality is a system of categorical imperatives, obligations, or duties, laying down what ought to be done, irrespective of the further consequences, with 'rights' correlating with the person whose interests are intended to be served by fulfilling these duties. What are called 'rights-based moralities' fit this model, but difficulties with this model are discussed in the following sections.

But are human rights really rights?

Human rights are certainly regarded as entitlements: people should not have to beg for that to which they have a human right. Human rights exclude, or trump, other considerations more than do ordinary rights. Moreover, human rights can readily be identified as protecting important, perhaps vital, human interests. In most cases, they can be viewed as claim rights that correlate with the duties of others and they may be regarded as immunity rights, because they cannot be taken away by the power rights of other people.

But some uses of human rights discourse are no more than affirmations about the importance of human interests, such as sustenance, relief from suffering, and autonomy, which do not address the question of who, if anyone, is responsible for protecting and furthering these interests. In this case, human rights may be important values that are relevant to determining what rights we ought to have, but they are not, in themselves, really rights at all, because no legitimate expectations as to the conduct of others are involved.

We might look to human rights law to discover the obligations correlative to human rights. Certainly, human rights are commonly identified with human rights law, but they cannot, in fact, be reduced to any system of positive law, which may fail in many respects to express and implement human rights adequately and effectively. Human rights are primarily a moral and political discourse about what positive laws (and other measures) ought to be in place, in order effectively to protect and promote the most important interests of all human beings. It may be argued that human rights actually exist in a rights-based moral realm that consists of rules establishing entitlements, whether or not these are recognized in any society. But the existence of controversy between reasonable people in the same, and in different, cultures as to what constitutes the form and content of these sort of moral human rights casts doubt on whether there really are rights that have an independent existence or being, or, if there are, whether they can be known to us. In this case, there are grounds for scepticism about whether the relatively abstract moral affirmations that make up the bulk of bills and conventions of rights should be considered to be rights at all—whether they should be viewed instead as declarations of values that are thought to be a basis, along with many other factors, for deciding what rights everyone ought to have.

Are human rights really universal?

Any rights that all human beings have by virtue of status of being human are, in that sense, universal rights. It is a non-negotiable ingredient of human rights that they apply to human beings universally, irrespective of their race, their colour, their religion, or their nationality.

The inclusive universality of non-discrimination on specified grounds does not mean, however, that human rights allow for no differences between the basic entitlements of different categories of person. For example, the human rights of children differ from those of adults, and states have special human rights-related duties for the protection of children's special interests. In some cases, the universality of human rights is a matter of all human beings having the same rights at each stage of their development and decline, so that there are human rights for the old and the sick, as well as for children. Many human rights are conditional, in the sense that they apply only to those human beings who are in a particular situation, such as those accused of committing a criminal offence or those in need of medical care. So the universality of human rights means only that all human beings in certain situations have, or ought to have, certain rights. These situations may be defined in such a way as to effectively exclude or favour some human beings, such as property owners, over others. Some important human rights arise from differences, not similarities, between human beings. Thus, some gender rights are based on the distinctive characteristics of women, while indigenous rights belong only to members of an indigenous group. ➜ **See Chapters 7 and 12**.

Views about which differences between human beings are the basis of the differential treatment that is required to protect human rights vary from culture to culture. Human rights discourse allows for this, insofar as some human rights require recognition of cultural diversity in relation, for example, to language and religion, but there is an insistence on certain cultural particulars, such as the acceptance of homosexuality, abortion, gender equality, a secular state, and parliamentary democracy, which may be seen as cultural preferences rather than as universal truths. The problem of **cultural relativism**—that is, the view that right and wrong differs from culture to culture and that different cultural values are non-comparable—concerns not only the content of rights, such as non-discrimination in employment, but also the grounding of moral value in a rights-based system of thought that neglects, for example, such 'Asian values' as respect for old age, wise leadership, and social solidarity. This is apparent in efforts to introduce Western sexual values to traditional Muslim countries.

The universality of human rights as currently expressed may be similarly questioned on the basis of their perceived ideological bias. While there may be agreement that human beings are of equal importance and that they should be treated with a respect that recognizes their human dignity, there is disagreement about what this means, and this entails ideological disagreements that reflect competing economic and political systems. Human rights, as a whole, can be seen as an expression of liberal individualism—a philosophy that endorses all outcomes of social interaction that do not violate specified individual

KEY CONCEPTS

The 'Asian values' debate

In the 1990s, some Asian political leaders, such as Lee Kuan Yew of Singapore, argued that human rights are culturally biased in promoting individual freedom over general well-being. In contrast, Asian cultures are said to emphasize community values, such as social order, respect for authority, general welfare, and loyalty to family, state, and nation. In fact, there are major historical cultural and religious differences, even within South East Asia, and Western commentators often regard championing Asian values as no more than a way of justifying authoritarian government. There is, however, an emerging Asian consciousness that distances itself from the perceived selfishness and irresponsibility of Western capitalism.

rights (Nozick, 1974). Society is the framework that allows individuals to maximize their own advantage, by controlling the extent to which others may interfere with their actions and by limiting their obligations to other people. Communitarian ideologies seek to place more emphasis on values of cooperation, solidarity, and community, and seek to devise what they see as a more effective and fairer system of collective, as well as individual, rights that manifests a deeper respect for human beings than competitive capitalism. This is evident in the disagreement about whether to view free trade and intellectual property rights as exemplars of human rights.

Maybe the best that we can do to preserve the claimed universality of human rights is to express it in negative terms as having to do with excluding certain considerations—such as race, ethnicity, religion, sexual orientation, disability, or nationality—as a basis for denying someone or some group a human right, although there is much debate as to precisely what should be included in such a list. When it comes to the content of the rights that are to be available on the basis of non-discrimination, there is no agreement as to whether the same universal rights should apply in all societies and, if so, what these rights are, or should be.

Are human rights really overriding?

Rights are used to exclude other considerations from decision making. In many countries, the courts use the rights identified in bills of rights to override legislation. Arguably, human rights override other rights, just as bills of rights may override ordinary legal rights.

But a human right of one person may conflict with the same human right of another: for example, I violate your right to life when I kill you in self-defence—or your right is limited by my right, and vice versa. This sounds reasonable, but is difficult to implement fairly in practice. Further, a human right may clash with another, such as when my right to free speech conflicts with your right to a fair trial. When it comes to institutionalizing human rights, decisions have to be made about balancing human rights, which entails giving some a measure of priority over others.

Human rights may override all other types of consideration, such as promoting the general welfare. One person's right to life cannot be taken away simply because that would make a lot of other people happy. In actual bills and covenants of rights, however, it is common to distinguish between those rights that are absolute, or non-derogable, in the sense that they can never be overridden even by other rights—as in the case of the right not to be tortured—and those that can be subordinated to such considerations as security and public order '*in a democratic society*'. Moreover, some rights, such as the right to a fair trial, are absolute in that they are not conditional, for example, on the right holder not violating the rights of others; other rights, such as personal freedom, are not absolute at all. Some rights are thought to be absolute in another sense, in that they cannot be waived—such as the right to life and the right not to be enslaved—while most other rights, such as the right to privacy, may be waived. In practice, very few, if any, human rights are considered to be completely overriding of non-rights-based or utilitarian consequences. The most that can be affirmed is that human rights are generally morally weightier than other rights and that they are highly resistant to being limited or overridden by non-rights-based considerations.

Questions about the alleged overriding and absolute nature of human rights are sometimes answered differently according to the type of rights in question. Thus, civil and political rights—such as free speech and the right to vote—are often held to be more overriding than social and economic rights—such as the rights to an education and to a decent standard of living. While both types of right are enshrined in international covenants and officially given equal status by the United Nations, civil and political rights—which are often (misleadingly) presented as negative rights (correlating with the duties of others to refrain from action)—are given much more emphasis in practice than are economic, social, and cultural rights. Yet several social and economic rights, such as the right to subsistence, are more basic than most civil and political rights, in that if these materially basic rights are neglected, then those involved will not live to enjoy their other rights (Shue, 1996). It is also noteworthy that, currently, there is a trend of responding to terrorist attacks by restricting the status of civil and political rights, and arguing that the 'war on terror' requires major diminution of such 'absolute' rights as the right to a fair trial, and even the right, under ICCPR, Article 7, not to be subjected to '*torture or to cruel, inhuman or degrading treatment*'.

☆   **KEY POINTS**

- Rights are legitimate expectations that are usually based on socially or legally recognized entitlements.

- Rights may be classified according to their relationship to duties. In the case of claim rights, there are correlative duties that are owed to the right holder.

- Moral rights may be understood as the 'positivist' rights that we ought to have, or as the rights that we do have under a morality of rules or divine commands.

- Human rights are not really rights if they are only affirmations of important values without specified correlative duties.

- Human rights are only universal in the sense that they exclude discrimination.

- Human rights generally override other rights, but may conflict with each other. Most human rights are also limited by social and political considerations. Few human rights are taken to be absolute.

Justifying theories

Analysing human rights leads on to issues relating to their justification. This involves a mixture of metaphysical and moral reasoning. Thus, as we have seen, to make sense of a pre-social idea of moral rights, we may draw on the idea of natural law, according to which there are rules that either exist in, or can be derived from, nature.

For people who have religious belief, these rules can be identified with the commands of a god, or derived from their beliefs about the purpose behind that god's creation of human beings and nature in general (Finnis, 1980). Those who do not have religious or metaphysical beliefs of this sort, but still believe that there are moral rights above and beyond actual social and legal rules, may think of human rights as intrinsically good or valuable things that are important and worthwhile in themselves—such as life, liberty, and happiness—which ought to be protected and promoted within human society. As we have seen, these intrinsic values are not in themselves rights, but may be used to justify their creation. In Bentham's case, this positivist approach is combined with a utilitarian moral theory according to which acts and rules are justified by their consequences—in particular, their consequences for human happiness.

A pure utilitarian theory (**act utilitarianism**) holds that we should assess all of our individual acts in the light of their consequences and do only that which maximizes the general happiness. This morality has no place for rules other than as rough guides to what sort of conduct has, in general, good consequences. **Rule utilitarianism**, however, holds that conformity to some rules—whether or not the individual believes that following the rule in a particular case maximizes utility—does, in the long run, maximize utility, which gives a place for rights as those interests that are protected by the rules that, in the long term, maximize happiness. The main difficulty with this view is that it could lead to adopting rules that benefit the interests of the majority of people at the expense of statistical minorities, because even if each person counts equally in calculating what serves the general happiness, maximizing happiness does not rule out, for example, making slaves of some to serve the happiness of others—the very thing that human rights are committed to excluding.

Another non-religious approach to the idea of moral rights sees morality as a matter of following certain categorical commands or rules, such as 'do not steal' and 'tell the truth', the moral standing of which depends on the human relationships involved, rather than on whether or not they promote other intrinsic values. According to this deontological approach, moral rights are part and parcel of this rule-based morality, and exist when the rules in question directly benefit someone or, perhaps, when they involve someone being entitled to control the actions of others. Problems arise in establishing what the rules of deontological morality are. It may fit the right not to be tortured, which may be said to rest on our knowledge that it is never morally justified to torture someone, but there is little agreement about, for example, precisely what is involved in the right to life, which some intuit as compatible with the death penalty and waging pre-emptive war, while others do not.

Much political theory is concerned with making progress on such epistemological issues. John Rawls (1971: 1973; 1999) deploys a modernized version of the theory of social contract to suggest a method that can be adopted to work out our equal basic liberties.

He identified these as those rights that would be insisted upon by everyone in an **original position**—that is, a hypothetical form of the state of nature—when deciding the ground rules of their future social cooperation. Ronald Dworkin (1977) seeks to do something similar by drawing on the morality of '*equal concern and respect*' as a way of protecting human rights by judiciaries taking a moral approach to the interpretation of law.

Whatever philosophical methodology is adopted for settling moral disagreements, the substantive disagreement in justifications and definitions of human rights is between those who see human rights as essentially about human autonomy and those who have a broader conception of human well-being. To count as human rights theories, both approaches have to be seen as committed to the idea of equal human worth. Their disagreement relates to what it is about human beings that gives them such value. **Autonomy theory** (or neo-Kantian theory) focuses on the rationality of human beings with specific reference to their capacity to make moral choices, in relation to both what duty requires of them and the capacity to choose to do what their reason tells them to be morally right. Humans have material needs that must be met if they are to be moral **agents**, and social and political organizations enable them to live together as a community of individual moral agents—but their equal worth is a matter of their capacity to exercise moral agency (Gewirth, 1982). Hence the central significance of negative freedom, which leaves individuals to exercise their moral choices. This is the capacity in virtue of which humans deserve equal respect, so that while other rights may be more basic, in that they concern having things (such as food and education) that we need to become moral agents, it is autonomy rights that are the morally foundational human rights and essential to human dignity.

 KEY THINKERS

Immanuel Kant (1724–1804)

Kant held that human beings are 'autonomous' in making rational decisions about what is morally right and acting on this through their 'free will'. His test of moral rightness is whether the maxim of an action (such as truth telling) can be 'universalized', in the sense that a rational person could endorse everyone acting on that maxim. Kant holds that human beings are 'ends in themselves' and should not be treated only as means. As such, they should be 'respected' and enabled to act autonomously, thus having the dignity that is the grounding of their moral rights.

In contrast, well-being theorists such as John Stuart Mill, while accepting the central importance of autonomy (and not only **moral autonomy**) for human flourishing, take a wider view as to what is worthwhile (although not necessarily unique) to human life. Thus, Mill would oppose torture not only because it destroys human autonomy, but also because it inflicts great suffering and has bad consequences for the rule-governance of human society, with all of the benefits that this brings to humans generally. A neo-Millian approach to the justification (and analysis) might be to adopt a rule-utilitarian approach, identifying human rights with having non-discriminatory, and generally overriding, social and political arrangements for protecting and fostering the most vital and important and fundamental interests of human beings.

☆ **KEY POINTS**

- Some justifications of human rights depend on specific metaphysical beliefs about the existence of gods and the associated idea of the moral nature of the universe.

- Utilitarian justifications of human rights take them to be positive rights that are instrumental in protecting fundamental human interests.

- Deontologists believe that we can discover certain moral rules by reasoning or intuiting, which constitute the overriding duties that are correlative with human rights.

- The contemporary social contract theory of John Rawls sets out a method for determining basic rights by combining impartiality and rational choice, using the construct of the 'original position'.

- Much disagreement about the content of human rights involves a tension between the moral choice approach of Kant and the consequentialist position of John Stuart Mill.

Implementing human rights

The competing moral bases of human rights all point to the need for adopting some social and political means for deciding what rights are human rights, and for achieving human rights objectives. For some purposes, human rights may be identified by the means that are used to identify and implement them. Thus, we may answer the question 'which rights are human rights?' by saying that they are the rights to which the special protection provided by a **bill of rights**, with strong judicial review, should be given. In other words, a right should be considered a human right if it is best secured by being included in a bill of rights, which is to be used by courts to override legislation. For purposes of international law, human rights might be seen to be those rights the violation of which legitimates the use of sanctions or armed intervention by states. Alternatively, human rights may be identified as those rights the violation of which negates political obligation and justifies rebellion. But while it is certainly true that it is difficult to be precise about the content and scope of human rights without being clear about the use to which they are to be put, the implementation of human rights, in broad terms, can be approached by identifying core human interests and the most common threats thereto, and then asking which forms of institutionalization are best suited to furthering human rights objectives.

When the Universal Declaration of Human Rights was adopted by the United Nations in 1948, it was assumed that such rights were already embodied in the common law and legislation of many jurisdictions. Because of well-entrenched legal rules and principles based in traditional practice, codification, or legislative provisions, it made sense to see human rights as representing prized individual rights, well protected by existing law in some—but by no means the majority—of states. The vision was to see that these rights were implemented in other countries, and that new legislation would be introduced in all states to realize economic, social, and cultural rights in a more effective and universal manner through the welfare state. The assumption (embodied in the ICCPR) was that this would be a democratic state, the government of which would be accountable to the opinion and, ultimately, the votes of the people, and operated through the medium of law—that is, general rules administered by executives responsible to elected ministers that, when controversy or non-compliance were at issue, were subject to the judgement of impartial courts. It was envisaged that these democratic processes would be further developed, and that elected governments would work to implement social and economic rights through legislation. The international aspect of this scenario involved the cooperation of democratic states in containing the use of force to settle international conflicts and in giving effect to the process of decolonization that recognized the self-determination rights of currently dependent peoples.

In democratic countries, this approach to human rights was somewhat complacent, but, in many ways, effective, with major developments in welfare, universal education, and administrative law (to control bureaucratic mismanagement), and progressive changes relating to such matters as capital punishment, abortion, women's rights, and equality of opportunity in general. In all of this, the discourse centred as much on justice, equality, and social welfare as it did on human rights, which some continued to associate with reactionary attempts to stem social progress by countering democratic majorities with affirmations of individual freedoms and property rights.

The easy harmony of political democracy and a broad conception of human rights implemented through progressive legislation were halted by a growing awareness of the relative deprivation of racial and cultural minorities. In the USA, from the 1960s, the civil rights movement developed to counter the problem of racial discrimination, especially in southern states, and this was bolstered by several decisions of the US Supreme Court on the desegregation of schools and other state-funded institutions—an issue that was matched in the UK by growing awareness of systematic discrimination against Catholics in Northern Ireland. All of this gave impetus to constitutional courts in their interpretation and application of bills of rights (in the USA), the European Convention on Human Rights, and the Canadian Charter of Rights and Freedoms. The justification for these institutions stemmed from a criticism of representative democracy as giving too much power to electoral majorities and their governments, who use their power to benefit themselves at the expense of minorities. Full implementation of human rights, especially in relation to equality, seemed to require protection of minorities, which was thought to be best provided by giving courts the power to override discriminatory legislation, and to initiate affirmative action to restore social and economic equality.

These developments set the scene for the current controversy over whether human rights ought to be implemented, at least in part, through the interpretation and application of very generally worded statements of rights, as set out either in a constitution or in an Act of Parliament, to reinterpret radically or actually override ordinary legislation. This seems necessary to protect minorities and to keep politicians within the rule of law, but it seems to be contrary to the democratic rights set up in these same bills and charters, because judges are not elected and yet are being asked to make controversial moral decisions about what human rights are to mean in practice. Fundamental political issues arise in relation to the role that courts and other unelected bodies ought to have in filling in the details in relation to what such abstract moral rights as *the right to subsistence* or a *right to family life* are to mean when they are enforced within a political system. If there is a right to self-determination, then arguably everyone should have an equal say as to what their universal rights are to be. If everyone's right of self-determination is to be respected, it seems wrong to have such matters decided by majority voting.

This critique of human rights focuses on the increased political power that is given to the judiciaries when human rights are entrenched in constitutions, or when judiciaries are given the power to interpret laws in line with their individual or collective view of what human rights mean, how they are to be interpreted, and what weight is to be given to them, and do so in a way that is designed to reduce the power of elected assemblies and governments. Thus, in the USA, political debate and decision making in elected assemblies is seriously circumscribed by the need to stay within the bounds established by the Supreme Court in relation to such issues as abortion, freedom of speech, campaign finance, family law, and equality at work. This removes the right of each individual to have an equal share in the process by which the decisions that bind him or her are reached. It turns the discourse of human rights from a language of political debate into a specialized matter that is falsely represented as being a matter of legal argument. Voting in the Supreme Court displaces voting in the Congress as the locus of political power.

In the international sphere, human rights are pursued largely through the monitoring of international treaties, a process under the United Nations that leads to the criticism, and sometimes the sanctioning, of states following Resolutions of the Security Council. This is predominantly a process of exerting diplomatic pressure, with only rare applications of sanction and even rarer UN-backed interventions. Nevertheless, the proliferation of international courts—both regional and global—is developing a large body of international human rights law that is increasingly drawn upon in domestic courts, especially in countries with a bill or charter of rights, in a way that is only remotely connected with any democratic process.

The implementation of human rights is still rightly regarded as a matter of changing the conduct of states, which are the chief violators as well as the best hope of human rights. But there are significant moves to have individuals who have participated in gross crimes against humanity, such as genocide, tried by international courts, such as the recently established International Criminal Court. It is, as yet, not clear if the work of such courts is an aid to achieving and sustaining peace, and whether it is possible to distinguish individual and collective guilt in the cases that come before them.

There is also a growing realization that large transnational corporations are also sources of human rights violations and, possibly, of human rights succour. Human rights, as they are currently institutionalized, emphasize mainly the role of the state as both the violator and the defender of human rights. This ignores the extent to which human individual and collective interests are vulnerable to the activities of economically powerful and hugely wealthy corporations in a world that is dominated by liberal capitalist institutions. While corporations are regarded as having duties to respect the human rights of those living in the countries within which they operate and, occasionally, experience a decline in market share as a result of loss of moral reputation, they are largely able to carry on their business without giving much regard to the well-being of persons beyond their own shareholders and cannot be brought to account through current human rights instruments. In a global economy, few states are in a position to make any significant progress in subjecting corporations to the discipline of human rights goals, such as extreme poverty and environmental degradation. Any progress that has been made on such matters has been largely the work of NGOs such as Amnesty International and Human Rights Watch. The naming-and-shaming pressures brought to bear on human rights violators, by what is loosely referred to as civil society, has become the primary mode whereby human rights are currently implemented.

Conclusion

There is no doubt that the concept of human rights is a strong moralizing focus in contemporary politics, based on deep conviction as to the equal worth of human beings, commonsense knowledge about what is needed to live a tolerable human existence, and the role of legal and political institutions, and the force of public opinion, in meeting these needs. Its weakness, intellectually, is its difficulty in making sense of the idea of moral rights in a secular world, beyond saying that they are values that are often best realized through establishing positive rights as part of an interlocking set of public institutions and widespread social expectations. Internationally, human rights are beset by lack of enforcement, which is partly due to the independence of states and partly to the diversity of cultures. Given the failure of bills of rights, domestically, to offer any significant protection for civil and political rights in times of crisis, at which they are most endangered, the widespread neglect of social and economic rights, and the evident inability of states and the United Nations to

KEY CONCEPTS

Human rights intervention

The established legal principle that states should not interfere in the internal affairs of other countries is challenged by the emerging doctrine of humanitarian intervention, whereby military action may be undertaken to prevent mass slaughter within a sovereign state. The United Nations occasionally imposes economic sanctions against states that inflict serious human rights wrongs within their borders, but is reluctant to approve armed intervention, because this may be practised by powerful states to advantage themselves. It is generally agreed, however, that there were grounds for humanitarian intervention in situations such as those that existed in Uganda in 1979, in Rwanda in 1994, in Bosnia in 1995, and in Kosovo in 1999. ➔ See Chapter 10.

regulate global corporations, it may be that normative political theorists should promote a vision of human rights that relies principally on political participation, progressive human rights legislation, and morally informed international diplomacy, rather than the transfer of political power from governments to courts.

 CASE STUDY

Torture and counter-terrorism—by Jeremy Williams

Among our most fundamental human rights is surely a right not to be tortured. But is this right *absolute*, in the sense that torture is strictly never morally permissible, and ought never to be legally tolerated, whatever the circumstances? Many people argue that it is. And categorical prohibitions on the use of torture are enshrined in a number of international human rights documents. Notably, Article 2 of the United Nations Convention against Torture (1984) requires of state parties that they ban all torture, adding that '[*n*]*o exceptional circumstances whatsoever, whether a state of war or a threat of war, internal political instability or any other public emergency, may be invoked as a justification of torture.*'

Yet, as Tom Campbell noted earlier in this chapter, the view that there is an absolute right not to be tortured has not gone unchallenged, particularly in the wake of the 9/11 attacks and the subsequent 'war on terror'. Some argue that, at the level of moral principle, torture is occasionally morally justified—notably in emergency situations in which counter-terrorist agents are trying to extract intelligence that will enable them to avert an imminent large-scale attack. And others argue, further, that domestic and international law ought to make room for that possibility, by protecting such agents' activities. This case study examines the controversy over the use of torture by security and counter-terrorist forces in greater detail. In doing so, it touches upon some issues of general theoretical interest in the study of human rights—in particular, the forfeiture of rights, the overriding of rights to prevent a greater evil, and the relationship between moral rights and the law.

Torture and morality

Does torture always represent a wrongful violation of the victim's human rights? Those who are categorically morally opposed to torture in both principle and practice are routinely challenged to explain how they would respond, were they in a suitable position of authority, in the so-called *'ticking bomb case''* (hereafter 'TBC'). This hypothetical case is derived from a scenario imagined by Michael Walzer (1973), and is usually described as involving a terrorist who is known to have planted a nuclear bomb in an urban area, which will kill thousands—if not millions—of people unless defused in time. The terrorist has been captured, but refuses to divulge the bomb's location. The question, then, is whether it would be morally permissible to torture him until he reveals the information. Most people intuitively believe that torture would indeed be permissible in this case.

A number of explanations for the moral permissibility of torture in the TBC are possible, of which, for space, we shall consider only some of the most prominent. The most straightforward explanation comes from *act consequentialist* moral theories, such as *act utilitarianism*. As you will recall from the chapter, act consequentialism holds that an act is morally required if it would produce the greatest overall sum of well-being of any act available. Moreover, there are no act types, according to the act consequentialist, that are intrinsically wrong or forbidden, independent of their consequences for the sum of well-being, including those which contravene what we think of as fundamental human rights. The act consequentialist, then, will endorse the use of torture in the TBC on the grounds that the bad effects of the torture are more than outweighed by the bad effects that would accrue if the bomb went off. Notoriously, however, act consequentialism is likely to justify torture in cases that go well beyond the TBC. Suppose, for instance, that, in some depraved society, millions of people could be given significant pleasure by witnessing the torture of an innocent child on television. In this case, if overall well-being would indeed be maximized by the torture, act consequentialism does not merely permit but mandates it. It is precisely because of its implications in cases like this that act consequentialism is criticized for failing to take human rights seriously.

Rather than discussing other versions of consequentialism, let us turn now to its principal theoretical rival—*deontology*. It may seem difficult, initially, to see how torture could ever be justified on a deontological view, for deontologists, as Campbell explains, believe that human rights trump the goal of maximizing societal well-being, and may not be transgressed just because the consequences of doing so would be overall better. Yet perhaps it is a mistake to think that the terrorist, in fact, *has* the human right not to be tortured. This conclusion has been argued for by deontologist Jeff McMahan (2008; see also Steinhoff, 2013). On McMahan's view, because of his wrongful actions in setting the bomb, the terrorist should be seen as having *forfeited* his right against torture. Torturing the terrorist in the TBC, McMahan argues, is somewhat analogous to defending an innocent person, who is about to be murdered, by killing her assailant. In both cases, we have a wrongdoer who culpably threatens to violate the human rights of others. And in both cases, therefore, they forfeit their own rights that we not inflict necessary and proportionate harm on them to prevent their threats from becoming a reality. Note that an important implication of McMahan's view is that torturing the terrorist would be permissible even if his bomb would only claim one victim, rather than thousands. For the crucial moral feature of the TBC, according to McMahan, is not the number of victims, but the fact that the terrorist has forced a choice between harms, whereby either he harms the innocent, or we harm him. Under those circumstances, McMahan concludes, justice requires that the terrorist be made to bear the harm.

McMahan's argument is directed at the standard version of the TBC, in which our choice is whether or not to torture the terrorist himself. Philosophers also sometimes discuss a revised TBC, however, in which the terrorist refuses to crack, even under torture, but we know we could break his resolve, and learn the location of the bomb, by torturing his innocent child instead. Notice that the revised TBC is even more stylized than the original, in that it is extremely difficult to imagine ever facing a case where torturing the terrorist's child would have the desired effect, if torturing him would not, much less that we could be confident of that. That point aside, however, we can still ask whether, in principle, torture would be permissible here. And given the extremely high stakes, many people say, albeit with great misgivings, that it would. If so, what is the reason? Deontologists cannot claim that the child's right not to be tortured has been forfeited. But they might say that torture, however unspeakable, is justified here on grounds of being the *lesser evil*.

To explain: although, as we have seen, deontologists hold that human rights may not be ignored just because respecting them leads to bad consequences, they are not generally strict absolutists about rights either. Rather, they commonly say that there are some catastrophes that are so great that overriding a person's rights is justifiable as a means to avert them. Unlike act consequentialists, deontologists do not think that rights can be overridden just because the consequences of doing so are marginally better, overall, than any alternative—the situation must be an emergency, in which the consequences of failing to act would be *much worse* (although it is a tricky question precisely *how* much worse they must be). At the same time, transgressing a right that has not been forfeited is still an evil, even when it is the lesser evil, and, thus, deontologists are likely to argue that we must make amends to the victim in the revised TBC, in the form of an apology and compensation.

Torture and the law

Reflection on the TBC has led many philosophers to the conclusion that in principle, at least, torture might occasionally be permissible. But does that highly unusual hypothetical case have any implications in practice? In particular, should it inform what the law on the use of torture should say? Harvard law professor Alan Dershowitz (2002, 2003) has courted significant controversy with his proposal for 'torture warrants', whereby if an emergency situation like the TBC were to arise in real life, a court would have the power to authorize the use of torture on a one-off basis to avert the threat. This is intended to mirror the practice of granting police and security agents warrants to perform other acts, like wire tapping, that are generally illegal, but that may be justified in special cases to prevent serious crimes. In support of his controversial conclusion, Dershowitz makes two key claims. First, that it is more in keeping with liberal values to subject the use of torture to open scrutiny, rather than allowing it to carry on unofficially behind closed doors, as it inevitably otherwise would. Second, that if the case for using torture has to be presented in front of a judge, we are more likely to be able to prevent its use from spreading. Hence, Dershowitz thinks, those whose aim is to minimize torture should support his proposal.

This, however, is a claim that proponents of a blanket legal ban on torture strenuously deny. In their view, any exceptions to a general prohibition of torture, however restrictive, will only succeed in further breaking down the already precarious taboo against its use, and lead to more widespread violations of the human right not to be tortured. Defenders of this view argue that the details of the TBC are so fantastic that it would be a serious mistake to design our laws with it in mind (Shue, 2006; McMahan, 2008). Instead, we should design our laws on the basis of the threats to human rights that we regularly face. And one of the most serious such threats, faced by people around the world, is that of being detained and tortured unjustly. To minimize that threat, we should make it as difficult as possible for any regime abroad, or security agent employed by our government at home, to engage in torture. But if our laws send the message that torture can sometimes be justified, however infrequently, this aim would be fatally undermined, for many counter-terrorist agents, even though they act in good faith, will be liable to form the mistaken conclusion that they face circumstances in which torture is justified. And others, whose aims are unjust, will use the legal exceptions as a veneer for their activities. Even placing the power to authorize torture in the hands of judges, as in Dershowitz's proposal, would not be a sufficient safeguard, for it is likely that judges would grant any requests made to them, rather than risk being held to blame for failing to give the security services the authorization they needed to prevent a terrorist attack. Finally, if we allow torture on the part of our own security agents, we lose all moral authority to criticize other regimes who do so, however brutally. Our words of censure against such regimes would, in McMahan's words (2008: 126), *'be no more effective than a proselytizing defense of vegetarianism by someone complacently enjoying a steak.'* Hence, this argument concludes, torture must, without exception, be banned.

Between Dershowitz's proposal for torture warrants and a blanket ban, other legal arrangements are obviously possible. Uwe Steinhoff (2013), for example, rejects the *institutionalization* of torture, via torture warrants, on grounds of the danger of judges granting those warrants too lightly, but he endorses its *legalization*, in the sense of allowing those who take it upon themselves to use torture with adequate justification to escape prosecution and punishment. Steinhoff argues that, albeit that it is exceptionally rare, torture can be morally justified in real as well as in hypothetical cases. In particular, he cites (2013: 14) a pair of striking German cases in which a kidnapper, under torture (or threat thereof) revealed the whereabouts of a child whom he had imprisoned in a confined space, and who was in danger of suffocating if not rescued. (Tragically, in only one of the cases was the child found in time.) Steinhoff argues that to prosecute those who use torture when genuinely necessary and justified would be an injustice to them. And he doubts that legalizing torture in such cases would encourage its wider use, any more than legalized self-defensive killing encourages murder. The debate about torture and the law seems set to continue, then. But all sides do at least agree that wrongful transgressions of the human right not to be tortured already occur with scandalous frequency, and that the law ought to be framed in whatever way seems most likely to prevent such violations in the future.

QUESTIONS

1. To what extent are Enlightenment conceptions of natural rights relevant to contemporary politics?

2. Are human rights too focused on the interests of individuals?

3. How is it possible for the idea of human rights to encompass both the value of cultural diversity and the imposition of universal standards?

4. How does the idea of non-discrimination feature in the UN Declaration of Human Rights?

5. What are the important differences between civil and political rights, on the one hand, and economic, social, and cultural rights, on the other?

6. What does it mean to say that human rights are based on 'respect for persons'?

7. Are there good consequentialist reasons for adopting human rights?

8. Who should determine how human rights, such as 'the right to life', are to be understood when applied to specific policy issues?

9. How far should duties to uphold and protect human rights be extended from states to corporations?

10. Is the United Nations an appropriate organization to establish and enforce global human rights standards?

11. What role should courts have in promoting the right to self-determination?

FURTHER READING

■ Bedi, S. (2009) *Rejecting Rights*, Cambridge: Cambridge University Press A critique of the use of rights in political justification to the detriment of liberty and democratic debate.

■ Beitz, C. R. (2009) *The Idea of Human Rights*, Oxford: Oxford University Press Argues that 'human rights' is not so much a normative idea as an emergent political practice.

■ Brandt, R. (1992) *Morality, Utilitarianism, and Rights*, Cambridge: Cambridge University Press A collection of useful essays, including treatments of consequentialism and rights.

- Campbell, T. (2006) *Rights: A Critical Introduction*, London: Routledge A positivist analysis of human rights, including a discussion of the institutions of rights and explorations of freedom of speech, sustenance, and self-determination.

- Donnelly, J. (2003) *Universal Human Rights in Theory and Practice*, 2nd edn, London: Cornell University Press Presents a theory of rights in terms of equal concern and respect, and discusses cultural relativism and international human rights in practice, including humanitarian intervention.

- Dworkin, R. (1977) *Taking Rights Seriously*, London: Duckworth Contains the classic analysis of 'rights as trumps' in the context of legal philosophy, with discussions of discrimination.

- Finnis, J. (1980) *Natural Law and Natural Rights*, Oxford: Oxford University Press A modern statement of human rights within the traditional natural law framework.

- Gewirth, A. (1982) *Human Rights: Essays on Justification and Applications*, Chicago, IL: University of Chicago Press An influential neo-Kantian theory, expounded and applied to a range of topics.

- Glendon, M. A. (1991) *Rights Talk: The Impoverishment of Political Discourse*, New York: Free Press A contemporary critique of the overuse of the concept of rights in political discourse, which includes a feminist viewpoint.

- Griffin, J. (2008) *On Human Rights*, Oxford: Oxford University Press A restrictive analysis of human rights in terms of 'personhood'.

- Ivison, D. (2008) *Rights*, Stocksfield: Acumen A wide-ranging and positivist approach to rights in general, including dignity, recognition, and terrorism.

- Shue, H. (1996) *Basic Rights: Subsistence, Affluence and US Foreign Policy*, Princeton, NJ: Princeton University Press Analyses and justifies the concept of economic human rights in the context of international obligations.

WEB LINKS

- http://www.hrw.org Human Rights Watch offers a collection of data on human rights performance worldwide.

- http://plato.stanford.edu/entries/rights-human/ Entry by James Nickel on 'Human rights' in the Stanford Encyclopedia of Philosophy.

- http://www.umn.edu/humanrts/index.html The University of Minnesota's Human Rights Library contains human rights treaties, other materials, and a list of other human rights sites.

- http://www.un.org/rights Providing comprehensive coverage of UN human rights material.

 Visit the Online Resource Centre that accompanies this book to access more learning resources: http://www.oxfordtextbooks.co.uk/orc/mckinnon3e/

9

Global justice

GILLIAN BROCK

Chapter contents

- Introduction
- Rawls' Law of Peoples
- Some critical responses to Rawls' Law of Peoples
- Some grounds for scepticism about global justice: authority in the global domain and global governance
- Conclusion

Reader's guide

What would a globally just world look like? How could we begin to make improvements towards a more globally just world? One central debate concerns what the principles governing interactions among the world's diverse people should be. Should we be aiming at more equality among people? What responsibilities do we have to ensure people are well positioned to enjoy prospects for a decent life, or at least to reduce poverty worldwide? What should the aim of redistribution be? Because of its enormous influence, we discuss John Rawls' answers to these and other questions, but we also canvass several highly critical responses to Rawls' views. How could we begin to make improvements towards a more globally just world? Because we need to have more systematic ways of managing our collective interests, we need to introduce better global governance arrangements. We discuss arguments concerning the desirability of attending, and obligation to attend, to global governance in a more concerted way and—in the case study—discuss further ways in which to realize global justice.

Introduction

Any student who has read a newspaper that covers contemporary affairs must have been struck by the existence of at least some injustice in our world today. In some places, people live in constant fear of attack because of their ethnic affiliations, or are being forced from their homes because of civil war, or are suffering the threat of starvation on a massive scale because of staggering levels of poverty. In other places, leaders are accused of 'crimes against humanity': genocide, corruption, or a failure to attend to the basic needs and liberties of their people. Sometimes, people seem too eager to intervene in the affairs of other states, such as when they go to war or press for 'regime change'. In other cases, they appear too passive and are accused of not doing enough, such as when an apparent case of genocide, ethnic cleansing, or massive violation of basic **human rights** is at issue.

What would a globally just world look like? Various theorists propose different models of global justice, which might consist of diverse components (which are not necessarily mutually exclusive), such as advocating that every person be well positioned to enjoy the prospects for a decent life, the universal promotion of human rights, global equality of opportunity, a more equal distribution of resources globally (or, at least, ensuring that all have enough to meet their basic needs), or promoting the **autonomy** of peoples who stand in relations of equality to one another. There is also debate about how best to realize the desired elements, what principles should govern our interactions at the global level, and how to improve the management of our global affairs.

Contemporary theorizing on this topic has been enormously influenced by John Rawls' work, especially his book *The Law of Peoples* (1999), and also by the position known as **cosmopolitanism**. In apparent contrast to nationalists, who believe that we have stronger obligations to members of our nation than to non-members, cosmopolitans believe that all individual human beings have equal moral worth and that national borders do not importantly diminish the strength of our moral obligations to others. There is considerable debate among contemporary cosmopolitans concerning what are our obligations to others, but one area of considerable agreement is that Rawls' account of our obligations to others in the global arena is defective.

The term cosmopolitanism originated with the Stoics. **Stoicism** rejected the idea that one should be importantly defined by one's city of origin, as was typical of Greek males of the time. Rather, it insisted that all were '*citizens of the world*'. The Stoics' idea of being a citizen of the world neatly captures the two main aspects of cosmopolitanism, especially as it is understood today: a thesis about identity, and another about responsibility (Scheffler, 1999). As a thesis about identity, being a cosmopolitan indicates that one is a person who is marked or influenced by various cultures. As a thesis about responsibility, cosmopolitanism generates much discussion, as we will come to see. Roughly, the idea is that, as a cosmopolitan, one should appreciate that one is a member of a global community of human beings. As such, one has responsibilities to other members of the global community. As Martha Nussbaum (1996) elaborates, one owes allegiance '*to the worldwide community of human beings*' and this affiliation should constitute a primary allegiance. As a thesis about responsibility, cosmopolitanism guides the individual outward from local obligations and prohibits those obligations from crowding out responsibilities to distant others.

Cosmopolitanism highlights the responsibilities that we have to those whom we do not know, but whose lives should be of concern to us.

 KEY CONCEPTS

Cosmopolitanism

Cosmopolitans see themselves as citizens of the world—as members of a global community of human beings, with robust responsibilities to others in the global community. Cosmopolitans believe that all individual human beings have equal moral worth and that the strength of our moral obligations to others is not, importantly, diminished by national borders.

Rawls' Law of Peoples

In *A Theory of Justice* (1971; 1999), Rawls sets out to derive the principles of justice that should govern liberal societies (see Box 9.1). By employing all of the apparatus attached to the **original position**—that is, the hypothetical choosing situation—he famously endorsed two principles: one, a **principle of equal basic liberties**, and another, permitting social and economic inequalities when, and only when, they are both to the greatest benefit of the least advantaged (known as the **difference principle**) and attached to positions that are open to all under conditions of fair equality of opportunity (the **principle of fair equality of opportunity**). In *A Theory of Justice*, Rawls' focus is on the principles that should govern closed communities—paradigmatically, nation states. Some cosmopolitans—first, Charles Beitz (1979), and then, Thomas Pogge (1989)—argued that these two principles should apply globally, because the same kind of reasoning that led to their endorsement at the domestic level should apply to the global case.

 KEY THINKERS

John Rawls (1921–2002)

John Rawls was an American liberal who is widely credited with reviving the discipline of political philosophy through the publication of *A Theory of Justice* (1971; 1999). In this work, Rawls develops the social contract tradition to justify principles guaranteeing equal liberties, equal opportunity, and a distribution of economic goods that makes the worst off as well off as possible. These principles apply within a state, but not across them. *The Law of Peoples* (1999) extends the idea of a social contract to deal with the global context. In this book, Rawls argues for general principles that both liberal and non-liberal societies should be able to accept as the defining norms to regulate their interactions.

It was something of a disappointment, then, when Rawls later weighed in on the issue, explicitly against such a suggestion. He argued that, although the two principles should apply within liberal societies, they should not apply across them. Rather, in the international arena, Rawls thinks that different principles would be chosen—and we discuss his reasoning next.

BOX 9.1 RAWLS' EIGHT PRINCIPLES GOVERNING HIS LAW OF PEOPLES

1. Peoples are free and independent, and their freedom and independence are to be respected by other peoples.
2. Peoples are to observe treaties and undertakings.
3. Peoples are equal and are parties to the agreements that bind them.
4. Peoples are to observe a duty of non-intervention.
5. Peoples have the right to self-defense but no right to instigate war for reasons other than self-defense.
6. Peoples are to honor human rights.
7. Peoples are to observe certain specified restrictions in the conduct of war.
8. Peoples have a duty to assist other peoples living under unfavorable conditions that prevent their having a just or decent political and social regime.

(Rawls, 1999: 37)

 KEY CONCEPTS

A people

A 'people' is a group of persons that are united by sufficient commonalities in areas such as: culture; tradition; a sense of kinship; history; sentiments; world views. Although they may be politically organized, they may or may not occupy a distinct state—for example, some indigenous people, such as the Basque people, may think of themselves as distinct people, but may not have their own state. This concept figures heavily in Rawls' discussions of global justice.

 KEY TEXTS

John Rawls, *The Law of Peoples* (1999)

In this text, Rawls extends the idea of a **social contract** to deal with the global context. He argues for general principles that both liberal and non-liberal societies should be able to accept as the defining norms that can regulate their interactions. These include principles acknowledging the independence of peoples (rather than of individual persons), their equality, that they have a right to self-defence, and that they have duties of non-intervention, to observe treaties, to honour a limited set of rights, to conduct themselves appropriately in war, and to provide limited assistance for peoples living in certain kinds of unfavourable conditions.

In *The Law of Peoples* (1999), Rawls aims to derive the laws to which well-ordered peoples would agree. For Rawls, well-ordered peoples include reasonable liberal peoples and '*decent non-liberal peoples*' (further on this to follow). Rawls argues that the **Law of Peoples** that he endorses is a realistic utopia. It is realistic in Rawls' view because it takes account of many real conditions, by (for example) assuming that a fair amount of diversity exists in the actual world and that not all peoples of the world do, or can reasonably be made to, endorse liberal principles.

Rawls' derivation occurs in several stages. First, he concerns himself only with liberal peoples and the principles that they would endorse. He employs two 'original positions' to derive his Law of Peoples for liberal peoples: the first grounds the social contract of the liberal political conception of a constitutionally democratic regime; the second operates among representatives of liberal peoples. In the first original position, parties must decide the fair terms of cooperation that will regulate the **basic structure** of society. After the principles governing the liberal society have been derived, Rawls moves to the international level. At this stage, the second original position is employed to derive the foreign policy that liberal peoples would choose. The representatives of peoples are subject to an appropriate **veil of ignorance** for the situation: for example, they do not know the size of the territory or how powerful they are.

In addition to the Eight Principles that Rawls believes would be chosen by liberal peoples, he believes that three organizations would be selected:

- one aimed at securing fair trade among peoples;
- one that enables people to borrow from a cooperative banking institution; and
- one that plays a similar role to that of the United Nations, which he refers to as '*a Confederation of Peoples (not states)*' (Rawls, 1999: 42).

And having posited that liberal peoples would select the Eight Principles and three organizations, Rawls shows how **decent peoples** would select the same principles and organizations.

What is a decent people, according to Rawls? The main criteria that must be satisfied for a people to count as a decent one, according to Rawls, are: first, the society must not be aggressive: it must conduct its affairs in ways that are peaceful and respectful of other societies. Second, the system of law and its idea of justice must secure basic human rights for all members of the people. It is, however, important to realize that the list of particular rights that must be secured is short. It is commonly thought to include only:

- the right to life, by which he means the rights to the means of subsistence and **security**;
- the right to **liberty**, which equates to freedom from slavery or forced occupation, but also includes some liberty of conscience—enough to ensure freedom of religion and thought;
- the right to personal property; and
- the right to formal equality, by which he means that similar cases be treated similarly.

Third, a decent people must have a '*decent consultation hierarchy*', in which the significant interests of all members of the people are taken into account.

Rawls then suggests that decent people would accept the Law of Peoples that he earlier derived. Indeed, he points out that decent people would have to be committed to it, given the very definition of what counts as a decent people.

So what might be an example of a decent, non-liberal people that Rawls would be prepared to count as 'well-ordered'? Rawls describes a case of a hypothetical decent hierarchical people—'Kazanistan'—which he considers meets his requirements (see Box 9.2). Rawls believes that Kazanistan can be admitted to the society of well-ordered peoples. In terms of its foreign policy, liberal societies should tolerate states such as Kazanistan. For those who have trouble with the idea that such a society should be considered as a member of the

> BOX 9.2 RAWLS ON 'KAZANISTAN'
>
> Imagine an idealized Islamic people named 'Kazanistan.' Kazanistan's system of law does not institute the separation of church and state. Islam is the favored religion, and only Muslims can hold the upper positions of political authority and influence the government's main decisions and policies, including foreign affairs. Yet other religions are tolerated and may be practised without fear or loss of most civic rights, except the right to hold the higher political or judicial offices . . . Other religions and associations are encouraged to have a flourishing cultural life of their own and to take part in the civic culture of the wider society.
>
> (Rawls, 1999: 76)

Society of Peoples—by which Rawls means something like the international community of peoples in good standing, and more precisely, the group of peoples who follow the principles of the Law of Peoples in their relations—Rawls believes that *'something like Kazanistan is the best we can realistically—and coherently—hope for'* (1999: 78). Moreover, he thinks that liberal peoples should *'try to encourage decent peoples and not frustrate their vitality by coercively insisting that all societies be liberal'* (1999: 62). By way of further defence of the view, Rawls argues that it is crucial that we maintain *'mutual respect among peoples'* (1999: 62).

Another crucial area of difference between cosmopolitans and Rawls relates to our duties of assistance (see Box 9.3). According to Rawls, some societies *'lack the political and cultural traditions, the human capital and know-how, and, often, the material and technological resources needed to be well-ordered'* (1999: 106). Well-ordered peoples have a duty to assist such societies to become part of the society of well-ordered peoples. He then offers some further thoughts on the duty of assistance. The aim of assistance is to:

> help burdened societies to be able to manage their own affairs reasonably and rationally and eventually to become members of the society of well-ordered peoples. This defines the target of assistance. After it is achieved, further assistance is not required, even though the now well-ordered society may still be relatively poor.
>
> **(Rawls, 1999: 111)**

The aim is to realize and preserve just (or decent) institutions that are self-sustaining. According to Rawls, the political culture of a burdened society is all-important to the levels of prosperity experienced in particular societies: wealth owes its origin and maintenance to the political culture of the society, rather than to, for example, its stock of resources (1999: 108). Indeed, he says:

> I believe that the causes of the wealth of a people and the forms it takes lie in their political culture and in the religious, philosophical, and moral traditions that support the basic structure of their political and social institutions, as well as in the industriousness and cooperative talents of its members, all supported by their political virtues.
>
> **(Rawls, 1999: 108)**

Rawls does engage directly with central claims made by some (although not all) cosmopolitans, who maintained that the principles of justice that applied in *A Theory of Justice*—particularly the difference principle—should apply globally. He takes up Charles Beitz's claim that, because a global system of cooperation already exists between states, a global difference principle should apply across states as well. Rawls argues against this, for

---

BOX 9.3 RAWLS ON THE DUTY OF ASSISTANCE

Two liberal or decent countries are at the same level of wealth (estimated, say, in primary goods) and have the same size population. The first decides to industrialize and to increase its rate of (real) saving, while the second does not. Being content with things as they are, and preferring a more pastoral and leisurely society, the second reaffirms its social values. Some decades later the first country is twice as wealthy as the second. Assuming, as we do, that both societies are liberal or decent, and their peoples free and responsible, and able to make their own decisions, should the industrializing country be taxed to give funds to the second? According to the duty of assistance there would be no tax, and that seems right; whereas with a global egalitarian principle without target, there would always be a flow of taxes as long as the wealth of one people was less than that of the other. This seems unacceptable.

(Rawls, 1999: 117)

---

a couple of reasons, but notably, as we have just seen, because he believes that wealth owes its origin and maintenance to the political culture of the society, rather than to its stock of resources, for example. Furthermore, any global principle of **distributive justice** that we endorse must have a target and a cut-off point, which are secured by ensuring the requirements of political autonomy. When a people are able to be self-determining and can manage their affairs *reasonably and rationally*, we have discharged our duty of assistance.

☆ **KEY POINTS**

- Rawls argues for the laws to which both liberal and non-liberal peoples could agree.
- He argues, first, that liberal peoples would endorse his Eight Principles and three global organizations, governing trade, loans to countries, and other common affairs.
- Decent peoples must satisfy at least three important conditions: they must be peaceful; they must secure limited basic human rights; and there must be mechanisms of consultation.
- Decent peoples are legitimate members of the Society of Peoples. We must not coercively insist that all societies be liberal.
- We have a duty of assistance to help burdened societies to manage their affairs 'reasonably and rationally'.
- Rawls argues against the application of a global difference principle on several grounds, such as that it does not contain a target and a cut-off point, and also that the causes of prosperity are traceable to local factors, such as culture, values, and character.

Some critical responses to Rawls' Law of Peoples

One of the most frequently raised objections is that the background picture that Rawls invokes incorporates outmoded views of relations among states, peoples, and individuals of the world. Rawls presupposes that states are (sufficiently) independent of one another, so that each society can be held largely responsible for the well-being of its citizens. Furthermore, according to Rawls, differences in levels of wealth and prosperity are largely attributable to differences in political culture and the virtuous nature of its citizens.

Critics, especially cosmopolitan critics, point out, however, that Rawls ignores both the extent to which unfavourable conditions may result from factors that are external to the society and also that there are all sorts of morally relevant connections between states—notably, that they are situated in a global economic order that perpetuates the interests of wealthy developed states, with little regard for the interests of those that are poor and developing. We who live in the affluent, developed world cannot thus defensibly insulate ourselves from the misery of the worst off in the world, because we are then complicit in keeping them in a state of poverty.

Pogge has done much to show the nature and extent of these incriminating connections (see, for example, Pogge, 1994, 2001, 2002). According to Pogge, two international institutions are particularly worrisome: the **international borrowing privilege** and the **international resource privilege**. Any group that exercises effective power in a state is recognized, internationally, as the legitimate government of that territory, and the international community is not much concerned with how the group came to power, or with what it does with that power. Oppressive governments may borrow freely on behalf of the country—that is, the international borrowing privilege—or dispose of its natural resources—that is, the international resource privilege—and these actions are legally recognized internationally. These two privileges have enormous implications for the prosperity of poor countries, because they provide incentives for coup attempts, often influence the sorts of people that are motivated to seek power, facilitate oppressive governments being able to stay in power, and, should more democratic governments get to be in power, leave them saddled with the debts incurred by their oppressive predecessors, thus significantly draining the country of resources needed to firm up fledgling democracies. All of this is disastrous for many poor countries.

 KEY CONCEPTS

The international borrowing privilege and the international resource privilege

- The international borrowing privilege refers to the ability of governments to borrow amounts of money on behalf of the country and the obligation of the country to repay the debts.
- The international resource privilege refers to the ability of governments to dispose of a country's natural resources in a way that is legally recognized internationally.

Because foreigners benefit so greatly from the international resource privilege, they have an incentive to refrain from challenging the situation (or worse, an incentive to support or finance oppressive governments). For these sorts of reasons, the current world order largely reflects the interests of wealthy and powerful states. Local governments have little incentive to attend to the needs of the poor, because their being able to continue in power depends more on the local elite, foreign governments, and corporations. We, in affluent developed countries, have a responsibility to stop imposing this unjust global order and to mitigate the harms that we have already inflicted on the world's most vulnerable people. As an initial proposal for us to begin to make some progress in the right direction, Pogge suggests that we impose a global resource tax of roughly one per cent to fund improvements to the lives of the worst off in developing societies.

 KEY THINKERS

Thomas Pogge (1953–)

Pogge is one of the most influential contemporary theorists to have developed a cosmopolitan account of our global responsibilities. In *World Poverty and Human Rights* (2002), Pogge asserts that people in high-income economies should be more concerned with eradicating global poverty than they are at present. Pogge stresses the increasing importance of global rules and social institutions, the design of which greatly affects the lives of people around the globe. He argues that, by imposing unjust global institutional arrangements—which foreseeably and avoidably perpetuate severe poverty and diseases in the less developed regions—today's affluent countries and their citizens are massively violating the human rights of the global poor.

Critics point out, then, that Rawls ignores the extent to which societies suffering unfavourable conditions frequently result from global factors or, at any rate, from factors that are external to that society, and that national policies are often shaped, or even decided by, international factors. They also argue that the boundedness and separateness of political communities is difficult to sustain in today's world, due to phenomena such as globalization and **integration** (Hurrell, 2001). Rawls assumes that we can talk coherently of bounded political communities that can constitute self-sufficient schemes of political cooperation—but critics argue that this is an untenable assumption. Some authors concentrate on showing that we actually have a system of global cooperation between societies and how this would give rise to obligations to the worst off (Hinsch, 2001). Others believe that it is insulting to characterize the relations between states of the world as cooperative, because, in reality, the relationship is rather one of domination and **coercion** (Forst, 2001 and Box 9.4).

Several critics argue that the basic global structure is a scheme of coercive institutions that importantly affects individuals' life prospects. Many cosmopolitan critics urge that it should be transformed so that it becomes a fair scheme of cooperation among all citizens of the world.

One commonly voiced complaint is that the notion of a people is not sufficiently clear or important to do the work that Rawls thinks it can do (Pogge, 1994; Kuper, 2000). Rawls often takes the boundaries of states to mark off distinct peoples, and so his view runs into difficulties. If we take a people to be constituted by commonalities such as shared language, culture, history, or ethnicity, then the official state borders and peoples do not coincide well. National territories are not typically comprised of a single people, nor is it clear that each individual belongs to one, and only one, people.

Furthermore, several critics charge that Rawls' reasons for excluding more socio-economic equality are unconvincing. As Pogge (1994) notes, Rawls assumes that representatives of peoples are interested in the justice of domestic institutions and care nothing about the well-being of members beyond what is essential for just domestic institutions.

BOX 9.4 FORST ON GLOBAL DOMINATION

[I]n the contemporary world the degree of globalized interdependence has reached a point where it is impossible not to speak of this context as one of justice: in addition to a global context of trade, there is now also a global context of production and of labor, and important actors in those spheres are to be characterized as 'transnational' (especially large companies); there is a global ecological context with all the problems of scarcity of resources, pollution, and so on; there is a global context of institutions from the United Nations to the International Monetary Fund (IMF) as well as of nongovernmental institutions (Greenpeace and Amnesty International, for example); there is a global context of legal treaties and obligations, of technological interdependence (just think of the consequences of an aggressive virus emerging in the World Wide Web), of military co-operations as well as conflicts, of migration within and across continents; and there is, of course, an ever-growing global context of cultural production, consumption, and communication.

But in order to come to a realistic global perspective when thinking about transnational justice, one must take a closer, critical look at these phenomena. For once one takes the history and concrete character of these multiple relations into account, it is a euphemism to refer to them as 'cooperation' or 'interdependence' without further qualification, since such terms imply relations of reciprocity that are obviously absent. Rather, what emerges is a complex system of one-sided and largely coerced cooperation and dependency rather than interdependence. In other words, one sees a context of force and domination.

(Forst, 2001: 165–6)

But why assume this? It is more plausible to assume that each delegate is interested not only in just domestic institutions, but also, all else being equal, in having '*a higher rather than a lower average standard of living*' (Pogge, 1994: 208). Even if this interest were only slight, the representatives would be inclined to adopt, at the very least, something like Pogge's global resource tax proposal. If delegates also know that great international inequality can negatively affect the institutions of domestic justice in poor countries, however, representatives would have at least a '*tie-breaking reason to favour a more egalitarian law of peoples over Rawls's*' (Pogge, 1994: 214). Critics also note substantial tension in the reasoning that Rawls offers for our interest in socio-economic equality at the domestic level and our apparent disinterest in this at the international level, claiming that the reasons for our interest in equality at the domestic level apply, as well, to the global.

Another common observation is that Rawls provides very little argument for why decent societies would endorse the set of human rights that he thinks would become part of the central Eight Principles defining the Law of Peoples. Pogge claims that he can see no reason '*historical or philosophical*', for believing that decent societies '*would incorporate these human rights into their favoured law of peoples*' (1994: 214–15). Liberal societies, by contrast, would want to add more to the list of human rights—for example, freedom of speech, democratic political rights, and equal liberty of conscience. In neither the case of decent peoples nor that of liberal ones would the precise list that Rawls offers be chosen and, moreover, it is noted that the attempt to find such a politically neutral Law of Peoples acceptable to both is not promising (Pogge, 1994: 215).

Rawls argues for a respectful relationship between states, as representatives of peoples. Indeed, he argues that liberal democratic regimes have an obligation to deal with illiberal decent regimes as equals and not to endeavour to impose their values on them. Some might think that Rawls' views appropriately acknowledge the importance of our cultural or national affiliations. Andrew Kuper (2000) argues that Rawls may take cultural pluralism seriously, but that he does this at the expense of taking seriously the reasonable pluralism of *individual persons*. Decent societies may well contain individuals who hold liberal ideas; Rawls' account incorporates the wrong kind of toleration for such societies at the expense of liberal values. Rawls' view is not sufficiently sensitive to the individuals within states. Indeed, it would seem that Rawls, in defending non-liberal states as he has, would be forced to defend the rights of states to impose inegalitarian policies on their citizens, even if a majority of the citizens were vigorously against such policies (Blake, 2005: 23).

Rawls gets into this kind of bind, according to some critics, because of a mistaken view about what tolerance demands. There is also a debate about what the appropriate unit of toleration should be: legitimate differences among individuals or among peoples. ➡ **See Chapter 3**. Liberalism does, in certain cases, require commitment to tolerance of views that are not liberal—but critics argue that the appropriate object of toleration should be legitimate differences among individual persons, not peoples, because this ensures better tolerance of legitimate differences where they matter most.

Rawls aims at a realistic utopia, but critics charge that the result is neither sufficiently realistic nor utopian (Kuper, 2000: 653). First, you might think that he has not taken account of all of the relevant realities: for example, of interdependence or domination in the global arena. To the extent that he has not captured all of the salient realities, his Law of Peoples is not as workable and likely to sustain ongoing cooperative political arrangements and relations between peoples. Furthermore, the view is not very utopian in that the ideals used are too tame to constitute much of an advance over the status quo. In his bow to **realism**, Rawls has tried to ensure that the Law of Peoples results in stability; yet according to critics, the Law of Peoples that he endorses might be unstable, because it allows

---

☆ KEY POINTS

- One of the most common objections to Rawls' Law of Peoples is that he incorporates outdated views of relations among states, peoples, and individuals.

- Cosmopolitans, such as Thomas Pogge, highlight some of the moral connections that we have to people in developing countries. Pogge argues that our failure to reform key aspects of the international order, such as the international resource privilege and the international borrowing privilege, implicates us in the misery of those suffering from poverty in developing countries. We, in affluent developed countries, must also make amends for the harm already inflicted, by implementing a global resource tax.

- Critics suggest that the notion of a people is not sufficiently clear or morally important to play the kind of role that Rawls assigns it in an account of global justice.

- Critics question whether the arguments for the Eight Principles are persuasive, especially those concerning limited assistance, the very short basic human rights list, and the omission of democratic rights.

- Critics argue that Rawls has not offered a realistic utopia, in that his account fails to be sufficiently realistic or utopian.

tolerance of unjust regimes. Rawls' focus on getting agreement seems to lead him to tailor steps in his argument to produce a result that enjoys wide agreement. Indeed, according to Darrel Moellendorf (2002: 15), Rawls '*sacrifices full justice for wider agreement*'.

Other critics charge that Rawls' failure to include democratic rights is quite mistaken. Amartya Sen (1999: 147–8, 154–5), for example, provides extensive evidence to support the claim that non-democratic regimes have severely adverse consequences for the well-being and human rights of those over whom they rule. Sen also argues that respect for human rights and ideas of **democracy** are not simply Western values, but rather, that substantial elements of these ideas can be found in all major cultures, religions, and traditions.

Some grounds for scepticism about global justice: authority in the global domain and global governance

There are some who are more sceptical of the idea of global justice, at least given our current circumstances. Grounds for such scepticism include the fact that since there is no way in which to enforce obligations of justice at the global level, there can be no such obligations (Nagel, 2005). Another concern revolves around fears that often accompany undesirable results, which can ensue when there is a concentration of power (Kukathas, 2006). An assumption is often made that global justice must entail a world state, and we have reason to fear the potential for world government to lead to oppressive consequences. Many resist this assumption, and differentiate between global government and global governance. Although we may need some ways in which to coordinate management of our transnational affairs, this need not amount to world government.

Global governance refers to how we manage interests affecting residents of more than one state in the absence of a world government or state with a legitimate monopoly on the use of force (or with the ability to enforce laws or rules with legitimate **authority**). Although the United Nations Security Council has some authority to impose peace, its sphere of activity is limited and its legitimacy is often questioned (because decisions are made by a very small number of nations, rather than giving all nations an equal vote, for example). Moreover, theorists of global governance attend to a multiplicity of our interests besides securing peace. Those who write about global governance are often concerned with interests in areas such as the economy, trade, the environment, or health. Even though one particular body may not currently have legitimate authority to enforce rules, there may be several mechanisms for encouraging compliance and accountability (such as those concerning consumer choices in the market, citizens' decisions, the activities of non-governmental organizations (NGOs), professional codes of conduct, and self-regulation of industries).

There are two main kinds of argument that can be marshalled to show why global governance is desirable:

- that global governance is necessary, in practice, to deal effectively with our global problems; and
- that global governance is required by considerations of justice.

The two sets are hard to separate sometimes, because they often rely on each other.

1. Many pressing problems have global reach

Various significant collective problems have global reach or implications. Collectively, we face threats to well-being and security on a variety of fronts. One obvious case is that of environmental concerns. Some of our decisions, actions, and interactions create conditions that affect us all. Chlorofluorocarbon (CFC) use in a particular country can destroy the ozone layer, which means that our shield from harmful radiation is ruptured and rendered ineffective, which can significantly affect people who live in an entirely different part of the world from that in which those chemicals are released. An AIDS, SARS, or avian flu epidemic in one country can easily spread to others. Someone who has access to weapons of mass destruction in one region can threaten the security of millions in another region. And an economic setback in one country can easily spread to others, causing a global crisis. Global problems require global cooperation for effective solution.

2. Interdependence

As just noted, interdependencies of various kinds exist. We are internationally interdependent in several areas: for example, in security, health, trade, travel, and communication. One notable area of interdependence is economic—especially under globalization. This global economic interdependence produces significant benefits, such as a higher rate of economic growth and greater efficiency in production. However, participation in the world economy is by no means on equal terms. Some participants have vastly more power than others, depending on a variety of factors, such as the range of products available for export and the perceived value of those exports. A notable example here is the way in which oil-producing countries enjoy significant power in the world economy.

3. Benefiting from injustice

As we have already seen in the previous section, some argue that we are situated in a global economic order that perpetuates the interests of wealthy, developed states, with very little regard for the interests of those that are poor and developing (see Box 9.5). By participating in a global economic order that is governed by unfavourable terms for the worst off, we are complicit in keeping those who live in desperate poverty from moving out of this condition. If we make no reasonable efforts at institutional reform, benefiting from unjust institutional schemes implicates us in them. According to Pogge, everyone has duties to everyone else not to cooperate in imposing an unjust institutional scheme on others. Our responsibilities must keep track with the fact that we are now all part of one

> ### BOX 9.5 YOUNG ON EXPLOITATION
>
> Some scholars argue that the current wealth of Europe and North America compared to socie-ties of Africa, Latin America, and South Asia is due in part to the persistence of colonial relations between North and South. The economies of the South depend on capital investment controlled from the North and most of whose profits return to Northern-held corporations. Their workers are often too poorly paid by multinationals or their local contractors to feed their families, and farmers and miners of the South obtain unfavorable prices on a global resource market.
>
> Such deprivation has forced many economies and governments of the southern hemisphere into severe debt to Northern banks and international finance agencies. This indebtedness restricts the effective sovereignty of many Southern states, because powerful financial institutions outside them exercise effective control over their internal economic policies. The standard of living and well-being of many people within their jurisdictions declines because of structural adjustment policies outsid-ers press them to adopt for the sake of foreign investor confidence or international financial stability.
>
> (Young, 2000: 248)

global institutional scheme. We cannot insulate ourselves from moral culpability for the practices that we support and the institutions in which we participate.

But rather than simply benefiting from unjust institutional *schemes*, some argue that we benefit (or have benefited) more directly from historical or current exploitation.

4. Associational relations

Some view duties of justice as generated by our associational relations and so argue for global duties of justice in this way. A good representative argument is that of Darrel Moe-llendorf (2002). His view is that associational relations generate duties of justice—in particular, our economic associations do this. Duties of justice are conventional: they do not arise from the nature of personhood or in virtue of what each person owes all oth-ers. Rather, '*duties of justice arise between persons when activities such as politics or com-merce bring persons into association*' (Moellendorf, 2002: 32). People can be in association whether or not they intend this association, and this is especially so in the case of economic association. Moellendorf believes that we are now in a situation of owing global duties of justice, because of the global nature of economic association.

But although there is much that is certainly plausible about this kind of argument, it is also vulnerable to criticism such as: why think that the mere fact of interaction should generate duties (Blake, 2005)? Perhaps it is not mere economic association that generates the necessary obligations, but a conjunction of facts: for example, the scope of economic association, that it is no longer voluntary, and that it is sometimes heavily exploitative.

5. What all humans are owed as humans

In contrast to the view that associational relations generate duties of justice, others argue that our duties of justice stem from the nature of personhood, or humanity—or, at any rate, apply to all human beings, irrespective of our associational relations to them. All humans are owed certain kinds of treatment simply in virtue of their being human beings, and the basic threshold of adequate treatment includes duties of justice. A common cosmopolitan way in which to launch the argument proceeds from the observation that vast differences in wealth, power, distribution of natural resources, etc. mean that there are huge asymmetries in the prospects that people have for decent lives and in what those lives consist. The society into which you happen to be born—which is arbitrary from a moral point of view—can be a major factor in the sort of life chances that you are likely to enjoy, and the life expectancy, job, income, and level of unemployment, etc. that you can anticipate. According to this kind of argument, we should care about what all humans are owed as humans, and so we cannot be unmoved by such considerations. ▣ **See Chapter 8**.

The human rights approach captures the key ideas reasonably well here, although it is not necessary to appeal to human rights to make this kind of argument.

6. Concerns about power, and its effects on freedom and democracy

Differences in levels of power between states mean that there are significant differences in prospects for domination among people in the world. Power differences also entail significant differences for authentic democracy.

7. Ensuring that burdens are more evenly shared

Without proper global governance, some can perform morally heinous actions with impunity: for example, multinationals that are neither fully accountable to home or host country governments, and which refuse to take appropriate responsibility for their actions (for example, Union Carbide's actions in Bhopal or Nestlé's marketing of infant feeding formula in less-developed countries). Without a concerted effort to create a universal system of norms with reasonable enforcement, some may find it rational not to pay the costs associated with a more level playing field. Moreover, because there is already something that approximates a system of global governance, surely we should ensure that it is a fair one, in which the benefits—and especially burdens—of cooperation and interdependence are fairly shared? The concern is a more general one, as I discuss next.

 KEY TEXTS

Held, *Democracy and the Global Order* (1995)

Held argues that nation states are embedded in complex interdependence and power relations, making them no longer always capable of guaranteeing democracy, autonomy, or, sometimes, even the basic well-being of citizens. Held reconstructs an account of democracy, whereby the goal of international institutions and organizations should be to oversee democratic progress. He also discusses various mechanisms that could help us to approximate the ideal of democracy more closely: for example, making greater use of referenda and allocating public funding for deliberative bodies, such as a second chamber of the United Nations, only for democratic nations in which representatives would be elected and accountable directly to democratic peoples.

8. We already have a system of global governance

The significant amount of interdependence that exists has already led to the development of a global regulative structure that governs the world economy and the system of trade. Besides these formal regulations, a variety of informal practices and expectations, built up through repeated transactions, order our interactions at the global level. Because these shared practices, rules, and institutions already exist, we can defensibly investigate whether the terms that govern these (and their consequences) are fair ones. According to this line of argument, we already have a system of global governance, so why not ensure that it is fair?

Many argue that although there is an effective system of governance in place to promote trade and investment worldwide, this governance system is quite contrary to democracy and the interests of billions of people whose lives it influences. We need to ensure that our de facto system of global governance better serves these important interests. This would involve, for example, making the system of governance that regulates trade and investment more inclusive, accountable, and democratic, but it should also include the setting up (or reform) of alternative governance structures to complement this emphasis on economic prosperity.

What models are there for systems of global governance that better realize these desiderata? Those developing the project called 'cosmopolitan democracy' or 'global social democracy' have much to say on this topic.

☆ **KEY POINTS**

- A prominent kind of scepticism about global justice concerns legitimate authority in the global domain.

- Global governance refers to the management of interests affecting residents of more than one state, in the absence of a single body that has legitimate authority to enforce rules.

- Arguments for the desirability of global governance include that many pressing problems have global scope and our fates are interdependent in many domains. Moreover, because we already have a de facto system of global governance, we ought to ensure that it is fairer than it currently is. We have duties to ensure a fairer system of global governance (it is variously argued), given our associations with others in the global economic order, the benefits we derive from it, what all humans are owed as humans, concerns about power, and its effects on freedom and democracy, ensuring that burdens are more evenly shared, and the fact that our current system of global governance is unfair.

Conclusion

What would a globally just world look like? Would it consist of self-governing autonomous peoples who respect each others' rights to introduce laws of their choosing, even if they violate key liberal ideas, such as freedom from discrimination in holding political office, as

Rawls' Law of Peoples allows? Does Rawls' limited duty of assistance—that is, ensuring the essentials of political autonomy, even though people may still be quite poor—adequately capture the extent of what we owe one another? Alternatively, would a globally just world have a more cosmopolitan character and possibly include redistribution according to a global difference principle, such that inequalities in socio-economic goods would be justified only when they serve to improve the position of the world's worst off? Might global justice require a commitment to global equality of opportunity or a global resource tax, as some of Rawls' critics maintain?

As we have seen, there is a vigorous debate on such questions between Rawls and his critics. A key difference between the parties is whether the unit of equality should be peoples or individuals. For Rawls, we must promote equality among peoples; cosmopolitans believe each individual person deserves a certain kind of equal treatment and respect that Rawls' account seems to ignore. Another main point of difference revolves around different views about the relations among states, peoples, and individuals, and different views concerning the causes of prosperity—whether they are ultimately traceable to local or global factors. Rawls hopes to have presented a realistic utopia, but his critics argue that he has not succeeded, in that his account is neither sufficiently realistic nor utopian.

Whatever vision of global justice you endorse, the extent of global poverty must constitute one of the central obstacles to realizing global justice in the world today. The case study will suggest important reforms to current practices that could considerably alleviate one of the most important stumbling blocks to a globally just world, such that we can better enable the poor in developing countries to help themselves better.

Although some are sceptical about the concept of, or prospects for, global justice, there is at least a practical need to ensure that we have global governance arrangements in place to deal with a variety of common problems. Many pressing problems have global scope and our fates are interdependent in many domains. We have duties to ensure a fairer system of global governance (it is variously argued), given our associations with others in the global economic order, the benefits we derive from it, what all humans are owed as humans, concerns about power, and its effects on freedom and democracy, and ensuring that burdens are more evenly shared. Moreover, because we already have a de facto system of global governance, we ought to ensure that it is fairer than it currently is. Again, the case study will suggest ways in which reforms to our current global accounting, taxation, and disclosure practices might easily be introduced, and how such reforms would help to close the gap between theory and practice in realizing global justice.

CASE STUDY

Funding to address global poverty

Global poverty continues to be a massive issue. The latest World Bank statistics estimate that about 25% of the world's population subsists below the international poverty line.[1] Those living in this condition have lives that are characterized by severe deprivation, as evidenced by their being unable to meet their basic needs—because, for example, they lack access to safe drinking water, basic sanitation, adequate shelter, or are severely undernourished. Half of the population of the world—nearly 3 billion people—live on less than US$2 per day. As Kofi Annan, ex-UN Secretary General, said (2000): '[Y]et even this statistic fails to capture the humiliation, powerlessness and brutal hardship that is the daily lot of the world's poor.'

Current global poverty is one of the most pressing obstacles to realizing global justice. There are several ways in which we can assist those in poor countries to help themselves better. Small reforms to international practices can better promote a culture of more accountability and responsiveness to the needs of those suffering from such severe poverty. In this case study, I show relatively simple ways in which we can promote the interests of the world's worst off by simple reforms to some of our current practices, such as those governing the sale of resources and those governing accounting practices in the world today. We first discuss our international double standards in the sale of resources and why we should aim for consistency.

International double standards: why we should aim for consistency

Foreign aid, although desirable, is by no means always necessary to finance improvements for the worst off. In many cases, the revenue that would be derived simply from resource sales, if it were actually to be received and properly spent, would be more than enough to finance the necessary provisions for helping people to meet their needs (*New Zealand Herald*, 2002). This is especially clear if we look at the case of oil and the crippling corruption that sometimes surrounds its sale.

Consider how, for example, US$1.4bn in oil revenue disappeared in Angola in 2001—an amount equal to about a third of state revenue. Because the international oil companies refuse to disclose how much money they paid for oil in Angola, it is impossible for Angolans to monitor where money paid for oil actually went. Natural resources should be held in trust by the state for the benefit of (at least) all citizens of a country. Citizens, thus, should be entitled to information concerning the sale of their resources. Moreover, **recognition** of ownership of these resources is acknowledged in the law of developing countries. For example, Angolan law establishes that all underground or continental shelf liquid and gaseous deposits of hydrocarbons within the national territory are the property of the Angolan people. If they do so belong, those people are entitled to information about how their resources are being managed. Such information helps citizens to keep governments accountable for the sale of their resources and the management of revenues that are thereby generated. This information is standardly disclosed in the developed world and the extension to the developing world is long overdue. A promising way in which to prevent such corruption is to ensure that oil payments become more transparent. This is standard practice in the developed world, for example when oil companies operate in Europe's North Sea or the Gulf of Mexico.

This problem is very serious. For example, in Angola, oil revenue makes up about 90% of the state budget. It is estimated that, during the last five years, about a third of the entire state budget has disappeared. The United Nations has been relied on to assist with the shortfall. A similar picture emerges in many other developing countries—notably, Nigeria and Equatorial Guinea. Not only does this theft halt the progress of development, but also the connection between corruption and restrictions on political and civil rights is well established (McFerson, 2009).

Regulation is clearly needed. Relying on voluntary disclosure tends to punish the more scrupulous and risks their business being transferred to less scrupulous operators. Indeed, when BP announced that it intended to publish what it had paid for oil, it was threatened with termination of its contract. Required payment disclosure is the only fair option, because it levels the playing field for all and eliminates the current international double standard between required levels of transparency in the developed and developing worlds. Companies can be made to publish what they pay by various mechanisms: for example, it might easily be made a condition for the listing of oil companies on major stock exchanges (such as those of London or New York) that they adopt the transparency practice.

The lessons that we learn from the case of oil seem quite generalizable. More transparency in payments and in the flow of money to less developed countries, more generally, would eliminate the ease with which corruption can flourish and would ensure that payments intended to benefit the citizens of a country actually do so.

Tax avoidance, tax havens, and transfer pricing: how they exacerbate global poverty

There are many ways in which reforms to our tax laws can better assist with the goal of alleviating global poverty. By understanding some of the current tax practices that are widely used in the world today, we can see that many of the beneficiaries of globalization are shirking their responsibilities, both to their home societies and to the societies in which they do business, through avoiding paying taxes. Failure to pay taxes has a dramatic effect on all countries, but especially on developing ones. States are not usually able to collect all of the taxes that they are owed—especially from powerful multinational corporations—which results in substantial losses in revenues. Receiving more of the taxes that poor developing countries are owed will allow these countries enormous sources of funds with which they could do much to address some of the structural causes of local poverty, which might include having more resources for education, job training, health care, infrastructural development, capital investment, and so on. In this way, we would be better enabling those in poor countries to help themselves.

It seems to be quite easy for at least some people to avoid paying taxes in today's world. It is estimated, for example, that at least $255bn in tax revenue is lost worldwide, each year, on account of tax havens (Addison, 2009). It is further estimated that *about half of all world trade* passes through tax haven **jurisdictions**, as profits are shifted to places where tax can be avoided.[2] The policy of transfer pricing and other complex financial structures—which I will discuss shortly—reduce transparency, thus facilitating tax evasion. It is estimated that, through such schemes, developing countries lose revenue that is greater than the annual flow of aid (Oxfam, 2000: 3). Locating just 0.5% of the holdings in tax havens could be enough to finance fully the United Nations' Development Goals for 2015, thereby halving global poverty (Christian Aid, 2005: 11).

Tax evasion threatens both development and democracy, especially in developing countries. Because large corporations and wealthy individuals are effectively avoiding taxation, the tax burden is frequently shifted onto ordinary citizens and smaller businesses. Governments often thereby collect much-reduced sums that are insufficient to achieve minimal goals of social justice, such as providing decent public goods and services. Cuts in social spending are inevitable and these cuts can have a dramatic effect on other goals, such as developing and maintaining robust democracies. Moreover, because most developing countries are in competition in trying to attract foreign capital, offering tax breaks or tax havens may seem to provide an attractive course. But as states compete to offer tax **exemptions** to capital, the number of tax havens increases, thereby making all developing countries worse off. Corporations pay much-reduced, if any, taxes, and ordinary citizens have to bear more of the cost of financing the social and public goods necessary for sustaining well-functioning communities.

The use of tax havens is an important channel for tax evasion and constitutes a major reason why many corporations pay very little, or even no, income tax. Economic activity is often declared as occurring in places within which taxes are low or non-existent, rather than accurately recorded as occurring where it actually took place.

Transfer pricing is a recognized accounting term for sales and purchases that occur within the same company or group of companies. Because these transactions occur within the company, there is wide scope to trade at arbitrary prices, instead of at market-attuned ones. If a multinational company has a factory in one country, but sells its products to foreign subsidiaries in other countries, it can artificially construct the 'buy and sell' prices to record a loss, because the trade occurs within the same company. A multinational company, for example, may have a factory in country F. The factory produces products—say, microwave ovens—for US$50 and sells these to a subsidiary in the same group that is based in country T, which is a tax haven. The company's accountants might define the price of the transfer as the cost of production: in this case, US$50. Then, the subsidiary in T sells the product to a foreign subsidiary in country S for US$200. If the price of the good to consumers in country S is US$150, the good has then been sold at a loss of US$50, technically. Because the cost of the good from the tax-haven country, S, is US$200 and the sale price is US$150, a net loss of US$50 may be recorded in country S—a loss that can be offset against other taxes to be paid (in country S). Despite a real profit of US$100 (US$150–US$50—that is, the actual sales price less the actual cost of production), the company ends up declaring a net tax loss. These accounting schemes, and variations on these general themes, are extremely widespread and currently perfectly legal. About 60% of all world trade occurs within multinational corporations, with about 50% passing through tax havens (Sikka, 2003: 11). If such corporations can manipulate their accounts sufficiently, they may even qualify for government assistance. Several of the US corporations to receive bailout money, including General Motors, operated subsidiaries in tax haven jurisdictions (Larudee, 2009).

The Tax Justice Network calls for the initiation of a democratic global forum, comprising representatives from citizen groups and governments across the world, which should engage in widespread debate on these issues and the possibility of implementing policies such as the following:

1. We should develop systems of unitary taxation for multinationals to put a stop to the entirely false shifting of profits to countries with low or no taxes.

2. States should cooperate with each other to reduce the destructive effects of tax competition between themselves.

3. They should consider the possibility of '*establishing regional and global tax authorities that can represent the interests of citizens*'.[3]

The events of 9/11 and the global economic crisis have led to a greater appreciation of the interconnected nature of the global economy. As a result, there is now considerable international interest in phasing out tax havens. Loopholes in international taxation greatly assisted in financing terrorist organizations. In light of this, there is substantial support for setting international standards for transparency in accounting and for better monitoring of all flows of money.

Global taxes: some possibilities

As we have seen, Thomas Pogge suggested that we introduce a global tax to begin to make amends for the unjust global order that we have been imposing on the poor in developing countries. So what prospects are there for introducing global taxes in the world today?

In fact, we do already have some global taxes—for example, on deep seabed mining, which were incorporated in the UN Law of the Sea Convention in the 1980s. Furthermore, recommendations for various global taxes have a fairly long history and there have been a number of proposals for such. There has been much research on these various taxes, including on how they could be fairly implemented and their predicted effects, and several governments—such as those of France, the Netherlands, Brazil, and Austria—have given their support to the idea for some time now. In general, much support for these taxes has been expressed, but powerful interest groups in many rich countries have sometimes reacted negatively towards these ideas. Recently, however, the global economic crisis has exposed the instabilities of the world's financial system and the desirability of regulation. This provides a crucial opportunity for advocates of such taxes.

Two taxes, in particular, have gained attention:

- a tax on the carbon content of commercial fuels—commonly referred to as a 'carbon tax';
- a currency transaction tax—often referred to as a '**Tobin tax**', after James Tobin, who first floated the idea in the 1970s.

It is estimated that well over half of the US$4tn in currency transactions that occur every day are speculative and, as such, are potentially destabilizing to local economies. Local currencies can devalue rapidly, causing major financial crises, such as those that occurred in East Asia in 1997–98, Brazil in 1999, and Argentina in 2001. When the local economy is in the grip of such crises, millions of people can be significantly harmed.

In the 1970s, James Tobin suggested a small tax on currency trades to ward off such eventualities, to '*throw sand in the wheels*' of the markets, slowing down speculation and promoting more long-term investing. The purpose of such a tax would be to reduce destabilizing trades, and the order of magnitude proposed is considerably less than 1% on each trade. The tax would promote more stability and the conditions for development, and, depending on how low it was set, this might be achieved without damaging positive market operations (Paul and Wahlberg, 2002: 6–9).

The USA, Japan, the European Union, Switzerland, Hong Kong, and Singapore account for 90% of currency exchange transactions. It is hard to believe that we could not collect the tax effectively from such countries if the will were mobilized to do so, because the tax could easily be imposed at the point of settlement, and could be levied through computer programs installed in banks and financial institutions. Currency deals already carry an administrative charge in most countries—certainly, in the main currency exchange countries—so the administrative feasibility of such a tax is already plain. A tax of just 0.05% is predicted to raise about US$33bn annually (Schmidt, 2008).

The tax has had considerable support from NGOs and also gained mass backing from politicians and others—including George Soros, who himself made billions through speculative trades. Former British Prime Minister Gordon Brown, German Chancellor Angela Merkel, and French President Nicholas Sarkozy have all endorsed the concept. Public support is also strong, and has recently been boosted by the UK-based 'Robin Hood Tax' campaign.

A number of other proposals have been made, but have not received the same levels of support and attention as the Tobin and carbon taxes, although some seem clearly worthy of much support. These others include an email tax, a tax on world trade, a tax on international arms trade, and aviation fuel taxes.

? QUESTIONS

1. What principles does Rawls argue might regulate the interactions of liberal and non-liberal peoples in the world?

2. What does Rawls mean by 'decent peoples'?

3. What duties of assistance do we have, according to Rawls?

4. Why does Rawls argue against the endorsement of a global difference principle?

5. Do you think Rawls' example of Kazanistan constitutes a decent people who should be admitted to the society of well-ordered peoples?

6. How does Thomas Pogge argue that we, in affluent developed countries, are morally connected to global poverty in developing countries? What actions does he suggest we take?

7. How do critics challenge the Eight Principles that form the basis of Rawls' Law of Peoples?

8. Has Rawls offered a realistic utopia? Why does Rawls think that he has? Why do critics think that he has failed?

9. In what ways do cosmopolitans disagree with Rawls' account of justice at the global level?

10. What is 'global governance'? Why is it desirable?

FURTHER READING

■ Caney, S. (2005) *Justice beyond Borders: A Global Political Theory*, Oxford: Oxford University Press Examines the principles that should govern global politics.

■ Held, D. (2004) *Global Covenant: The Social Democratic Alternative to the Washington Consensus*, Cambridge: Polity Press An accessible overview of ways in which we could improve the global order, such that the result is a more democratic and just basic institutional structure.

■ Jones, C. (1999) *Global Justice: Defending Cosmopolitanism*, Oxford: Oxford University Press Argues for a form of cosmopolitanism involving protecting human rights, while also defending the view from several varieties of critics.

■ Kuper, A. (2004) *Democracy beyond Borders: Justice and Representation in Global Institutions*, Oxford: Oxford University Press Develops an account of representation so that we can ensure that the global order is more responsive to the interests of the world's people.

■ Mandle, J. (2006) *Global Justice*, Cambridge: Polity Press One of the best, most accessible, introductory books on global justice, surveying core concepts and central debates, while also promoting a distinctive view about an account of global justice, inspired by Rawls' Law of Peoples.

■ Martin, R. and Reidy, D. (2006) *Rawls's Law of Peoples: A Realistic Utopia?*, Malden, MA: Blackwell A good, balanced mix of critical and defensive essays on Rawls' Law of Peoples.

■ Moellendorf, D. (2002) *Cosmopolitan Justice*, Boulder, CO: Westview Press One of the best contemporary comprehensive accounts of global justice published to date, covering theoretical and public policy issues.

■ Nussbaum, M. (2006) *Frontiers of Justice: Disability, Nationality, Species Membership*, Cambridge, MA: Belknap Press In which Nussbaum, one of the most influential contemporary cosmopolitans, develops her capabilities approach to issues of justice, including global justice.

■ Pogge, T. (2002) *World Poverty and Human Rights*, Cambridge: Polity Press Contains some of Pogge's most influential writing on our global responsibilities, including more details of the global resources tax that he recommends.

■ Tan, K.-C. (2004) *Justice without Borders: Cosmopolitanism, Nationalism and Patriotism*, Cambridge: Cambridge University Press Argues that cosmopolitan justice can adequately take account of the appropriate nationalistic and patriotic commitments that people have.

 WEB LINKS

● http://www.cceia.org The Carnegie Council is a resource that declares itself '*the voice for ethics in international policy*'.

● http://www.ceedweb.org/iirp The Tobin Tax Initiative provides a range of resources on the Tobin Tax proposal.

● http://www.globalpolicy.org The Global Policy Forum contains a good range of current articles relating to progress towards global justice or suggestions for reform.

● http://www.international-political-theory.net International Political Theory is a resource that includes links to excellent, recently published, scholarly articles on topics in international political theory.

 Visit the Online Resource Centre that accompanies this book to access more learning resources: http://www.oxfordtextbooks.co.uk/orc/mckinnon3e/

 ENDNOTES

[1] See Chen and Ravallion (2008).

[2] French Finance Minister Dominique Strauss-Kahn speaking to the Paris Group of Experts in March 1999, quoted in Christensen and Hampton (1999).

[3] Declaration of the Tax Justice Network, p. 4, available online at http://www.taxjustice.net/cms/ front_content.php?idcat=3

10

War and intervention

HELEN FROWE

Chapter contents

- Introduction
- The just war tradition
- Theoretical approaches to the ethics of war
- *Jus ad bellum*
- *Jus in bello*
- *Jus post bellum*
- Conclusion

Reader's guide

War is one of the most morally difficult, and morally pressing, aspects of human existence. It nearly always involves killing and maiming on a vast scale. It destroys social infrastructure, political systems, and important cultural sites, and can cause catastrophic environmental harm. And yet, war persists: despite the rise of rights talk on the international stage and the spread of democracy across large parts of the world. ➡ **See Chapters 4 and 9**. The last twenty years have seen wars in Kosovo, the Falklands, Iraq, and Afghanistan, as well as ongoing civil conflicts in Chechnya, Sri Lanka, Syria, Libya, and Sierra Leone, to name but a few. In this chapter, we will explore the main theoretical approaches to war, and consider the circumstances under which it is permissible to wage war.

Introduction

Since the 9/11 attacks on the World Trade Center in 2001, and the ensuing wars in Afghanistan and Iraq, there has been a surge of interest in the ethics of war amongst both scholars and the general public. War brings into sharp focus many of the political and philosophical issues covered in this textbook. With the spread of democracy, we have become more responsible for the wars that our leaders fight. As we become increasingly concerned to recognize and fulfil universal human rights, we must determine whether, for example, this extends to waging wars of humanitarian intervention to rescue people from grave suffering abroad. And, as wars are fought against non-state groups, we must think about the role of political authorities in legitimizing violence and our obligations to obey those who might order us to fight.

It is common, in the face of these most pressing debates, to hear people talk of 'just war theory', and to make claims about what that theory permits or prohibits. But this is misleading, for it suggests that there is a single theory of what makes a war just, and that we can judge wars by reference to this single theory. In reality, of course, there are various competing theories about what makes a war just or unjust. And, whilst there is some consensus concerning the kinds of things to which we ought to pay attention when judging the morality of war (such as whether the war is proportionate), there is considerable disagreement about what exactly it *means* for a war to meet these criteria—what it is for a war to be proportionate, or to count as a last resort, and so on. In addition, recent years have seen deeper disagreement emerge between just war scholars concerning the moral foundations of a state's apparent right to employ force to achieve certain ends. These fundamental differences in approach produce markedly different conclusions about central issues in the ethics of war.

 KEY TEXTS

Frowe, *The Ethics of War and Peace: An Introduction* (2011)

Frowe's text offers a critical overview of the most important debates in recent just war theory. It covers the relationship between war and self-defence from collectivist and individualist perspectives, the three main stages of war (*jus ad bellum*, *jus in bello*, and *jus post bellum*) with detailed discussion of just causes for war, the moral status of combatants, and the principle of non-combatant immunity. It includes a chapter on the role of terrorism in contemporary just war theory and the permissibility of using interrogational torture on (suspected) terrorists. It also contains an annotated guide to further reading.

The just war tradition

Historical roots

The just war tradition with which most people are familiar has its roots in Catholic writings, particularly the works of Aquinas and Augustine. Aquinas and Augustine were concerned with how an activity like war could be reconciled with the Church's teachings about the wrongness of killing. Although less extensive than Aquinas's writings, Augustine's claims about just causes for war were particularly influential, holding that wars may be fought for the purposes of defence, correcting wrongs (for example, the re-taking of stolen goods), and punishment.

The **doctrine of double effect (DDE)**—a key part of various aspects of traditional just war theory—originates in Aquinas's work on self-defence. Aquinas argues that one can sometimes permissibly bring about harm as a foreseen side-effect of pursuing a good. In the case of using defensive force, then, the idea is that one does not intend harm to one's attacker (which would be immoral), but intends only to save one's own life, foreseeing that this will involve harm to the attacker. Even though many philosophers are sceptical about the DDE, its role in just war thinking has been significant.

 KEY CONCEPTS

The doctrine of double effect

The doctrine of double effect holds that, whilst it is wrong to aim at harm, it can be permissible to foreseeably cause harm as an unavoidable side-effect of pursuing a proportionate good end. So, when one's action will have multiple effects (for example, the death of an attacker and the saving of one's own life), one must aim only at the morally permissible effect (saving one's life).

The next major developments in just war thinking came with the early scholars of international law, such as Hugo Grotius (2004), Samuel Pufendorf (2005), and Francisco Suarez (1994). Despite its largely religious roots, much of the just war tradition is essentially secular. Much of what we call the 'Laws Of Armed Conflict' (LOAC) is made up of customary law—that is, law established through long practice—although some key elements have been formally codified in treaties such as the 1899 and 1970 Hague Conventions and the 1949 Geneva Conventions and their Additional Protocols. But, as already indicated, given the disagreement amongst just war theorists about how we ought to judge the justness of war, it would be a mistake to take the existing LOAC as the definitive guide to the morality of war. Whilst looking at the law can be a useful starting point for assessing aspects of war, much of the philosophical opinion about war will diverge from those laws.

It is with the development of international law that just war theory begins to develop its distinct branches. *Jus ad bellum* (justice prior to war) sets the conditions under which it is just to declare war. *Jus in bello* (justice during the war) sets the 'rules of engagement', governing the conduct of combatants during a conflict. *Jus post bellum* (justice after war) deals with topics like war reparations and punishment of aggression and had, until recently, received comparatively little attention in the just war literature. But the aftermath of the wars in Iraq and Afghanistan has led to renewed interest in this field: these wars have taught us that what happens after an initial invasion can be just as important for securing the just cause of a war as how the war is fought.

We should notice that, in using the term 'just' to describe some wars, we are not committing ourselves to the claim that such wars are *good*. Most just war theorists, especially those working today, will agree that war is a very bad thing—this is precisely why we spend so much time thinking about how to limit its use. To say that a war is just, then, is to claim that it is morally permissible or required as a necessary means to achieve some important good. Under these circumstances, it can be a good thing that the war is fought, but not even just wars are desirable in themselves.

Alternatives to just war theory

What unifies just war theorists, if not their views about when war is just? Essentially, just war theorists share two beliefs: that wars can, at least in theory, sometimes be just, and that the fighting of war is governed by moral rules.

But not all those who engage in moral theorizing about war share these two beliefs. **Pacifists** reject the idea that the use of force can ever be just, and therefore think that the just war theory project is misguided because we should always eschew violence (even in the face of violence by others). **Realists** comes in various guises, but typically reject the idea that concerns of justice apply to war at all—not because war is always wrong, but because war is a political tool designed to serve the interests of states (or other groups). When one ought to wage war, and how one ought to fight it are not, according to this view, moral questions at all.

Not many people are absolute pacifists, although there has been a rise in the popularity of a position within just war theory known as *contingent pacifism* (Bazargan, 2014). Contingent pacifists believe that the use of force is not inherently wrong, and that there could, in theory, be such a thing as a just war (at both the *ad bellum* and *in bello* levels). But, as a purely contingent matter, the methods of fighting war that are currently available are too crude to allow us to fight justly. We simply do not possess sufficiently precise weapons or sufficiently reliable information to ensure that we only ever strike legitimate targets and inflict only proportionate collateral harm. Since we therefore know in advance that our war will inevitably involve inflicting wrongful harms, war is, in practice, always unjust.

This chapter will focus on just war theory, rather than realist or pacifist approaches to war. As I described earlier, just war theorists disagree about pretty much all aspects of the ethics of war. But they do at least believe that there can be such a thing *as* ethical warfare, and that we should try to understand what such warfare would entail.

⭐ **KEY POINTS**

- Just war theorists believe that war is, at least in theory, sometimes just.
- Just war theory is usually divided into *jus ad bellum*, *jus in bello*, and *jus post bellum*.
- Pacifism and realism offer alternative approaches to the ethics of war.

Theoretical approaches to the ethics of war

Collectivism

Just war theory has, for most of its history, been dominated by a position that I will call the **collectivist** approach to war. This view makes two central claims. The first is that war

KEY TEXTS

Walzer, *Just and Unjust Wars* (1977; 2000)

Just and Unjust Wars is the most developed recent defence of the traditional, collectivist account of just war theory. It makes extensive use of historical examples to illustrate its claims. Walzer's human rights-based account reflects long-held views about the moral independence of *jus ad bellum* and *jus in bello*, the distinction between combatants and non-combatants, and the essentially state-based nature of war. Controversially, Walzer also develops the 'supreme emergency' exception to his otherwise stringent prohibition on the attacking of non-combatants, arguing that it can be permissible to intentionally target non-combatants if doing so is necessary to avert a genuine catastrophe.

is a relationship between collectives—essentially, states—rather than between individuals. The second, related, claim is that we cannot, therefore, judge the morality of war by looking to the morality of ordinary life. This is partly because war is a relationship between collectives, and, according to this view, this relationship gives rise to considerations that cannot be captured by thinking about the individual people who make up those collectives. We see this most clearly at the *ad bellum* level. The kinds of goods that are typically thought to give rise to a just cause for war—say, the protection of a state's territory or its political integrity—seem to be collective goods. But the belief that war cannot be judged by the morality of ordinary life also stems from a view about the nature of war itself. War involves the intentional transgression of some of our most fundamental moral prohibitions. It is about killing and maiming as a means of achieving an end, knowing that both the guilty and the innocent will suffer as we pursue our goal. This concern speaks most obviously to *jus in bello*: to how a war is fought. Since war essentially comprises activities that we ordinarily prohibit, we cannot judge war by our ordinary standards of morality.

 KEY THINKERS

Michael Walzer (1935–)

In 1977, Walzer published *Just and Unjust Wars*, which has come to represent the 'traditional', collectivist account of just war theory in much of the recent literature. In Walzer's view, war is an essentially political activity, not a relationship between persons. He is particularly concerned in his work on the ethics of war to reflect the experiences of soldiers engaged in fighting. His view that it is the common life that is defended in war ties in with his broader Communitarian view of political philosophy. His other books include *Arguing About War* (2004) and *Spheres of Justice* (1983).

International law defines an act of aggression between states as an act that violates, or threatens to violate, the victim state's *sovereignty*. Sovereignty is the label given to a state's political and territorial integrity—that is, its control over its political system and land.

Even though collectivists reject the idea that we should judge war by the moral rules of ordinary life, they have nonetheless made use of what is called *the domestic analogy* as a way of understanding and recognizing instances of aggression:

> Every reference to aggression as the international equivalent of armed robbery or murder, and every comparison of home and country or of personal liberty and political independence, relies upon what is called the *domestic analogy*. Our primary perceptions and judgements of aggression are the products of analogical reasoning. When the analogy is made explicit, as it often is among the lawyers, the world of states takes on the shape of political society the character of which is entirely accessible through such notions and crime and punishment, self-defense, law enforcement, and so on.

(Walzer, 1977: 58)

We can make use of comparisons between the sorts of wrongs that states can commit against one another, such as invading and occupying each other's land, and the sorts of wrongs that individuals inflict on one another, in order to understand when aggression has taken place. And, according to Walzer, what justifies a state's armed response to aggression is its right (and obligation) to defend its citizens' 'common life'.

The common life is the way of living that citizens create between themselves. It refers to communities and cultures—to the bonds between people that arise from their shared values, practices, beliefs, and language. Since the common life depends on the connections *between* individuals, it is an essentially collective good, irreducible to the individuals themselves. Walzer believes that the protection and flourishing of the common life requires freedom from outside interference. This is why sovereignty matters so much—without it, states cannot enable their citizens to enjoy a common life.

So, the rights of states to use force to defend their sovereignty are, ultimately, grounded in the rights of their citizens to enjoy and defend their common life. But this does not mean that we can judge what states may do to defend their sovereignty by thinking about the defensive rights of individual citizens. The domestic analogy might help us to recognize an act of aggression, Walzer says, but when it comes to the *conduct* of war, we lack any domestic activity to which we can helpfully compare war. There is simply nothing in ordinary life that is like fighting a war, and so there is nothing in ordinary life that can tell us the right way to go about it.

The collectivist position has influenced many of the laws of war pertaining to both *jus ad bellum* and *jus in bello*. As we noticed earlier, the kinds of good that are recognized by international law as providing a just cause for war are collective, state-based goods: the defence of political and territorial integrity. And, the *ad bellum* condition of legitimate authority effectively restricts the legal power to declare war to heads of state.

Since they have the legal capacity to declare war, states also enjoy certain *in bello* legal privileges that are not typically afforded to non-state groups. For example, imagine that a state, Alpha, decides to unjustly invade another state, Beta. Under international law, Alpha can order its combatants to attack Beta combatants and, provided that they obey the rules of *jus in bello*, the Alpha combatants will have legal immunity for the harms they inflict. This privilege obtains even though Alpha is fighting an illegal unjust war. The leaders of Alpha may be prosecuted for the crime of aggression, but their combatants are not liable to prosecution for fighting in the aggressive war. They have what Christopher Kutz has described as 'essentially *political* permission to do violence' that is grounded in their membership of the collective—in this case, their state (Kutz, 2005: 173). This permission can, in Kutz's view, make it permissible for them to do things that would normally be impermissible. In serving the collective's will, they act not as individuals but as agents of the collective. In assessing the morality of their actions, therefore, we must treat them not as individuals but as agents of the state.

Individualism

Over the last two decades, the collectivist approach to war has been subjected to sustained and influential criticism, most notably in the writings of Jeff McMahan. McMahan defends a reductive individualist account of the morality of war. It is *reductivist* because it holds that the moral principles that govern both the declaring and fighting of war are the same moral principles that govern the use of force in ordinary life. It is *individualist* because it holds that individuals, not collectives, are the proper focus of moral evaluation in war.

 KEY TEXTS

McMahan, *Killing in War* (2009)

Killing in War offers the first book-length defence of the reductive individualist view of war. McMahan develops an account of moral liability to defensive harm that holds that a person forfeits his or her usual rights against being harmed when that person is morally responsible for an unjust threat of harm, and harming him or her is necessary to avert that threat. He then builds upon this account to defend his claim that unjust combatants are not morally equal to just combatants.

A central tenet of this view is that states, or indeed any groups that engage in political violence, do not enjoy special moral permissions to cause harm simply because they are collectives, or because their violence is political. For a start, we would presumably have to limit the sort of collective that gets to sanction the inflicting of harms—we do not think that the Mafia, or a group of Manchester United fans, or the University Rock Climbing Society should enjoy this kind of power. Christopher Kutz suggests that we might set this limit by restricting the power to groups that are properly organized, with political aims that they have a reasonable prospect of achieving. But McMahan is sceptical:

> The suggestion, then, is that by organizing themselves politically, with internal norms of authority and obedience, individuals can somehow authorize each other to use violence for political reasons, thereby making it permissible for each to do what none would otherwise be permitted to do. This, however, presupposes a form of moral alchemy to which it is difficult to give credence. How can a certain people's establishment of political relations

among themselves confer on them a right to harm or kill others, when the harming or killing would be impermissible in the absence of the relevant relations?

(McMahan, 2007: 52–3)

McMahan's objection, then, is that if individuals are not permitted to pursue a certain goal, they cannot simply, by deciding to form a group, give themselves licence to
pursue that goal. What matters for the permissibility of harming in pursuit of a goal is
not whether the goal is political, but whether it is *just*, and whether its pursuit warrants
inflicting harm on people. Political goals can be deeply immoral—ethnic cleansing, for
example—and the mere fact that some people decide to form a group to pursue such
goals cannot make it permissible to pursue them. If, in contrast, a goal is just, it is its
justness, not its being political or pursued by a particular sort of group, that makes it
permissible to pursue it.

If we reject the idea that groups, including states, have special permission to do violence,
it seems that we can understand the morality of warfare only by thinking about the permissions that individuals have to do violence. The most obvious circumstance in which
individuals are permitted to use force is in defence of themselves and their property, and
other people and their property. The reductive individualist view holds that by analysing these conditions of self-defence and other defence, along with other moral principles
familiar from ordinary life, we are able to capture and explain the moral permissions that
obtain in war.

 KEY THINKERS

Jeff McMahan (1954–)

Over the past twenty years, McMahan has published a substantial body of work undermining
the traditional, collectivist approach to the ethics of war. McMahan defends a reductivist individualist account of war, according to which the moral rules governing war are simply the moral
rules of ordinary life, most obviously the rules of self-defence and other defence. His work has
important implications for, amongst other things, the relationship between *jus ad bellum* and
jus in bello, and the moral status of combatants. Much of his work to date is summarized in his
Killing in War (2009).

☆ **KEY POINTS**

- Just war theory has been historically dominated by the collectivist view that war is a relationship between states, not individuals.
- The domestic analogy holds that, whilst we can use comparisons with ordinary life to recognize aggression, we cannot judge behaviour in war by thinking about the morality of ordinary
life.
- Recent work by individualists challenges this view, arguing that collectives do not enjoy special moral permissions to do violence.

Jus ad bellum

In a conventional just war theory account, whether one can justly declare war is determined by whether one's war meets the following conditions:

- legitimate authority
- just cause
- last resort
- proportionality
- right intention
- public declaration
- reasonable prospect of success.

The conditions are not ranked in terms of importance, since (on a conventional view) one must meet all of them in order to count as justly declaring war. But legitimate authority and just cause have priority in the sense that they must be satisfied before the others can be addressed.

As we have just seen, many just war theorists believe that being a legitimate authority—a head of state, who represents his or her citizens on the international stage, or perhaps a governing body like the US Congress—is a condition not only of declaring a *just* war, but of declaring war *at all*. But this condition has been somewhat undermined in recent years by the rise of non-state military organizations such as Al Qaeda. The rise of **asymmetric wars**—wars between a state and a non-state group or groups—have caused some just war theorists to reject the idea that wars require a legitimate authority, or at least to reject conventional understandings of what counts as a legitimate authority.

The requirement that one have a just cause—a just goal that the war is intended to secure—is much less controversial. Several of the other conditions (proportionality, last resort, reasonable prospect of success) make sense only when one has a just cause to judge them against. The paradigm just causes for war are self-defence or collective defence. Self-defence is the defence of one's own sovereignty against an act of aggression. Collective defence is the defence of an ally with whom one has a mutual defence treaty. Article 51 of the UN Charter protects the rights of nations to self and collective defence.

Remember, though, that 'aggression' includes both an actual violation of one's sovereignty and the *threat* of such a violation. Wars that respond to mere threats to sovereignty are described as *pre-emptive* wars. Such wars count as self-defence and are legal (strictly speaking, all self-defence is pre-emptive, since one cannot defend oneself against a harm that has already been inflicted). Pre-emptive wars are distinguished from *preventive* wars. Although it is hard to draw a clear line between pre-emption and prevention, we might say that pre-emptive wars try to curtail threats before they eventuate in harm, whereas preventive wars try to curtail a state's capacity to do harm even in the absence of any threat. For example, we might destroy a hostile state's nuclear factories even if we do not believe they are currently planning to wage war or are even capable of making nuclear weapons. Here, we do not respond to an existing threat but, rather, try to ensure that they cannot pose a future threat.

Paradigm unjust causes for war include expansion of one's own territory, the imposition of regime change, and ethnic or religious persecution. Those fighting wars for unjust causes are engaged in aggression, and their behaviour can give rise to a just cause for a defensive war on the part of those against whom they are aggressing. Once one has a just cause for war—that is, one is the victim of aggression—one can consider whether a war fought to secure that cause of defeating the aggression would meet the other *ad bellum* conditions. To count as a last resort, one must have reasonably explored feasible, non-violent alternatives to war, such as diplomacy and negotiations, economic sanctions and trade bans. In order to judge whether war is proportionate, one must determine whether securing the just cause is sufficiently important to justify the costs and harms that war is likely to entail. The requirement of a reasonable prospect of success reflects the view that one ought not to fight a war that has very little chance of achieving the just cause, since wars inevitably involve widespread harm to combatants and non-combatants. It is wrong to inflict such harms if one has only a slim prospect of victory. This can mean that a less wealthy nation can be required to appease a nation with a much more powerful military, even if the poorer nation is the victim of aggression and has a just cause.

We can see why this is plausible, even though it involves permitting injustice, by thinking about self-defence. Imagine that an attacker is going to kill you. Your only means of defence is to throw a grenade at him or her (you never go out without your grenade). But, your aim is rather poor. It is likely that the attacker will be able to dodge the grenade, but wherever the grenade lands, the explosion will badly burn a child who is standing nearby. Whilst it might be permissible for you to throw the grenade and burn the child if doing so is very likely to save your life, many people would think that you ought not to throw the grenade if it has only a slim chance of saving your life. You should not risk such serious harm to an innocent person in a likely futile bid to prevent injustice to yourself. The same sort of reasoning explains the success requirement: since wars always involve killing and maiming people—often innocent people—there must be at least a reasonable prospect that the war will achieve its goal in order for the war to be just.

The requirement of right intention holds that one must declare and fight the war for the reasons that genuinely motivate it. It is a slightly odd condition, since it is hard to know how we would judge what really motivates a head of state (and this gets even more difficult if the legitimate authority is made up of a group of people, all of whom might have different motivations for wanting to fight the war). This is probably why international law does not include a right intention condition. But, nonetheless, the condition is not without its appeal. Prior to (and during) the invasion of Iraq in 2003, many people expressed scepticism about the motivations of the Bush and Blair administrations. It was popularly thought that even if the leaders *said* they were fighting to obtain Saddam Hussein's weapons of mass destruction, they were really trying to secure their own countries' access to oil. The criterion of right intention is probably at least partly motivated, then, by thoughts about what leaders owe their citizens and, especially, what they owe the combatants who will be fighting the war. A state should not deceive its armed forces into fighting in a war motivated by illicit ends, even if there exist genuinely just ends that the war could pursue.

Finally, wars need to be publicly declared. One reason for this is that being at war changes the legal status of a state's behaviour in the manner described earlier. Declaring war, therefore, signals that the laws of war now govern one's relationship with the enemy state.

A public declaration also makes possible, at least to some extent, the evacuation of non-combatants from likely target zones. Additionally, it serves as further support for the claim that war is a last resort. Declaring one's intention to wage war gives the enemy a final opportunity to surrender and desist in its aggression.

KEY CONCEPTS

Legitimate authority and asymmetric war

Traditionally, being a legitimate authority has been thought to be a prerequisite, not of fighting a just war, but of fighting a war *at all*. Only those appropriately situated with respect to a state (such as the head of state) have been regarded as capable of declaring war. But this view has been undermined in recent years by the growing importance of non-state military organizations such as Al Qaeda. The prevalence of asymmetric wars—wars between a state and a non-state group or groups—has caused some just war theorists to reject the idea that conflicts must be fought upon legitimate authority in order to count as a war.

Recently, the idea that humanitarian intervention might be a just cause for war has gained considerable popularity (see Box 10.1). Armed humanitarian intervention is the use of force by an external group (usually a state) to protect a group of citizens from harm within their own state, without the consent of their government. Sometimes these are harms being perpetrated against the citizens by their own government, but sometimes the government is simply unable or unwilling to protect the citizens from being harmed by people within the state.

Humanitarian intervention is legally complex. As we have seen, international law places enormous weight on the importance of sovereignty. Defence of sovereignty is the only legally recognized just cause for war. Humanitarian intervention challenges this importance in two ways. First, it suggests that there can be other just causes for war—that the defence of human life can justify war even if their states' sovereignty is not at risk. Second, it implies that the value of sovereignty is not absolute, since humanitarian interventions take place without the consent of the government of the state in which one intervenes. Thus, it looks like such interventions require transgressing the sovereignty of the state in which one intervenes.

However, in recent years, the 'conditional sovereignty' view has gained credence amongst scholars of international law and war. This view holds that statehood is independent of sovereignty. Whether or not a state enjoys sovereignty—rights over its land and political system—is conditional on whether it protects its citizens' basic human rights. States that fail to protect these rights lack sovereignty. This means that when there are widespread human rights abuses taking place in a state and the state's leaders either encourage these abuses or fail to accept assistance to end them, the state lacks sovereignty. Taking this view, then, it is not the case that the sovereignty of a state is justifiably overridden by the need to save lives. Rather, there is no sovereignty that can be violated by a war of humanitarian intervention in such a country.

BOX 10.1 THE KOSOVO INTERVENTION

The political landscape surrounding humanitarian intervention shifted significantly as a result of the Kosovo intervention in 1999. Peace talks aimed at ending the ethnic cleansing of Kosovars by Serbs repeatedly failed. As the violence worsened, large numbers of people began to flee, resulting in widespread displacement and homelessness. But whilst the United Nations Security Council issued resolutions condemning the violence, it did not authorize the use of 'all necessary means'—the crucial wording that sanctions the use of military force. Whilst nations have the independent right to engage in self-defence and collective defence, other uses of force—including force to protect those with whom one has no mutual defence treaty—are subject to UN authorization. Strictly speaking, then, the NATO intervention, which took the form of an aerial bombing campaign between March and June 1999, was illegal under international law. But, helped, no doubt, by its comparatively rapid success in forcing a Serbian withdrawal from Kosovo, many people believed that the intervention was morally justified.

☆   **KEY POINTS**

- The paradigm just causes for war are self-defence and collective defence.

- But wars must meet a range of further conditions—in addition to having a just cause—in order to be just.

- Wars of humanitarian intervention are wars that seek to militarily defend people against abuses perpetrated or permitted by their own state.

- Historically, such wars have been thought to violate a state's sovereignty and constitute illegitimate interference in another state's domestic affairs.

- More recently, scholars have argued that states' sovereignty is conditional on their protecting their citizens' basic human rights. Thus, when humanitarian interventions are necessary, they do not violate sovereignty.

Jus in bello

Three central moral principles underpin the rules of *jus in bello*:

- discrimination (between combatants and non-combatants)
- proportionality
- military necessity.

The requirement to discriminate between combatants and non-combatants holds that whilst combatants are legitimate targets of attack, it is impermissible to intentionally harm non-combatants or civilian infrastructure (the requirement is also known as the principle of non-combatant immunity). This means that certain types of weapons, such as firebombs, are prohibited because they are essentially indiscriminate—once one drops a firebomb, one cannot control its spread.

Unlike non-combatants, combatants are typically thought to have forfeited their usual rights not to be attacked by enemy soldiers, and combatants on all sides of a war therefore enjoy a mutual licence to kill each other. Exactly why and how combatants forfeit their right not to be attacked is the subject of some dispute. Some just theorists argue that, by joining the armed forces, combatants agree to be attacked by the enemy in war. Others hold that since combatants threaten and are threatened, they have rights to kill each other on grounds of self-defence. An important claim of the individualist view, however, is that just combatants do not forfeit their usual rights against attack. We return to this later.

 KEY CONCEPTS

Qualifying as a combatant

The 1949 Geneva Convention holds that for a person to qualify as a combatant, he or she must:

1. be part of a hierarchical group, such that there is a recognizable chain of command
2. wear a distinctive emblem that is visible from a distance
3. bear arms openly
4. obey the rules of *jus in bello* as laid out in the Convention.

The second and third conditions were revised in 1977 to take account of the fact that under some circumstances, it is very dangerous, or otherwise impractical, for a combatant to openly identify him or herself. The new conditions grant a person combatant status provided that he or she bears their arms openly during combat and immediately prior to combat, thereby distinguishing him or herself from the non-combatants.

Non-combatants are thought to retain their usual rights not to be attacked. But this does not mean that non-combatants may not be harmed at all in war. On the contrary: it is predictable and inevitable that non-combatants will be harmed, and, in some conflicts, non-combatant casualties outnumber those of combatants. In order to meet the requirement of discrimination, these harms must be merely foreseen, but not intended. This invokes the kind of double-effect reasoning we discussed earlier. As long as the amount of harm inflicted on non-combatants during an offensive is both necessary and outweighed by the good of securing the military objective, such harming is permitted by the rules of *jus in bello*.

The moral equality of combatants

As we have seen, traditional just war theory holds that combatants may kill and be killed with impunity, provided that those killings adhere to the *in bello* rules. According to this view, it is only political leaders who are responsible for whether the *ad bellum* conditions are met. It would, therefore, be unfair to condemn soldiers simply for fighting in an unjust war, since they have no control over the sort of war in which they are ordered to fight. All that they can control is whether they fight well. On the traditional model, *jus in bello* is morally independent of *jus ad bellum*. A just war can be unjustly fought, and an unjust war can be justly fought. We call this the 'moral equality of combatants thesis'.

The idea that combatants can fight justly, even if their war lacks a just cause, has been the focus of much of the individualist critique of traditional just war theory. Again, it is McMahan who has most powerfully articulated these concerns (McMahan, 2006). It is, he says, deeply implausible to think that a person who is unjustly attacked, and who then uses force in legitimate defence, somehow becomes the moral equal of her attacker. Rather, a person who engages in necessary and proportionate defence against an unjust attacker does not forfeit any of her usual rights not to be harmed. If the attacker kills the victim, he or she therefore violates the victim's right not to be killed (see Box 10.2). The attacker, in contrast, *does* forfeit his or her usual rights against being harmed. If the victim's defence harms the attacker, this does not violate the attacker's rights. There is moral inequality between unjust attackers and their innocent victims. And, according to McMahan, this is no less true when the attackers and victims are combatants. When unjust combatants kill just combatants, they violate the just combatants' rights. But when just combatants kill unjust combatants, they act in self-defence, and do no wrong.

So, this argument rejects the idea that we can separate how combatants fight (*jus in bello*) from whether their country's war is just (*jus ad bellum*). A combatant's moral status, and the moral status of the killings she carries out, depend on whether she is fighting a just or an unjust war. Furthermore, McMahan argues that unjust combatants cannot meet the *in bello* proportionality principle. Recall that this principle governs the inflicting of collateral harms on non-combatants during an offensive. Such harms are justified if they are warranted by the securing of a particular good. But when combatants are fighting on the unjust side of a war, they are not pursuing good ends. They are pursuing *unjust* ends, such as the wrongful expansion of their state's territory. They therefore lack any good ends that can outweigh the collateral harms they cause. This means that all collateral harms that unjust combatants inflict fail the proportionality condition and are impermissible. So, according to McMahan, it is nearly always impossible for unjust combatants to fight well.

BOX 10.2 PRISONERS OF WAR

The Geneva Convention includes rules for the treatment of captured enemy combatants, commonly known as prisoners of war (POWs). Entitlement to POW status is one of the main privileges afforded combatants. This is partly why there is so much contention about whether non-state actors (e.g. members of terrorist groups) are entitled to be treated as combatants, since, if they are, they should also be granted POW rights. These rights include that one must not be punished for fighting, be subjected to dangerous, degrading, or inhumane treatment, be coerced into revealing information, or be forced to contribute to the detaining power's military effort. POWs should be evacuated from dangerous places and kept with their fellow combatants, and their own military should be informed of their capture. Crucially, they must be released once the war is over.

Non-combatant immunity

Although most people believe that it is wrong to intentionally attack non-combatants in war, it is difficult to explain exactly why such attacks are wrong. This is because it is hard to point to a morally significant difference between combatants and non-combatants that will explain why all combatants may be attacked, but no non-combatants may be attacked. We can, of course, point to various non-moral differences between combatants and non-combatants; combatants wear uniforms, for example, whilst non-combatants do not. But to show why the requirement of discrimination has *moral* force, we need a morally relevant difference, and it is not clear that wearing different clothes is the right sort of difference to explain why some people may be intentionally killed whilst others may not (May, 2005).

We might think that it is easy to capture the difference between combatants and non-combatants, because combatants are the ones posing threats, which is surely morally significant. Walzer, for example, says that a combatant 'has allowed himself to be made into a dangerous man' (Walzer, 1977: 145). But this will cover all combatants only on a very broad notion of what it is to pose a threat. Most combatants are not on the front line firing guns. Many threaten indirectly, by providing logistical, technical, and intelligence support. If these combatants are to count as legitimate targets, we must grant that people making only these indirect contributions count as posing a threat. But once we adopt this broad notion of what it is to pose a threat, many non-combatants will count as legitimate targets as well. Non-combatants often make important contributions to their country's military capacity—think of the Land Girls or Women's Timber Corps in World War Two, or of scientists developing nerve gas to be used at Ypres, or engineers building drones to bomb militants in Pakistan.

In light of this sort of difficulty, George Mavrodes has argued that the requirement of discrimination does not, in fact, reflect an important moral feature of non-combatants (Mavrodes, 1975). Rather, it is a useful convention that has been adopted because it is mutually beneficial for all sides of a conflict. Since war is terribly damaging and costly, it is morally important to try to restrict this damage as much as we can, whilst recognizing that people are going to fight wars. The ideal solution would be the 'champion' model of conflict resolution, where each party to a conflict sends out a representative to fight in single combat. If we agree that the winner's country will be taken to have won the conflict, we can resolve the conflict without having to resort to war. But Mavrodes argues that this model is impractical because the losers would not abide by the result: it is likely that they would simply fight the war anyway.

Since the single combat model is out, then, the next best thing is to divide the population into legitimate targets and illegitimate targets, since then the harms of war will, at least, be somewhat restricted. We make the legitimate targets wear uniforms and call them 'combatants', but our doing so is grounded in the moral requirement to limit harm, not some moral fact about non-combatants that warrants giving them special protection.

In Mavrodes's view, therefore, it is morally important not to attack non-combatants, but this is because having a convention of non-combatant immunity limits the overall harms of war. We might wonder, then, what we should do if one party to a conflict violates the convention and begins to attack non-combatants. Something is a convention only if people follow it: once people cease to adhere to it, it is no longer a convention. If the prohibition on attacking non-combatants rests solely on the importance of the convention for limiting the harms of war, it is hard to see what, if anything, could ground the prohibition if the convention is erased. And, indeed, whilst Mavrodes emphasizes that conventions can be reinstated, he is ultimately forced to concede that, in the face of others' persistent deviance from the convention, the moral reasons for adhering to it oneself evaporate.

> ☆ **KEY POINTS**
>
> - The rules of *jus in bello* prohibit targeting non-combatants and civilian infrastructure.
> - Any harm to non-combatants must be a proportionate and necessary side-effect of pursuing a military goal.
> - Reductive individualists reject the claim that just and unjust combatants are morally equal, since just combatants act in legitimate self-defence. This means that, contrary to the traditional view, *jus in bello* is not independent of *jus ad bellum*.
> - It is hard to identify a morally significant difference between combatants and non-combatants that explains their different treatment, leading some writers to suggest that the requirement of discrimination is merely a useful convention.

Jus post bellum

Until very recently, the study of justice after a war—*jus post bellum*—had been somewhat neglected by scholars working on just war theory. What has emerged in the wake of the wars in Iraq and Afghanistan is a much more patchwork set of guidelines than we see *ad bellum* and *in bello*. The field of *jus post bellum* covers reparations, rebuilding, the obligations of victors, reconciliation, and punishment, and these myriad topics do not lend themselves to a neat set of principles.

But *post bellum issues* are connected to both *ad bellum* and *in bello* concerns. A central *post bellum* interest must be that of securing and bolstering the just cause of the war. If, for example, the war was fought to stop an unjust expansion of territory, it is unlikely that merely driving the aggressors back to their own territory will suffice. The victors might also need to limit and partially disarm the aggressor's armed forces in ways that remove their capacity to recommence war. Of course, this assumes that the victors are the just side: one cannot secure the just cause if one has fought a victorious unjust war. Just as McMahan argues that *jus in bello* is robustly connected to *jus ad bellum*, Brian Orend argues that *jus post bellum* cannot be divorced from whether the victors had a just cause (Orend, 2007). Justice after war is only possible, he argues, when the just side are the victors.

We can distinguish between minimalist and maximalist accounts of *jus post bellum* (Bellamy, 2008). Minimalist accounts focus on the rights of victors, seeking to limit the harms that victors might inflict upon a defeated enemy. Historically, victors would demand the unconditional surrender of an enemy and then help themselves to the 'spoils of war', including people and property. Minimalist accounts hold that victors may act only to secure the just cause of the war and punish aggression. Maximalist accounts, in contrast, focus upon the obligations of victors. Brian Orend suggests that those who win the war incur at least some of the following obligations:

1. The peace terms must be proportionate and publicly declared.
2. The rights that were threatened by aggression must be secured.
3. The burdens of the peace terms should not disproportionately burden non-combatants.

4. Those responsible for the aggressive war must be punished.

5. Those responsible for war crimes must be punished.

6. Ensure that the victims of the aggression are fairly compensated.

7. Ensure the political rehabilitation of the aggressive government.

We can now see why Orend thinks that only a just victor can meet the *post bellum* conditions. An unjust aggressor can hardly secure the rights that justified their war, and can hardly punish itself for that war. Nor is an aggressor likely to fairly compensate its victims or rehabilitate itself.

But notice that the obligations Orend lists could be very demanding—especially the obligation of political rehabilitation, which Orend concedes could require the removal and replacement of the existing regime. Regime change is not, itself, a just cause for war, but Orend believes that such change could be required as a means of securing the just cause for war. And, he argues that victors may not leave the citizens of a defeated state without the infrastructure they need to meet their basic human rights. Such reconstruction could be expensive and administratively burdensome, and it is not obvious why the victors of a just war—that is, those who have repelled an aggressor—must take on these burdens.

☆ **KEY POINTS**

- *Jus post bellum* covers a wide range of moral issues that arise in the aftermath of a conflict, including the prosecution of war crimes, the imposing of reparations, and the securing of the just cause.

- Some authors believe that only the victors of a just war can bring about a just peace.

- Historically, the focus of *post bellum* accounts has been to limit the excesses of victors.

- More recent accounts, in contrast, argue that extensive obligations befall the victors, including an obligation to ensure that a defeated state is able to meet its citizens' basic human rights.

Conclusion

Just war theory covers a range of issues in moral and political philosophy, and has had significant influence on the drafting of laws designed to regulate the harms of war. The traditional, collectivist approach to war has dominated the political and legal discourse, as reflected in the state-based goals that are established as just causes for war. Combatants who fight for states are afforded legal protection for the harms they inflict and are entitled to prisoner of war status if they are captured. The importance of group membership—of whether one is a combatant or a non-combatant—also underpins many of the *in bello* rules that govern the fighting of war.

But this collectivist account of war, that affords groups special permissions to engage in political violence, has been substantially undermined by the reductive individualist account. Traditional just war theory was largely developed during periods of history when states consisted of subjects and rulers, and when vast chunks of the population had no political representation, education, or wealth. In modern democratic states, we do not typically believe that the justness of our country's war is a matter only for our leaders, and that ordinary citizens, including those serving in the armed forces, need not concern themselves with whether that war is just. The rise of human rights legislation reflects growing awareness of injustice and suffering that many people believe gives rise to obligations of assistance, irrespective of whether that assistance requires intervening in another state. And, the growing role of non-state groups in international affairs makes it increasingly difficult to judge the ethics of violence on a state-based model. The challenge for just war theorists, now, is to show how the principles that have been traditionally thought to govern warfare can be revised to illuminate the moral features of conflicts in the twenty-first century.

 CASE STUDY

Afghanistan and the 'war on terror'

On the 11th of September 2001, terrorists hijacked four planes in US airspace. Two of the planes were flown into, and destroyed, the twin towers of the World Trade Center in New York City. The third crashed into the Pentagon in Washington DC. The fourth plane missed its target, but was possibly intended for the White House. Thousands of people were killed in the attacks, which were the trigger for the 2001 war in Afghanistan and the broader 'war on terror'.

The US government identified a violent Islamic group, Al Qaeda, as the group responsible for the 9/11 attacks. They demanded the extradition of the group's leader—a Saudi Arabian national, Osama bin Laden—from Afghanistan. Afghanistan's Taliban leadership refused to extradite bin Laden without evidence of his involvement in the attacks; the US, although insisting that they had such evidence, refused to supply it. Declaring that they would recognize no distinction between terrorists and 'those who harbor them', a coalition of the US, the UK, and Australia began the military action 'Operation Enduring Freedom' in Afghanistan on October 7th, 2001.

Just cause?

The 9/11 attacks were certainly the appropriate sort of wrong to trigger a debate about whether war might be a justified response. If a state had perpetrated these attacks, we would consider them a clear violation of US sovereignty—an act of aggression. Military action aimed at ensuring that the responsible state could not, or would not, perpetrate similar attacks in future could meet the criterion of just cause. But things were made more complicated by the fact that Al Qaeda is a non-state organization, and such organizations are not usually thought to be capable of engaging in aggression because aggression is a crime between states. This is why the assertion that those who harboured the perpetrators would be treated as if they, themselves, were the perpetrators, is so important—because it connects the Afghan state to the attacks.

It is not implausible to think that states giving shelter to people carrying out these kinds of attacks may be treated as accomplices to those attacks. What many people disagree about is whether Al Qaeda, and specifically bin Laden, was in fact responsible for the 9/11 attacks, and whether the US and the UK had sufficient evidence of this responsibility. Bin Laden initially denied involvement (although he later revoked this, claiming responsibility), and much of the case for Al Qaeda's involvement focused on its record of comparable attacks, its clear willingness to be involved in attacks on the US, and the improbability of anyone else's having had the willingness and capacity to carry out such attacks. But, as Darrell Moellendorf argues, whether there was a just cause for war really turns not on whether the US had sufficient reason to declare bin Laden guilty, but on whether there was sufficient reason to demand his extradition to stand trial (Moellendorf, 2002). If US evidence met a standard sufficient to warrant demanding his extradition, Moellendorf argues that it would be 'inappropriate' to then deny that it was permissible for the US to respond forcefully to a refusal to extradite, especially given the concern that bin Laden posed an ongoing threat to US citizens (Moellendorf, 2002).

Proportionality and a reasonable prospect of success

Moellendorf argues that, in order to know whether the war in Afghanistan was proportionate, we must know how likely it was to succeed in achieving the just cause of preventing future attacks. He maintains that if the war was unlikely to succeed, it was unlikely to produce more good than harm, and, therefore, unlikely to have been proportionate (Moellendorf, 2002).

But I think Moellendorf's characterization of how we assess *ad bellum* proportionality is mistaken. The proportionality requirement is distinct from, and must be assessed independently of, the prospect of success requirement. The proportionality requirement governs *means*: it tells us whether a use of force is a proportionate way of securing a good. But only on the assumption that force is successful can we compare the good (to be) secured with the harm (to be) inflicted—that is, do a proportionality calculation. In determining the proportionality of defensive force, we must ask whether, *if successful in securing the good*, the force would be a proportionate means of securing that good. When we ask whether a war would be *ad bellum* proportionate, then, we are asking, 'Would war, fought with the permitted means at our disposal, be a proportionate way of securing the just cause?' But this means that we build an *assumption* of success—of securing the just cause—into our calculation. The calculation cannot, therefore, also be sensitive to the *probability* of success, which is what the reasonable prospect of success condition asks us to judge.

If there were reason to believe that further attacks, comparable to the 9/11 attacks in terms of scale and impact, would be perpetrated if the leaders of Al Qaeda were not imprisoned or killed, military force could be a proportionate means of preventing such attacks, assuming that the coalition forces had military measures at their disposal that would not inflict harms that exceeded the good to be secured. I think that the war in Afghanistan may, therefore, have satisfied the *ad bellum* proportionality condition.

But, even if the reasonable prospect of success condition is not a component of proportionality, this condition must still be satisfied if a war is to be deemed just. The harms to combatants and non-combatants can make it impermissible to wage a war, even to secure a proportionate just cause, if the war is unlikely to succeed. Part of the problem of waging a war to prevent a non-state group like Al Qaeda from perpetrating future attacks is that it is not clear that ordinary military methods can be effective in achieving this sort of goal. Al Qaeda had training camps and personnel, but little else in the way of infrastructure, the targeting of which could disable their capacity to launch attacks. The inhospitable terrain and presence of sympathetic parties in neighbouring countries made it feasible that members of the group could leave Afghanistan (and, unlike a head of state fleeing in the face of an invader, the departure of Al Qaeda operatives would not constitute a victory, but rather a failure, for the invaders). It also seems reasonably predictable that a war in Afghanistan would alienate people living there and increase radicalization, particularly given the hostility towards the US even prior to the invasion. This increase in radicalization undermines the just cause of preventing future terrorist attacks. Given the rather low prospect of success, then, it seems unlikely that the war in Afghanistan was, all things considered just, even if pursuing those responsible for the 9/11 attacks provided a just cause.

The 'war on terror'

The war in Afghanistan was part of a broader initiative that US President George W. Bush famously described as a 'war on terror'—a campaign of military force aimed at eradicating (or at least seriously depleting) the capacities of terrorist organizations thought to threaten the US and its allies. It would be a mistake, though, to think of this as the sort of war that can be judged as a whole by just war criteria. The war on terror consists of a range of activities and events, including (but not limited to) the war in Afghanistan, the war in Iraq, the killing of Osama bin Laden, the detaining of hundreds of suspected terrorists in Guantanamo Bay, and drone attacks in Pakistan. Whilst it might be possible to judge at least some of these activities using just war criteria, it is likely that some parts of the war on terror are just and other parts are unjust.

A particular difficulty for just war theorists, and indeed for legal scholars, has been incorporating the role of the non-state actors, who are often the targets of the war on terror, within the statist framework of traditional just war theory and international law. This has been most starkly illustrated by the treatment of suspected terrorists by coalition forces. The 'detention centre' in Guantanamo Bay has become notorious as the home of suspected terrorists from Afghanistan, Iraq, and elsewhere, not least as a result of the allegations of abuse and torture of prisoners at the hands of their captors. One of the many important questions raised by the detaining of suspects in Guantanamo is whether we should treat individuals who fight as part of non-state groups as combatants or as criminals. If we deem members of Al Qaeda to be combatants, this has the 'benefit', in strategic terms, of making it lawful to kill them by virtue of the very fact that they are combatants, and to detain them without trial for the duration of the conflict (which, in the war on terror, is a rather indeterminate period of time). But combatant status also affords those combatants some privileges: they cannot, for example, be prosecuted or punished simply for fighting, and they are entitled to prisoner of war status if they are captured. This means, amongst other things, that they should not be tortured, insulted, humiliated, paraded in public as 'objects of curiosity', or required to give up information other than their name, affiliation, date of birth, and rank. It would certainly not be lawful to water-board a prisoner of war.

If, in contrast, we class members of Al Qaeda as criminals, we set the bar for lawfully harming them very high. In order to kill or imprison a person suspected of a crime, one would normally need to demonstrate, in a fair trial and beyond all reasonable doubt, their complicity in a sufficiently serious crime. One cannot kill a suspected criminal simply for being a member of a particular group, or because one thinks that he or she will commit (further) crimes in the future.

In an attempt to navigate this legal minefield, the US government has adopted a third category of 'unlawful combatant' to describe the status of members of terrorist groups. John C. Yoo and James C. Ho (2003) argue that this category describes people who fight, but who fail the conditions for qualifying as a combatant laid out in the 1949 Geneva Convention. Recall that these conditions originally stated that to be a combatant, a person must:

1. be part of a hierarchical group, such that there is a recognizable chain of command
2. wear a distinctive emblem that is visible from a distance
3. bear arms openly
4. obey the rules of *jus in bello* as laid out in the Convention.

Members of Al Qaeda can probably meet the first condition. Although some experts argue that Al Qaeda is a fairly loosely-organized network of cells, rather than a single hierarchical group, any particular cell is still likely to have a leader and subordinates. The fact that members of groups such as Al Qaeda tend not to wear distinctive emblems to distinguish them from non-combatants, and that they do not bear their arms openly would have precluded their being granted combatant status under these original Geneva Convention rules. But under the revised conditions of 1977, it is sufficient for claiming combatant status that a fighter bears his or her arms openly immediately prior to and during combat. A person need not also wear a distinctive emblem, such as a uniform, and carry their arms openly at *all* times. There is no reason why members of Al Qaeda could not meet these revised conditions (although it may be contingently true that they often do not).

However, we might think that members of Al Qaeda will always fail the fourth condition of obeying the rules of *jus in bello*, vindicating Yoo and Ho's claim that they are unlawful combatants. Al Qaeda is identified as a terrorist group because its members target non-combatants—a clear violation of the principle of discrimination. But even here, the law does not clearly state that this precludes their being granted combatant status. The Geneva Convention holds that 'violations of these [*in bello*] rules shall not deprive a combatant of his right to be a combatant, or, if he falls into the power of an adverse Party, of his right to be a prisoner of war.' (1977). Moreover, a detaining power—that is, a state that captures an enemy combatant and holds him or her as a prisoner of war—is not supposed to prosecute a prisoner of war for crimes committed prior to capture (although this is controversial—see International Committee of the Red Cross (ICRC) at http://www.icrc.org/applic/ihl/ihl.nsf/b466ed681ddfcfd241256739003e6368/5cd83e96981e1ee0c12563cd00427ee4). The detaining power is thus in something of a catch-22 situation: in order to deny a person combatant status, one must show that he or she fails to meet the qualifying conditions—in this case, that the person has violated the principle of discrimination. But to be tried for crimes committed prior to capture, one must have already shown a person not to be a combatant, since captured combatants are prisoners of war, and detaining powers should not prosecute prisoners of war.

? QUESTIONS

1. Is there a morally significant difference between harms that I intend to inflict and harms that I foresee will be a side-effect of my action?

2. Is war a relation between political entities or between individuals?

3. Can a war be justly fought even if it lacks a just cause?

4. Can preventive war sometimes be just?

5. Do just combatants forfeit their usual rights against being attacked?

6. Is there a morally significant difference between a combatant who shoots at enemy soldiers and a non-combatant munitions worker who makes guns for the army?

7. Do the victors of a war against unjust aggression have an obligation to bring about the political rehabilitation of the aggressive state?

8. Are members of Al Qaeda entitled to prisoner of war status?

9. Do wars of humanitarian intervention violate sovereignty?

10. Is it morally wrong to embrace pacifism?

FURTHER READING

■ Bellamy, A. (2008) 'The responsibilities of victory: *Jus Post Bellum* and the just war', *Review of International Studies,* 34: 601–5 Bellamy's paper outlines the history of *jus post bellum* and argues that we ought not to regard it as part of just war theory.

■ Frowe, H. and Lang, G. (eds) (2014) *How We Fight: Ethics in War*, Oxford: Oxford University Press This collection of ten essays explores theoretical issues relating to *jus in bello*, including the doctrine of double effect, non-combatant immunity, and the distribution of risk between combatants and non-combatants.

■ Frowe, H. (2011) *The Ethics of War and Peace: An Introduction*, New Abington: Routledge Frowe's introduction to just war theory focuses on contemporary debates concerning the moral equality of combatants, non-combatant immunity, the moral status of terrorists, and the legitimacy of humanitarian intervention.

■ Kutz, C. (2005) 'The difference uniforms make: collective violence in criminal law and war', *Philosophy and Public Affairs,* 38, No. 2: 148–80 Kutz's influential paper defends the claim that certain groups have licence to engage in political violence.

■ May, L. (2005) 'Killing naked soldiers: distinguishing between combatants and non-combatants', *Ethics and International Affairs,* 19, No. 3: 39–53 May's paper explores the difficulty of identifying morally significant differences between combatants and non-combatants that might underpin the principle of distinction.

■ McMahan, J. (2009) *Killing in War*, Oxford: Oxford University Press This is McMahan's book-length defence of the reductive individualist position. It outlines his account of individual liability to defensive harm and draws together key arguments from his earlier papers.

■ Moellendorf, D. (2002) 'Is the war in Afghanistan just?', *Imprints,* 6, No. 2 Gives an analysis of the justness of the war in Afghanistan, focusing on just cause, last resort, proportionality, and a reasonable prospect of success.

■ Scheid, D. E. (ed.) (2014) *The Ethics of Armed Humanitarian Intervention,* Cambridge: Cambridge University Press This is a collection of original papers by philosophers, legal scholars, and political theorists on the morality and legality of armed humanitarian intervention.

■ Walzer, M. (1977; 2000) *Just and Unjust Wars: A Moral Argument with Historical Illustrations*, New York: Basic Books Walzer's book is the most influential piece of just war scholarship of the twentieth century. It defends the traditional collectivist position, and has been the inspiration for, and target of, much of what has been written since.

■ Yoo, J. C. and Ho, J. C. (2003) 'The status of terrorists', *Virginia Journal of International Law,* 44: 207–28 Yoo and Ho argue that terrorists ought to be viewed as illegitimate combatants.

 WEB LINKS

● http://www.carnegiecouncil.org/index.html This is the website of the Carnegie Council for Ethics and International Affairs.

● http://plato.stanford.edu/entries/war/ Brian Orend's entry in the Stanford Encyclopaedia gives an overview of just war theory.

● www.stockholmcentre.weebly.com The website for the Stockholm Centre for the Ethics of War and Peace has links to various sources of information and events on just war theory.

- http://www.justwartheory.com/ This is a list of readings and other information about just war theory.

- http://www.icrc.org/eng/war-and-law/index.jsp The website of the International Committee of the Red Cross contains all the articles of the Geneva Convention and its Additional Protocols, along with useful commentary on each article.

 Visit the Online Resource Centre that accompanies this book to access more learning resources: http://www.oxfordtextbooks.co.uk/orc/mckinnon3e/

11

Environment

DALE JAMIESON

Reader's guide

Academic writing about the environment in the late 1960s and early 1970s centred on whether democracies are able to cope with serious environmental threats. Some theorists responded with green utopian theorizing; others put their faith in ecological modernization; still others remained sceptical. What is clear is that problems of global environmental change, such as climate change, pose serious challenges to democratic political systems as they are currently constituted. Deliberative democracy, ecological citizenship, and the green virtues have been discussed as potential solutions, but the latter two approaches appear to challenge some core commitments of liberalism by demanding that the state adopt value-committed, non-neutral policies that may efface the distinction between other- and self-regarding action. But this critique, in its extreme form, rests on a misunderstanding of liberalism. Indeed, environmentalism, like liberalism, has justice at its centre, but extends this concern to future generations and non-human nature.

Introduction

The philosophy of nature is an ancient subject. From the pre-Socratics to the present, philosophers have sketched diverse pictures of nature and held various views about nature's relationships to human flourishing. For Aristotle, nature and goodness were closely allied. For Hobbes, the **state of nature** was something to be overcome, but the laws of nature directed us how to do it (1651; 1968; 1994; 1996). Mill was avid in his appreciation for nature, but wrote that *'nearly all the things which men are hanged or imprisoned for doing to one another are nature's every-day performances'* (1861; 1962; 1969: 396). Rousseau (1997) idealized the state of nature and thought that it was required for human flourishing.

Despite these debates, the environment, in the modern sense of the term, plays almost no role in the history of political theory. However much Hobbes, Locke, and Marx (1982) may have disagreed in other respects, their views about the environment are not appreciably different. Locke (1690; 1924; 1952; 1980; 1988) spoke for all three when he wrote that *'land that is left wholly to nature, that hath no improvement of pasturage, tillage, or planting, is called, as indeed it is, waste'* (1952: 25). For most in the tradition, nature untouched by humanity is utterly without value. Value arises only when people mix their labour with nature.

Part of the explanation for this devaluing of nature may be because nature was seen as an overwhelming and inexhaustible force that was a continual threat to humanity. The idea that nature might, in some way, be vulnerable to humanity would have seemed strange to most thinkers in the tradition. This insight—that humanity has the potential to profoundly affect nature—can conveniently be attributed to the US politician and polymath, George Perkins Marsh, who argued in his book, *Man and Nature*

 KEY TEXTS

Carson, *Silent Spring* (1962; 2002)

This book is generally regarded as launching the modern environmental movement. The book's title evoked a spring that was silent because all of the songbirds that died from pesticide poisoning. Carson accused the chemical industry of spreading disinformation and public officials of accepting industry claims uncritically. She was viciously attacked by the pesticide industry, but the book became a bestseller. Within a decade of the book's publication, the pesticide, DDT, had been banned in the USA. A trained scientist and gifted writer, Carson's commitment to the public's right to know became a hallmark of the environmental movement.

Meadows et al., *The Limits to Growth* (1972)

This text models the consequences of a rapidly growing world population with finite resources. The book appeared at a time when growth was uncritically considered to be good, and the authors' warning that we were rapidly heading for limits shocked many people and led to calls for resource conservation. Many economists were critical of the study, complaining that the authors model population, capital, and pollution as growing exponentially, but technologies for expanding resources and controlling pollution as growing only arithmetically, if at all.

(1864; 2003), that Mediterranean civilizations collapsed as a result of their abuse of the environment.

In the wake of the Industrial Revolution, attitudes towards nature began to change. In the nineteenth and early twentieth centuries, John Ruskin (1992), John Muir (1997), Albert Schweitzer (1987), and others articulated many of the concerns that would come to prominence in the second half of the twentieth century. After World War II, environmental concerns were eloquently expressed by such writers as Aldo Leopold (1987), Rachel Carson (1962; 2002), and Barry Commoner (1980). It was the environmental movement of the 1960s and 1970s that was mainly responsible for bringing these concerns to political theory and philosophy.

Doom and gloom

Academic writing about the environment in the late 1960s and early 1970s was full of doom and gloom. In 1968, Paul Ehrlich published *The Population Bomb*, in which he forecast hundreds of millions of people starving to death in the 1970s and 1980s, because of overpopulation. In 1972, a group of MIT researchers (Meadows et al.) published *The Limits to Growth*, in which they seemed to suggest that humanity would soon exhaust the resource base of the planet. Robert Heilbroner (1980) and William Ophuls (1977) introduced these ideas to political and social theory, arguing that scarcity and environmental crisis would make unprecedented demands on our democratic political institutions.

In an extremely influential 1968 paper, Garret Hardin provided an elegant analysis of the structure of environmental problems. Hardin invited us to imagine a pasture shared by herders. Each herder individually benefits from grazing an animal, while the costs are spread between all of the herders, since each animal slightly degrades the common pasture. Each herder has an incentive to keep adding animals, because he gains all of the benefits while the costs are spread over all those who use the commons. The result is overgrazing and the degradation of the pasture. Hardin's idea was that many of our environmental problems have this structure: individuals benefit from acts that pollute, degrade the land, change the climate, and stress fisheries, but the costs are spread over the entire population. Each of us acts in our immediate self-interest, but, together, we produce outcomes that are worse for all of us.

What are the possible solutions? Hardin considers appeals to conscience, but dismisses them for several reasons. He assumes that such appeals must rest on inducing feelings of guilt and that it is generally bad for people to feel guilty. Moreover, asking people to act from conscience is asking them to act irrationally, contrary to their own interests. Finally, appeals to conscience will, in any case, not succeed, because those who act in this way will be taken advantage of and such behaviour will eventually be eliminated from the community. The only possible alternative that can forestall our environmental problems, according to Hardin (1968: 1247), is '*mutual coercion, mutually agreed upon*'. He admits that such a system may be unjust, but concludes that '*the alternative of the commons is too horrifying to contemplate. Injustice is preferable to total ruin*'.

KEY THINKERS

Garrett Hardin (1915–2003)

Hardin was a US human ecologist, who wrote influential essays in the 1960s and 1970s against overpopulation, immigration, and altruism, and in favour of abortion, assisted suicide, and environmental protection. The central theme of his work was that common property resources would inevitably be depleted or degraded, and that the only viable solutions were privatization or coercion. Perhaps most importantly, Hardin was an early advocate of the need to situate all human institutions, whether political, economic, or social, in an ecological context.

Green utopianism

Some theorists responded to the gathering storm by arguing that the environmental crisis can be successfully addressed only by a new system of political organization, based on new values. An early site of this debate was an exchange between two Australian philosophers, Richard Routley (1973) and John Passmore (1974). Routley (later called 'Sylvan') delivered a paper to the 1973 World Conference of Philosophy meeting in Sofia, Bulgaria, in which he asked the question: 'Is there a need for a new, environmental ethic?' Routley's answer was a qualified 'yes' and he went on to devote a great deal of attention to working out a deep green version of anarchism. While Passmore granted that one strand of the Western tradition—that is, 'dominion'—was implicated in the environmental crisis, he argued that another strand—that is, 'stewardship'—provided the moral, cultural, and religious resources for successfully addressing the crisis. Thus, Passmore was optimistic that our environmental problems could be successfully addressed from within the Western tradition, without turning to new values or forms of political organization.

Such discussions took on greater urgency when the Green Party entered the German Federal Parliament in 1983. The Greens popularized the slogan '*neither left nor right, but ahead*', and were committed to the 'four pillars' of ecology, social responsibility, **democracy**,

☆ KEY POINTS

- Academic writing about the environment in the late 1960s and early 1970s was full of doom and gloom.

- According to Garret Hardin, the only possible solution is '*mutual coercion, mutually agreed upon*'.

- Some theorists responded to the gathering storm by arguing that the environmental crisis can be successfully addressed only by a new system of political organization, based on new values.

- Such discussions took on greater urgency when the Green Party entered the German Federal Parliament in 1983.

- The energy of the Greens, combined with the collapse of the traditional left, led to a burst of utopian political theorizing.

and non-violence. This stimulated discussion about whether these pillars reflected a distinctive political vision, a 'greening up' of alternative political perspectives, such as anarchism or socialism, or simply represented a rebalancing of social and political values within a broadly liberal perspective. The energy of the Greens, combined with the collapse of the traditional left, led to a burst of **utopian political theorizing**—that is, theorizing that advocates an ideal society, independent of the likelihood of our actually being able to achieve it. Theorists such as Ted Benton (1993), Murray Bookchin (1982), Andrew Dobson (2003), Robin Eckersley (1992), Warwick Fox (1990), and Val Plumwood (1993) defended various versions and permutations of Marxism, anarchism, ecologism, socialism, and feminism.

Democracy and environmental crisis

The dark question posed by Hardin and others was whether political democracies are able to cope with serious environmental threats. Heilbroner (1980: 158) poses the question in this way: '*Is there hope for man?*' He answers by saying that, if we mean by this question '*whether it is possible to meet the challenges of the future without the payment of a fearful price, the answer must be: "no, there is no such hope"*'.

From the beginning, many thought that the concerns of the pessimists were exaggerated. Critics claimed that Ehrlich (1968) and Meadows et al. (1972) simply repeated the mistakes of the eighteenth-century cleric, Thomas Malthus (1999), who argued that mass starvation was inevitable, because population and consumer demand would increase exponentially, while natural stocks and production would remain constant or increase only arithmetically. What Malthus did not take into account was the dynamism and resourcefulness of human creativity and social organization. Rates of population growth and consumption do not ineluctably march on, but vary, due to all sorts of social and cultural factors. Economic innovation and technological change produce substitutes for resources that are in short supply. For example, whale oil was commonly used as a fuel for lighting houses and streets in the nineteenth century. Many reasons remain for wanting to save the whales, but concern about lighting our houses and streets is not one of them. Markets have provided substitutes for these uses of whale oil.

Similarly, many critics have thought that Hardin's '*tragedy of the commons*' misrepresents the actual shape of our environmental problems. As a matter of fact, the practice of grazing individually owned animals on common pasture persisted for centuries. Communities regulated the use of commons by various methods of informal control that lay somewhere between the extremes of conscience and **coercion** (Ostrom, 1990). Moreover, herdsmen often identified their own interests with those of the community, rather than thinking in terms of individual self-interest. Today, we have sophisticated policy instruments, such as congestion pricing and pollution taxes, which allow us to hold individuals responsible for the costs that they impose on others when they exploit a commons. Hardin describes a real problem, but whether it is as ubiquitous and devastating as he imagines is open to dispute.

Ecological modernization

In the late 1980s, the idea that we would naturally move into a brighter environmental future came to the fore as the notion of ecological modernization became prominent in Germany and other Western European countries—especially the Netherlands. In its simplest form, the idea is that, as countries modernize economically, politically, and socially, environmental challenges are internalized into the prevailing systems of governance and production. According to this view, modernization is the ultimate solution to environmental problems.

This idea reflects some important insights. Air pollution, for example, is more prevalent in societies in the early stages of industrialization than in those that are further along this road. Water quality is generally better in rich countries than in poor countries. Advanced capitalist countries, such as Germany, have extremely demanding laws requiring producers to take responsibility for their products once their useful life is over, resulting in much higher levels of recycling, reuse, and pollution prevention than occurs in less-developed countries (see Box 11.1).

Despite these examples, there are reasons to be suspicious about the idea of ecological modernization. Modernization is one of those terms that has a nice ring to it, but an obscure meaning. Indeed, 'modernism' was one of the labels that was used to market fascism in the first half of the twentieth century, when it was presented as the shiny new futuristic political system that would soon replace the outworn idea of democracy. We might wonder what anti-democratic tendencies lurk behind the idea of ecological modernization.

Even if we embrace a sympathetic idea of ecological modernization, it appears that this thesis may be true in relation to some environmental problems and some countries, but false in relation to other problems and other countries. Scholars have suggested that the

---

 KEY CONCEPTS

Sustainability

Sustainability is what we should be aiming at, according to many environmentalists, but it is not easy to say exactly what this is. One common distinction is between strong and weak sustainability. Strong sustainability focuses on preserving 'natural capital', while weak sustainability aims at preserving welfare. A further question concerns how much preservation is required in order to achieve sustainability. While these and other questions must be answered if we are to aim our policies at sustainability, it is often easier to identify practices as unsustainable than it is to provide definitions.

BOX 11.1 GERMAN ENVIRONMENTAL LAWS

Environmental law in Germany developed rapidly after the Green Party entered Parliament in 1983. In 1986, the Federal Ministry for the Environment was created and Germany became a leader in environmental protection. The 'precautionary principle' emerged in Germany in the 1970s and, in the early 1980s, it was used to promote vigorous policies in response to acid rain and pollution of the North Sea. Since 1991, Germany has implemented the 'polluter pays' principle in waste disposal, requiring manufacturers or retailers to take responsibility for recycling or disposing of the products that they market.

thesis is more plausible in relation to Germany and the Netherlands—the countries in which it emerged—than in the USA. There is also reason to believe that this thesis is more applicable to local or regional environmental problems than it is to the emerging problems of global environmental change.

☆ KEY POINTS

- The question posed by Hardin and others was whether political democracies are able to cope with serious environmental threats.
- From the beginning, many thought that the concerns of the pessimists were exaggerated.
- In the late 1980s, the idea that ecological modernization would solve environmental problems became prominent.
- But ecological modernization, on its own, is unlikely to solve such problems as climate change.

Global environmental change

The best way in which to understand problems of global environmental change is by contrasting them with other problems. Many environmental problems are local in scale, such as the common practice in medieval Europe of tossing sewage into the street. My neighbour, who insists on playing loud music at all hours, causes a local environmental problem. A much more serious local environmental problem is exposure to tobacco smoke, which claims thousands of lives each year.

Local environmental problems can be contrasted with those in which people act in such a way as to degrade the environment over a region, thus producing harms that may be remote from the spatio-temporal location of their actions. Rather than one event simply producing another event in the same locale, these actions involve complex causes and effects that are spread over large areas. For example, when I drive in the Los Angeles basin, pollutants discharged by the tail pipe of my car mix with other pollutants and naturally occurring substances to produce harmful chemicals that are transported over the entire area. My behaviour, when joined with that of others, produces serious health risks to many people. In recent years, global environmental problems, such as climate change and stratospheric ozone depletion, have captured a great deal of attention. These are problems that would not have existed without modern technologies and population densities.

Ozone depletion is caused by chlorofluorocarbons (CFCs)—a class of chemical that was invented in 1928 for use as a refrigerant, fire extinguisher, and propellant in aerosol cans. CFC emissions, through a complex chain of chemistry, lead to the erosion of stratospheric ozone, thus exposing living things on Earth to radically increased levels of life-threatening ultraviolet radiation. The climate change that is now under way is largely caused by the emission of greenhouse gases which include CFCs, methane, and carbon dioxide (which is a by-product of the combustion of fossil fuels). The massive consumption of fossil fuels fed the Industrial Revolution and continues to support the way of life of industrial societies. The Earth has already warmed at least 0.8°C (almost 1.5°F) since the pre-industrial era and is likely to warm at least another 0.7°C (1.26°F) over this century (Intergovernmental Panel on Climate Change – IPCC, 2013). Because emissions of carbon dioxide and other climate-changing gases continue to increase, we are bequeathing, to future generations, the most extreme and rapid climate change to have occurred since the age of the dinosaurs. While, to some extent, everyone has contributed to this problem, it is the richest people who contribute the most—but it is the poor descendants of today's poor people, and the non-human natural world that will suffer most.

While there are difficulties in motivating democratic societies to respond to local and regional environmental problems, the problems involved in responding to a global problem, such as climate change, are much more difficult, for many reasons. Climate change is a problem that requires a great deal of technical sophistication to understand, thus people tend to ignore it or easily fall prey to misinformation. Climate change has complex causes and effects. We cannot simply point to a single factor in the way that we can when we say that exposure to raw sewage causes cholera, for example. The effects of climate change are probabilistic, rather than deterministic. Climate change 'loads the dice' in such a way as to increase the frequency of extreme climatic events, but it is very difficult to attribute the occurrence of any single such event to climate change. Climate change is a long-term problem. A carbon molecule emitted today can remain in the atmosphere for centuries and affect climate for even longer. The effects of climate change are dispersed through space, as well as time. Carbon emissions are local, but the climate that they affect is global. Climate change can cause floods or drought, heat waves or cold snaps. It can have indirect effects, such as wars, famines, and refugee flows. Perhaps most importantly, the effects of climate change can be invisible: climate change may kill many people, but it is unlikely that an obituary in a newspaper will ever say that a particular individual died as a result of climate change.

In addition to these features that affect the way in which we perceive and respond to climate change, climate change is a global problem beyond the purview of a single nation or society to address fully. Each democratic society is a single nation in a world of many nations, some democratic and some not. The contribution of any single democracy to combating climate change can be swept away by the behaviour of others.

Furthermore, an analogue of Hardin's *'tragedy of the commons'* extends to relations among generations. Each generation suffers from the climate change imposed on it by previous generations. Bearing costs to mitigate climate change will primarily benefit future generations, rather than one's own. Thus, each generation has an incentive to continue

---

☆ KEY POINTS

- Problems of global environmental change, such as climate change and ozone depletion, could not have existed without modern technologies and population densities.

- Problems such as climate change are difficult to address because of their scientific and technical complexity.

- Problems such as climate change are difficult to address because they involve both intra- and inter-generational collective action problems.

emitting greenhouse gases from which it will benefit and impose the costs of doing so on those who will come later. Because each generation finds itself in this situation', each generation has the same incentive to take the benefits now and defer the costs to the future (Gardiner, 2003).

Climate change and democracy

Whatever the plausibility of the general thesis that environmental problems pose serious challenges to democracy, it seems undeniable that a certain class of these problems—problems of global environmental change—poses serious challenges to democratic political systems, as they currently exist. One way in which to understand these challenges is by distinguishing political action that is based on values from political action that is based on interests and preferences. These terms are ambiguous and often used in cross-cutting ways, so a certain regimentation is required in order to make some important distinctions.

Values, as I use the term, are close to the core of a person's identity and are relatively stable: they reflect how someone wants the world to be, not merely what the person may want for him or herself. Preferences, on the other hand, reflect what people want at a particular moment. Preferences and values can come into conflict in our behaviour. Someone may both value an egalitarian distribution of wealth and prefer to be very rich. This may express itself in his or her voting for egalitarian political candidates, while seeking to make the sharpest possible financial investments. Unless irony is at work, a similar conflict can be seen in people who decorate their gas-guzzling automobiles with green bumper stickers. The term 'interest' is often ambiguous between what a person may currently want and what is good for that person. We can speak of someone's interest in health, while at the same time noting his or her interest in smoking. Bringing these thoughts together, we can say that values express people's views of how the world ought to be, interests concern what is good for them, either in the short or long term, and preferences express what it is that they currently want.

It is a commonplace assumption among many political scientists that the US political system, and those of most other Western democracies, are based on interest-group politics. Indeed, politics is sometimes defined as 'who gets what, when, where, and how'. Insofar as this is true, it will be difficult to respond politically to climate change, because many of those who will be most harmed by climate change do not participate in the reigning political systems. These include the non-human natural world, future generations, citizens of other countries, and even the disenfranchised and alienated citizens of one's own countries. In reply, it is sometimes said that these interests gain political representation through the active participation of those who care about them and assert their interests. To some extent, this is true, but it is obvious that, at best, these marginalized interests are represented only as shadows, rather than in their full vivacity. This can be seen by comparing the case in which my interests are represented by someone with many interests of their own, who also cares about me, with the case in which I assert my own interests.

But it is not entirely true that Western societies are interest-group democracies. It is often remarked, in electoral analyses, that voters do not always express their interests at the ballot box. ➡ **See Chapter 4.** For example, poor people often vote for rich people who will give themselves tax cuts at the expense of their poor supporters; soldiers often vote for leaders who will put their lives at risk; even criminals sometimes vote for candidates who want to crack down on crime. There are many ways of trying to explain such behaviour, but one is to say that people often act politically on the basis of their preferences or values, rather than their interests. This is not surprising, because there are many cases outside of political life in which preferences and interests diverge, and in which we find our preferences compelling. For example, I may want to eat tiramisu, even though it is not in my interest to do so. Even more strongly, I may want to smoke, although it is counter to my interests. And I may want to drive my sport utility vehicle, despite my valuing of nature and future generations.

One reason that people act politically on the basis of preferences, rather than interests, is the power of branding. By and large, parties and candidates do not seek to convince the public of the wisdom or justice of their policies; instead, they attempt to make themselves a 'brand' with which people want to associate (Postman, 1985). In doing so, they exploit deep facts about the psychology of social animals like us, who evolved in small societies and are largely dependent on emotion, rather than reason, in guiding our behaviour. Because asserting positions and making arguments are, at best, not part of the branding process and, at worst, antithetical to it, political campaigns have become the last place in which to find serious discussion of important public issues. It is tempting to blame politicians and their handlers for this, but we citizens are also to blame. We tend to punish politicians (of whatever political stripe) who take strong, understandable positions on important public issues.

☆ **KEY POINTS**

- Problems of global environmental change pose serious challenges to democratic political systems, as they currently exist.

- One way in which to understand these challenges is by distinguishing political action that is based on values from political action that is based on interests and preferences.

- Values express people's view of how the world ought to be, interests concern what is good for them either in the short or long term, and preferences express what it is that they currently want.

- People often act politically on preferences, rather than on interests or values, because of the power of branding.

Democratic responses

When branding, rather than reasoning, is the main point of public discourse, it is not surprising that a political system that is based on preferences and anchored in branding should fail to come to terms with an issue as complex as that of global warming. There is another way of thinking about how a democratic political culture should function: one centred on deliberative engagement with values, rather than on branding. The deliberative ideal is reminiscent of the Enlightenment views that dominated European and US political thought in the eighteenth century. It is centred on the idea that the best society is one that is a democratic expression of the reflective views of its citizens, based on their most fundamental values. These views require constant examination, which is why free speech is important, and also a foundation in our best understandings of the world, which is why education matters.

Some theorists, rather than emphasizing deliberative processes, advocate changing our conception of citizenship (Dobson, 2003). They argue that the dominant conception of citizenship—which emphasizes paying taxes, obeying the law, defending the nation, and perhaps voting—is too thin. In their view, we need a thicker conception of citizenship that governs a much broader set of relationships. **Environmental citizenship** would obligate citizens in relation to every aspect of environmentally relevant behaviour, whether public or private. Duties of environmental citizenship would concern the welfare of people across national boundaries, future generations, and even perhaps animals. It might also require *'thinking like a mountain'* (Leopold, 1987).

So what would such people be like? How could they be produced by a democratic society? In answer to this question, we can return to an ancient strand in the philosophical tradition of both the West and the East that concerns the idea of character and the notion of virtue. From this perspective, we might ask what sort of person would be an environmentally responsible citizen, who would engage deliberatively in a democratic society in such a way that would contribute meaningfully to confronting such problems as climate change (Sandler, 2007; Lane, 2012).

 KEY CONCEPTS

Anthropocentrism

Some environmentalists say that anthropocentrism is the ultimate source of environmental problems. Generally, the term refers to the fact that our moral and political systems are human-centred—but there are many different versions of this view. Strong versions of anthropocentrism say that any human preference, however weak or trivial, takes precedence over any non-human interest. Weak versions of anthropocentrism give priority to human interests, but also find a place for non-human interests. Weaker still is an anthropocentrism that holds that, without humans, there are no values, but that, once this condition is satisfied, anything—human or not—can be valuable.

The following are some brief suggestions about what we might call the 'green virtues':

- Humility is a widely shared moral ideal that is not often connected to a love of nature or the importance of living lightly on the Earth. Yet indifference to nature is likely to reflect the self-importance or lack of self-acceptance that is characteristic of a lack of humility. A person who has proper humility will be horrified at the prospect of changing Earth's fundamental systems and will act in a way that minimizes the impact of his or her behaviour.

- Temperance is an ancient virtue that is typically associated with weakness of will. But conceived more broadly, temperance relates to self-restraint and moderation. A temperate person does not overconsume; he or she *'lives simply, so that others may simply live'*.[1]

- Finally, we can imagine a virtue that we might call 'mindfulness'. Behaviour that is performed by rote and without thinking, as is the case with much of our environmentally destructive behaviour, is the enemy of mindfulness. A mindful person will appreciate the consequences of his or her actions that are remote in time and space. He or she will see him or herself as taking on the moral weight of production and disposal when purchasing an article of clothing, for example. The mindful person will make him or herself responsible for the cultivation of the cotton, the impacts of the dyeing process, the energy costs of the transport, and so on. Mindful people will not thoughtlessly emit climate-changing gases.

If we bring together these reflections on **deliberative democracy**, ecological citizenship, and the green virtues, a picture may begin to emerge of what our society, and we ourselves, would have to be like in order to address such problems as climate change. But this may give rise to another worry that we are now in the domain of Aristotle, rather than that of Mill: would the sort of society that we are sketching be a recognizably liberal society?

> ☆ **KEY POINTS**
>
> - When branding, rather than reasoning, is the main point of public discourse, it is not surprising that a political system based on preferences and anchored in branding would fail to come to terms with an issue as complex as that of global warming.
>
> - One response is deliberative democracy, which is based on the idea that the best society is one that is a democratic expression of the reflective views of its citizens, based on their most fundamental values.
>
> - A second approach is environmental citizenship, which would obligate citizens in relation to every aspect of environmentally relevant behaviour, whether public or private.
>
> - A third approach is green virtue theory, which asks what sort of person would be an environmentally responsible citizen who would engage, deliberatively, in a democratic society in such a way that would contribute meaningfully to confronting such problems as climate change.

Environmentalism and liberalism

In one characteristic liberal view, the proper role of the state is in relation to other-regarding actions that occur in the public domain (especially those that cause harm), and the principles on which the state acts must be neutral between different ways of life and conceptions of the good. Environmentalism seems to challenge the importance and tenability of such distinctions by demanding that the state adopt value-committed, non-neutral policies that, in some cases, seem to efface the distinction between other- and self-regarding action. Thus, environmentalism seems to set itself against some core ideas of liberalism.

Much of the challenge comes from the environmentalist idea that 'everything is connected to everything else' (Commoner, 1980). In this account, almost no action is innocent: it is either part of the problem or part of the solution. Consider land-use policy: some people like to hike quietly in the wilderness, while others prefer to drive off-road vehicles. Liberalism, one might think, is committed to the idea that each should be allowed to do as they please: 'different strokes for different folks' might be the liberal slogan. Indeed, that is the position of the off-road vehicle enthusiast: he or she does not mind if some people want to hike, as long as he or she gets to ride a dirt bike. But the environmentalist hiker is not happy with this 'live and let live' solution: he or she wants off-road vehicles banned. The only uses of the wilderness that the hiker wants to allow are those that he or she prefers—and this does not sound like the voice of a liberal.

But this critique, in its extreme form, rests on a misunderstanding of liberalism (Dworkin, 2011). It is possible for liberals to have value commitments that are expressed in public policy. Indeed, the liberal commitment to toleration and diversity is, itself, such a commitment. Of course, not all substantive value commitments are consistent with liberalism—not a commitment to intolerance and uniformity, for example. The difficult question here is whether a commitment to environmental values is the sort of commitment that is consistent with a broadly liberal perspective.

This large question cannot fully be pursued here. It is clear, however, what shape a liberal environmentalist argument would have to take. Promoting environmental values would have to be necessary for human survival or flourishing, or it would, at least, have to be consistent with the possibility that people who do not share green values can live their lives in their own preferred ways. There is a plausible case in relation to all of these possibilities. When it comes to protecting the ozone layer, for example, life on the planet is in the balance. While climate change does not threaten humanity with extinction, much that we treasure may well be lost as a result of the warming that is now under way—and this is as

---

☆ **KEY POINTS**

- Liberalism is often regarded as implicating a set of important distinctions: public/private; neutral/non-neutral; other-regarding/self-regarding. In one characteristic liberal view, the proper role of the state is in relation to other-regarding actions that occur in the public domain (especially those that cause harm), and the principles on which the state acts must be neutral between different ways of life and conceptions of the good.

- Environmentalism seems to challenge the importance and tenability of such distinctions by demanding that the state adopt value-committed, non-neutral policies that, in some cases, seem to efface the distinction between other- and self-regarding action.

- But it is possible for liberals to have value commitments that are expressed in public policy.

- The difficult question here is whether a commitment to environmental values is the sort of commitment that is consistent with a broadly liberal perspective.

true for those who do not care much about nature as it is for those who do. A case can also be made that some degree of environmental preservation is required for human flourishing. Finally, as long as some parts of the wilderness are preserved for hiking, species diversity, and wildness, and other parts are opened to those who like to drive off-road vehicles, protecting environmental values is consistent with those who reject these values being able to live according to their own preferences and desires. In the messy world of actual politics, however, it is often difficult to strike such a balance.

Environmentalism and justice

Justice is one of the values that liberals are most concerned to promote and, in my view, a concern with justice is also close to the heart of environmentalism (see Box 11.2). Indeed, while environmentalism takes justice seriously, liberal political theorists have been remiss in not taking the environment seriously (an early exception is Barry, 1995).

BOX 11.2 A CONSTITUTIONAL RIGHT TO ENVIRONMENTAL QUALITY

In 1970, Senator Gaylord Nelson proposed adding the following amendment to the US Constitution: '*Every person has the inalienable right to a decent environment. The United States and every State shall guarantee this right.*' The proposal failed, but, subsequently, Sixteen US states and about 130 countries enshrined environmental protection in their constitutions, ranging from China and India, to Papua New Guinea and Vanuatu. Few of these, however, embody fundamental rights that are enforceable by affected individuals. Because most of these constitutional provisions are less than a decade old, it remains to be seen how transformative they may become (Hayward, 2005).

What exactly is environmental justice? Aristotle distinguished two types of justice: **distributive justice** and corrective justice. Distributive justice concerns how various benefits and burdens should be distributed; corrective justice is about punishment and compensation. It is plausible to suppose that some instances of environmental justice involve corrective justice. For example, if some have caused harm to others by appropriating what is rightfully theirs (resources from a global commons, or perhaps habitat, in the case of wild animals), then duties of corrective justice may be owed. The larger temptation, however, is to think of environmental justice as primarily a kind of distributive justice (as does Wenz, 1988).

In this view, the environment is a resource, the distribution of which should be governed by principles of justice. Because many aspects of the environment cannot physically be transferred from one community to another, this view is more precisely thought of as advocating the distribution of the benefits and costs of environmental resources according to principles of justice. From this perspective, environmental resources are, in principle, no different from money, food, health care, or other distributive goods over which people have claims of justice. It is an open question as to how, exactly, environmental resources are defined, how benefits and costs are assessed, what principles of justice are appropriate for governing their distribution, and who are the subjects and beneficiaries of these duties.

The idea that duties of environmental justice are global in scope has been around since the 1970s. At the United Nations Conference on the Human Environment in Stockholm in 1972, the notion of global environmental justice was introduced as the developing world's answer to the industrialized world's growing concern to preserve pure environmental goods, such as species and ecosystems, many of which exist primarily in developing countries. The idea began to gain momentum in 1991 with the publication of *Global Warming in an Unequal World: A Case of Environmental Colonialism* by the Indian environmentalists, Anil Agarwal and Sunita Narain.

 KEY THINKERS

Anil Agarwal (1947–2002) and Sunita Narain (1961–)

Anil Kumar Agarwal founded the Centre for Science and Environment, India's leading environmental NGO, in 1980. He spent his life advocating participatory policies in natural resource management, that were rooted in India's own traditions. Sunita Narain joined the Centre in 1982 and became its Director in 2000. Together, in 1991, they wrote *Global Warming in an Unequal World*, which put the question of justice at the centre of the global conversation on climate change.

Poor countries often argue that rich countries committed various environmental injustices during the course of their development and continue to commit injustices by appropriating more than their share of the Earth's resources. For example, they point out that not only is the USA the world's second largest emitter of greenhouse gases, but on a per capita basis, Americans emitted, in 2011, about two and a half times as much greenhouse gas as Chinese, ten times as much as Indians, and almost twice as much as Germans.[2]

Viewing global environmental issues from the perspective of distributive justice can certainly be a useful analytical approach, as the case of greenhouse gas emissions illustrates. The Framework Convention on Climate Change, which now has been ratified by 194 countries including the USA, commits the parties to the goal of stabilizing '*greenhouse gas concentrations in the atmosphere at a level that would prevent dangerous anthropogenic interference with the climate system*'. There are many ways of reaching this objective, but any successful attempt would impose costs in forgone development opportunities, and in economic and social restructuring. Different regimes would distribute these costs differently. One approach would be to establish an annual global ceiling on greenhouse gas emissions, allocate permissions to emit, and then allow unlimited emissions trading. This approach has the potential to be highly efficient, but whether it would be just would depend, to a great extent, on how permissions to emit are initially allocated.

However useful and intuitive it may be to see global environmental problems in this way, it is also clear that the idea of environmental justice is not exhausted by the notion of distributive justice. In an insightful early article, Iris Marion Young (1983) argued that it was **participatory justice**—that is, justice that ensures the fair distribution of rights to take part in collective decisions that affect one's interests—not distributive justice, that was the primary demand of US environmental justice activists in communities such as Afton, North Carolina. People objected, not only to the fact that they were being subjected to risks, but also to the fact that the exposures were without their consent and without institutional mechanisms that would allow them to articulate their opposition. This was also the case in the late 1970s, at Love Canal in New York State, when white, working-class homeowners became so frustrated by the lack of governmental responsiveness to their concerns, that they detained officials from the US Environmental Protection Agency, who had come to allay their fears about the fact that their community was built on top of a toxic waste dump.

The centrality of participatory justice to environmental justice is also indicated by the fact that the Principles of Environmental Justice adopted by the First National People of Color Environmental Leadership Summit in 1991 emphasized **self-determination** and respect for diverse cultural perspectives, rather than distributive justice. Indeed, distributive justice is mentioned in only two of the seventeen Principles adopted.

Participatory justice is also important at the global level. Those who suffer most from environmental insults are often not at the table. For example, sea-level rise caused, in part, by climate change, is likely to destroy, completely, such countries as São Tomé and Princípe, Kiribati, Maldives, and Tuvalu. These countries may cease to exist, because their land mass will be under water. Other small countries in the Caribbean and elsewhere may be ravaged by more intense, frequent storms and hurricanes. Seventy million farmers and their families in Bangladesh will lose their livelihoods when their rice paddies are inundated by sea water. Yet, despite the vast number of people around the world who will suffer from climate change, most of them are not at the table at which decisions are being made. Poor people and those who live on the margins are effectively voiceless in many environmental debates.

In some cases, participation is denied not because of institutional or political failure, but because those in question are not recognized as in the domain of justice. Historically, at various times and places, slaves and women have been denied justice, not only in the sense that they have borne disproportionate burdens or that their voices have been muted, but also in that they have not been regarded as the proper subjects of justice. Not only were African American slaves not getting their fair share, but they were excluded from the community over which justice was supposed to prevail. Poor people and those at the margins are not alone in being disenfranchised. Future generations are not at the table to defend their interests and the use of standard economic tools, such as the **discount rate**—that is, the rate at which the value of future benefits and costs are reduced in comparison to present benefits and costs—are often used, effectively, to dismiss even their most important interests. Again, this can be seen clearly in the case of climate change. It is rich people who are currently alive who reap the greatest share of the benefits of emitting greenhouse gases; it is those poor people who will live in the second half of this century and beyond who will bear most of the burdens. It is difficult to believe that we would behave so irresponsibly if we had to defend our actions directly to those who will suffer from them.

Some of those who speak of global environmental justice also believe that we owe duties of justice to other entities that cannot speak for themselves: individual plants; individual animals; populations; species; ecosystems; geological formations; even planets. Various cases are made for including such entities in the domain of justice, but they typically appeal to criteria of inclusion, such as naturalness, wildness, teleological organization, and sentience (Agar, 2001; Callicott, 1989; Regan, 1983; Rolston III, 1988; Taylor, 1986; Varner, 1998). While there are many difficult and controversial issues here, it seems clear to me that the case for recognizing duties of justice to some non-human animals is as strong as is the case for recognizing such duties to some human animals. The other great apes, for example, have complex social systems and lives that can improve or worsen in a way that matters to them. The same reasons that we have for recognizing duties of justice to some humans apply to them as well. Once this point is granted, it becomes clear that many other non-human animals also qualify as beneficiaries of duties of justice (Jamieson, 2002).

☆ KEY POINTS

- Justice is one of the values that liberals are most concerned to promote and it is also close to the centre of environmentalism.
- Environmental justice includes corrective and distributive justice, but also participatory justice.
- Environmental justice also extends to future generations and elements of the non-human natural world.

Conclusion

The environmental challenge to political theory will become increasingly prominent as the problems of global environmental change become more severe. The Earth's fundamental systems are being altered by climate change and biodiversity loss. Wild nature is everywhere in retreat. The world that we bequeath to our children will be dominated by humanity in an unprecedented way, whether measured in terms of human population or levels of consumption. As biotechnology continues to develop, the world will become one that we make, rather than one that we discover. Will this new world reflect our values and political will, or will we see it as foreign and alienating? This will depend on the expressiveness of our behaviour and the responsiveness of our institutions. Whether we will need new values, principles, concepts, and theories remains to be seen.

Environmental problems—especially those that involve global environmental change—are not only challenges to our politics, but also have the potential for improving them. Successfully responding to climate change can make us better citizens and help us to reclaim our democracy. This connection between the state of our souls and the fate of the Earth was clearly seen by Walt Whitman, the sage poetic observer of US democracy, when he wrote: '*I swear the Earth shall surely be complete to him or her who shall be complete*' (from 'A song of the rolling earth' in *Leaves of Grass*, available at: http://classiclit.about.com/library/bl-etexts/wwhitman/bl-ww-rollingearth.htm). This should give us heart, because large changes are caused and constituted by small choices—and in the end, however things turn out, it is how we live that gives meaning and significance to our lives.

CASE STUDY

Managing climate change

The possibility of anthropogenic (human-caused) climate change has been recognized since at least 1896, when Svante Arrhenius, the Swedish Nobel Prize-winning physicist, speculated that burning fossil fuels (such as coal and oil) might increase atmospheric carbon dioxide, thereby affecting both climate and terrestrial biological systems. Arrhenius estimated that a doubling of atmospheric carbon dioxide would increase the Earth's mean surface temperature by about 4–6°C—an estimate that is very close to those produced today by sophisticated climate models. In 1963, a Conservation Foundation meeting warned of '*potentially dangerous atmospheric increases of carbon dioxide*' and a 1979 report from the US National Academy of Sciences stated that '*a wait-and-see policy may mean waiting until it is too late*' to avoid significant climate changes. In light of this history, no one can say that we have not been warned about the possibility of climate change.

In 1992, the Framework Convention on Climate Change (FCCC) was officially opened for signature at the Rio Earth Summit. It came into force in 1994 and has now been ratified by 194 countries. Its objective is to '*prevent dangerous anthropogenic interference with the climate system*'. In recognition of the fact that the developed countries of Europe and North America had emitted about four-fifths of the greenhouse gases that were then in the atmosphere, the FCCC adopted the principle of 'common, but differentiated' responsibilities. The developed countries agreed voluntarily to stabilize greenhouse gas emissions (GHGs) at 1990 levels by the year 2000, while developing countries agreed to various monitoring and reporting requirements.

It soon became apparent that most-developed countries would not fulfil their commitments. In 1995, the parties to the FCCC adopted the Berlin Mandate: they pledged that, by the end of 1997, they would reach an agreement establishing binding '*quantified, limitation, and reduction objectives*' for developed countries and that no new obligations would be imposed on other countries during the compliance period. Later that year, they fulfilled this mandate by adopting the Kyoto Protocol.

Four provisions are central to the Kyoto Protocol, as follows.

1. The rich countries agreed to differentiated, binding targets among themselves that would reduce GHGs to about 5% below 1990 levels sometime between 2008 and 2012.
2. Performance in meeting these targets would be assessed on the basis of 'sinks' (for example, tree planting) as well as 'sources' (emissions), and virtually all GHGs, not only carbon dioxide, would be taken into account.
3. Emissions trading among developed and developing countries would be permitted.
4. The Protocol reaffirmed that developing countries would not be subject to binding emissions limitations before 2012.

The guiding vision behind the Kyoto Protocol was that the developed countries that had produced most of the warming would demonstrate their commitment to addressing the problem by taking some modest first steps. After 2012, they would undertake more stringent commitments and developing countries would follow by undertaking some modest commitments of their own. This adaptive process would be responsive to the emerging science and would force technological change. Led by the developed countries, the nations of the world would succeed in preventing '*dangerous anthropogenic interference with the climate system*'.

Unfortunately, these hopes have not been realized. The Clinton administration negotiated and signed the Protocol on behalf of the USA, but did not seek its ratification and did almost nothing to control emissions. In 2001, the Bush administration renounced the Protocol altogether. Because the Protocol required ratification from fifty-five countries, responsible for 55% of 1990 GHGs, in order to come into force, the US renunciation seemed likely to sink the Protocol. But the European Union stood firm and eventually persuaded Russia to ratify. On 16 February 2005, the Kyoto Protocol came into effect.

Despite the diplomatic activity, carbon dioxide emissions have continued to increase annually and, by 2010, were 50% greater than they were in 1990. Much of this increase is attributable to developing countries, such as China, but emissions in developed countries also continue to increase. Despite a downturn associated with the recession that began in 2008, the USA is now emitting about 14% more per year than it did in 1990. While the European Union reached its Kyoto reduction goals (in part by buying 'carbon credits' from developing countries), there are serious questions about its commitment to further reductions. For the foreseeable future, global emissions are likely to be controlled by the domestic politics of each country and, even within the EU, these are quite various. For example, the politics of Poland are much less green than those of Germany; the UK has reduced its carbon emissions about 18% from 1990–2009, while Spain's emissions increased by more than 30% during the same time period.[3]

The Earth responds on different timescales from those of political systems. Once carbon dioxide is emitted, it may remain in the atmosphere for centuries, while other GHGs may remain for millennia. Even if emissions of GHGs are dramatically and radically reduced, atmospheric concentrations can continue to increase. In the mid eighteenth century, there were 275 parts per million (ppm) of carbon dioxide in the atmosphere; today, we are approaching 400 ppm. Since the signing of the Framework Convention on Climate Change, concentrations have increased at an average of about 2 ppm per year. Because GHGs have such long residency times in the atmosphere, we are already committed to a substantial warming in addition to the warming we have already experienced, even if all emissions were to immediately cease. Our behaviour will have to change radically and we will have to be very fortunate to keep the warming at less than 2°C—the figure that has become the benchmark for '*dangerous anthropogenic interference with the climate system*'. Any rapid warming, including that which we have already experienced, causes harm to people and nature, but once we cross the 2°C threshold, the harms become much more widespread and acute, and the risks of a catastrophic climate change grow exponentially.

There are those who would like to treat climate change as only a technical or economic problem, and to evade questions of politics and ethics, but this strategy is bound to fail. Climate change is a global problem that divides the rich from the poor, the present from the future, and humans from nature. The values are close to the surface and no policy can succeed that fails to acknowledge them (Jamieson, 2014).

The people who will suffer most from climate change are those who have done the least to cause the problem. Poor countries will suffer more from climate change than rich countries, just as they suffer more from climate variability and extreme events. Honduras suffers more from hurricanes than Costa Rica; Ethiopia suffers more from drought than the USA; and probably no country is more affected by floods than Bangladesh. A one-metre sea-level rise (which is just beyond the upper bound of the IPCC's projection of what could happen this century) could inundate 11.5% of the land of Bangladesh and 12–15% of Egypt's arable land. Poor people in poor countries will bear the brunt of the climate change burden. They suffer most under 'normal' conditions and often need only a good shove to plunge into catastrophe.

Climate change also divides the present from the future. Each generation benefits from its own emissions, but the costs are borne by those who come after. Our parents and grandparents largely caused the climate change that we are experiencing; our much greater emissions will affect our grandchildren and their grandchildren. Because restricting emissions primarily benefits those who come later, it is, to some extent, altruistic—and while altruism is not always easy for individuals, it is even more difficult for governments. ➔ **See Chapter 13.**

When we bring these facts together, we can see how great the challenge is that we face. What is required to '*prevent dangerous anthropogenic interference with the climate system*' is for those of us who are rich, by global standards, to restrict our emissions radically, in order to benefit future generations of poor people. Given how little most of us do to help our poor contemporaries, it is not surprising that it is difficult to motivate us to benefit their descendants.

In addition to the divisions that climate change tears in the human community, it also divides humans from nature. The biggest losers will be the plants and animals that are now hanging on by a thread. Consider the fewer than 800 remaining mountain gorillas who cling to life in two small areas of misty, densely vegetated forest in Uganda and Rwanda. What will happen to them when their reserves dry out and warm up due to climate change? Even our attempts to respond to climate change often have paradoxical results. Orang-utan habitat is being destroyed in Indonesia in order to plant palm oil for biofuels. Scientists predict that a quarter of all species face extinction by the mid twenty-first century as a result of climate change.

What it will take to make a difference is extreme reductions in GHGs and aggressive action to adapt to climate change. Political leaders in Europe, North America, and Australasia do not seem to have the stomach for what would be required. If they did, they would almost certainly be punished by voters. China, which is now the world's largest carbon emitter, may have installed more solar panels in 2013, alone, than the USA has installed in its entire history, yet the share of renewables in its total energy remains less than 10%, and most of that is hydroelectric power. In addition, China remains the world's largest importer of coal.[4] Despite unprecedented increases in energy production, there are still about three million Chinese without access to electricity. In India, there are more than 300 million people who are off the grid.[5]

Increasingly, the pressing question is one of adaptation and compensation (McKinnon, 2012). Unless truly catastrophic climate change occurs, rich countries will largely be able to adapt. They will build sea walls to protect their coastal areas, compensate the farmers and foresters who lose their livelihoods, and invest more in developing and maintaining water resources. Poor countries, however, do not have the resources to adapt. Will the developed countries that have largely caused the problem be willing to finance adaptation in the poor countries? They may have some self-interested reasons to do so: climate change will cause environmental refugees and political instability in a world that is already uncertain—but nations do not always act on the basis of their rational self-interest, and such considerations only go so far. As the world becomes more chaotic and insecure, the temptation to try to geo-engineer climate will grow. We will hear more about launching space mirrors, injecting sulphate particles into the atmosphere, and creating vast fields of artificial trees. Each of these proposals, now only speculative, raises enormously complex issues of global governance.

Looming in the background are questions about our political systems and our values. Are Western democracies able to act on the timescale that is required to address climate change? Would liberal values have to be sacrificed? Would citizens have to change their values? Because climate change is a global problem, it also raises questions about the international order. Should it be addressed through the United Nations, the Framework Convention on Climate Change, or through a multilateral agreement among the largest emitters? Would any of these approaches—*could* any of these approaches—be effective?

Climate change is occurring and serious impacts are already being felt. Unless we radically cut emissions, the impacts will be severe and possibly catastrophic. In any case, we will have to adapt, and those already living on the margin have little capacity to do so. Can our political systems respond to this challenge? Over the next few years, the answer to this question will become increasingly obvious. In the meantime, GHG concentrations in the atmosphere continue to increase.

? QUESTIONS

1. What is 'the tragedy of the commons'? What are some possible solutions to it?

2. Why have some thought that the environmental crisis cannot be solved by democratic societies?

3. How have markets helped to solve environmental problems?

4. What is 'ecological modernization'? Is it a good idea, from an environmental perspective?

5. What is 'global environmental change'?

6. What is the difference between values, preferences, and interests? What is the relevance of these distinctions to thinking about the environment?

7. What is 'environmental citizenship'? Is it achievable?

8. Why do some think that there is a conflict between environmentalism and liberalism? Are they right?

9. What is 'environmental justice'?

10. What is the distinction between distributive and corrective justice? What is the relevance of the distinction to thinking about the environment?

FURTHER READING

■ Dobson, A. and Eckersley, R. (2007) (eds) *Political Theory and the Ecological Challenge*, Cambridge: Cambridge University Press An excellent collection, devoted to the themes of this essay.

■ Dryzek, J. and Schlosberg, D. (1998; 2005) *Debating the Earth*, Oxford: Oxford University Press The best available anthology on environmental politics.

■ Gardiner, S. (2011) *A Perfect Moral Storm: The Ethical Tragedy of Climate Change*, Oxford: Oxford University Press The most comprehensive single-volume treatment of the ethics and politics of climate change.

■ Goodin, R. (1992) *Green Political Theory*, London: Polity An early, philosophically sophisticated account of the subject.

■ Jamieson, D. (2008) *Ethics and the Environment: An Introduction*, Cambridge: Cambridge University Press An incisive introduction to the subject.

■ Passmore, J. (1974) *Man's Responsibility for Nature*, New York: Scribner's A good account of the cultural background to our environmental problems and the resources available for their solution.

WEB LINKS

- http://www.ecc-platform.org/index.php?option=com_content&view=article&id=2735%3Aharrison-program-on-the-future-global-agenda&catid=31&Itemid=272 The Harrison Program on the Future Global Agenda offers a wide range of resources on environmental politics.

- http://www.ecoequity.org EcoEquity offers reports and discussions on justice and climate change.

- http://www.realclimate.org Presents reliable climate science from climate scientists.

- http://www.humansandnature.org/ The Center for Humans and Nature presents thoughtful discussions of foundational issues.

- http://trillionthtonne.org/ An excellent website that explains the impact of various levels of carbon emissions.

 Visit the Online Resource Centre that accompanies this book to access more learning resources: http://www.oxfordtextbooks.co.uk/orc/mckinnon3e/

 ENDNOTES

1 This expression is attributed to Gandhi: see http://www.dropsoul.com/mystic-quotes.php

2 Based on data collated by the World Resources Institute, available online at http://cait2.wri.org/wri/Country%20GHG%20Emissions?indicator[]=Total%20GHG%20Emissions%20Excluding%20Land-Use%20Change%20and%20Forestry%20Per%20Capita&indicator[]=Total%20GHG%20Emissions%20Including%20Land-Use%20Change%20and%20Forestry%20Per%20Capita&year[]=2011&act[]=Albania&sortIdx=&focus=&chartType=geo

3 http://unfccc.int/resource/docs/2011/sbi/eng/09.pdf

4 http://www.eia.gov/countries/cab.cfm?fips=ch

5 http://www.worldenergyoutlook.org/resources/energydevelopment/energyaccessdatabase/

12

Gender

CLARE CHAMBERS

 Reader's guide

Feminism has a long history, encompassing both theory and action. Feminists have achieved enormous change in social and legal structures, and feminist philosophy continues to challenge prevailing orthodoxies. And yet many people, both women and men, are unwilling to call themselves 'feminist'. Even while they support the idea of equality between women and men, some people feel that feminism is either unnecessary or wrong. This chapter engages with the main themes of feminism and aims to show that feminism still has a distinctive role to play in political theory. Much progress has been made towards sex equality, but there is still a long way to go. Issues covered in this chapter include: defining feminism; the role of family life, and the distinction between public and private; and the relevance of sex and violence to feminism.

Introduction

Mainstream political theorists have often ignored the issue of gender difference, and so feminists have had to argue for its significance and importance. Ranging from Aristotle's exclusion of all women from political activity (along with slaves of both sex), to Rousseau's arguments for women to be educated differently from men and excluded from citizenship, to Nietzsche's claim that equal rights for women are evidence of a society in decline, political theory is full of examples of women being dismissed.

The history of political theory is also often taught as a history of male theorists. As with many cultural, literary, or historical matters, women's contributions are marginalized. Canonical feminists such as Mary Wollstonecraft, bell hooks, Simone de Beauvoir, Andrea Dworkin, Germaine Greer, Mary Daly, and Kate Millet are seldom taught in political theory courses. John Stuart Mill is a standard figure in political philosophy for his works *On Liberty* and *Utilitarianism*, yet his work *The Subjection of Women* (which argues for women's suffrage fifty years before it was granted) is relatively unknown (Mill, 1996).

Contemporary political philosophers are not always much better. In his canonical text, *A Theory of Justice* (1971; 1999), John Rawls argues that those in the **original position**, who are to decide on principles of justice, should be assumed to be heads of households, with justice within the family not discussed. As many feminists have pointed out, ignoring justice within the family is effectively to ignore women, and heads of households are usually assumed to be men.

Feminists have thus had a large task insisting on the importance of gender in general, and women in particular, to political philosophy. For some feminists, the ideas and values of male-focused political philosophy can be useful as long as some modifications are made. In other words, we can use existing theories as long as women are no longer excluded from consideration. This may result in changes to law and practice, but we do not need to rethink our fundamental values radically. This position is not shared by all feminists, however, or may not be applicable to all male-focused political philosophy. For some feminists, the very concepts and assumptions of mainstream political philosophy must be overturned and replaced with theories that take gender difference into account from the very start.

What is feminism?

There are many varieties of feminism, just as there are many varieties of liberalism or egalitarianism. But it is possible to identify three theses that all feminists support, in one form or another. These theses are:

- the entrenchment of gender;
- the existence of **patriarchy**; and
- the need for change.

The entrenchment of gender

The first feminist thesis is the idea that society is deeply gendered and that gender is (still) one of the most important **social cleavages** (factors that divide society). All feminists argue that an understanding of gender is crucial to an understanding of society. Gender might be one of the most significant features of an individual's identity, defining who she is and how she understands herself. It might be a key feature of resource distribution, determining or strongly influencing a person's relative wealth or poverty. Gender might also play a fundamental role in social hierarchies, explaining why some people enjoy greater status or respect than others.

Feminists differ on the specifics of the entrenchment of gender. For some, gender is the most important factor explaining these phenomena, whereas for others, it is one factor among many others, such as race or class.

The existence of patriarchy

The second feminist thesis claims that gender is not neutral in its effects, but casts women as inferior. All feminists argue that social structures based on gender disadvantage women. In other words, gender does not simply differentiate between women and men: it creates a hierarchy with men at the top and women at the bottom—or a patriarchy. The word 'patriarchy' literally means 'rule of the father', but its most common meaning in feminism is simply a society that advantages men and disadvantages women, regardless of who are the formal leaders. It is, therefore, possible to describe a society as patriarchal even if it has a woman leader (such as the Queen or former British Prime Minister, Margaret Thatcher). ➡ **See Chapter 14.**

Again, the existence of patriarchy is compatible with a range of feminist thought. It need not imply that men consciously act to maintain their dominance, or that they conspire or desire to keep women inferior. Patriarchy may be maintained through informal or opaque structures, such as **social norms**—that is, informal rules about how people ought to behave.

The need for change

Finally, all feminists argue that patriarchy is unjust and needs reform. Feminism is, thus, an essentially **normative** movement, demanding reform or revolution. The third thesis of feminism distinguishes feminists from others who believe that a gender hierarchy exists, but who do not criticize that fact. Such people may advocate gender hierarchy for reasons of religion, tradition, or apparent biological necessity.

Again, feminists differ in their views as to the sorts of changes that are necessary. For some, legal change is sufficient—for example, so that women are protected by anti-discrimination legislation. For others, change in social norms is needed, such that women are no longer seen as destined for motherhood and domestic work, for example. For still other feminists, even deeper change is needed, because patriarchy is rooted deeply in our attitudes and preferences. Nonetheless, all feminists share the goal of gender equality. They want women and men to have an equal status, and to enjoy equal respect. For most feminists, an important part of gender equality is equality of opportunity and, for many, greater **equality of resources** is also needed. ➡ **See Chapter 5.**

Feminists are also concerned to increase or protect women's freedom. For many feminists, women should be free to choose their own ways of life and should not be constrained by traditional or stereotypical rules about 'feminine' behaviour. ➔ **See Chapter 2.**

Feminist methods

When theorizing or campaigning, feminists may use methods that are common to other philosophies or causes. Thus, feminists use familiar methods of gathering and using evidence, criticizing and developing philosophical arguments, and political activism. But there are some methods that feminists have particularly pioneered, and two of these are worth discussion.

One strategy for feminism has been to ask what Katherine Bartlett calls 'the Woman Question' (1990). This asks how existing laws or theories are affected once the particular position of women is taken into account. The aim is to identify the way in which these theories or laws are based on a male norm and, thus, disadvantage women. For example, we might critically examine the fact that many professions require the most commitment from their workers just at the point at which female workers are most likely, and most biologically able, to have children. For example, it is during the childbearing years of the 20s and early 30s that academics must publish extensively in order to get tenure, lawyers must work hard to secure partnerships, and junior doctors are required to be on call for long periods. Because women are more likely than men to take responsibility for carework, and women face stricter biological time constraints on their fertility than do men, the Woman Question reveals that apparently gender-neutral employment practices disadvantage women. The Woman Question can also be asked of philosophical theories (for an example, see Okin, 1989).

The second unique feminist strategy is consciousness raising. Consciousness raising is particularly associated with second-wave feminism. It involved a group of people—usually women (although there were also consciousness-raising groups for men)—meeting regularly to discuss issues of importance or concern in their lives. Consciousness-raising groups operated on strict norms of equality, with no hierarchical structure or leadership. Their aim was to allow each member to talk about her own experiences and, through

---

☆ **KEY POINTS**

- The entrenchment of gender states that gender remains one of the most significant social cleavages.

- The existence of patriarchy states that gender norms are not neutral, but cast women as inferior.

- The need for change states that gender hierarchy is not natural, desirable, or inevitable, but should be changed. Feminists thus argue for equality between women and men, and for women's freedom.

- Feminists use philosophical and political methods that are common to other theories or campaigns, but there are some distinctively feminist methods, such as the Woman Question and consciousness raising.

interaction with other members and their stories, to develop a more critical understanding of those experiences. With this critical understanding of experiences would come new perspectives on social structures, particularly those relating to gender inequality. Ultimately, the aim was transformative: through consciousness raising, many women instigated changes in their own lives, the lives of their families, and their interaction with society and political institutions.

 KEY CONCEPTS

First-wave feminism

First-wave feminism refers to the women's suffrage movements of the late nineteenth and early twentieth centuries. First-wave feminists, such as Sylvia, Emmeline, and Christabel Pankhurst, Mary Wollstonecraft, John Stuart Mill, and Sojourner Truth, argued that the rights that men enjoyed should be extended to women. Some first-wave feminists based these arguments on claims that women were men's equals; others argued that women's reason was superior to that of men. All argued that women's interests were not reducible to those of their husbands and that women, consequently, needed to be able to vote for themselves.

Second-wave feminism

Second-wave feminism refers to the resurgence of feminist activism, particularly radical feminism, in the 1960s and 1970s. It is associated with feminists such as Shulamith Firestone, Andrea Dworkin, Germaine Greer, and Mary Daly. Key themes of second-wave feminism include: the attack on male violence towards women, particularly sexual violence; the rejection of 'feminine' norms such as sexual submissiveness and participation in beauty practices; the critique of enforced female domesticity; a critique of heterosexuality as inherently hierarchical, with political lesbianism sometimes advocated; and the insistence on female solidarity and sisterhood.

Post-feminism

Post-feminism signifies resistance to the themes of second-wave feminism. Feminists such as Camille Paglia, Katie Roiphe, and Pat Califia are associated with post-feminism. Key themes include the ideas that: women must see themselves as **agents**, not as victims, and that a focus on violence undermines women's agency; sexuality should be thought of as liberating and that all consensual sex should be celebrated; feminism should focus on women's material equality, rather than on symbolic aspects of gender; and femininity, including participation in beauty practices and gendered dress, is compatible with equality.

Natasha Walter's book *The New Feminism* (1998) is a key post-feminist text, but Walter recants her post-feminism in her most recent book *Living Dolls: The Return of Sexism* (2010).

The sex/gender distinction

A key theme of feminist theory has been the idea that it is vital to distinguish the terms 'sex' and 'gender'.

Feminism aims to identify and criticize the disadvantages suffered by women. In order to do so, feminists need to tread a careful line between arguments that focus on *difference* between men and women, and arguments that focus on *sameness*. Feminists recognize, and often try to celebrate, the fact that women are different from men, but they also criticize aspects of this difference and argue in favour of equality. Arguing in favour of equality is sometimes supposed to require a claim of sameness, because, in order for two things to be equal, there must be some respect in which they are the same.

One feminist technique for dealing with this problem has been to argue that there is a crucial distinction between biological *sex* difference and social *gender* difference. On this account, 'sex' refers to those differences that are an inevitable part of biology. These are primarily differences in the physical size and shape of men and women, with the most significant differences concerning the organs and functions of reproduction. On the other hand, 'gender' refers to those differences that are imposed only by social norms, such as the norm that baby girls should wear pink and baby boys should wear blue, or the norm that women should be kind and emotional, whereas men should be tough and rational.

Many feminists argue that patriarchal societies confuse social gender differences with biological sex differences. Thus, John Stuart Mill, for example, argued in 1859 that '*What is now called the nature of women is an eminently artificial thing—the result of a forced repression in some directions, unnatural stimulation in others*' (1996: 135). Thus, one task for feminists is to identify which differences are true sex differences and which are mere gender differences. A second task is to determine which gender differences are objectionable and unjust, and which (if any) are not. For example, we might say that it is a difference of sex, and not of gender, that women and not men give birth and breastfeed children. It is, however, a difference of gender, and not sex, that women are far more likely to stay at home to look after children on a full-time basis than are men. Whether this gender difference is unjust depends on further features of the case: whether women are able to choose alternative options; whether caring work has social status; whether full-time mothers have financial independence; etc.

The sex/gender distinction faces attack from several angles. Some are hostile to feminism, claiming that much of what feminists attribute to gender is, in fact, attributable to sex. If this is the case, then the feminist thesis of the need for change is undermined, because if gender differences are natural, this suggests they are unproblematic or inevitable. But the sex/gender distinction has also been criticized from within feminism. Some feminists, such as Catharine MacKinnon (1989) and Germaine Greer (1970; 1991), argue that it is misleading to talk as though so-called sex differences are purely biological and have no social basis. First, it is not really possible to identify two discrete and concrete biological sexes. Sex difference encompasses a number of biological features, such as the visible external genitals (vulva or penis), the internal reproductive organs (uterus or testes), and the chromosomal make-up of the person (XX or XY). In the paradigmatic male and female, these distinctions are aligned, but there are many people who have some features of one sex and some features of another. The biological 'truth' of sex is, thus, less clear-cut than it first appears.

Second, some feminists point out that biological features are not significant in and of themselves. Rather, they assume significance only when societies point to those biological features as significant. Why should an entire system of social category be constructed around sex differences, as opposed to any other biological differences? Thus, Catharine MacKinnon argues that gender is a matter of politics and power, rather than a matter of

> ### 📖 KEY TEXTS
>
> #### Simone de Beauvoir, *The Second Sex* (1949)
>
> This text argues that women are defined by their sex, which is, in turn, defined relative to male-ness: a woman is a 'not-man'. Men, on the other hand, are defined independently of their sex and of women, as autonomous and rational beings. This imbalance underpins the inequality between men and women. In order to bring about equality between men and women, women must be redefined as, like men, having freedom and **autonomy**. The autonomous woman needs civil liberties and economic independence, but, beyond this, she also needs to overcome the ideals of passive femininity and sexual submission.

biology or psychology. As she puts it (1989: 219): '*Distinctions of body or mind or behavior are pointed to as cause rather than effect, with no realization that they are so deeply effect rather than cause that pointing to them at all is an effect. Inequality comes first, difference comes after.*' If MacKinnon is right, there is no real difference between sex and gender.

> ### ☆ KEY POINTS
>
> - The sex/gender distinction has, historically, been important to feminist thought. According to the distinction, 'sex' refers to biological differences and 'gender' refers to social differences.
> - Feminists have used the sex/gender distinction to argue that many observable differences between men and women are differences of gender, rather than of sex. They are, thus, not inevitable and can be changed.
> - But some feminists criticize the sex/gender distinction. The biological categories of 'male' and 'female' are not as distinct as they seem—and it is society, not biology, that makes these categories so significant.

Feminism, liberalism, and the law

We have seen that feminists argue in favour of women's equality with men and in favour of women's freedom. The ideas of freedom and equality can be seen as fundamentally *liberal* ideas, and so some feminists can be described as liberal feminists. Liberal feminists are those who argue that feminism is best served by applying the values and methods of liberalism to the situation of women. Often, this involves campaigning for laws that formally recognize gender equality—particularly equality of opportunity.

Perhaps the most famous liberal feminist struggle in Western countries is the women's suffrage movement of the late nineteenth and early twentieth centuries. Women's struggle for the vote is an example of the feminist movement insisting that the liberal values of **liberty** and equality should apply to women, as well as to men. ➡ See Chapter 2. For example, the US National Woman Suffrage Association, formed by Elizabeth Cady Stanton and Susan B. Anthony, published a weekly newspaper, between 1868 and 1872, with the motto '*The true republic—men, their rights and nothing more; women, their rights and nothing less*'.

Other campaigns that can be understood in a liberal framework include campaigns for anti-discrimination legislation—such as the UK's Equal Pay Act 1970, Sex Discrimination Act 1975, and Equality Act 2010 (see Box 12.1), and the ongoing campaign in the USA for an Equal Rights Amendment to the US Constitution, which would explicitly forbid any denial of equal rights on account of sex. ➡ **See Chapter 8.**

Campaigns such as these are clearly justifiable with reference to the liberal values of freedom and equality. The task of feminists involved in these campaigns has been to show that societies already committed to liberal values, such as the UK and the USA, were harbouring practices antithetical to those values. Women should be included as among those citizens who were equal and deserving of liberty, and legal reform was required to make good on the founding principles of liberal societies. But the philosophical task of applying liberal equality to the position of women and men is not straightforward. Equality sometimes seems to require treating people the same—and this is problematic in the context of difference. As a result, as mentioned earlier, feminists have been conflicted as to whether the right form of equality for women focuses on difference or sameness. ➡ **See Chapter 5.**

Feminism that focuses on sameness argues that treating women equally means treating them the same as men. In other words, if we are trying to pursue gender equality, we need to allow women to do the same jobs as men, to enjoy the same rewards as men, and to compete on the same basis as men. If a man and a woman apply for the same job, for example, they should be judged on the same criteria.

BOX 12.1 LEGISLATION FOR SEX EQUALITY

- In the UK, the Equal Pay Act 1970 gives an individual a right to the same contractual pay and benefits as a person of the opposite sex in the same employment, if the man and the woman are doing like work, or work rated as equivalent, or work that is proved to be of 'equal value'.

- The British Sex Discrimination Act 1975 outlawed discrimination in employment, education, advertising, or when providing housing, goods, services, or facilities. It is unlawful to discriminate because of sex or marital status, and it is also illegal to discriminate in employment on grounds of pregnancy, maternity, or gender reassignment.

- The Equality Act 2010 supersedes the previous legislation. It includes permission for political parties to use women-only shortlists for election candidates, requires private-sector employers to publish information about the relative pay of women and men, and makes it unlawful to treat a woman '*unfavourably because she is breastfeeding*'.

- In the USA, the Equal Rights Amendment (ERA) to the Constitution proposed by Alice Paul in 1923 stated: '*Men and women shall have equal rights throughout the United States and every place subject to its jurisdiction.*' The proposed ERA was amended in 1943 to read: '*Equality of rights under the law shall not be denied or abridged by the United States or any State on account of sex.*' But, although the ERA was passed by Congress in 1972, it was not ratified by all of the states in time to pass into law. It has been before Congress ever since 1982, but has not yet been passed.

But the sameness approach has two problems. First, it takes men as the standard for which women should aim and implies that women can be considered equal only in so far as they are like men. It implies that any way in which women are different from men is a way in which they are worse than men and undermines the idea that femaleness is valuable. It does not, in other words, encourage equal respect. By imposing the standard of maleness, women's status is undermined. The second problem with the sameness approach to equality is that it fails to take adequate account of the ways in which women and men are different. It is all very well requiring women and men to meet the same criteria, but some criteria might be inherently biased towards one gender. For example, treating women the same as men might mean denying or drastically curtailing maternity leave, because men do not give birth to babies and have traditionally not taken time off work when they become fathers (a tradition that has started to change). Treating women the same as men might, therefore, fail to treat them equally, because women face different constraints from those of men.

Feminism that focuses on difference is an attempt to avoid these problems. This approach argues that treating people equally does not always mean treating them the same. Instead, if we are to treat people equally, we need to take account of their differences: perhaps women need more parental leave than men, because they are the ones who give birth, for example. Indeed, difference-based approaches may go further and argue that women and men have different strengths that justify different careers and lifestyles. Equality, on this understanding, is secured not by sameness, but by awarding equal value, respect, or **recognition** to the different skills of women and men. ➡ **See Chapter 3**. Thus, women might be more suited to childcare than men, and this should be recognized, but equality requires that childcare is given equal status to other, male pursuits.

The problem with this approach is that it paints a very essentialist picture of male and female roles. It assumes that all women are alike, and may trap them into gendered roles by questioning their claims to have the same skills and abilities as men. Difference feminism appears to stereotype women which would undermine their equality rather than respect it.

For Nancy Fraser (1997), the solution to this problem is to deconstruct gender: to envisage a world in which gender divisions are blurred or non-existent. One way to do this, in the context of debates over childcare, is to move away from both the idea that women must be able to be breadwinners *like men* and the idea that women's role in childcare must be emphasized. Instead, men might become more *like women*: combining both caring roles and paid employment. The aim of such an approach would be to ensure equal *respect*.

Arguments such as Fraser's are helpful in understanding why it is that liberal legal reforms have not, in practice, secured equality for women. Although pay discrimination is illegal in the UK, for example, the gender pay gap is 22% (on the government's preferred measure of comparing the pay of all men and women in work and looking at the median). Research by the Government Equalities Office (Olsen et al., 2010) concludes that much of the pay gap is explained by issues such as occupational sex **segregation** and the negative effects on women's salaries of taking time out of the labour market to look after family. However, it concludes that discrimination is the most likely explanation for 36% of the pay gap.

What issues such as the pay gap demonstrate is that formal equality before the law is not enough to secure genuine sex equality. The causes of inequality are set deep in the social structure and institutions, outside the realm that has traditionally been thought to comprise the **political sphere**. Arguments along these lines form the basis of the archetypal feminist slogan: '*The personal is political*.'

☆ **KEY POINTS**

- Liberal feminists argue for laws that give women formal equality of opportunity and freedom from discrimination.

- Equality and anti-discrimination law has been an essential part of feminist change—but such law does not eliminate inequality.

- A problem for liberal feminism is whether equality requires a focus on difference or a focus on sameness. A focus on difference emphasizes how women are different from men. A focus on sameness insists that they must be treated the same as men.

'The personal is political'

'The personal is political' was a rallying cry of radical second-wave feminism. The slogan aimed to capture the sense that women's oppression occurs everywhere, in areas that had not previously been subjected to scrutiny. The slogan can be understood as a critique of the traditional liberal separation between the political or **public sphere**—that is, government and politics—and the personal or **private sphere**—that is, family and personal relationships—with legitimate state interference confined to the former, so as to protect individual liberty.

Susan Moller Okin (1989) argues that 'the personal is political' comprises four separate claims. First, it highlights the fact that the private sphere is a sphere of *power*. One definition of the 'political' is that it is the sphere in which there is power, or the sphere in which rights and duties, advantages and disadvantages, are distributed. The statement draws attention to the fact that power and advantage also characterize areas of life that are not usually thought of as political—areas such as family life and personal relationships. Domestic violence is one example of power pervading the private sphere and has, thus, been a key area of feminist analysis, as discussed later. ➡ **See Chapter 14**. If the personal is political, it follows that family life and personal relationships should be subject to normative scrutiny.

The second way in which the personal is political is that the explicitly political sphere defines and infiltrates the personal. Institutions such as the family are not immune from state interference; rather, they are defined by the state. For example, the state defines marriage. It declares who may marry (heterosexual couples only, or homosexual couples as well), what the requirements for marriage are (how old the marrying partners must be, whether they may have more than one marriage at a time), what legal rights and duties apply to married couples (tax benefits, parental responsibilities, ownership of property), and the conditions for ending the marriage (whether and when divorce is allowed, and what it entails). These conditions of marriage are defined by the state and imposed on married couples, regardless of their wishes: it is not possible to marry but agree on unique conditions for divorce, for example. Marriage is just one of the ways in which the state is intricately involved in the private sphere. As a result, it does not make sense to say that individual liberty requires that the private sphere be left immune from state interference. There is no such thing as a private sphere without such interference.

KEY TEXTS

Okin, *Justice, Gender and the Family* (1989)

This text examines how much contemporary political philosophy ignores women, gender inequality, and the injustice of the family. Okin notes that it is not enough simply to answer the woman question in philosophy by using gender-neutral language, such as 'he or she'. Although such shifts in language perform the useful task of uncovering the male bias in much of our current and traditional thinking, changing the language is not enough to undo the bias. Much of *Justice, Gender and the Family* is devoted to exposing the way in which contemporary political philosophers fail to take sexual difference into account, despite their use of gender-neutral language.

Third, the personal is political in that the private sphere—and particularly family life—creates the psychological conditions that govern public life. Another way of putting this is to say that the family is a crucial arena for **social construction**—that is, the process by which social norms affect our lives, either by shaping the options that are available to or appropriate for us, or by affecting the way in which we interpret society, understand ourselves, and form preferences. In patriarchal societies, social construction is deeply gendered. For example, there are very different norms governing the way that men and women are supposed to look: norms of clothing, make-up, deportment, and beauty are profoundly sex-specific. The family or personal sphere is an important arena in which we develop our attitudes to these norms. Children grow up watching men and women conform to these, and other, gendered norms (such as norms about housework and childcare). Part of the process of growing up involves children internalizing these norms and applying them to their own lives: for example, girls and boys come to understand what sorts of clothes and toys are appropriate for their gender, and, in time, develop 'appropriate' preferences. Similarly, Okin argues that if children grow up in a household that is characterized by the gendered division of labour, they will internalize these gendered differences and apply them in ways that undermine gender equality. In particular, they will internalize the idea that women are nurturers and should have ultimate responsibility for childcare, as opposed to the male role of breadwinning. As a result, gender differences are instilled in the next generation and perpetuated in society.

The fourth and final aspect of 'the personal is political' is the claim that the gendered division of labour within the private sphere, with women taking on most or all of the domestic and caring tasks, creates barriers for women in every other sphere and, thus, spills over into all other areas. Some of these barriers occur as a direct result of the gendered division of labour, in the sense that women's material and mental resources are diminished by the need to take on all of the domestic work in a household. But women's concentration in the private sphere also spills over into public life, in the sense that women are underrepresented in positions of power, such as government, the judiciary, and business. For example, in 2010, only 22%

> ### 🔖 KEY TEXTS
>
> #### Friedan, *The Feminine Mystique* (1963)
>
> This text discusses '*the problem that has no name*': the unhappiness, loneliness, and shame of the suburban housewife in the USA. Friedan argues that, after World War II—during which many women had worked in traditionally male jobs, such as manufacturing—women were persuaded that they would be fulfilled only by domesticity, motherhood, and femininity. This persuasion was backed up by supposedly scientific theories, such as crude Freudian analysis and evolutionary theory, and was reinforced by women's magazines and advertising. As a result, the US woman's life was confined to the home, with her only involvement with the outside world being via her husband and children.

of UK members of Parliament, and 17 % of members of the US Senate and House of Representatives, were women. In turn, women's relative lack of involvement in political, judicial, and economic decision making hinders progressive change.

Feminism and family

As is evident from this discussion, a critique of family life has been central to many feminists. Criticisms of women's confinement to the family can be found in the work of early feminists such as Mary Wollstonecraft and John Stuart Mill, continuing, through Simone de Beauvoir and Betty Friedan, to contemporary feminists. For many of these theorists, paid employment for women has been thought to be necessary to their equality and **emancipation**.

Employment outside the home might be necessary for women's equality for several reasons, including the following:

- It provides women with the financial resources necessary for them to be independent, able to make their own decisions, and to live without a male partner if they so wish.
- Paid employment enables women to use their skills and may be more rewarding than repetitive domestic work.
- Paid employment is awarded more status than is domestic work, so if women are to enjoy equal respect, then they must have access to employment.
- If women are confined to domestic work, then they are not able to exercise influence in important areas, such as politics, law, and business. Only by leaving the home and domestic demands can women gain positions of power that enable them to change society in significant ways.

But, in recent years, some feminists have become critical of the idea that women's equality requires that women work outside the home. Some of these critiques are part of an attempt to value domestic life and what is seen as women's particular role in it. A good example of this approach is the ethics of care, discussed in the next section.

Other critiques from within feminism point to the fact that paid employment may not be as emancipatory for women as feminists hoped. Housework, and caring for children and the infirm, always have to be done. Paid employment is only liberating for women if these domestic tasks are performed by someone else, because paid work is organized in ways that assume that workers have somebody else to perform domestic work, particularly childcare. The working day is much longer than the school day and the holiday entitlement of most jobs does not cover the school holiday. Moreover, childcare is very expensive. And yet, while women are now more likely to go out to work, there has not been a corresponding increase in men taking responsibility for childcare and domestic work.

☆ **KEY POINTS**

- A key claim of feminism is that 'the personal is political'. This claim criticizes the traditional liberal separation of public and private spheres, with state action and justice thought to be a matter only for the public sphere.

- The private sphere contains power. Hierarchy, injustice, abuse, and violence can occur within the private sphere—and, therefore, it is subject to politics.

- The private sphere is a political creation. The state defines institutions such as family and marriage. It is, thus, not the case that the private sphere can remain separate from the state.

- We develop a sense of justice as we grow up in a family. Injustice learned in the family will be transferred to our understanding of what justice requires in all areas of life.

- The gendered division of labour undermines gender equality. It means that women are financially dependent on men, and makes women unable to take up positions of power and influence.

- Paid employment may be a means of women gaining influence and independence—but the problem of domestic work remains.

The ethics of care

Not all feminists have criticized women's traditional association with the domestic sphere and caring work. In 1982, Carol Gilligan published *In a Different Voice*, which argued that the gendered family schools men and women into different methods of moral thinking. Through interviews with college students, Gilligan identified two different ways of thinking about morality, which she characterized as 'justice' and 'care'. While almost all men focused on justice, women were fairly evenly spread between justice and care. Rather than downplaying women's involvement in caring, the ethics of care suggests that feminists ought to re-emphasize the specific moral outlook that caring gives women.

Liberal theories of justice, such as those of John Rawls and Ronald Dworkin, focus on individualistic ideas of rights, understood in the abstract. The focus of such theories is on developing principles of justice that can apply universally (or at least universally within a particular society), and that are impartial and emphasize individual autonomy. Justice encourages us to think about our individual entitlements and to prioritize the claims of the individual above claims of the group. ➡ **See Chapters 5 and 8.**

In contrast, the ethics of care focuses on human connectedness, self-sacrifice, and obligations to others. It takes account of the relationships between people, and the need sometimes to focus on emotions and support for particular others with whom we are in close relationships. The claim of the ethics of care is that this approach is crucial to morality: we should not contrast morality and care, but should, rather, consider care to be part of what morality requires.

Justice has often been seen as superior to care: as being based on rationality rather than emotion; as focusing on the abstract not the specific; as applicable in general and free from bias. The claim of the ethics of care is that care is an important part of moral reasoning—and may even be superior to justice in some ways. In place of justice, care emphasizes peace, compromise, and stability. How might the demands of justice and care differ? Imagining a case within which the demands of family conflict with the demands of other people in general can best answer this. For example, a woman who works for a children's charity might face competing demands from her job and her family. The demands of abstract principles of justice might require that she devote most of her time and energy to her job, while the demands of care might require that she prioritize her own children, even if they are much better off than the children she would be helping at work.

Of course, approaches based on justice do not usually claim that we are never justified in prioritizing our own family. The usual strategy is to attempt to delineate a sphere of legitimate partiality that can be justified in universal terms: all people are justified in granting a set amount of priority to those close to them, but no further. For example, justice might allow us to give our close friends career advice, but not to give them a job if they are not the best candidate. The first partiality (the advice) is compatible with justice, but the second (the job) is not. In order to be distinct from justice, then, the ethics of care must go beyond this sort of partiality, which is delineated and permitted in advance. According to the ethics of care, partiality to particular others that goes *beyond* what justice allows is sometimes necessary and morally legitimate. One way of thinking about this claim is that certain relationships, such as those with our children, are so important that they should never be subjected to abstract rational analysis.

Criticisms of the ethics of care

An important criticism of the ethics of care claims that justice is, in fact, the most crucial value for women's equality. As we have already seen, feminists insist that the personal is political, and one meaning of this claim is that relationships that are supposedly characterized by care can be characterized by power and abuse. Feminists have, thus, insisted that justice should apply in every sphere, not exempting family and other personal relationships. Thus, Martha Nussbaum (1999b) argues that feminists must strengthen, not undermine, the focus on the individual and her rights. In other words, liberalism is not too individualistic to take account of women's rights and equality; if anything, it is not individualistic enough. Women suffer many forms of oppression in the family, ranging from domestic violence, to forced marriage, to financial dependence or poverty. For Nussbaum, the solution is to insist that each and every person is considered an individual worthy of rights and respect: a focus on care, family, and obligation risks putting the needs of women below the interests of men and children.

> ☆ **KEY POINTS**
>
> • The ethics of care is a moral approach that is contrasted with justice. Whereas justice prioritizes abstract individualistic rights, care prioritizes situated relational empathy.
>
> • Justice-based approaches typically allow for partiality towards particular others only within certain universally defined limits. Care-based approaches emphasize that partiality may take precedence over more general, or universal, demands of justice.
>
> • Carol Gilligan suggests that both women and men use justice-based approaches, but that the ethics of care is associated with women only. For Gilligan, morality requires both justice and care.
>
> • Not all feminists are convinced that the ethics of care helps women. It may enhance nurturing stereotypes and confine women to the domestic sphere, or it might distract attention from the role of individualistic justice in securing women's rights and equality.

Sex and violence

A key part of feminism, particularly of second-wave feminism, has been the analysis and criticism of male violence towards women, and the connection of that violence with sex.

The statistics about violence towards women are shocking. The UK British Crime Survey of 2009 found that women are the victims in 77% of cases of domestic violence, and that, in 2008–9, the police recorded 12,165 rapes and 19,740 sexual assaults on women, as compared with 968 rapes and 2,323 sexual assaults on men.[1] One in four UK women experiences domestic violence in her lifetime. Amnesty International (2004) reports that one in three women, worldwide, experiences violence, abuse, or rape in her lifetime, and that 70% of female murder victims are killed by their male partners.

These statistics reinforce the feminist arguments that the private sphere of family and personal relationships is a sphere of power, because a great deal of violence against women is committed by men with whom women are in a relationship. This fact is true of crimes that are not usually thought of in this way. For example, a 2013 government report into sexual offending found that '90 per cent of victims of the most serious sexual offences in the previous year knew the perpetrator, compared with less than half for other sexual offences'.[2] Moreover, the prosecution rate for rape is particularly low: according to a Home Office Research Study in 2005, it is 5.6% (Kelly et al., 2005).

Radical feminists are those who argue that the extent of violence against women is key to understanding patriarchy. Rather than an abhorrent exception, violence against women should be recognized to be routine—an integral part of the way in which women and men relate under conditions of sex inequality. For radical feminists, it is not possible to secure equality and freedom for women until violence against them is stopped.

The claim that violence against women is routine does not mean that it is acceptable or that it is inevitable; rather, it means that violence is part and parcel of gender inequality. It is both the *result* and the *cause* of inequality: rape and other violence happen because women are unequal to men, and rape and other violence keep women unequal to men. Thus, Susan Brownmiller (1977: 14–15) argues: '*From prehistoric times to the present, I believe, rape has*

> ### KEY TEXTS
>
> #### Greer, *The Female Eunuch* (1970; 1991)
>
> The central argument of this text is that women's liberation requires the rejection of the idea that women's libido is 'merely responsive'. Women are effectively rendered eunuchs by a social structure that denies their sexuality and freedom in several ways. In physical terms, many of the features that characterize a supposedly female body are labelled as such only by stereotype and biased assumptions. These stereotypes extend to norms about sex, family, and love. In general, women are required to be passive and submissive, recipients of male energy and power. Greer uses a variety of literary, pornographic, and other sources to illustrate that '*Women have very little idea of how much men hate them*'.

played a crucial function. It is nothing more or less than a conscious process of intimidation by which all men keep all women in a state of fear.'

Claims such as this—as well as the claim sometimes attributed to radical feminists that 'All men are rapists'—are often misunderstood. The claim is not that each individual man is, in fact, or has the tendency to be, a rapist; the claim is, rather, that women do not know which men are rapists and which men are not. So, from a woman's point of view, each man whom she encounters might, possibly, be a rapist. Women are, thus, encouraged to live in fear of attack: a situation that leads them to limit their activities and their confidence. Women might be afraid to go out after dark or to walk the streets alone. Despite the fact that men are more likely to suffer violence in a public place than women (because men are more likely to get into fights or suffer violence on the streets and because most attacks on women occur inside a private home), it is women who are warned to be careful of venturing out alone. Rape and violence thus cause women to be afraid of acting independently, even though the real place of danger is the home.

In confronting rape and violence against women, feminists have debated whether rape is a crime of violence or a crime of sex. One feminist interpretation of rape is to say that, properly understood, it has nothing to do with sex. Sex is an intimate act between two equals; rape, on the other hand, should be understood as an act of violence. Instead of being motivated by sexual desire, rape is motivated by a male desire for power. ➔ See Chapter 14.

But radical feminists argue that it is problematic to try to distinguish sex and violence, because the two are intimately linked. Sexual violence is the main driver of sex inequality, and it occurs because patriarchal societies eroticize female submission and male domination. Norms about appropriate male and female roles during courtship, romance, and sex all emphasize that men should be active and in control, whereas women should be passive. For example, it is customary that men should invite women to go out on dates or to get married. Sexually, women are supposed to want sex less than men and are supposed to refuse casual sex so as to protect their reputations. Romantically, men are supposed to woo women by buying flowers and paying for dinner. This eroticization of female submission and male domination underpins patriarchy, and partially explains why rape and violence occur. Radical feminists make similar arguments in condemning pornography (see the case study).

Liberal feminists also strongly criticize rape and other forms of violence against women—but they are less likely to focus on the eroticization of inequality and more likely to focus on the need for legal reforms to increase the prosecution rate for rape. There are many reasons why rape is so difficult to prosecute. Perhaps the largest problem is the problem of evidence. Advances in DNA testing mean that it is usually possible to prove, scientifically, whether intercourse took place. Alleged rapists are, thus, more likely to appeal to the defence of consent than the defence of denial: they accept that intercourse took place, but claim that the woman consented to it. This defence makes evidence harder to obtain, because the charge turns on the fact or otherwise of consent—and this is hard to prove.

Another problem with prosecuting rape is that many women are afraid to take their case to court, because they fear (or are told by law enforcement agencies) that it will be a deeply traumatic experience. Moreover, this fear is well founded: inequalities in the rules for questioning alleged victims and alleged perpetrators of rape mean that women may be subjected to intense questioning about their sexual history, with the implication being that a sexually active woman cannot be raped, whereas any previous offences or accusations of rape committed by the alleged attacker are not revealed in court. Many feminists campaign for these sorts of rules to be changed so as to increase prosecution rates for rape.

☆ KEY POINTS

- Violence against women is prevalent. Contrary to popular opinion, however, women who suffer violence or rape usually suffer it at the hands of men whom they know, inside a private home, rather than at the hands of strangers, in a public place.

- For radical feminists, the prevalence of violence against women is part and parcel of sex inequality. It is because women are unequal to men that they suffer violence, and the fact that women suffer violence helps to keep them unequal. In patriarchal societies, heterosexuality involves the eroticization of male dominance and female submission.

- Liberal feminists are more likely to see male violence against women as an injustice committed by a minority. The solution is improved policing, court procedures, and rape laws, to ensure that rapists are convicted.

Conclusion

Feminists have many challenges for political philosophers. Most basically, feminists ask why it is that the equality and liberty that liberal philosophers advocate has not, in fact, materialized for women. At the very least, women's equality requires changes to law and society, so that women really do have equal opportunities and freedoms to men. But these simple changes may not be enough. For some feminists, most political philosophy simply lacks the conceptual resources needed to take adequate account of the differences between men and women: either the differences that exist naturally, or the differences that are imposed by society.

Support from within feminism can, thus, be found for a variety of changes. The distinction between public and private must be broken down, because family and personal life is of crucial relevance to justice. Women's access to employment, and men's contribution to domestic work and caring responsibilities, must be rethought. The problem of male violence towards women is grave and poses considerable barriers to justice—barriers that are not taken seriously by non-feminist philosophers. Issues of sex and pornography demonstrate problems with liberal concepts such as freedom of speech. And the ethics of care suggests that justice itself may be insufficient. Gender, therefore, is not something to be added on to political theories after they have been developed: it is something that must be considered from the very beginning.

 CASE STUDY

Pornography

Pornography is an issue of deep controversy within feminism. For some feminists, pornography is a result and a cause of sex inequality, the objectification of women, and violence against women. For others, pornography should be protected as part of freedom of speech, and any censorship undermines the values that feminists should be defending. This case study considers the feminist arguments for and against pornography.

Defining pornography

The first step in an analysis of pornography is to define it. It is useful to distinguish three concepts: obscenity, pornography, and erotica. In the UK and the USA, the law that deals with explicit sexual material uses the concept of obscenity. Obscenity is material that has a bad effect on people—specifically, material that undermines morality when it is viewed. The UK Obscene Publications Act 1959 defines obscenity as material that '*is such as to tend to deprave and corrupt*' those who are likely to encounter it. Obscenity is, thus, a moralized concept, which refers to the effect of the material rather than its content. Explicitly sexual material need not be obscene and material can, in principle, be obscene without being sexual.

Pornography, in contrast, is a concept that refers to content. Bernard Williams (1981) defines pornography as a representation of sexual activity that is intended to arouse. Thus sexy lingerie is not pornographic, even if it is intended to arouse, because it is not a representation of sexual activity; a sex education book is not pornographic, even if depicts sex, as long as it is not intended to arouse.

A third term, erotica, is controversial. Some question its use, suggesting that it is used merely to indicate pornography and by people who find the label more palatable—that is, 'what turns you on is pornography; what turns me on is erotica'. But some feminists have a more specific definition of pornography as material that eroticizes sexual hierarchy, and use the term 'erotica' to describe sexually arousing material that does not depict inequality.

Pornography and freedom of speech

A central issue concerning pornography is freedom of speech. Freedom of speech is often thought to be vital to liberal societies. For example, the First Amendment of the US Constitution states:

> Congress shall make no law respecting an establishment of religion, or prohibiting the free exercise thereof, or abridging the freedom of speech, or of the press; or the right of the people peaceably to assemble, and to petition the Government for a redress of grievances. This right is either absolute or it does not exist.

Similarly, John Stuart Mill (1996) argues that freedom of speech is essential to progress. Unless ideas may be expressed freely, we have no means of sorting the good ideas from the bad and we risk suppressing the truth. Both defences of free speech stress the dangers of censorship: it may suppress worthy material and it lends too much power to the government, undermining democratic accountability and equality.

Some feminists, such as Nadine Strossen (2000) and Alison Assiter (1989), use these liberal defences of free speech to defend pornography. They argue that, however unappealing some pornography may seem to women, the dangers of censorship are far greater. It would encourage tyrannical government and undermine individual freedom. And anti-pornography laws might censor legitimate literary, or even feminist, material, because state censorship has a history of being used against those who are disempowered or who challenge the status quo.

Andrea Dworkin (1997) argues that liberal arguments defending free speech do not apply to pornography. Mill argues that free speech must be protected, because the free exchange of ideas is necessary for progress and truth—but, according to Dworkin, pornography does not express ideas and so is not relevant to truth or progress. As Dworkin puts it, '*we are told all the time that pornography is really about ideas. Well, a rectum doesn't have an idea, and a vagina doesn't have an idea, and the mouths of women in pornography do not express ideas*' (1997: 129).

 KEY THINKERS

Andrea Dworkin (1946–2005)

In all of her work, Dworkin argues that male violence against women is both the most shocking and the most common aspect of patriarchy. She documents and analyses many varieties of male violence, including rape, domestic violence, the abuse of women in pornography, and racial violence, and argues that women can never be free until men's violence against them is stopped. Dworkin sees male violence as intricately related to patriarchal sexuality, according to which heterosexuality is female submission and male domination. One of her books, *Intercourse* (1987), explores heterosexuality as it is constructed under conditions of patriarchy. Another, *Pornography: Men Possessing Women* (1981), discusses the role that pornography plays in perpetuating sexual hierarchy and violence.

Catharine MacKinnon (1987) has a further argument against the idea that free speech protects pornography. For MacKinnon, it is pornography itself that constrains speech. Specifically, it silences women by emphasizing that they are inferior to men and that women are properly thought of as sexual objects for male consumption. If women themselves are to be able to speak freely, MacKinnon argues, they need to have equality—and that equality is incompatible with pornography (see Box 12.2).

Pornography and sex

A central part of Dworkin and MacKinnon's argument against pornography is that pornography depicts sexual hierarchy. Indeed, their Anti-Pornography Civil Rights Ordinance defines pornography as sexual material depicting women as inferior or violated. For Dworkin and MacKinnon, this sexualization of hierarchy is part of what makes pornography so antithetical to feminism. They argue that much of pornography depicts women as enjoying abuse or humiliation, and that this reflects—and perpetuates—the real abuse that women experience every day. The fact that pornography is supposed to be sexually arousing demonstrates the deep nature of inequality: the abuse and inferiority of women is portrayed as erotic and exciting. Thus, MacKinnon argues that pornography *'makes hierarchy sexy and calls that "the truth about sex" or just a mirror of reality. Through this process, pornography constructs what a woman is as what men want from sex. This is what the pornography means'* (1987: 171).

These objections to the way in which sex is depicted in pornography have led other, anti-censorship, feminists to depict writers such as Dworkin and MacKinnon as prudish: Assiter (1989) describes them as 'anti-sex' and Strossen (2000) accuses them of causing a 'pornophobic' 'sex panic'. According to Assiter and Strossen, feminists who object to pornography have no basis for their arguments other than a dislike of sexual explicitness. Anti-censorship feminists have, therefore, argued that pornography, or sexually explicit material, is a healthy expression of adult sexuality. For these feminists, it is misleading to describe pornography as necessarily subordinating women. It is quite possible to see pornography as an expression of mutually enjoyable sex.

This disagreement is partly empirical, partly a matter of terminology, and partly normative. It is empirical in that it reflects a disagreement about what proportion of pornography depicts acts that all feminists would agree are degrading to women—or, at least, acts that depict violence against women. It is partly a matter of terminology in that Dworkin and MacKinnon define pornography as material that is hierarchical: if Strossen and Assiter are right that some 'pornography' is not hierarchical, then Dworkin and MacKinnon would simply say that it should not be called 'pornography' (that perhaps it should be called 'erotica'). But there remains a normative aspect to the disagreement: there is a disagreement between feminists as to whether certain images do, in fact, portray women as inferior or not.

Pornography and violence

The connection between pornography and violence is perhaps the most controversial aspect of the debate. There are several parts to this issue:

- pornographic depictions of violence;
- violence and harm caused to women who appear in pornography; and
- pornography encouraging its audience to commit acts of violence.

Pornographic depictions of violence

Much feminist debate concerns the question of violence depicted in pornography. In part, this is because pornography that is explicitly violent seems difficult for anti-censorship feminists to defend. Many such feminists thus argue that, while some pornography is violent, most pornography is not, and that, consequently, approaches such as that of Dworkin and MacKinnon are misleading, and the examples of violent pornography that they use are unrepresentative.

It is certainly true that many anti-pornography feminists do analyse explicitly violent pornography. It is also certainly true that such material exists. Quite how prevalent it is, however, is unclear, although there have been some studies. A recent study examined fifty films from the bestseller lists (in shops and online) of the industry journal *Adult Video News*. It found that *'48% of scenes portrayed verbal aggression, and a full 88.2% portrayed physical aggression . . . nearly 90% of scenes contained at least one aggressive act, with an average of 12 acts of aggression per scene'* (Bridges et al., 2008). The Criminal Justice and Immigration Act 2008 introduced a new offence of *'possession of extreme pornographic images'* in England, Wales, and Northern Ireland. In defence of the legislation, the government noted that the internet makes severely violent

BOX 12.2 THE DWORKIN/MACKINNON CIVIL RIGHTS ORDINANCE

In the 1980s, Andrea Dworkin and Catharine MacKinnon drafted a Civil Rights Ordinance. As civil rights legislation, the Ordinance would not censor pornography or prevent it from being published; instead, it would allow people—particularly, but not only, women—who had been harmed by pornography to sue its makers for damages. The Ordinance thus intended to allow action by those coerced into appearing in pornography, those on whom pornography is forced (for example, in the workplace or at home), and those who are raped by men acting on the influence of pornography or copying scenes from violent pornography. In the case of women coerced into pornography, for example, prevailing US law does forbid the **coercion** but protects, as free speech, the pornography depicting the rape.

The Ordinance was passed in Indianapolis in 1984. In 1985, it was struck down by the Seventh Circuit Court for violating the First Amendment of the US Constitution, which prohibits laws that abridge freedom of speech. In 1986, the Supreme Court declined to hear the case, leaving the Seventh Circuit judgement in place.

The Ordinance defines pornography as:

> the graphic sexually explicit subordination of women through pictures or words that also includes women dehumanized as sexual objects, things or commodities, enjoying pain or humiliation or rape, being tied up, cut up, mutilated, bruised or physically hurt, in postures of sexual submission or servility or display, reduced to body parts, penetrated by objects or animals, or presented in scenarios of degradation, injury, torture, shown as filthy or inferior, bleeding, bruised or hurt in a context that makes these conditions sexual.

material much more commonly available. Gail Dines, who has studied contemporary pornography and interviewed many producers and others in the pornography business, reports that:

> images today have now become so extreme that what used to be considered hard-core is now mainstream pornography. Acts that are now commonplace in much of online porn were almost nonexistent a couple of decades ago. As the market becomes saturated and consumers become increasingly bored and desensitized, pornographers are avidly searching for ways to differentiate their products from others.

(Dines, 2010: xvii)

Harm to women appearing in pornography

Dworkin and MacKinnon argue that pornography causes real harm to the real women who appear in it. Wherever pornography depicts a woman in a position of humiliation or bondage, a woman has had to experience humiliation or bondage. Moreover, they point out that some women are coerced into appearing in pornography. One important example of a woman coerced into appearing in pornography is the woman known as Linda Lovelace, who appears in the best-selling pornographic film *Deep Throat*. Lovelace has described how she was trapped and brutally coerced into appearing in that and other films, suffering rape and torture from the man who incarcerated her and made the films (Lovelace and McGrady, 1981).

Against these examples, some feminists point out that rape and violence are already illegal. Cases such as that of Linda Lovelace thus do not justify censorship of pornography, because it is the violence rather than the pornography that is the problem. While this is true, it is worth noting

KEY THINKERS

Catharine A. MacKinnon (1946–)

Catharine MacKinnon is the Elizabeth A. Long Professor of Law at the University of Michigan Law School. She has written many books, covering a wide range of feminist issues, such as sexual harassment, pornography, rape and domestic violence, law, the state, and international human rights. MacKinnon is a radical feminist, arguing that male violence and the eroticization of inequality are central to patriarchy. MacKinnon is a practising lawyer, as well as an academic. Her work pioneered the legal treatment of sexual harassment as a form of sex discrimination in the USA, and the treatment of rape, forced prostitution, and forced impregnation as legally-actionable acts of genocide.

that laws against rape are not the same as laws against pornography showing a rape. In the USA, *Deep Throat* is protected as freedom of speech, regardless of the circumstances in which it was filmed. Dworkin and MacKinnon thus argue that it is necessary to change the law such that pornography depicting real-life rape is not legally protected.

Pornography as incitement to violence

The question of whether pornography incites men who view it to commit acts of sexual violence against women and children is hotly debated. Two kinds of evidence are offered. The first is anecdotal: examples of attacks in which pornography was used, or of women or children who were forced to copy pornographic images, or of rapists who had a large collection of pornography. For example, in the hearings for the Dworkin/MacKinnon Ordinance, one Native American woman described how two white men raped her. During the attack, they repeatedly referred to a computer game called 'Custer's Revenge', in which the aim of the game is to rape Native American women (MacKinnon and Dworkin, 1997). The second sort of evidence offered to support the claim that pornography incites its audience to violence is that provided by experimental studies, of which there are many. Another example described at the Ordinance hearings exposed US volunteer male college students to one film per day for five days. Some saw 'slasher' films (combining sex with explicit gory violence), some saw non-violent pornography, and a control group watched a law school documentary. The study found that the men viewing the violent material became increasingly desensitized to the violence.

The significance of these sorts of evidence is contested. One problem is that different experiments have conflicting results; another problem is that anecdotal evidence is evidence only of a correlation between pornography and violence. It does not prove that the pornography caused the violence: many men view pornography and do not become violent. On the other hand, it is uncontroversial that people's behaviour is affected by the media that they encounter—after all, companies spend vast sums of money on advertising on precisely this assumption. Nonetheless, there is no consensus about whether pornography causes violence and, if it does so, what the implications of that would be. Opponents of censorship argue that, even if some violence is caused by pornography, the correct response is to tackle violence rather than pornography. Opponents of pornography argue that violence against women is not, in fact, prosecuted with any regularity, that part of the problem is that pornography helps to make violence against women seem normal and sexy, and that pornography is increasingly viewed by young people who assume that it does depict what real sex is, or should be.

QUESTIONS

1. What is 'feminism'?
2. What does it mean to say that 'the personal is political'?
3. How is the family relevant to feminism?
4. Is there a difference between 'sex' and 'gender'? Is the difference important?
5. What is the difference between feminism based on sameness and feminism based on difference?
6. Is the ethics of care a good alternative to justice?
7. What is the significance of violence against women?
8. How can feminists be both for and against pornography?
9. What is the difference between liberal feminism and radical feminism?
10. What changes do feminists think are needed in order to bring about gender equality?

 FURTHER READING

■ Abbey, R. (2011) *The Return of Feminist Liberalism*, Durham: Acumen Publishing Analysis of recent works of feminist liberalism.

■ Bryson, V. (1999) *Feminist Debates: Issues of Theory and Political Practice*, Basingstoke: Palgrave A useful introductory text on feminism.

■ Chambers, C. (2008) *Sex, Culture, and Justice: The Limits of Choice*, University Park, PA: Penn State University Press Argues that a theory of justice cannot ignore the role that culture plays in shaping choices.

■ Dines, G. (2010) *Pornland: How Porn has Hijacked our Sexuality*, Boston, MA: Beacon Press A feminist analysis of pornography.

■ hooks, b. (1982) *Ain't I a Woman? Black Women and Feminism*, London: Pluto Press Argues that feminism often ignores the situation of black women and underestimates the significance of differences between women.

■ Jeffreys, S. (2005) *Beauty and Misogyny: Harmful Cultural Practices in the West*, London: Routledge Explores the link between beauty practices and women's inequality.

■ MacKinnon, C. A. (2006) *Are Women Human? And Other International Dialogues*, Cambridge, MA: Belknap Press Argues that international human rights theory and practice ignores the position of women.

■ Walter, N. (2010) *Living Dolls: The Return of Sexism*, London: Virago Argues that girls are being brought up in an increasingly sexualized and sexist culture.

 WEB LINKS

● https://www.gov.uk/government/organisations/government-equalities-office The Government Equalities Office is a UK government agency. It describes itself as working 'to take action on the government's commitment to remove barriers to equality and help to build a fairer society, leading on issues relating to women, sexual orientation and transgender equality'.

- http://www.fawcettsociety.org.uk The Fawcett Society is a British organization, campaigning to 'close the inequality gap' between women and men.

- http://www.feminist.org The website of the Feminist Majority Foundation contains information and resources about global feminism.

- http://www.object.org.uk Object is a UK pressure group that challenges 'sex object culture'.

- http://ukfeminista.org.uk UK Feminista is 'a movement of ordinary women and men campaigning for gender equality'.

- http://www.now.org The National Organization for Women (NOW) is a US feminist pressure group.

- http://www.thefword.org.uk The F Word is a website devoted to contemporary UK feminism.

 Visit the Online Resource Centre that accompanies this book to access more learning resources: http://www.oxfordtextbooks.co.uk/orc/mckinnon3e/

 ## ENDNOTES

1 British Crime Survey 2009: http://webarchive.nationalarchives.gov.uk/20110314171826/http://rds.homeoffice.gov.uk/rds/pdfs09/hosb1109vol1.pdf

2 See Ministry of Justice, Home Office, and Office of National Statistics, 'An overview of sexual offending in England and Wales: statistics bulletin' (2013) available at: https://www.gov.uk/government/uploads/system/uploads/attachment_data/file/214970/sexual-offending-overview-jan-2013.pdf

13

Generations

AXEL GOSSERIES[1]

Chapter contents

- Introduction
- Government for the living only?
- Responsibility for the past?
- What (if anything) do we owe to future generations?
- We all age
- Conclusion

Reader's guide

How we relate to our ancestors and descendants is crucial to our identity. The succession of generations and the passage of time raise questions in democratic theory. There are also challenges with respect to the existence, justification, and content of our obligations to future and past generations. This chapter begins by examining whether and how our constitutional democracies should be redesigned to take into account the intergenerational dimensions of justice. It then moves on to consider whether meaningful accounts can be provided of the idea of responsibility for our ancestors' deeds. In a third section, the other side of the issue is explored: do we have obligations to *future* generations, and if so, how can they be accounted for? We close the chapter by investigating whether 'age' should be seen as a distinct focus point for theories of intergenerational justice and what differentiates it from, for example, gender or 'race'.

Introduction

Social life confronts us with a variety of issues of intergenerational and trans-generational justice: how should we adjust our pension schemes to population ageing? Should age discrimination be dealt with less strictly than gender discrimination? Should radioactive waste be disposed of in a non-retrievable way? Should young Germans be blamed for what their grandparents did during World War II? Should economists now rely on a zero **discount rate** when calculating the impact of climate change on future generations? All of these issues, and many others, involve, at their heart, questions of intergenerational justice. Surprisingly, theorists have devoted less attention to these questions than to, for example, global justice. And yet, there is no doubt about both the practical significance and the philosophically challenging nature of problems of trans-/intergenerational justice and democracy.

When looking into questions of generations, we are dealing with what the time dimension entails for our obligations of justice as well as for the design of our democracies. Time has a connection with *power*. We are unable to force past generations to have acted differently from the way in which they did. Moreover, even if we can sometimes prevent future generations from doing certain things (such as spreading a virus that we irreversibly destroy), we fully depend on them to transfer our political, linguistic, and artistic cultures, and all sorts of other resources, to even more remote generations. Time also holds a relationship with *investment* because things are never produced instantaneously. However, those who invest and put in the work effort—for example, by engaging in blue skies research—will not necessarily end up being those who reap the rewards, which has implications for justice. Time also connects with *uncertainty*: the future has not yet taken place and remains open—and even more so when it is remote. There are many things that we do not know for sure: the precise future impact of our actions; whether there will still be people around in 500 years and how many; what their preferences and their vulnerabilities will be; etc. As uncertainty tends to lead to short termism, and considering the possibility that our societies may be experiencing growing uncertainty at several levels, we can see, as well, how this may be crucial for those concerned about the long term. Finally, time is associated with *genesis*. We are mortals. Yet, while those living in the future will not be us, they will be the outcome of our reproductive choices, which could, in turn, affect the nature of our obligations towards them. This is so if we believe, for example, that parents have special duties towards children that non-parents do not have, because of the reproductive choices that they respectively made. These are just a few examples of significant ways in which the temporal dimension of our shared lives connects with the demands of justice and **democracy**.

The chapter will address four issues. We will first examine the notion of generational **sovereignty** and what is required for a democracy to take the interests of future generations into account. Next, we will look at whether groups of people today—typically, nations—should be held responsible for the actions or abstentions of their predecessors, and what would follow if they should not. We will explore our obligations to future birth cohorts from the perspective of various theories of justice. Finally, we will analyse the dimensions of justice between age groups and ask whether it raises issues irreducible to an approach in terms of justice between birth cohorts.

Government for the living only?

Let us begin with democracy. In his seminal letter to James Madison (1789), Thomas Jefferson insisted on the fact that '*We seem not to have perceived that, by the law of nature, one generation is to another as one independent nation to another*'. For Jefferson, this concern for generational sovereignty was mainly directed at the weight that past generations' decisions may have in the present. What he had in mind is the fact that the rigidity of a constitution—that is, the incorporation of provisions that make it harder to revise than a standard legislative act—strongly constrains possibilities for action for subsequent generations, despite the fact that none of them were involved in its enactment. Jefferson's concern—shared by Condorcet (2012)—is an invitation to reconsider our democratic procedures. In the late eighteenth century, the weight of the past—typically through an inherited constitution—was a key source of concern. However, in the early twenty-first century, it is the insufficient weight given to the future—typically through lack of specific representation for future voters—that worries those who assess the ability of our democracies to take the intergenerational dimension seriously. Is there a case for reducing the power of the living over future people? If so, how should this be done?

One of the questions addressed by democratic theory is how to identify who should take part, either directly or through representatives, in the deliberation, as well as in the vote, on a given issue—that is, who should be part of the *demos*. One proposal is the 'all affected principle'. Roughly, it states that all those who are potentially and significantly affected by a given decision should take part in the decision-making process. Whenever a decision is likely to impact on future generations, this principle calls for the inclusion of future generations in the demos. The problem is, of course, that future people do not exist yet; hence, they are unable to deliberate with us or to exercise any power themselves, today. However, making sure that power is exercised *by* the current generation *for* both current *and future* generations is still an option: it simply requires that we limit the power of the living. This might be done in two ways: by placing *substantive* constraints on the actions of living people—typically through constitutional provisions—and/or by enacting specific *procedural* mechanisms.

Consider substantive constitutional constraints first. Jefferson insists on the fact that constitutions give too much power to the dead over the living. Indeed, if constitutions are to have any rigidity, they will inevitably bind the next generations unless, for example, a qualified majority obtains within them to revise it. A constitutional democracy is one that operates within a constitutional structure and with a set of rights that have been defined by others. To use Jefferson's analogy with nations again, this is as if Dutch people were to have to live under a **bill of rights** drafted, debated, and adopted by German people. Note, however, that if a constitution is to bind generations at all, it would be overly risky to count on each succeeding generation to re-enact such a constitution afresh and to bind itself. Hence, while the power of constituent past generations can be seen as a problem, it can also be considered in a different light. Dead constituent generations can indeed be seen as allies both of vulnerable minorities within each succeeding generation and of defenceless future generations in general, in the face of potential abuses of power by the living. This is especially the case if such constitutions contain specific protections for future generations.

Admittedly, the interests of minorities are not always aligned with those of future generations. Even the interests of remote future generations may differ from those of proximate ones. Be that as it may, one may share Jefferson's worry about the power of the dead as such, especially given that they cannot be affected by our decisions. Yet one may consider this to be a lesser evil if one is also concerned about the excessive power that the living have towards both their own minorities and future generations.

 KEY CONCEPTS

Mayfly generations

Political philosophers have long been using insect-based metaphors to explore the significance of intergenerational overlap. For Hume (1994: §23), it is because *one generation of men [does not] go off the stage at once, and another succeed, as it is the case with silk-worms and butterflies* that *it is necessary, in order to preserve stability in government, that the new brood should conform themselves to the established constitution*. Burke (1790; 1993: §162) insists, in the same vein, on the benefits of following tradition. If each generation were *changing the state as often, and as much, and in as many ways, as there are floating fancies and fashions, the whole chain and continuity of the commonwealth would be broken… [M]en would become little better than the flies of a summer*. As to Mulgan (2001: 283–4) he asks us to imagine a *mayfly people [who] do not have overlapping generations*, to test the ability of a set of theories of justice to justify obligations to the next generation in the absence of overlap.

Constitutions are one way in which the power of the living over future people can be reduced, by limiting the power of *all* generations, except the first one before constitutional enactment. However, the power of the living can also be constrained without necessarily giving *substantive* power to the dead, through the use of *procedural* constraints, typically enacted in future impact assessment requirements, or by setting up a special representative for future generations acting as an interpreter and reminder of their interests (see Box 13.1). This raises interesting questions for democratic theory. In particular, we need to understand the sense in which such a commissioner acts as representative. Clearly, representation cannot be of a mirror type here—that is, such as when we require that black people, women, etc. be present in parliamentary assemblies, assuming that members of a group will best be represented by those belonging to the very same group. Because future people do not exist yet, this is not an option here. Moreover, no actual interaction with the people represented is possible either. ➔ **See Chapter 4.** If it were, it could guarantee that, despite not being a future person him- or herself, the representative would have a good idea of what those whom he or she represents actually think. For these two reasons, society, at large has greater responsibility than in more standard representation cases to figure out what *substantive mandate* the representative for future generations should have. Such procedural mechanisms for constraining the actions of living people need explicit substantive goals, more than in cases in which mirror representation can obtain, and in which there is room for interaction between representatives and those they represent.

BOX 13.1 THE HUNGARIAN OMBUDSMAN FOR FUTURE GENERATIONS

In 2007, Hungary launched an Ombudsman for Future Generations. It became, in 2012, a Deputy of the General Ombudsman for Fundamental Rights, with powers in the environmental field, including: to participate in the preparation of legislation as a consultative institution to the Parliament, to initiate proceedings before the Constitutional Court when the right to a healthy environment is at stake, and to intervene in court proceedings to promote environmental protection or the interest of future generations. With a staff of around fifteen people, it initiates investigations upon complaints and ex officio. During 2013, it reviewed and/or participated in the investigation of over 400 complaints, reacted to more than fifty legislative proposals, initiated research on several critical issues related to the right to a healthy environment, and intervened in two court cases.

☆ **KEY POINTS**

- There is a democratic case for reducing the power of the living over future people.
- Constraining the power of the living through constitutional rigidity may be intergenerationally justifiable, despite giving power to the dead.
- Limiting the power of the living through setting up a representative of future people does not give substantive power to the dead, but requires the definition of a clear substantive mandate.

Responsibility for the past?

There are at least four ways of looking at *earlier* generations with justice and democracy in mind. One relates to whether we have duties towards dead people—for example, to respect their reputation or to honour the fruit of their labour, as we do through preserving major paintings or remarkable monuments. Another relates to whether our obligations towards the future are to be derived from duties towards the past—for example, when one claims that it is because we received something from the past that we owe something to the future. A third issue is whether it is avoidable and/or acceptable that the actions and choices of earlier generations restrict our freedom—for example, through constitutional rigidity. Finally, we can ask whether current members of a community are liable towards the current members of another community because of commitments made, or wrongful acts performed, by the former's ancestors. Here, alleged obligations exist *because of the past* rather than being obligations *to (people in) the past*. This will be the focus of discussion here. In contrast with the previous section, the concern here is not with the power of the dead on the living; rather, it has to do with the lack of power of the living on the dead when the latter were alive.

There are a set of issues related to this question, ranging from black reparations for slavery in the USA, to World War II reparations for Jews, arising from the Holocaust, to Third World debt cancellation, and to compensation for historical CO_2 emissions. Rather than being concerned with what one generation owes the previous or the next one, these issues typically involve two groups (A and B) across two generations (1 and 2). The central question is whether what one generation of one group (A2) owes the other group (B2) is generated or affected by what its ancestors (A1) did, or by what it (A1) committed its descendants (A2) to through, for example, making a contract with the ancestors of the other group (B1).

KEY THINKERS

Thomas Jefferson (1743–1826)

Thomas Jefferson was one of the American Founding Fathers and the third President of the US (1801–09). He adopted questionable positions on issues such as the rights of Native Americans, the enfranchisement of women, and slavery (while a slave owner himself, he also contributed politically to the abolition of the international slave trade). He also wrote and was politically active on issues such as federalism and state–church separation. His letter of September 6, 1789, to J. Madison makes important claims on three intergenerational fronts: on the intergeneration-ally problematic nature of constitutions, on inheriting debts, and on **usufruct** as an account for the nature of our intergenerational rights and duties.

Two cases arise. First, a *wrongful act* (such as enslaving, torturing, or killing people with no justification) is committed in the past, with consequences today—for example, in terms of poverty or adverse environmental conditions: should the wrongdoers' descendants be held responsible for repairing the consequences of these acts performed in the past, despite the fact that these descendants were not alive when the act was committed? Providing compensation makes sense only if one acted or abstained wrongly. There is nothing that present people could have done or abstained from doing in the past. Therefore, someone abiding by 'ought implies can' should provide a negative answer to this question, because these descendants could not have done anything to change their ancestors' behaviour. Even if they are *able* to do so, why expect these descendants, alone, to 'repair' the consequences of wrongful acts that they were unable to oppose and for which they are, therefore, no more responsible than the rest of their contemporaries?

KEY CONCEPTS

Common but differentiated responsibility

States shall cooperate in a spirit of global partnership to conserve, protect and restore the health and integrity of the Earth's ecosystem. In view of the different contributions to global environmental degradation, States have common but differentiated responsibilities. The developed countries acknowledge the responsibility that they bear in the international pursuit to sustainable development in view of the pressures their societies place on the global environment and of the technologies and financial resources they command.

(UN Rio Declaration, 1992: Principle 7)

Through referring to differences in contributions to environmental degradation, this Principle also incorporates a dimension of historical responsibility.

In the second case, a *contract* is signed between two groups in the past (for example, an inter-state borrowing contract): are the descendants bound by such a contract? Taking the notion of consent seriously, as a source of liability, and giving it a standard meaning delivers a negative answer. How can someone who did not exist have consented to anything? And why expect him or her to honour contractual obligations to which he or she was unable to consent?

In both cases, it is the relationship between time and power that is at stake. One has no power over events occurring before one's conception, which means that one lacks the power to consent, to refuse consent, or to object to past people consenting in one's name, and also that one lacks the power to prevent past people from acting wrongfully. ▶ See Chapter 14.

We, admittedly, often feel proud of or ashamed for what our ancestors did, despite not having in any sense contributed. Yet, philosophically speaking, defending historical responsibility presupposes a rejection of moral individualism (see, for example, Thompson, 2002). 'Moral individualism' is the view that individuals—rather than, for example, communities or corporations as such—are the core units of moral concern, and the only possible bearers of moral responsibility. A commitment to historical responsibility entails a rejection of moral individualism because people are held responsible for actions or abstentions despite their lack of individual agency with respect to these actions or abstentions.

Note, however, that the rejection of *historical* responsibility does not need to entail a rejection of the idea of *collective* responsibility altogether. In a group of contemporaries, it may make sense to say that I can be held responsible for the outcome of actions of other group members if membership in such a group entails some power over each other. Consider the family: when parents are held legally responsible for the wrongful actions of their children, it is assumed that, through various means, they were able to prevent their children from acting in certain ways and should have done so. In the intergenerational case, however, the circumstances are reversed, in so far as the focus is on holding descendants responsible for their predecessors' actions. What marks the difference between the two cases is the absence of overlap in the latter, which reduces the power of the present on the past to zero: there is nothing that any current member of a group could do to change the way in which past members of that group acted, and, therefore, the possibility of collective responsibility in this context makes no sense.

Endorsing moral individualism nevertheless leaves open the possibility that alternative intuitions of justice be relied upon in historical injustice cases, thereby making an appeal to collective responsibility unnecessary. To see this, consider the case of US 'black reparations' and affirmative action as a means of addressing the injustices of the past that African Americans suffered through slavery, racial **segregation**, and other forms of unfair treatment. There are three avenues of justification for affirmative action in this context, and only the first one implies a rejection of moral individualism:

1. **Historical responsibility**

   Descendants of slave owners and of other European-American wrongdoers should be held responsible for what their ancestors did. They should *fully repair* the harm suffered by African-American descendants as a result.

2. Free riding

Descendants of slave owners and of other European-American wrongdoers are not morally responsible for what their ancestors did. However, they widely benefited from these wrongful actions. To that extent, they can be said to free ride on costs imposed on others—that is, African Americans of the past, as well as their descendants. It is the extent of such benefits only for which current descendants of such wrongdoers should be held liable for reparations.

3. Inherited inequality

Today's European Americans are not responsible for what their ancestors did. Moreover, there is no reason to limit ourselves to one specific source of inherited wealth. What matters is that today, *for a variety of inherited reasons*, European Americans are more wealthy than African Americans. It is to the extent that African Americans are, on average, less well off, for reasons beyond their responsibility, that affirmative action policies should be adopted. Affirmative action is better understood as redistribution rather than as reparation.

As we can see, the rejection of the first justification does not leave us without resources to address the issue. The two other avenues remain available to account for our sense of injustice when considering the situation of current African Americans. The third justification is the most robust one. It is compatible with moral individualism and does not presuppose that some sources of our inherited wealth be treated differently from others, which makes sense since all of them are beyond our control. Yet its policy implications differ significantly from the two other possible justifications. To illustrate this, consider a case in which the descendants of victims of past wrongs end up being much better off than the descendants of the wrongdoers themselves—that is, a case unlike that of African Americans and European Americans, in which the former remain far less well off than the latter. In this illustration, contrary to the African-American case, the descendants of wrongdoers *do not owe anything* to the descendants of their victims under the third approach. Conversely, it allows for very significant transfers, even in cases in which no benefits accrued to the wrongdoers' descendants, which clearly differs from the second approach.

However, there is one central difficulty associated with the rejection of historical responsibility and to which the third approach is especially vulnerable. The case to be considered is debt cancellation. In the first generation, B1 lends money to A1. Then, one generation later, B2 asks for the money back. A2 may refuse on the grounds that it did not sign anything and ought not to be bound by anything signed by its ancestors. It may also want to refuse by showing that it did not benefit at all from the money borrowed by its ancestors. And it may finally refuse on the grounds that B2 is a much richer community than A2 anyway. Thus, in the debt cancellation case, if we abandon the idea of historical responsibility, there is a practically significant range of cases in which the two other approaches will not command any reimbursement duties on A2. The failure of even the third justification in this context is particularly worrying, because it is likely to make potential lenders reluctant to lend money as long as the descendants of the borrowers are likely to remain poorer than those of the lenders. For those who consider that lending is essential in improving the situation of the poor, this issue of disincentive is crucial.

⭐ **KEY POINTS**

- Responsibility for the acts or omissions of our ancestors is incompatible with moral individualism.
- Abandoning historical responsibility does not preclude alternative accounts of our obligations of justice towards the descendants of our ancestors' victims.
- A good test for the various views is one in which the descendants of the victims end up being wealthier than the descendants of wrongdoers.
- Alternatives to historical responsibility face a challenge of incentives.

What (if anything) do we owe to future generations?

Let us now turn to what theories of justice tell us about the obligations of a generation to subsequent ones. Earlier in the chapter, we raised questions about inequalities of *power* between generations. Here, we will look at what justice requires more generally. Rather than examining the defensibility of generational sovereignty, let us look into the substantive implications of transgenerational impartiality. Moreover, while rejecting *responsibility for the past* still leaves open the possibility of *obligations to the past*, we shall focus here almost exclusively on our obligations *to the future*. It will nevertheless become apparent that both the power that some generations have over others and the obligations of living people to those in the past have a role to play for some of the theories accounting for our obligations to the future.

Consider a diversified basket of goods (including natural resources, technology, political institutions, cultural heritage). Let us ask two questions:

1. Do we owe anything to the next generation with respect to that basket of goods, and if so, why? (The 'whether and why' question.)
2. What do we owe the next generation with respect to this basket of goods? (The 'what' question.)

Do we owe *anything* to future generations?

There are various challenges to the very *possibility* of being obliged to the future. We will leave some of these challenges aside here. One of them connects with the fact that future people do not exist yet (the 'non-existence' challenge). How could we possibly justify current obligations in the absence of correlative rights to be had by future people? One answer consists in claiming that *future* rights may suffice to justify *current* obligations (see, for example, Gosseries, 2008). Another challenge arises from the fact that our allegedly wrongful actions also affect the very identity of who will come into existence in the future (the 'non-identity' challenge) (Parfit, 1984). Here, we will assume that both the 'non-existence' and the 'non-identity' problems can be addressed successfully. Our focus will be on further challenges to the existence of obligations to the future, arising from specific theories of justice.

KEY THINKERS

Derek Parfit (1942–)

Parfit is a British philosopher who has written seminal papers on ethics, including—from 1976 onwards—on four dimensions of intergenerational justice. Parfit wrote one of the early papers on the social discount rate (1983). In *Reasons and Persons* (1984), he touches upon the complete-life approach (Chapter 15, § 117) and devotes a full chapter to the non-identity problem (Chapter 16). He also brings to light (in Chapter 17) an associated problem, referred to as the 'repugnant conclusion', that challenges the very idea of an optimal population size. Put briefly, in response to the argument that it would be better *for the next generation* to control population, we must ask 'for *which* individuals is it better?', given that some of those individuals will be brought into existence only if we decide to go for a larger population.

One prominent conception of justice is mutual advantage contractarianism. It rests on the idea that obligations of justice arise only in a context in which social cooperation can be mutually beneficial. Such a theory of justice will then be concerned with the fair allocation of the cooperative surplus—that is, the allocation of what none of the cooperators could have produced alone, in the absence of interactions with others. For such a theory, the very possibility of intergenerational obligations presupposes the possibility of intergenerational interactions benefiting *all* generations involved. Although he was not a mutual advantage contractarian, Kant (1784; 1970; 1991) was worried that such benefits of cooperation could never benefit all of the generations involved:

KEY CONCEPTS

The non-identity problem

The non-identity problem arises when an action x, that is allegedly harmful to a person y, is also a necessary condition for this person's very existence. This means that had action x not taken place, person y would not have existed. Since establishing a harm usually implies a comparison between the state in which a person x finds him or herself as a result of an action and the one in which he or she would have found him or herself had the allegedly harmful action not taken place, such a comparison cannot be made in non-identity cases. The key question is then: does it follow that whenever an action is a necessary condition for its victim's existence, it cannot be morally objectionable towards that victim? Philosophers have extensively explored both the scope and the possible solutions to this problem (Heyd, 1992; Parfit, 1984; Roberts and Wasserman, 2009).

What remains disconcerting . . . is firstly, that the earlier generations seem to perform their laborious tasks only for the sake of the later ones, so as to prepare them for a further state from which they can raise still higher the structure intended by nature; and secondly, that only the later generations will in fact have the good fortune to inhabit the building on which a whole series of their forefathers (admittedly, without conscious intention) had worked without themselves being able to share in the happiness they were preparing.

(Kant, 1784; 1970: 44)

Kant points to the fact that only later generations can benefit from the work of earlier ones, not the reverse. As Rawls puts it, benefits '*flow only in one direction*' (1999: 254). While there can thus be an intergenerational cooperative surplus, it cannot benefit *all* generations. A further problem arises from the fact that even if we could make it possible that benefits be mutual, we would still need to guarantee the mutuality of such benefits, which requires compliance and the possibility of credible mutual threats. But here, again, consider the threats that future generations could make against us if we were to violate our obligations. First, in the absence of generational overlap, such threats are not credible because current people will no longer exist at the point in time at which the threats could be acted upon. Second, even in overlap cases, we should realize that sanctioning one generation often amounts to sanctioning the next one too, which, in fact, means that future generations would shoot themselves in the foot. If your parents have to sacrifice some of their wealth as a compensation for not transferring enough to the next generation, it is likely that this will, at least partly, reduce what you will end up inheriting.

The prospects of defending intergenerational obligations on mutual advantage grounds are bleak.[2] There is another view, however, that has been explored by Barry (1991), and draws on the value of reciprocity. Rather than relying on the idea of mutual advantage, the idea of reciprocity rests on the intuition that justice not only allows, but even requires, the absence of net positive or negative transfers between people. We need to make sure that none of us has received more from society than he or she has given, and vice versa. In the intergenerational realm, the concept of reciprocity is opened up to include third parties. Rather than having to reciprocate to the very person or group whose activities create initial benefits for me, I could reciprocate to a third party. If a generation (G1) does something for the next one (G2), the latter could reciprocate to the following one (G3), rather than to its predecessor. Rather than being direct (G1–G2–G1), reciprocity would then be indirect (G1–G2–G3).

The indirect reciprocity view plays a twofold role: first, it helps us to identify what we owe to the next generation(s); second—and more importantly here—it provides us with an account of whether, and why, we would owe anything to the next generation. *Ex hypothesi*, the latter has done nothing for us and, thus, we have no *direct* obligations of reciprocity to it. The idea is that we owe it something *because* we received something from the previous generation. Although it is relatively robust, this view faces several difficulties. A general one is that the core idea of 'no net debt, no net benefit' is far from intuitive as a general principle of justice. For example, we generally feel bound to ensure, out of justice, that heavily handicapped persons have, at the very least, enough income for a decent living, even if it entails them being net beneficiaries of social transfers. A specific difficulty is that an indirect reciprocity view is unable to address the situation of a hypothetical first generation (which received what it has from no one) or of a last generation (which has no one onto whom to discharge its debt). Still another issue is how to account for the fact that receiving something without having asked for it can give rise to a duty to return (Barry, 1991). The justification for an indirect obligation of reciprocity to the next generation qua third party is, thus, far from obvious.

If one is convinced neither by mutual advantage, nor by indirect reciprocity, other options remain, perhaps the most promising of which is an egalitarian view. According to this view, making members of future generations worse off than we are is unjust because the circumstances that create their disadvantage (that is, the point in time at which they were born) are not something for which they can be held responsible. This is what fundamentally drives an egalitarian, distributive account of our intergenerational obligations, especially one that is sensitive to issues of responsibility. Treating other human beings impartially, as equals, entails obligations towards them, regardless of whether interacting with them makes us net beneficiaries of or net contributors to an intergenerational scheme of cooperation.

What do we owe the next generation?

Let us take for granted that we *do* have obligations towards the coming generations: what is their content and nature? In the past, the language of law was often used to answer this question: for example, '*the Earth belongs in usufruct to the living*' (Jefferson, 1789) or '*we do not inherit the Earth from our ancestors; we inherit it from our children*' (anon.). Relying on legal metaphors such as usufruct, loan, co-ownership, mortgage, and the like, is one way of trying to give substance to our intergenerational obligations. Yet it is also possible to use established theories of justice in the intergenerational realm. In order to contrast these theories against one another, let us assume a constant population and use the simple language of (generational) savings and dis-savings. Dis-savings obtain whenever a generation transfers to the next one *less* than what it inherited. Savings obtain whenever a generation transfers to the next one *more* than what it inherited from the previous one. The differences between various accounts of what we owe to future generations can be brought out by reference to what they require of any generation in terms of savings and dis-savings.

First, consider plain **utilitarianism**—that is, the view that what matters is maximizing the total amount of well-being in society, independently of the pattern of its distribution. If there were only one generation, it may require imposing a major cost on some for the sake of a greater benefit to others or a comparable benefit to many others. In an intergenerational setting, the total amount of well-being over all of the generations involved should be maximized. One fact is significant: renouncing a certain amount of consumption today may enable us to invest it in such a way that much more future consumption will be made possible with the same amount of capital. Of course, such benefits are likely to fall on future generations rather than on those sacrificing their consumption. However, this is not a concern for an aggregative theory such as utilitarianism.

It follows that utilitarianism will adopt, as a principle, an obligation for each generation to transfer *more* than what it inherited, hence rendering savings compulsory, to the extent that such savings will maximize well-being over generations. This raises various difficulties, one of them being that if the number of coming generations is indefinite, we may actually be sacrificing all generations to come to the benefit of none: savings imposed on each generation may never materialize into maximum intergenerational well-being if we do not know which generation will be the last.

The social discount rate

A key debate among economists is whether we should discount the future. A positive discount rate means that we give less value to one unit of future consumption or welfare than to a current one. If driven by *pure time preference*, it certainly violates the requirement of intergenerational impartiality. However, Rawls (1999: §45) has stressed that adopting a positive social discount rate (SDR) on an *ad hoc* basis may be desirable as a second best, *if* one sticks to an aggregative view. Moreover, a positive SDR might be defended on grounds other than pure time preference, such as uncertainty about the very existence of people in the future or the assumption that future people will be better off than we are. We should thus always ask: '*what* are we discounting *for what?*' For instance, discounting *future consumption* for *diminishing marginal well-being* is quite different from discounting *future well-being* for *uncertainty about the existence of people in the future*.

Interestingly enough, utilitarianism is not the only theory of justice advocating compulsory savings. Rawls defends it too. Yet his idea of an accumulation phase differs in various respects from that of utilitarian. First, the accumulation phase is limited: it does not go on indefinitely. Rawls writes that '*once just institutions are firmly established and all the basic liberties effectively realized, the net accumulation asked for falls to zero*' (1999: 255). Second, Rawls is perfectly aware that requiring an accumulation phase will violate the requirement that an intergenerational rule be such that the least well off under it be better off than the least well off under any alternative one—which lies at the heart of his principle of **distributive justice**, the '**difference principle**'. Rawls questionably assumes that the difference principle is inapplicable to the intergenerational realm. It could be applicable beyond the accumulation phase. And its violation during the accumulation phase might be justifiable by reference to what Rawls calls the 'priority of **liberty**': securing basic freedoms matters even more than achieving distributive justice with the difference principle. Because a minimum level of material wealth may arguably be needed to guarantee such basic freedoms, this would justify the need for an accumulation phase up to that 'sufficiency for supporting institutions' threshold (Gaspart and Gosseries, 2007).

We have just seen that some advocate compulsory savings, either as a general rule (utilitarianism) or as a principle for a limited accumulation phase (Rawls, 1999). A mere prohibition on dis-savings (authorizing savings while not making it compulsory) is still another option. Indirect reciprocity advocates would have reasons to adopt such a principle of 'authorized savings, prohibited dis-savings': if a generation were to transfer less to the next one than it had inherited, it would actually end up receiving more than it gave back. In short, such a generation would be a net beneficiary, which would mean that the general prohibition on net transfers that is central for reciprocity defenders would be violated. As to Rawls, his position regarding the principles applicable beyond the accumulation phase differs from this. He *allows* for *both* savings and dissavings—as long as, in the latter case, they do not bring us back to a level lower than the 'sufficiency for supporting institutions' threshold. While utilitarians advocate 'compulsory savings', and while a reciprocity-based view defends an 'authorized savings, prohibited dis-savings' view, Rawls calls for 'limited compulsory savings'—up to the 'sufficiency for supporting institutions' level—followed by an 'authorized savings, authorized dis-savings if above institutional sufficiency' principle. Surprisingly enough, insofar as the steady state is concerned, Rawls defends a form of intergenerational sufficientarianism—admittedly not a 'basic needs' one, but one that focuses on the material preconditions of just institutions. A sufficientarian view claims that justice is about securing *enough* for each of us, rather than about reducing inequalities as such or maximally improving the situation of the least well off. Sufficientarianism may *authorize both savings and dis-savings* provided that we remain above sufficiency.

From an egalitarian perspective that takes seriously, the possibility of applying the difference principle intergenerationally, there is a further option: a *prohibition* on *both* generational savings and dis-savings. While the prohibition on dis-savings may be grounded directly in intergenerational impartiality concerns, the prohibition on savings is less intuitive for one may ask: could there be anything wrong with transferring *more* to the next generation than we inherited from the previous one? The answer is 'yes': there is an **opportunity cost** (that is, the cost corresponding to the difference between the savings and the no-savings option) in doing so for the least well off members of the current generation. In other words, if a generation has a surplus on top of what it inherited from the previous ones, it should give it to the least well off among its own members rather than to the next generation. This does not imply any form of generational partiality; rather, it takes seriously, the fact that if each generation were to stick to an intragenerational difference principle, as well as to this 'neither dis-savings, nor savings' intergenerational rule, we would end up with an intergenerational path on which the least well off are better off than under alternative intergenerational rules.

KEY TEXTS

The Brundtland report (1987)

Our Common Future (1987) was written by the World Commission on Environment and Development (WCED) and named after its chair, Gro Harlem Brundtland. It provides one of the most influential definitions of sustainable development, understood as '*development that meets the needs of the present without compromising the abilities of future generations to meet their own needs*'. The intergenerational dimension is clearly central in this definition. Given its focus on 'essential needs', it also provides us with an intergenerational instance of basic needs *sufficientarianism*. Finally, it does not define what we owe the future totally independently of what we inherited. It is sensitive to the fact that the efforts of the present generation to meet the intergenerational standards should not jeopardize its own ability to meet its needs.

It is now clear that not all theories converge on savings and dis-savings. Some make it compulsory to transfer more than we inherited (utilitarianism; Rawls in the accumulation phase). Others prohibit dis-savings only while allowing for savings (indirect reciprocity view). Still others allow for both savings and dis-savings within limits (Rawlsian and non-Rawlsian sufficientarians). Yet, one may also defend a stricter rule in the steady state, of a 'neither less, nor more' type, out of concern for the least well off. Each of these views is significantly different from the others and leads to quite different practical implications. This becomes even more visible when we introduce complications such as population change or the fact that the number of future people is indefinite.

☆ **KEY POINTS**

- Both mutual advantage and indirect reciprocity views have difficulties accounting for the very existence of obligations to future generations.
- Utilitarianism tends to justify compulsory savings.
- Liberal egalitarianism—Rawlsian in spirit—is able to account both for the fairness of a (limited) accumulation phase and for the need for a 'neither savings, nor dis-savings' principle in a steady-state phase of development.

We all age

So far, the word 'generation' has been used to mean 'birth cohort'. However, it can also refer to the idea of 'age group'. For example, a person who was aged fifty during the eighteenth century and one who has the same age today are part of the same age group. This raises a difficult question: are there issues of justice that are best understood as governing relations between age groups as opposed to birth cohorts? Are there any genuine issues of justice *between age groups*? Let us approach this in two steps, looking first at the 'complete life view', and then, more broadly, at possible justifications for age limits.

🔑 **KEY CONCEPTS**

Age groups and birth cohorts

A birth cohort is a group of people born during a given period. The 1970 birth cohort includes all those born between Jan 1st and December 31st, 1970. An age group is a group of people sharing the same age, regardless of their date of birth. People who are 40 in 2010 and those who will be 40 in 2040 belong to the same age group. Social scientists, and demographers in particular, try and separate out age from cohort effects in explaining social phenomena. For political theorists interested in generational issues, this is crucial to understand the rationale of certain policies. For instance, age discrimination may aim at reducing inequalities between birth cohorts (e.g. age-based compulsory retirement). And it is also central to understand the nature of our goals. For example, should we give priority to equality between age groups or to equality between birth cohorts whenever they conflict?

Take, as a starting point, an egalitarian view. Should we be concerned about making sure that equality, in the relevant respects, prevails at each period in time (whatever the age of those involved), within each age group (regardless of inequalities between age groups), or, more broadly, over people's complete lives (e.g. McKerlie, 2013)? Most people sharing the view that age-based differentiated treatment is often justified are likely to adopt the complete life approach. It limits itself to the requirement that people end up having had equal opportunities as they reach the end of their life, differences in the temporal distribution of such opportunities being only relevant to the extent that they can affect total, complete life opportunities.

At least two questions follow. First, even for those exclusively concerned with equality over complete lives, it may still be the case that reducing inequalities between age groups could help, in practice, to reduce inequalities over complete lives. Second, there might be reasons of principle to consider equality over complete life insufficient. One such concern is delivered by sufficientarianism. Access to certain things—shelter, decent food, etc.—may have to be granted *throughout* a person's life, regardless of whether guaranteeing such an access may increase or reduce inequalities over complete lives. This would require, in most cases, banning forms of age-based differential treatment whenever access to these goods and services is at stake.

Let us now look at age limits more closely. We rely on them to a great extent: those below the age of 18 are usually excluded from the right to vote; those over the age of 65 are sometimes denied access to jobs (compulsory retirement) or to some health care services (organ transplant), etc. Age is certainly a feature that people do not choose. However, we often have the feeling that age-based differential treatment is not as problematic as gender-based or 'race'-based differential treatment. Is that intuition justified?

One hypothesis is that age is a better proxy than gender or 'race' for certain physical, affective, and intellectual abilities. The passage of time—with which age is associated—matters for the processes that affect the level of these abilities (learning, maturation, degradation). It is certainly the case that age is a good predictor at the extremes, definitely for very early ages, probably less so for more advanced ages. Insofar as the use of proxies can be justified, this can account for part of our moral intuitions about the acceptability of age limits. However, it cannot be the whole story. For in a very racist or very sexist society, it is also true that—as a matter of *fact*—'race' and gender are reliable proxies for certain competences. For instance, if we know that black people are excluded from the best schools, 'race' will correlate well with the level of competences that people acquire at school. And yet, we would not automatically conclude that the use of 'race' as a proxy is *morally* acceptable in such a context. We thus need to dig deeper.

A second important feature of age is that, on top of being a reliable proxy at the extremes, age limits will not necessarily entail any inequalities over complete lives, provided that certain conditions are met ('complete life neutrality' argument). In other words, even though, at a given point in time, a person aged 16 will not have the right to vote whereas another aged 40 will, this may not constitute any form of unacceptable differential treatment once we consider their complete lifespans. This is probably a central element that accounts for the extra leniency of our legal systems towards age limits as opposed to gender or racial discrimination. There are at least three problems with this argument though. First, one may find the complete life metric insufficient, as we have seen. Second, and more importantly, in a lot of cases, age limits *will* generate differences in treatment over complete lives. They do so whenever either the age limit changes or a constant age limit operates in a changing environment (e.g. in a labour market that experiences significant fluctuations in its unemployment rates). Third, even if they were not to generate any inequalities over complete lives, age limits reduce people's freedom and require justification. If we were to tell people to take turns along gender lines, men leading during one year, and women during the year after, it may not produce any gender inequalities either. But we would still ask what is to be gained from such an alternation.

Here are three extra reasons that, in conjunction with the other two arguments already considered, may justify the imposition of some age limits and, as a result, lead to inequalities between age groups at a given moment in time. The first extra reason is plainly *paternalistic*. We prohibit children from doing certain things (e.g. buying alcohol) because we believe that they do not yet have sufficient abilities to do particular things on their own. Some level of paternalism towards young children is good, and even required. The second reason has to do with the *efficiency* of certain time sequences. We think that it is more efficient that people learn certain things before they engage in specific activities. We send children to school *before* we allow them to work or vote. Several age limits serve this purpose. They constrain the order in which people do things, because we believe that there are very significant efficiency gains attached—gains that may, for example, benefit the least well off, in turn. The third reason is that age limits, rather than being merely neutral from the point of view of equality over a complete life, may in fact *promote* it. This is so, for instance, when upper age limits tend to shift resources towards the beginning of people's lives. In a world of significant differences in life expectancy, age rationing in health care through upper age limits may, all else being equal, contribute to reducing inequalities over complete lives in the relevant respects.

In the end, a theory of justice between age groups will, thus, tell us when age limits are acceptable and when they are not. It is more likely to accept inequalities between age groups than, for example, a theory of gender justice would accept inequalities between people of different genders. For those adopting the complete life view, age limits will have to be justified with reference to their complete life neutrality and/or benefits. Inequalities between age groups may be desirable if they are associated with efficiency gains—that can, for example, benefit the least well off over complete life—or if they can help reduce inequalities over complete lives.

☆ KEY POINTS

- The idea of equality over complete life is central to understanding what is special about age limits and why they could be less problematic than, for instance, gender criteria.

- Justice between age groups may insist on the reliability of age as a proxy and on the frequent 'complete life neutrality' of age criteria. While being key, the conjunction of these two arguments is insufficient.

- Additional justifications for age limits include: (1) justifiable paternalism in some cases; (2) efficiency gains from organizing our lives along a given sequence; and (3) the fact that some age limits may positively contribute to an increase in complete life equality.

Conclusion

Taking generations seriously entails a set of challenging questions for normative political theory. We have seen how, as democrats, we should design our institutions to govern not only for the present, but also for the future. We also showed how endorsing moral individualism affects the way in which issues of historical injustice should be addressed. Justifying and defining what we owe the next generation, in terms of justice, is not an easy task either. As indicated, on the basis of a very simple dichotomy—'savings/dis-savings'—various theories of justice lead to very different positions on intergenerational justice. We completed this panorama with an examination of age discrimination issues and of how much importance should be granted to the complete life view. This is a field of theoretical complexity and of practical significance that will no doubt keep requiring all of our attention in the decades and centuries to come.

 CASE STUDY

Intergenerationally fair pensions

Pension benefits raise both issues of intragenerational and intergenerational justice. One issue is whether, for example, poor and rich people are being treated fairly in the calculation of their contributions and the amount of benefits that they end up having received. The rich may defend their higher monthly benefits on the grounds that they contributed more, but this often does not take account of the fact that they are likely to receive such higher benefits over a longer period of time because of significant differences in life expectancy between rich and poor. In some extreme cases, one may actually end up with a pension system in which the poor fund the rich. A related issue arises, *mutatis mutandis*, due to the fact that women tend to live longer than men. While this gender gap in life expectancies is gradually shrinking, it remains significant.

Besides such intragenerational issues, there are properly intergenerational ones too. One of the distinctions often invoked is the one between pay-as-you-go and funded pension schemes. In the former case, I ensure, during period 1 (P1), the funding for my own pension at period 2 (P2). In the latter, I contribute at P1 to fund the pension of those retired at P1, and the same will happen at P2, P3, P4, etc. In fact, while being significant, the intergenerational importance of the 'funded/pay-as-you-go' distinction should not be overstated. Putting your own money aside for your old age is not like accumulating chunks of wood for the winter. Unlike the future caloric value of your wood, the value of the money that you save for later, in a funded scheme, will fully depend on the state of the economy at that time. Under both funding schemes, you will depend on the future active population—that is, on its willingness to stick to the expected contribution rates (pay-as-you-go scheme) or, more plainly, on its willingness to work (funded scheme). If the future economy crashes, both the funded scheme and the pay-as-you-go scheme will experience difficulties.

This is not to say that there are no genuine intergenerational issues at stake. One often points to the fact that the first generation to receive a pension in a pay-as-you-go scheme is a 'free lunch' generation, which may raise a problem of justice for those who are concerned about reciprocity: why should a cohort benefit from a pension while not having contributed in the first place? One way of addressing the free lunch challenge consists in broadening the focus to include the whole basket of what the free lunch generation transferred to its successor. One may then assess to what extent the cohort that is active when the pay-as-you-go pension scheme begins can be expected to have benefited in any way, over its complete life, from more wealth than that which its free lunch parents did.

There is, however, a more interesting difficulty than the free lunch one, and this has to do with the way in which pension schemes spread economic risks across generations. It becomes apparent, when we follow Musgrave's (1981) three models in this respect, spread over two periods. The first model, referred to as 'defined benefits' (or fixed replacement rate), usually—but not *necessarily*—associated with pay-as-you-go pension schemes, consists in guaranteeing to those working today (P1) retirement benefits (P2) corresponding with a defined proportion of their *current* wages. If the economy experiences a declining trend, all of the adjustment effort will have to be supported by tomorrow's active population (P2). The benefits that the retirees at P2 will get will still correspond to the same percentage of their wage at P1. The only ones who will have to adjust are the active people at P2. Through an increase in their contribution rate—that is, because wages have dropped in P2—contributors in that period will have to devote a larger percentage of their own wages to retirees than they would have done had the economy not declined. Prima facie, this seems unfair, because the economic decline is not necessarily something for which a given cohort ought to be held responsible.

The second model, referred to as 'defined contribution' (or fixed contribution rate) is usually associated with funded schemes. It guarantees, to the currently active population, that their retirement benefits (P2) will correspond with a predefined proportion of *future* wages (P2). In such a case, if the economy goes down, the adjustment will exclusively take place through reducing retirement benefits in order not to exceed the fixed contribution rate. Future contributors will not have to bear any extra costs in order that future retirees receive the benefits that had been promised by the scheme. This is prima facie as unfair as the previous rule, since it is not clear why one cohort alone should bear the full costs of a change that may not be either of the two cohort's specific responsibility.

Musgrave's own proposal is an intermediary one. It is referred to as 'fixed relative position' and keeps constant, for each period, the ratio between net contributions per head from which retired people will benefit at P2 and the net income per head of future workers at the same P2. This rule spreads the risks associated with population and economic evolutions across the various succeeding birth cohorts. In the case of a negative trend, adjustments will comprise both an increase in contribution rate of future workers (P2) and a decrease in benefits level of future retirees (P2).

At first sight, Musgrave's more balanced rule seems fairer, especially with respect to the possibility of economic decline. At a national level, at least, there are indeed economic shocks for which one generation should not be held exclusively responsible.

However, we should emphasize that—contrary to such economic shocks—demography results, in part, from choices of specific generations. Therefore, we should not treat that dimension as a mere risk generated by nature or by a third party. Each generation partly chooses the size of the next one in so far as it has control over its own birth rates. If such a choice makes it heavier for the next generation to fund pensions at P2, this extra burden should arguably be mostly supported by those who made such a choice, if objectionable. This suggests that if demography were the only factor influencing the evolution of retirement pensions, the *defined benefits* model would be fairer if strict replacement rate were defensible as a normative demographic target.

Of course, a smaller working population at P2 will have to suffer a higher contribution rate if we are to preserve the same level of pension benefits for retirees at P2. Consider, now, the fact that what we are transferring to the next generation is not made up only of a set of retirement pension funding obligations: it also includes, for example, a stock of natural resources. And we have intergenerational obligations in that respect, too. Now, if we look at the natural resources aspect, a declining population actually makes it easier for the current generation to meet its natural resource obligations towards its own successors. It will also tend to increase investment in education per head, which could make members of the next generation wealthier. What follows from this? In a case of population decline, while the pension burden on the next generation may increase, its educational and renewable natural resources per head may actually increase. If the net effect on the next generation is positive, there may actually be a case for privileging the *fixed benefits* rule in the realm of pensions.

As we can see, Musgrave's three models illuminate the central intergenerational question that pensions funding schemes raise. However, we should not conclude, too quickly, that the one privileged by Musgrave is necessarily the fairest simply because it proposes a mix of the other two. Such issues need to be assessed by considering the full package of intergenerational transfers.

QUESTIONS

1. Can constitutional rigidity be justified on grounds of intergenerational fairness?
2. What are the challenges in setting up a commissioner for future generations?
3. Should a generation apologize for the harms caused by its ancestors three generations ago?
4. Does the rejection of responsibility for the actions of our ancestors entail the absence of obligations towards our descendants' victims?
5. Considering the problem of disincentive to lend, can a Third World debt cancellation policy remain pro-poor?
6. Can an accumulation phase ever be intergenerationally fair?
7. Is there a case for prohibiting both generational savings and generational dis-savings?
8. What is special about age discrimination compared with racial or gender discrimination?
9. Does the fact that age limits will not necessarily lead to differential treatment over complete lives suffice to justify them?

FURTHER READING

■ Asheim, G. (2010) 'Intergenerational equity', *Annual Review of Economics*, 2: 197–222 A survey of the axiomatic treatment of the issue by one of the leading experts in the field.

■ Barry, B. (1991) *Liberty and Justice: Essays in Political Theory 2*, Oxford: Clarendon Press Contains three of his most important essays on the topic, focusing on reciprocity (1979), on the asymmetry of power between generations and the design of the original position (1977), and on the ethics of exploiting non-renewable resources (1983).

■ Daniels, N. (1988) *Am I My Parents' Keeper? An Essay on Justice between the Young and the Old*, New York/Oxford: Oxford University Press An important book on justice between age groups.

- Gauthier, D. P. (1986) *Morals by Agreement*, Oxford: Clarendon Press Chapter IX contains a seminal discussion from the perspective of mutual advantage contractarianism, echoing Rawls' worries.

- Gosseries, A. and Meyer, L. (2009) *Intergenerational Justice*, Oxford: Oxford University Press A recent collection of original papers providing an updated account of issues of intergenerational justice from various perspectives.

- Jefferson, T. (1789) 'Letter to J. Madison', 6 September, available online at http://memory.loc.gov/cgibin/query/r?ammem/mtj:@field(DOCID+@lit(tj060008) An influential early statement of three problems of intergenerational justice.

- McKerlie, D. (2013) *Justice: the Young and the Old,* Oxford: Oxford University Press A good complement to Daniels's book on justice between age groups.

- Parfit, D. (1984) *Reasons and Persons*, Oxford: Oxford University Press One of the major books of twentieth-century ethics, with four full chapters devoted to future generations and others that are directly relevant too.

- Rawls, J. (1971; 1999) *A Theory of Justice*, revd edn, Cambridge, MA: Harvard University Press The reference book in twentieth-century political philosophy, with sections 44 and 45 devoted to intergenerational justice.

- Roberts, M. and Wasserman, S. (2009) (eds) *Harming Future Persons: Ethics, Genetics and the Non-Identity Problem*, Dordrecht: Springer A recent collection of essays on the non-identity problem.

- Sikora, R. and Barry, B. (1978) (eds) *Obligations to Future Generations*, Philadelphia, PA: Temple University Press One of the early collections of essays on the topic, containing some excellent papers.

- Thompson, J. (2002) *Taking Responsibility for the Past: Reparation and Historical Injustice*, Cambridge: Polity Press One of the recent books on responsibility for the past, influenced by a Burkean perspective.

 WEB LINKS

- http://www.ageuk.org.uk/ Age UK provides information about the issues central to those concerned with the rights of older people.

- http://www.apfc.org/home/Content/aboutFund/aboutPermFund.cfm The website of the Alaskan Permanent Fund Corporation provides information, including an annual report, on the activities of a fund that includes intergenerational justice as one of its key purposes.

- http://www.intergenerationaljustice.org/ The Foundation for the Rights of Future Generations (FRFG) is a German foundation that focuses on the rights of future generations in general, including through engaging with parliaments and publishing a journal (the *Intergenerational Justice Review*).

- http://jno.hu/en/ The official website of the Parliamentary Commissioner for Future Generations (Hungary) offers details about its 2007–2011 activities.

- http://www.worldbank.org/en/topic/environment The World Bank website offers data, per country, on one of the most interesting sustainability indicators for those aiming to operationalize the demands of intergenerational justice.

Visit the Online Resource Centre that accompanies this book to access more learning resources: http://www.oxfordtextbooks.co.uk/orc/mckinnon3e/

 ENDNOTES

1 The author wishes to thank D. Attas, C. McKinnon, N. Vrousalis, and three anonymous referees for comments and suggestions on an earlier version of this chapter. He also wishes to acknowledge the financial support of the *Action de Recherche Concertée* (ARC) project 09/14–018 on 'sustainability' (French-speaking community of Belgium) and of the *Fonds de la Recherche Scientifique* (FNRS).

2 For further developments on mutual advantage contractarianism, see Arrhenius (1999).

14

Power

DAVID OWEN

Reader's guide

Power is central to any understanding of politics but what roles does the concept of power play in such an understanding, and what different modes of power can be distinguished? Recent political theory has seen a variety of views of power proposed, with these views having significantly different implications for conceptualizing the scope and form of political activity. Two main views concerning power are the locus of contemporary debate. The first, 'agency-centred' view, emerges in the Anglo-American debate that follows discussions of community power in American democracy. The second, 'non-agency-centred' view, emerges from the post-structuralist work of Michel Foucault. At stake, in the debate between them, are how we distinguish between injustice and misfortune, as well as how we approach the issues of freedom and responsibility.

Introduction

Power is a basic concept of political theory. Its use encompasses both phenomena of empowerment (typically expressed in terms of freedom, rights, and capabilities) and of disempowerment (for which we have developed a rich vocabulary including, for example, servitude, exploitation, domination, oppression, marginalization, and powerlessness). In its most fundamental sense, power is a *dispositional* concept that refers to the capacity to affect some feature of the world (such as, for example, another person's ability to act as they choose) and the capacity to produce effects with respect to some feature of the world (such as, to continue the example, the range of choices available to another person). The concept of power is, as the parenthetic example illustrates, closely bound in social and political contexts to the concepts of freedom and responsibility. To reinforce this point and further illustrate why power is central to the concerns of political theory, consider that, for example, the possibility of drawing a distinction between injustice and misfortune requires the concept of power, since the point of such a distinction is to register whether or not a state of affairs is the product of effects for which some set of agents can reasonably be held accountable.

While in the most general use of the concept, power can be a property of objects, events, agents, institutions, or social structures, in social and political contexts, its use is bound up with issues of agency. However, the nature of this relationship is at the heart of the most important contemporary controversy over the concept of power. The debate concerns whether, in social and political contexts, power is best conceived as an agent-centred concept (that is, seen solely as a capacity of agents) or whether it can also encompass structural features of social relations, insofar as these are social or political in origin and capable of being altered through social or political action. This debate involves a critical exchange between 'post-structuralist' analysts of power, who draw on the work of Michel Foucault, and 'Anglo-American' theorists of power, most prominently Steven Lukes, whose reflections on power emerge from an earlier debate on the issue—the 'community power' debate—sparked by a dispute over the character of American democracy. I will address both of these debates but, before I do so, it will be helpful to reflect a little further on the point of the concept of power and its modes.

☆ KEY POINTS

- Power is central to the analysis of politics, encompassing phenomena of empowerment and disempowerment.
- Power is a dispositional concept.
- The concept of power is basic to drawing a distinction between injustice and misfortune.
- A key debate on the concept of power concerns whether it is an agent-centred concept.

The concept of power and modes of power

Let us start with a reflective question acutely raised by Peter Morriss (2002): 'Why do we need concepts of power?' Taking this as a question addressed to reflective actors in political society, we can follow Morriss in offering responses that align with three main types of context in which the question may arise for us:

- *Practical contexts*: In order to form, pursue, and reflect on our projects, we need to be able to make reasonable judgements about, on the one hand, what we can do or become as social and political agents, and, on the other hand, how the conduct of other agents, or the rules and norms of social structures, can affect what we can do or become.

- *Moral and/or political contexts*: We need to be able to judge who to hold accountable—or, more generally, how responsibility is to be assigned—for the effects of power on our lives and the lives of others: for example, what is injustice and what is misfortune? Who is accountable for what opportunities are available to us and them, and how is responsibility for the distribution of influence over social norms or political decisions to be assigned?

- *Evaluative contexts*: When we are concerned with judging a social or political context in terms of justice, democracy, or legitimacy, we need to be able to make reasonable judgements about questions such as who has access to membership, what its members have the power to do or become, and how power is distributed among members.

These responses are indicative rather than exhaustive, but they are sufficient to demonstrate why power is such a central concept for political theory. Let me draw attention to two further points in these responses. First, they highlight the link to freedom: 'x has (lacks) the power to do or become y' can be glossed as 'x is (is not) free to do or become y'. Second, I have pointed out that in moral and political contexts, concepts of power are bound up with issues of moral responsibility and political accountability. The link between the concepts of power, freedom, and responsibility entails both (a) that disputes concerning any of these concepts is liable to generate disputes concerning the others (it is often argued that such concepts are **essentially contested concepts**; see Gallie, 1956 and Connolly, 1974) and (b) that any coherent concept of power must invoke concepts of freedom and responsibility that are compatible with this concept of power. How we conceive of power is liable to be bound up with the normative and methodological commitments in terms of which political theorists understand, explain, and evaluate the social and political contexts that shape who and what actors are and what they can do or become. This point will be illustrated by both of the major debates to be addressed in this chapter—that between pluralists and elite theorists in the 'community power' debate, and that between 'Anglo-American' and 'Continental' theorists of power in the contemporary debate.

Knowing why we need concepts of power allows us to address the question of its modes. To do so, let us consider a very simple example. A democratically elected government passes a law removing a range of welfare benefits from those claimants with disability who are judged fit to work by a government appointed agency. In response to this act, a group of citizens protest collectively through petitions, demonstrations, and vigils, in order to bring this to the attention of the wider public, to mobilize more support for the protest, and to encourage the government to retract or revise its legislation. This simple scenario is, like politics generally, pervaded with power relations and helps draw attention to different *modes of power*:

- The government has the *power to* enact this law.
- In doing so, it exercises *power over* its citizens.
- They, in turn, exercise *power with* each other by acting in concert to protest.
- They do so utilizing the *power of* particular media of protest (petitions, demonstrations, vigils) to advance their cause.

This simple scenario should not be taken as offering a way of modelling power more generally, since it highlights only instances of power as a product of the *intentional actions of agents*. Rather, its purpose is, first and foremost, to draw attention to the point that it is helpful to distinguish these modes of power in analysing any given context of power. However, it also helps to foreground two important points about power.

First, the power of an agent is dependent on the context of power in which they are situated and, more specifically, on the relations in which they stand to other agents within broader social structures. This means that what I have the power to do in a given social or political context is, typically, liable to depend on how I am situated in relation to other agents and to social structures. Most obviously, for example, what I have the power to do will, typically, depend on whether you are seeking to exercise power *over* me, to structure my field of possible actions, or to exercise power *with* me, coordinating our efforts in joint pursuit of a shared goal. Notice, though, that there are contexts in which a given agent may be powerless, in that nothing they can do *as this agent*, in acting for or against another agent, can have any effect. A classic instance of such a case, with respect to formal decision-making power, is provided by the position of Luxembourg in the Council of Ministers of the EU between 1958 and 1973. In this period, Luxembourg held one vote, and a qualified majority of votes was defined to be twelve out of seventeen. Given that the other member states each held an even number of votes, Luxembourg was never able to make any difference to the outcomes of the voting process.

The phrase, *as this agent*, in the preceding comments, draws our attention to the important point that how the relevant agent of power is individuated need not be fixed. Suppose Luxembourg, Belgium, and the Netherlands engaged in a strictly binding agreement to always vote the same way. In such a context, the relevant agent of power in the Council of Ministers is 'the Benelux countries'—that is, Belgium, Luxembourg, and the Netherlands considered jointly, rather than severally. This small point has very significant implications because it points to two facts that are central to political life. The first is that in a situation in which a group of agents are each relatively powerless, they may combine to form an agent (a 'plural subject') who is more powerful. The second is that any agents who are relatively powerful in the initial situation, and wish to maintain their power advantage, have a clear interest in minimizing the chances of the relatively powerless successfully forming such a 'plural subject' and, if such a mutually binding coalition comes to pass, working to undermine it: the classic maxims of the powerful ('divide and rule') and of the powerless ('in unity, strength') both have their basis in this feature of power.

The second point is that exercises of power are always mediated—and, indeed, we often distinguish forms of social and political power in terms of prominent general media through which they are exercised: for example, economic power, legal power, political power, and cultural power. This directs us to the fact that what an agent has the power to do in social and political contexts is dependent on (a) the range of media (for example, speech and money) through which they can exercise power in relation to others, and (b) the power of the available media in the context of their agency. Thus, the actual power of an agent will, in part, be a function of the range of media through which they can choose to exercise power in a given context and the power of those media in the particular context in which they are situated. A politician who can draw on both skills of political organization and an ability to raise funds for electoral campaigns is better placed than a politician who possesses only one of these attributes.

☆ **KEY POINTS**

- The use of the concept of power is located in the contexts of an agent's project, the attribution of moral or political responsibility, and the evaluation of social and political systems.
- We can distinguish different modes of power: power to, power with, power over, power of.
- The power of an agent typically depends on their relation to other agents and social structures.
- The exercise of power is always mediated.

Three dimensions of power

In the Anglo-American context, the terms set by Steven Lukes' *Power: A Radical View* (1974; 2005) have been influential in structuring the normative debate concerning power. Lukes distinguishes three views of power: (what he calls) 'one-dimensional' and 'two-dimensional' views of power, and a radical 'three-dimensional' view that emerged (most notably) from the Marxist tradition. In this slim but powerfully argued volume, Lukes aims to defend the radical view.

According to Lukes, the one- and two- dimensional views emerge in the context of the 'community power' debate which addressed the issue of power in relation to the character of American democracy. At the end of the 1950s, the dominant view of American social science presented a picture of American municipal politics as the rule of **elites**. At the start of the 1960s, this view was challenged by a group of Yale-based political scientists, led by Robert Dahl, in a study of the city of New Haven that issued in a number of works, most prominently Dahl's *Who Governs?* (1961) ⮕ **See Chapter 4**. Dahl argued that, insofar as New Haven is a representative city, American municipal democracy is best considered 'pluralist' rather than 'elitist', that is, where decision making is not subject to the control of a well-defined group of powerful actors but, rather, is a product of contestation between a plurality of groups. Dahl's book, not unexpectedly and, perhaps, not unintentionally, immediately sparked controversy in respect of problems of concept, theory, and method with regard to the study of power.

The conceptual, theoretical and methodological commitments which guided Dahl's project were focused on addressing what he had earlier identified as a central problem with the methodological approach of sociologists and political scientists who presented the case that America was ruled by elites. What Dahl objected to in this approach was the apparent lack of attention to the exercise of power over actual decision-making processes. To test if there is a ruling elite (rather than, for example, a plurality of groups sometimes winning, sometimes losing), Dahl reasoned that we need to be able to identify the membership of the elite, to identify political decisions where the interests of the elite conflict with those of other groups, and to show that, in the majority of important cases, the decisions taken express the interests of the elite (Dahl, 1958).

KEY TEXTS

Dahl, *Who Governs?* (1961)

Robert Dahl's *Who Governs?* is a study of the city of New Haven, home to Yale University, published in 1961. It was awarded the 1962 Woodrow Wilson Foundation Award for the best book published on government, politics, or international affairs for the preceding year and was one of the most cited works in political science for at least the next twenty years. It argued, against the received wisdom that American municipal government was elitist, that the diverse sources of power were differentially distributed among various groups, with no one group able to control political decision making and, hence, was pluralist.

Dahl's intervention involves both a concept of power and a specific operationalization of that concept, and is an example of what Lukes calls a one-dimensional view of power. Dahl appeals to the following intuitive concept of power: 'A has power over B to the extent that he can get B to do something he would not otherwise do.' He then operationalizes this concept in terms of an analysis of the influence of actors over political decisions in cases of actual and observable conflict, on the grounds that this provides as clear a test of the comparative power of the actors as we can achieve in the messy world of real politics. Thus, the study of New Haven, conducted by Dahl and his collaborators, put into play (though it did not consistently exhibit) a view of power according to which the judgement that A has power over B is predicated on a focus on the observable behaviour of A and B in determining the outcomes of political decisions where A and B have an observable conflict of policy preferences (and such preferences are taken to reveal what these actors identify as their interests).

A powerful criticism of this view of power was rapidly advanced by Peter Bachrach and Morton S. Baratz in their 1962 article, 'Two faces of power', which starts from the same intuitive concept of power to which Dahl had appealed, but which offers what Lukes calls a 'two-dimensional' view of power. Their point was simple in form:

> Of course power is exercised when A participates in the making of decisions that affect B. But power is also exercised when A devotes his energies to creating or reinforcing social and political values and institutional practices that limit the scope of the political process

to public consideration of only those issues which are comparatively innocuous to A. To the extent that A succeeds in doing this, B is prevented, for all practical purposes, from bringing to the fore any issues that might in their resolution be seriously detrimental to A's set of preferences.

(Bachrach and Baratz, 1962: 948)

As a logical elaboration of the basic concept of power to which Dahl appeals, this point is compelling, but it has two important implications for the study of power. First, it entails that there may be covert conflicts in the political community which are not directly observable through a focus on political decision making because A has successfully exercised power over the agenda-setting process so that issues that threaten A's interests do not arise as matters for decision. This is what Bachrach and Baratz call *nondecision-making*; they suggest this is expressed within the political community through the appearance of 'subpolitical' grievances. Second, it challenges the claim, by Dahl and his colleagues, to focus on 'key' decisions because it points out that, given the second face of power, what count as key decisions are not simply those obvious decisions in notable policy areas, characterized by overt conflict. In laying down this challenge, Bachrach and Baratz put into play a second picture of power in which the analysis of power entails attending to potential, as well as actual, issues; to issues that reach the decision-making arena and ones that are choked before they can reach that point; and, hence, to both covert and overt observable conflicts.

Against these two views, Lukes proposes a three-dimensional view of power. As a theorist, Lukes saw clearly that the challenge laid down by Bachrach and Baratz was limited: 'A may exercise power over B by getting him to do what he does not want to do, but he also exercises power over him by influencing, shaping or determining his very wants.' (Lukes, 2005: 27) If A successfully shapes B's perception of B's interests, potential conflicts between A and B will remain latent rather than overt or covert. Would not the most effective, insidious, and economical form of power, Lukes reasons, be one in which no observable conflict, overt or covert, emerged because the persons over whom power is exercised have their perception of their interests shaped by either the direct intentional activity of powerful agents or, indeed, by the social and political practices in which these persons are situated? This type of claim was, of course, familiar from the Marxist tradition and, as a conceptual claim, it is well-made. Lukes summarizes the features of the behavioural focus of the three-dimensional view of power as:

(a) decision making and control over the political agenda (not necessarily through decisions);

(b) issues and potential issues;

(c) observable (overt or covert) and latent conflict;

(d) subjective and real interests.

For all its conceptual clarity, however, the question of the value of Lukes' three-dimensional picture of power is less obvious. What motivates this view is a puzzle: why do the oppressed and dominated not rise up and overthrow their oppressors? There are a range of reasons that might help explain this puzzle—lack of time and resources, effective divide and rule tactics, a position of comparative relative advantage in respect of others who are even more oppressed, difficulties of coordination, etc.—but one theoretically elegant solution to the puzzle is that the oppressed do not rise up because they do not see themselves as oppressed, and that this is explained by the fact that their perceptions of their situation have been shaped by the powerful. To demonstrate the value of this three-dimensional view, we need reasons to think that (a) it is plausible that there are such cases and (b) we can identify them and the mechanisms through which such power operates. Let us consider each of these elements.

 KEY THINKERS

Steven Lukes (1941–)

Steven Michael Lukes is a political and social theorist who is currently Professor of Politics and Sociology at New York University. He has written studies of Durkheim, the concept of individualism, and the difficult relationship of Marxism and morality, and has very wide-ranging interests across social and political philosophy, the history of ideas, and the philosophy of social science. He is best known in academia for his work on power and the three-dimensional view that he continues to defend, but he achieved a wider readership with his novel *The Curious Enlightenment of Professor Caritat.*

Do we have reason to think that there are such cases? One basis for scepticism emerges from James C. Scott's work, most notably in *Domination and the Arts of Resistance* (1990), which documents the ways in which apparent displays of deference by the powerless—displays that make it appear, to the powerful, that the powerless have internalized the outlook advanced by the powerful—are designed as deceptions to create that very impression. Elucidating the 'hidden transcripts' of the dominated, exploited, and powerless, Scott's argument suggests that the public performances encouraging the view that the powerless are characterized by ideological 'false consciousness' admit of a rather different explanation and, in effect, charges that political scientists and political theorists have been too readily deceived in the same way as (and perhaps more so than) the powerful, at whom these performances are directed. However, while Scott's argument suggests that many cases can be accounted for in this way, it does not fully underwrite the claim that the three-dimensional view of power has no 'real world' applications. Consider, for example, that while Scott's view can account for much of the (seemingly) compliant behaviour of slaves, it cannot account for why ex-slaves, interviewed years after they had been freed, would exhibit an attitude of self-blame with respect to their conduct as slaves. Yet, Patterson has noted that such an attitude is all too characteristic: '"De Massa and Missus was good to me but sometimes I was so bad they had to whip me," said Victoria Adams. "It was always for something, sir. I needed de whippin'," recalled Millie Barber.' (Patterson, 1982: 12). Whether or not it is commonplace, the form of power identified by Lukes is certainly real.

Given that there are such cases, can we identify them and the mechanisms through which they work? Both elements are needed. To demonstrate that A has shaped B's perception of his or her interests, in ways running contrary to B's real interests, requires both that the analyst can demonstrate that we have good reason to believe that B's interests are not what B perceives them to be and, also, that A's power is the cause of this discrepancy. Both of these are complex issues. While there is nothing mysterious about the thought that agents can misperceive their interests (we are all familiar with such experiences), nor that agents may be deliberately misled by other agents (at least most of us are probably familiar with this experience), to claim that an agent's real and perceived interests are distinct places a significant burden on the analyst. It does so because they have to show either that the perceived interest is one that the agent, as rational and reasonable, could not coherently hold as an interest, or that the agent can be brought, through a process of rational reflection, to recognize that what they had perceived as their interest was not their real interest. In both cases, this demonstration requires that a cogent account can be given of how they came to have this mistaken perception of their interests. For the three-dimensional view of power, this means establishing the counter-factual that, in the absence of A's power, B would not have come to misperceive their interests in this way. This is likely to be a demanding task but it is by no means impossible.

☆ **KEY POINTS**

- The community power debate invoked both a one-dimensional and two-dimensional view of power.
- Lukes argues for a three-dimensional view of power.
- The movement from a one-dimensional, to a two-, and then a three-dimensional view of power makes increasingly great methodological demands on the theorist.

An alternative view of power

Lukes' influential account of power is, as he now recognizes (Lukes, 2005), limited in at least two major respects. First, it focuses on one mode of power: 'power over'. This is understandable in terms of the debate into which it was intervening, but it also obscured the point that the basic sense of power is the capacity to do things. Second, it operated with a moralized understanding of power in which 'power over' is identified with domination. Each of these limitations was exposed by the emergence of a different analysis of power developed, revised, and refined by Michel Foucault (1977, 1978, 1982). There is a further significant difference between the two views which we will illustrate in this section but address, directly, in the following section: Foucault moves away from an agency-centred view of power to one that encompasses social structures.

We can take as a starting point for analysing Foucault's position, his concern that the political analysis of power was construed primarily in terms of a focus on 'power over' that pictured power in negative terms: in the image of sovereign law as coercively enforceable restrictions on action, or the image of alienation as the repression of the authentic self or ideological obfuscation of one's real interests. Foucault's point in drawing attention to this feature is to highlight the fact that both liberal and radical views of power implicitly presuppose a picture in which power operates to constrain, restrict, or repress the free actions of autonomous persons. But, Foucault points out, this view elides the point that to be free to do x is to have the power to do x, and to be autonomous involves having the power to direct whether, and how, to exercise one's powers.

More prosaically, Foucault's point is that the subject presupposed by liberal and radical pictures of power is a subject of power, a subject characterized by various capacities, but that liberal and radical analyses give us no account of the formation of the subject as a subject of power. His contention is that the analysis of power needs to account for this formation and, more controversially, that it can do so in terms of power relations. The latter claim has caused a major misunderstanding of Foucault's position, a misunderstanding encouraged by some of Foucault's own early formulations. However, the basic point being made is straightforward: (a) we acquire and exercise capacities through practice in the dual sense of practising and practices as norm-governed activities and (b) our acquisition and exercise of capacities is structured by the ways in which our conduct is governed. So, for example, the child playing a simple piece of music on the piano is practising playing the piano and engaging in the norm-governed practice of piano playing and, hence, acquiring and exercising the capacity (to some extent or other) to play the piano, where this involves the ability to engage a series of relatively precise bodily movements in a way that is normatively structured both by formal norms, expressed through the musical notation of the piece, and informal norms, relating to expressiveness, musicality, etc. The child may be playing the piano because he or she will be punished by his or her parents for not doing so, or because the child's self-perception is structured by social norms concerning the attributes expected of a young woman or man, or because the child is committed to a musical career, or simply because the child enjoys it. In the first two instances, the child's conduct is subject to government by others; in the latter two, the child is exercising 'power over' him or herself. In all these cases, the power exercised over the child's conduct is productive, in the sense of developing his or her capacity for playing the piano. Notice, though, that these four 'regimes' of power stand in rather different relations to the child's autonomy. The first two do not develop (but substitute for and, hence, may diminish) the child's power to engage in the self-directed exercise of his or her powers; the latter two, by contrast, are engagements not only in the practice of piano playing but also in the practice of the child directing their own activity by choosing to devote his or her time to practising the piano rather than, say, watching television.

 KEY THINKERS

Michel Foucault (1926–1984)

Michel Foucault was a French historian and philosopher who, in 1969, was elected to the College de France in which he held the Chair in the History of Systems of Thought until his death in 1984 from an AIDS-related illness. A self-consciously political thinker, Foucault engaged in exercises in historical philosophy that were designed to unsettle what he saw as contingent limits in contemporary social and political thought. His rethinking of the analysis of power is an example of such an exercise in the service of his substantive investigations of punishment, sexuality, and political governance.

In one of his major works, *Discipline and Punish* (1977), Foucault focused on what he termed 'disciplinary power' to show how the individuals who are subject to power could be induced to become themselves the agents through which the exercise of others' power over them was accomplished. To see this, imagine that our piano-playing child has been told to practise by his or her parents who have installed a video camera system so that they can check whether the child is practising without having to be present. In this context, the

KEY CONCEPTS

Disciplinary power

Disciplinary power is a form of power that acts on the subject through regimes of bodily regulation subject to surveillance, in order to bring their conduct into conformity with a norm. The exemplary diagram of such power is provided by Bentham's 'Panopticon' (Foucault, 1977), in which the permanent visibility of the prisoner is combined with their inability to know whether, at any given moment, they are being watched and judged in their performance of a norm. This mode of power spread from the prison to the workhouse, the hospital, the factory, and, Foucault argues, eventually permeated modern society.

child's conduct is rendered permanently visible to the parents, whether or not they actually watch him or her and, supposing that they do watch regularly at the start and pick up any initial slacking, the child is gradually induced to act as if the parents are watching, regardless of whether they do so. The child becomes, as Foucault puts it, a 'docile body' whose powers to play the piano are augmented and developed, but whose autonomy—the power to direct the exercise of his or her own powers—is diminished as he or she is habituated to exercise surveillance and discipline over him or herself to bring conduct into conformity with parental norms concerning piano practice.

At this stage, we can introduce a further central innovation in the analysis of power that Foucault proposes, namely, what he calls '**power–knowledge**' relations. The basic thought is again a simple one: the ways in which power is exercised are structured by the field of knowledge within which the exercise of power takes place and, in turn, this exercise of power provides material for this field of knowledge. Returning to our piano player, we can note that the child's practice is situated in a field of knowledge in which pedagogics inform, for example, the appropriate arrangement of the body in relation to the instrument; the selection of suitable pieces for beginning, intermediate, and advanced students; guidance on how much practice is required for a normal rate of progression in proficiency—and much else besides. These features, in turn, allow for judgement of the child's performance in relation to the norm and evaluations of his or her talent, dedication, technical proficiency, musicality, etc., which can (a) inform the fine-tuning of his or her training regime to address specific strengths and weaknesses and (b) provide material for reflective improvements of the existing pedagogic theory and practice. Such power–knowledge relations allow, for example, the piano teacher to discipline the child's formation as a pianist.

Drawing together these points allows us to highlight one of Foucault's central concerns with modern society to which he gave passionate expression in *Discipline and Punish*:

> We are in the society of the teacher-judge, the doctor-judge, the educator-judge, the 'social-worker'-judge; it is on them that the universal reign on the normative is based; and each individual, wherever he may find himself, subjects to it his body, his gestures, his behaviour, his aptitudes, his achievements.

> (1977: 304)

The concern is that the rise of the human sciences works in concert with, and facilitates the intensification of, the state-led governance of social relationships, to make society increasingly resemble our example of the child practising under the eye of the parental video camera in which we become the agents of social surveillance and social discipline.

KEY TEXTS

Foucault, *Discipline and Punish: The Birth of the Prison* (1977)

Originally published in French as *Surveiller et Punir* (1975), *Discipline and Punish* is a study of the emergence of modern penal systems. Foucault argues that the penal reformers who established imprisonment as the rational form of punishment were concerned that power should operate more effectively and economically on the subject than in prior regimes. Central to this account is the linking of discipline—a technical mode of controlling the body and its movements —to systems of hierarchical observation, normalizing judgement and examination to compose disciplinary power, which Foucault argues is a ubiquitous feature of modern society.

Whatever the merits of Foucault's substantive diagnosis of the power structure of modern society—and in his final works, he focuses more on issues concerning the government of self, which he had neglected in *Discipline and Punish*—it will already be apparent, from this brief overview, that Foucault widens the remit of the analysis of power very considerably. One important respect in which he does so is to shift the analysis of power from an agency-centred approach to encompass the role of social structures, that is, those norms that arise out of the interactions of agents without being the intentional product of those interactions and which, then, govern (but do *not* determine) those interactions. I have already acknowledged this in the piano-playing example by pointing to one possible regime of government being comprised of social norms concerning the attributes expected of a young woman or man, but it is time to say a little more.

Social structures are normative orders that arise as unplanned products of the interactions of a plurality of human beings and govern their interactions, but are also reproduced, or transformed, through the ways in which those interactions conform to, or depart from, the norms that regulate them. According to Foucault's view of power, the analyst must address the importance of such social structures in subject formation and the role of subjects in transforming social structures, as well as the role of various agencies and institutions that seek to maintain or transform specific social structures. Foucault takes up this task by providing **genealogies** of specific normative orders—for example, those focused on madness, punishment, and sexuality—in order to perform three tasks. The first is simply to demonstrate that there is nothing natural, necessary, or obligatory about these normative orders by recounting the contingent historical processes through which they emerge and are established. The second is to show that they facilitate forms of domination (where domination is conceived as forms of government that those subject to them are unable to transform) because insofar as they are seen as natural, necessary, or obligatory, they are not perceived as forms of domination. The third is to incite experiments with other ways of governing in these domains that aim to minimize domination. The normative core of Foucault's analysis of power is expressed thus:

> a system of constraint becomes truly intolerable when the individuals who are affected by it don't have the means of modifying it. This can happen when such a system becomes

intangible as a result of its being considered a moral or religious imperative, or a necessary consequence of medical science.

(Foucault, 1988: 294)

Foucault's work can, thus, be said to share Lukes' concern with autonomy but, in contrast to Lukes, Foucault resists (and dislikes) talk of 'false consciousness' and 'perceived and real interests' for two reasons. First, because he was philosophically sceptical about notions such as 'real interests' that he took (in an arguably too strong sense) to require appeal to a substantive model of human nature. Second, because he was concerned with what he saw as the political danger that such talk encouraged of privileging the view of the analyst, concerning the 'real interests' of the subject, over the views of the subject.

☆ **KEY POINTS**

- The analysis of power must include the agent's formation as a subject of power.
- Disciplinary power operates by inducing agents to exercise power over themselves, on behalf of another.
- Power and knowledge are intertwined.
- Foucault's analysis of power moves away from an agent-centred concept of power.

Power, freedom, and responsibility

I began this chapter by saying that the major contemporary debate in political theory concerning power concerned the argument between 'analytic' political theorists, who see power as an agency-centred concept, and **post-structuralist** political theorists, who deploy the concept of power in a wider 'non-agency-centred' sense that encompasses issues of social structure. To engage with this debate, we can begin by recalling that the concept of power is intimately bound up with the concepts of freedom and responsibility.

One reason, I have suggested, that we need concepts of power is to make it possible to draw a distinction between injustice and misfortune, because that distinction hangs on being able to distinguish cases where some party can be held responsible (injustice) from cases where there is no one to hold responsible (misfortune). In this context, it is a significant point that the agency-centred view aligns with our ordinary understanding of responsibility. This understanding, what we may call the *liability* model, is one in which we are typically concerned with whether an agent can be credited or debited with an outcome. Notice in this context that an agency-centred view is not restricted to a focus on the intentional and positive actions of agents; it can encompass power that is never exercised (but still has effects) and unintended (but reasonably foreseeable) effects, as well as including failures to act when action is possible. Indeed, Lukes' rationale for adopting this broader understanding of an agency-centred view of power is precisely that 'we can and often do hold agents responsible for consequences they neither intend nor positively intervene to bring about.' (Hayward and Lukes, 2008: 7).

The difference between this agency-centred view and the wider view is that the former restricts the understanding of power to effects 'caused by agents who are able to act in ways that predictably and significantly affect other agents,' while, on the non-agency-centred view, power also encompasses effects that 'are the unplanned net effect of the actions of multiple actors who could not—not through their individual choices, not through their coordinated efforts—control and direct the outcomes that, together, their actions produce.' (Hayward and Lukes, 2008: 9). This wider view is, it seems, able to focus on a more extensive range of significant social constraints on freedom but, for just this reason, it does not mesh with our ordinary understanding of responsibility since it encompasses power relations that can arise only as the unintended and unforeseen effects of the interaction of a plurality of agents.

Does this mean, then, that the wider view cannot perform the fundamental task of distinguishing injustice from misfortune? Not necessarily. Help is available here from the work of Iris Young who was concerned, precisely, that an agency-centred view of power failed to make visible forms of, what she called, '**structural injustice**':

> Structural injustice exists when the combined operation of actions in institutions put large categories of persons under a systematic threat of domination or deprivation of the means to develop and exercise their capacities, at the same time as they enable others to dominate or give them access to an abundance of resources. Structural injustice is a kind of moral wrong distinct from the wrongful action of an individual agent or the willfully repressive policies of a state. Structural injustice occurs as a consequence of many individuals and institutions acting in pursuit of their particular goals and interests, within given institutional rules and accepted norms.
>
> (**Young, 2007: 170**)

Structural injustice thus refers to forms of unfreedom and inequality that are products of social structures. Any social structure is liable to involve *positional differences*—that is, the differential distribution of resources, opportunities, and advantages across different persons within a society—but when ongoing patterns of positional differences align with *categories* of persons, this suggests that structural injustice is in play. Young illustrates this form of injustice by reference to the position of women, African Americans, and the disabled in the USA. Her claim is that these enduring patterns of positional difference can legitimately be seen as injustice, rather than misfortune, because the source of such patterns of positional difference is social and political interaction by multiple agents acting according to accepted norms —*and* they are amenable to transformation through social and political agency. But to underwrite that claim, she requires an account of responsibility that goes beyond the liability model as standardly construed.

To address this issue, Young proposes what she calls a 'social connection' model of responsibility:

> The social connection model of responsibility says that individuals bear responsibility for structural injustice because they contribute by their actions to processes that produce unjust outcomes. Our responsibility derives from belonging together with others in a system of interdependent processes of cooperation and competition through which we seek benefits and aim to realize projects.
>
> (**Young, 2011: 175**)

Where we, severally, conform to accepted social norms and expectations in pursuing our own interests and projects within a system of social cooperation, and the outcome of our so acting is an ongoing pattern of positional difference in which some category (or categories) of persons are dominated or disadvantaged, we can legitimately be held to share responsibility for such outcomes. This responsibility takes the form of placing us under a joint obligation to address the position of the dominated and disadvantaged. So, for example, if our society has evolved norms concerning the production of the built environment which effectively assume the capabilities of able-bodied persons and, thereby, produce various forms of disadvantage for disabled persons, we are under a joint obligation to take reasonable measures to alter these norms or their practical effects in ways that acknowledge disabled persons as *equal* members of society. Young's proposal provides one route (but not necessarily the only route) for those committed to the wider concept of power to be able to draw a distinction between injustice and misfortune.

Given that both agency-centred and non-agency-centred views of power can accomplish the fundamental task of grounding a distinction between injustice and misfortune, what hangs on the difference between them? To explore this question, we can consider a recent exchange between Steven Lukes (representing the agency-centred view) and Clarissa Hayward (representing the wider view) in which they consider the example of residential housing patterns in American cities. Hayward captures the distinction between the respective views of power in relation to this example by noting that Lukes' example directs us to consider what is only 'one subset of inegalitarian social constraints' namely, 'those caused by the action or inaction of agents who, in principle, might have "[made] a difference": for example, public officials who engage in exclusionary zoning' (Hayward and Lukes, 2008: 9). She then goes on to point out that this analysis does not treat as 'power effects' those housing patterns that are 'produced unwittingly by "multiple actors pursuing their varied respective interests". Presumably, Lukes would include in this category the processes signalled by the familiar phrases "urban economic restructuring" and "white flight". (Hayward and Lukes, 2008: 9).

In response, Lukes argues that 'Hayward is, of course, correct in asserting that "significant, inegalitarian and remediable social constraints on human freedom" are not always caused by what Lord Acton called the 'bad men' in power. These constraints, indeed, as in the case of white flight to the suburbs, may be best thought of structurally' but immediately goes on to suggest that those 'who are in a position to contribute to remedying them, perhaps by working to change the institutional framework, but who did not contribute to causing them, are, to that extent, responsible and thus powerful.' (Hayward and Lukes, 2008: 12) In other words, Lukes is arguing that to describe the position of those 'left behind' as misfortune, rather than injustice, would require it to be the case not simply that powerful actors cannot be held liable for causing the harms that befell those 'left behind' but also that they cannot be held liable for failing to prevent or mitigate the harms that result from this structural process.

We can express the key difference between the two views in this way:

- The agency-centred view takes the issue of *liability* to be primary in the analysis of power and, hence, focuses on making visible, situations where an identifiable (set of) powerful agent(s) can be held responsible for causing or, in the case of structural processes, failing to prevent, forms of unfreedom and inequality.

- The non-agency-centred view takes the issue of *freedom* to be primary in the analysis of power and, hence, focuses on making visible what Hayward nicely refers to as 'codified and institutionalized human actions that create patterned asymmetries in the social capacity to act.' (Hayward and Lukes, 2008: 12).

It is tempting to suggest that the agency-centred view of power has primacy in contexts in which we are concerned with holding political agents to account and that the non-agency-centred view has primacy in contexts in which we are concerned with evaluating a society in terms of freedom—and this temptation suggests an intriguing line of thought: why should we assume that the different contexts in which the question of why we need concepts of power arises call for a single view of power that is invariant across these contexts? We need concepts of power for different reasons in each of these contexts and, perhaps, the distinct purposes we have in each of these different contexts is best served by a different view of power?

☆ **KEY POINTS**

- Agency-centred and non-agency-centred views of power draw the distinction between injustice and misfortune differently.
- Agency-centred views are primarily focused on identifying responsible agents.
- Non-agency-centred views are primarily focused on identifying constraints on freedom.

Conclusion

The view that we take of power has significant implications for how we demarcate the realm of politics, for how we conceive of freedom and responsibility, and for how and where we draw the distinction between injustice and misfortune. It is true that power is a ubiquitous feature of political life; it is equally true that concepts of power shape our understanding, explanation, and evaluation of political life. If it is a central normative concern of political theory to articulate how to govern ourselves with the minimum of domination, the analysis of power is necessarily central to that endeavour.

  CASE STUDY

Racialized inequality in America

The history of African American–White inequality in the USA is a history replete with power in a wide variety of forms. It begins with slavery, perhaps the most fundamental form of human domination and one bound up with such brutality as murder, rape, and whipping (brought to dramatic expression in Steve McQueen's 2013 film *Twelve Years a Slave*). After the Civil War, it continued with Jim Crow laws and lynchings maintaining racial segregation in the South (1876–1965), structures held in place not least by the concerted use of supermajority rules by the representatives of the South in the Senate between 1870 and 1957 to block legislation designed to give African

Americans the genuine equality before the law for which the 14th Amendment (1868) called. But other forms of power were also in play, most notably the concerted exercises of power with one another of many American citizens (White as well as African American) that were manifest in the Civil Rights Movement.

Yet even today, fifty years after the Civil Rights legislation of the 1960s, African American–White inequality is a 'durable inequality' across a very wide range of measures encompassing health and life expectancy, income and wealth, employment, educational attainment, vulnerability to crime (especially violent crime), and susceptibility to criminal conviction. It offers a classic example of positional difference, reproduced through processes of racialization of bodies, behaviour, work, and space, in which African Americans are subject to ongoing forms of domination and disadvantage.

To focus in on just one measure, we can look at African American–White economic inequality on which the *Washington Post* published a series of charts to mark the fifty years since Martin Luther King's 'I Have a dream' speech in 1963.[1] We can summarize the main points thus:

- The ratio of African American to White unemployment was 2.2 in 1963 and 2.1 in 2013.
- The gap in household income between African Americans and Whites has barely changed.
- The wealth disparity between African Americans and Whites has grown between 1963 and 2013.
- Although the percentage of African Americans in poverty has declined from 42% to 28%, the ratio of African Americans to Whites in poverty remains the same (2.8 in 1963 and 2013).
- African American children are far more likely to grow up in areas of concentrated poverty: African American, 45%; White, 12%.
- The share of African American children in segregated (50-100% non-White) schools was 76.6% in 1963 and 74.1% in 2013.
- 52.1% of African American children live in one-parent homes compared to 19.9 of White children.
- The incarceration rate of African American men is six times higher than of White men, a slightly higher ratio than in 1960.

It is hard not to be shocked by these figures and the lack of progress since the 1960s, but what explains the durability of this inequality?

The most plausible account, provided by Elizabeth Anderson in *The Imperative of Integration* (2010), is that the linchpin for much of this inequality, and its durability, is the racialization of space, that is, 'racial segregation, understood as processes that prevent interracial contact or structure it on terms of inequality, and resulting conditions of spatial separation by race and disproportionate black occupation of subordinate social roles.' (Anderson, 2010: 25).[2]

Now, it is certainly the case that there are powerful agents responsible for the emergence of racial segregation in American cities. As Anderson notes:

> Current patterns of residential racial segregation can be historically traced to the collusion of federal, state, and local governments with white real estate agents, apartment owners, and homeowners to keep blacks out of white neighborhoods.
>
> (Anderson, 2010: 68)

However, the persistence of segregation today is not simply a matter of powerful agents, it is also the product of 'the unplanned net effect of the actions of multiple actors who could not—not through their individual choices, not through their coordinated efforts—control and direct the outcomes that, together, their actions produce.' (Hayward and Lukes, 2008: 9). Consider the phenomenon of 'white flight' to which Hayward refers in her exchange with Lukes:

Over the course of the last century, as is well known, industrial production in the country was not only automated; it was decentralized at the national level, as well, and, internationally, globalized. Together with technological advances in telecommunications and travel, deindustrialization helped to create an urban economic structure in which multiple individual and collective actors pursuing their varied respective interests—interests in protecting their investments, interests in obtaining an optimal package of public services while paying relatively low taxes—migrated to the suburbs of older cities and to the newer cities of the American West and Southwest. Neither deindustrialization, nor the exodus of middle-class whites from older central cities, was a consciously coordinated process. Their combined effects on those 'left behind' were largely unintended. However, together, they eroded the urban tax base at just that historical juncture when African-Americans migrated *en masse* from the rural South to the urban North, increasing dramatically demand for affordable housing in older cities.

(Hayward and Lukes, 2008: 9)

We can note both that this process has reinforced segregation and that it has exacerbated the effects of racial segregation in terms of its effects on access to goods and services and the ability to accumulate forms of economic, social, and cultural capital (Anderson, 2010: 23–43). These effects undermine the power of African Americans to breakdown segregation by acquiring the means to move to White neighbourhoods.

 KEY TEXTS

Anderson, *The Imperative of Integration* (2010)

Elizabeth Anderson's *The Imperative of Integration* (2010) is a study of why, more than forty years after the passage of civil rights and anti-discrimination laws, African American–White inequality endures and, on some axes, has worsened in recent years. Winner of the American Philosophical Association's Joseph B. Gittler Award in 2011, it is an incisive exercise in non-ideal political theory that draws on a wide range of findings in social science to identify segregation as a key cause of this durable inequality, and makes a powerful case for the policy of racial integration as an imperative of democratic justice.

But 'white flight' was itself already informed by (and, through its segregating effects, has further reinforced) the unconscious formation of stigmatizing racial stereotypes that encourage the reproduction of segregation and its attendant inequalities (Anderson, 2010: 44–66). It would be naïve and inaccurate to suggest that America lacks overtly racist agents who are powerful, but an important part of the central role of segregation is that it generates mechanisms that support the durability of African American–White inequality, even in the absence of widespread individual racism (conceived as self-endorsed racist attitudes). Consider the social psychology of **attribution biases** which come into play when explaining another's behaviour in terms of dispositional causes (characteristics of the person) or of situational causes (the environment in which they act) and focus on stigmatizing racial stereotypes that account for the behaviour of a racialized group in terms of negative characteristics of those identified as members of that group. By using these tools, Anderson is able to demonstrate that spatial segregation (predominantly African American neighbourhoods and predominantly White neighbourhoods) and role segregation (predominantly African American jobs and predominantly White jobs) support a range of stigma-reinforcing attribution biases that 'naturalize' African American inequality by encouraging ascription of its causes to the characteristics of these people. Once established, such stereotypes can be self-supporting in that they filter perceptions to pick out confirming evidence and may also induce those whom they stereotype to conform to them.

It is an important point here that those who exhibit these attribution biases and stigmatizing stereotypes need not be aware that they are doing so and need not (and often would not) endorse these stereotypes at a reflective level. These reflections apply as much to politicians as to ordinary citizens; they also apply to a range of social scientific explanations and public policy proposals that, in simply tracking the surface phenomena, reproduce these biases in their findings and policies (for example, attributing the inequality of African Americans to their culture). Dominating power operates here not simply through acting on the self- (and other-) perceptions of the dominated but, arguably more so, through acting on the other- (and self-) perceptions of those advantaged by this structure of domination.

Notice that, in this context, White Americans may follow the segregationist norm not because they are racist but because predominantly African American localities are likely to be characterized by low-class residents, high crime rates, and poor access to goods and services. Put pointedly, even well-meaning Whites 'are simply trapped in a prisoner's dilemma' in that 'any individual white who

 KEY CONCEPTS

Attribution bias

Attribution biases are the product of heuristics that we use in explaining another's conduct in terms of dispositional causes (characteristics of the person) or of situational causes (the environment in which they act), such that we are more prone to focus, in the case of the in-group (the group to which we belong), on dispositional causes when this generates a positive judgement and situational causes when this cancels a negative judgement, whereas in the case of the out-group (the group that contrasts with the group to which we belong), we are more prone to focus on dispositional causes when this generates a negative judgement and on situational causes when this cancels a positive judgement.

ignores the racial profile' of the neighborhood 'risks a large personal loss in access to advantage for a negligible positive impact on the neighborhood's access.' (Anderson, 2010: 71) As Anderson notes:

> One could argue that whites who avoid black neighborhoods for these reasons are not blameworthy . . . Individual whites can hardly be blamed for preferring to buy homes in neighborhoods that can promise decent public services, low tax and crime rates, few blighted lots, and steadily appreciating house values—especially when their individual choices can do little to improve the neighborhoods that suffer from these problems.
>
> (Anderson, 2010: 71)

The persistence of segregation need not involve appeal to the power of specific powerful agents who can be held accountable for producing this outcome. Rather, this type of prudential reasoning, by even well-meaning White Americans, will help to reproduce segregation and the durable inequalities that it supports. This matters because while it is plausible to argue that citizens—and especially politicians and public officials—have a responsibility to reflect critically on their own biases, they do not have a responsibility to be civic saints. At the same time, the widespread presence of stigmatizing racial stereotypes makes it difficult for segregation to be identified as a key linchpin of African American–White inequality. It does so since these stereotypes facilitate political receptivity to other explanations and, for the same reasons, limit the prospects for building the kind of African American–White movement needed to support political action on African American–White inequality.

Who should we hold responsible for this situation of enduring inequality? Recall that Lukes (Hayward and Lukes, 2008) argues that those who can make a significant difference are responsible, hence powerful. This view points us to federal, state, and local governments (who, let us not forget, colluded in the construction of segregation) as the agents of primary responsibility. Iris Young's (2007) view of structural injustice directs us to a wider constituency that would encompass the politics of civil society—churches, schools, universities, clubs, etc. But there is no need to choose between these alternatives, since a dual-track approach is not only reasonable but may be practically necessary for addressing this type of durable inequality. A politics of civil society directed at fostering sites of African American–White interaction may be necessary to break down the stigmatizing stereotypes to the extent needed to get a politics of the state off the ground, to build the coalitions needed for state policies of integration to be politically viable under the non-ideal conditions in which we must act.

I began by referencing Steve McQueen's 2013 film *Twelve Years a Slave*, which takes us back to the pre-Civil War era, but we can end by referring to another, slightly earlier, film that provides eloquent testimony to African American–White inequality in contemporary America—Spike Lee's 2006 documentary *When the Levees broke: a requiem in four parts* which focuses on New Orleans in the aftermath of the devastation wrought by Hurricane Katrina in 2005. In this film, Lee exposes the ongoing nature of African American–White inequality in the context of a disaster that throws that inequality into sharp relief.

? QUESTIONS

1. 'Politics is unimaginable without power.' Discuss.

2. What is the point of concepts of power?

3. Why is it important to distinguish modes of power?

4. Is power an essentially contested concept?

5. 'The community power debate was primarily methodological rather than conceptual.' Discuss.

6. 'Lukes' three dimensional view of power is conceptually cogent but has little practical significance.' Evaluate this claim.

7. How compelling is Foucault's critique of liberal and radical views of power?

8. In social and political concepts, the concept of power is best viewed as an agency-centred concept. Is it?

9. How should we distinguish between injustice and misfortune?

10. Durable inequalities point to the importance of moving beyond an agency-centred concept of power. Discuss.

11. Critically examine the presuppositions of structural injustice.

12. 'Power can only be exercised over free persons and only insofar as they are free.' Is this claim defensible?

FURTHER READING

■ Dowding, K. M. (1996) *Power*, Minneapolis: University of Minnesota Press Provides a refreshing introduction to the concept and study of political power that overcomes many of the old disputes over the nature and structure of power in society. Dowding develops the concept of systematic luck and explains how some groups get what they want without trying, while the efforts of others bring little reward.

■ Haugaard, M. (1997) *The Constitution of Power: A theoretical analysis of power, knowledge and structure*, Manchester: Manchester University Press Discusses the relationship between power, structure, and knowledge and offers vital insights into some of the core debates which have dominated contemporary social and political theory for the past twenty years.

■ Hayward, C. (2000) *De-facing Power*, Cambridge: Cambridge University Press Challenges the prevailing view of power as something powerful people have and use. Rather than seeing it as having a 'face', Hayward argues for a view of power as a complex network of social boundaries—norms, identities, institutions—which define individual freedom, for 'powerful' and 'powerless' alike.

■ Hindess, B. (1996) *Discourses of Power: From Hobbes to Foucault*, Oxford: Blackwell Publishing Provides a new interpretation of concepts of power within Western social thought, from Hobbes' notion of 'sovereign power' to Foucault's account of 'government'.

■ Scott, J. (2001) *Power*, Cambridge: Polity Press Gives a concise and coherent overview of the debates surrounding the analysis of social power. The concept of power is outlined, and its main dimensions are explored through consideration of various facets—command, pressure, constraint, discipline, protest, and interpersonal power.

 WEB LINKS

● http://foucault.info A useful site for Foucault bibliography and links.

● http://stevenlukes.net Steven Lukes' homepage, providing information about his many publications and activities.

● http://www.tandfonline.com/loi/rpow21#.Uvf7fHmN5g0 The *Journal of Political Power*.

● http://www.powercube.net Contains practical and conceptual materials to help us think about how to respond to power relations within organizations and in wider social and political spaces.

● http://cartome.org/panopticon1.htm An image of Bentham's 'Panopticon'.

 Visit the Online Resource Centre that accompanies this book to access more learning resources: http://www.oxfordtextbooks.co.uk/orc/mckinnon3e/

 ENDNOTES

[1] Available online at: http://www.washingtonpost.com/blogs/wonkblog/wp/2013/08/28/these-seven-charts-show-the-black-white-economic-gap-hasnt-budged-in-50-years/

[2] For a current mapping of spatial segregation see: http://demographics.coopercenter.org/DotMap/index.html

Glossary

active consent See **explicit consent**.

act utilitarianism Act utilitarianism is the view that all of our actions should aim to maximize the amount of collective utility of all persons or even sentient beings. For example, a hedonistic version of act utilitarianism would require that we act so as to maximize the amount of pleasure and minimize the amount of pain in the world. Cf. **rule utilitarianism**.

agent A being who has a will—although not necessarily a rational will—to do something.

aggregative justice An aggregative conception of justice is one that primarily focuses on the total amount of a given x. Imagine that this x was, for example, 'opportunity for well-being'. The aggregative approach will aim at maximizing its total amount, even at the cost of a more unequal distribution of it. Cf. **distributive justice**.

aggression International crime that covers the planning, preparation, and execution of an act of armed force by a state against the sovereignty, territorial integrity, or political independence of another state.

anarchy Literally 'without rulers', this term refers to a society in which the state has been abolished, or, more widely, in which all forms of hierarchy or oppression have been abolished.

anti-egalitarian sufficientarianism This is a **sufficiency principle** that attaches great importance to the universal attainment of a certain critical level of advantage, and denies the importance of equality or priority once such a level has been universally attained.

assimilation This term refers to a policy that encourages cultural minorities to lose their distinctive customs or norms in order to fit in more easily with the rest of society. Assimilation is often resisted by minority cultures. Cf. **integration**.

asymmetric war A war fought between a state and a non-state group, such as a terrorist organization.

attribution biases Biases that arise from attributing bad behaviour of out-group members to their character and of in-group members to the situation in which they find themselves, and vice versa with respect to good behaviour.

authority The power to issue commands that are or ought to be obeyed because of from whom they issue.

autonomy An individual has autonomy (or **individuality**) to the extent that he or she rationally chooses his or her acts and omissions in accord with his or her own judgement and inclinations—where 'rationality' implies at least a minimal capacity to understand and foresee the probable consequences of those acts and omissions. The individual may have autonomy without necessarily having **moral autonomy**.

autonomy theory This approach focuses on the rationality of human beings with specific reference to their capacity to make moral choices, in relation to both what duty requires of them and the capacity to choose to do what their reason tells them to be morally right.

basic liberty principle A principle of **social justice** defended by Rawls, that restricts inequality by insisting on upholding the fair value of rights to participate in the political system and not merely more familiar civil liberties. See **principle of equal basic liberty**.

basic structure A technical term employed by John Rawls to refer to a set of major social institutions that distribute rights and duties between individuals, and which exert profound influence on motivations and life prospects.

bill of rights A declaration of citizens' rights or **human rights**, normally incorporated in a constitution and sometimes used by courts to override legislation or executive action deemed to be contrary to the bill of rights.

brute luck This refers to luck inherent to the conditions faced by individuals and independent of the choices they have made. Cf. **option luck**.

capability approach An approach to the interpersonal comparison of advantage under which an individual's level of advantage depends on his or her capacity to function or to act in certain listed ways: for example, to be well nourished, mobile, and literate.

civil liberty An individual's civil liberty—or **liberty** in a **normative** sense—consists of a set of civil and political rights that are distributed to that individual as a member of a given civil society by the society's laws of justice. By distributing any such right, law makers recognize that the individual's liberty to do as he or she wishes has legal and social value in relation to a domain of conduct that is, at least implicitly, defined by the relevant right. This does not mean that the individual agrees with the law makers or that everyone assigns the same relative importance to different rights.

civil society The collection of voluntary associations in political societies that help to mediate between the state and the citizens.

claim rights These refer to one person's right to do or have something that correlates with other people's duties to allow, or enable, that person to have or do that to which her or she has the claim right.

classical liberalism Most commonly, the view that an important relationship exists between individual **liberty** and private property, such that possession of the latter is identical with, or the best means for, the protection of the former. Sometimes also used to refer to a form of liberalism that emphasizes the distinction between the **public sphere** and the **private sphere**.

classical utilitarianism A version of **utilitarianism** that posits that the morally right act is that which maximizes the greatest good of the greatest number. The idea is associated with Jeremy Bentham and Henry Sidgwick.

cleronomicity A theory of intergenerational justice is cleronomic when what a generation actually inherited is taken as a baseline in defining what we owe the next generation. It is non-cleronomic when the definition of what any generation owes to the next generation is independent of what the former actually inherited. An example of a non-cleronomic theory is one concerned only with the basic needs of the next generation in defining what the generation preceding it owes to it.

coercion The forcing of someone to do something by threatening him or her with an unpleasant outcome if he or she does not comply. Some theorists think that the threatened outcome must also be wrongful in order for the threat to count as coercive. The term is sometimes used more widely to refer to the use of force, both threatened and actual, to achieve some aim.

collectivism The view that war is essentially a relationship between collectives and cannot be morally reduced to the relationships between individual members of the warring parties.

common sense morality A core of values, rules, and prohibitions that are widely respected, although sometimes embodied differently. Some prohibitions on dishonesty, killing, and cruelty, and some honouring of parents, caring for children, and respecting of one's community and its laws appear to be common to many different cultures and historical periods.

comparative prioritarianism See **prioritarianism**.

conception of the good This refers either to (a) a person's full set of persisting and stable preferences, or (b) the package of substantive commitments (which include beliefs, preferences, and habits) relating to how to live life well.

consent theory The view that political **authority** and obligation are justified because citizens have consented to obey the law in one way or another. Cf. **contract theory**.

consequentialism A moral theory that bases the rightness or wrongness of conduct solely on the extent to which it maximizes good consequences and minimizes bad consequences.

consociational institutions These are institutions that require consensus among the various groups in society to make legislative and policy decisions. Cf. **federalist institutions**.

contract theory The view that political **authority** and obligation is justified because citizens have formed a contract with each other to obey the law. Unlike the term **consent theory**, the term contract theory is not usually used for the view that contemporary citizens give their **tacit consent** to obey the law, being more commonly used in relation to **hypothetical consent** theory.

cosmopolitanism Cosmopolitans see themselves as citizens of the world—as members of a global community of human beings, with robust responsibilities to others in the global community. Cosmopolitans believe that all individual human beings have equal moral worth and that the strength of our moral obligations to others is not diminished by national borders. The philosophy has its roots in the **Stoicism** of Ancient Greece.

crimes against humanity International crimes that cover inhumane acts such as murder, torture, rape, or enslavement, when committed as part of a widespread or systematic attack against the members of a certain group.

cultural identity This refers to an individual's sense of belonging to a cultural or ethnic group. The term is most often used to describe the content of that individual's identity—for example, 'wearing the veil is part of my cultural identity'.

cultural norms This refers to rules that exist within a group, including how to behave in social situations. For example, it is a cultural norm among young people in the UK that they aim to become homeowners. Cultural norms are not laws, but can be important to people.

cultural racism This refers to when racial prejudice is expressed by using 'cultural' insults—for example, 'Paki!' is often meant as a racist slur, although it does not overtly refer to a person's ethnic group or skin colour (see Modood, 2005).

cultural relativism The view that either (a) what is right or wrong is entirely a matter for cultural determination and/or (b) that there is no basis for saying that the values of one culture are better than those of another.

cultural rights The rights of members of a cultural group to engage in practices that are central to their culture and/or the rights of a cultural group to take measures to protect its continued existence. These rights can take the form of **exemptions** from requirements imposed on all other persons and/or groups.

customary international norms These are norms that come from a general practice that is accepted as law by states and that exist independent of treaty law. This means that states follow customary international norms not merely as a matter of habit, but out of a sense of obligation. All international legal subjects are bound by these norms.

decent people These are non-liberal societies, the basic institutions of which meet certain conditions of justice, including the right to play a role in making political decisions through a consultation process or hierarchy.

deliberative democracy A form of collective decision making, whereby laws and policies are legitimate to the extent that they are publicly justified to the citizens of the community. Public justification is justification to each citizen as a result of free and reasoned debate among equals.

deliberative polling Involves giving a group of citizens the opportunity to hear information about some policy issue, debate with one another, and question experts, before coming to a verdict.

democracy A method of group decision making that is characterized by a kind of equality among the participants at an essential stage of the collective decision making.

democratic equality A term for Rawls' conception of justice.

deontology A theory that grounds morality in imperatives that lay down moral obligations that are independent of the consequences of their being followed.

descriptive Concerned with how things actually are in the world or how they would be if something were to happen. Cf. **normative**.

difference principle A **principle of social justice** advocated by Rawls which prohibits inequalities in income and wealth that are detrimental to the least advantaged.

direct action A principled attempt to remedy an injustice by directly confronting the source of the injustice, rather than by asking someone else to take action on your behalf.

discount rate The discount rate is the rate at which the value of future benefits and costs are reduced in comparison to present benefits and costs. Even a very low discount rate has the consequence that very great benefits and costs in the distant future are worth very little compared to small benefits and costs that occur at present.

distributive justice A distributive conception of justice is one that primarily focuses on the distribution of the total amount of a given x in society. Imagine that this x were, for example, 'opportunity for well-being'. The distributive approach will care about how the 'pie' of opportunity for well-being is divided up, even if it means that we shall end up with a smaller 'pie'. Cf. **aggregative justice**.

doctrine of double effect (DDE) The claim that whilst one may not aim at harm, it can be permissible to bring about harm as a foreseen and unavoidable side-effect of pursuing a proportionate good.

elites Relatively well-defined groups of persons who possess the power to govern the rules, norms, and decisions of a particular domain of activity (culture, economic, politics).

elite theory A theory of **democracy** that argues against any robustly egalitarian or deliberative forms of democracy, positing that high levels of citizen participation tend to produce bad legislation, which is designed by demagogues to appeal to poorly informed and overly emotional citizens.

emancipation The freeing of an individual or group from slavery or bondage. Where such slavery or bondage is, in the first instance, legally recognized, emancipation has a clear meaning: either the abolition of the law, or the granting of rights under the law, when, for example, a slave is freed by his or her master. In contemporary use, emancipation is often more a matter of overcoming social or cultural bonds, rather than a grant of legal rights, and may be a matter of degree rather than absolute.

enforceability This refers to whether or not people can be made to follow a rule under threat of punishment. Enforceability may refer to the moral permissibility of enforcing a rule or the practicality of enforcing a rule. The former meaning is applied in this book.

environmental citizenship A conception of citizenship that involves responsibility for the environmental consequences of our actions as well as the familiar obligations of citizenship, such as voting, obedience to the law, and defending the nation.

envy test A device employed by economists to evaluate distributions. A distribution is said to pass the envy test if nobody prefers another's endowments to his or her own. Dworkin, among others, describes equality as a condition of envy freedom.

equal basic liberty, principle of A **principle of social justice** advocated by Rawls that grants individuals certain basic civil liberties, such as equality before the law and free speech, as well as rights to participate in the democratic process on a fair basis. It is also known as the **first principle**, because Rawls grants it the highest priority.

equality of resources A theory of social justice devised by Ronald Dworkin, which evaluates distributions by asking whether they could have emerged from a hypothetical market process.

essentially contested concepts Evaluative concepts whose proper use is contested, where such contestation does not arise from confusion but rather from the internally complex character of the concept and the fact that different persons are liable to weigh the diverse constituent elements of the concept differently. There is, consequently, no best exemplar of such concepts. Disputes concerning the use of such concepts are both genuine (not based on mistakes) and irresolvable by rational argument.

ethical pluralism The doctrine, of which there are many versions, that there are plural irreducible ethical values rather than a single ultimate value, such as general welfare. Berlin's version holds that plural basic values may sometimes conflict to the extent that there is no singular universal rational resolution of the conflict.

exemptions This refers to not being subject to a rule that normally applies to everyone. Religious groups often demand exemptions in relation to children's education.

explicit consent Consent expressed by clearly stating or writing down one's consent. An example would be saying, 'I consent to X', or signing at the bottom of a document to that effect. It is also known as **express consent** or **active consent**. Cf. **tacit consent**.

express consent See **explicit consent**.

external protections Rights that protect a culture from the policies of the wider society in relation to issues such as education and health care. Cf. **internal restrictions**.

extreme prioritarianism This is a form of **prioritarianism** that gives *absolute* priority—rather than some extra weight—to the interests of the less advantaged, over those of the more fortunate.

fair equality of opportunity, principle of This **principle of social justice**—advocated, inter alia, by Rawls—requires that governments ensure that similarly motivated and talented individuals enjoy the same prospects of success in the competition for jobs and political offices.

federalist institutions These are stratified institutions that allocate some powers to legislative assemblies deciding for the whole and some powers to more local assemblies. Cf. **consociational institutions**.

first principle See **principle of equal basic liberty**.

freedom of expression This refers to the freedom to express oneself in speech, writing, performance, appearance, etc., without fear of punishment or social censure. It is variously defended in the name of individual **autonomy**, self-respect, pursuit of truth and knowledge, and also scepticism about the existence of universal truths, or our ability to know them.

full compliance, theory of A theory that discusses the norms that justice or morality requires, on the assumption that those norms would be respected. It is also sometimes referred to as **ideal theory**.

genealogy A term introduced by Nietzsche and adopted by Foucault to refer to exercises in historical philosophy that attempt (a) to trace how we have been formed as the subjects we are (in some aspect, e.g. sexuality), (b) to demonstrate the contingent power-laden character of this process, and, thereby, (c) to open up space for critical reflection on the ways in which we currently understand and act on ourselves.

genocide International crime that covers the perpetration of crimes such as killing and causing serious bodily or mental harm, when committed with intent to destroy a national, ethnical, racial, or religious group.

human rights These refer to moral rights that belong to all human beings by virtue of their humanity, which override or generally outweigh other moral considerations. Human rights correlate with the duties of all human beings— and especially all governments—to respect, protect, and promote the interests identified by these rights.

hypothetical consent Consent that *would* be given in some imagined world, if certain conditions obtained that do not, in fact, obtain. Cf. **express consent** and **tacit consent**.

ideal theory See **full compliance, theory of**.

immunity rights These rights render their holders immune from having their rights and duties changed by another person.

implicit consent See **tacit consent**.

incomplete theory This refers to a theory that is restricted in its scope—for example, one such theory might deal only with social, but not global, justice.

individuality See **autonomy**.

integration The idea that different cultural groups within the same country can belong equally to it, but still have different social institutions and rights. The opposite of integration is **segregation**. Multicultural thinkers greatly prefer integration to the idea of **assimilation**.

interest group pluralism An approach to **democracy** that is partly motivated by the problem of democratic citizenship, but which attempts to preserve some elements of equality against the criticisms of **elite theory**.

internal restrictions This refers to group rights that limit the individual liberties of people within a culture. Cf. **external protections**.

international borrowing privilege This refers to the way in which governments may borrow freely on behalf of the country and the country is obliged to repay debts.

international resource privilege This refers to the way in which governments may freely dispose of the country's natural resources in a way that is legally recognized internationally.

judicial review A mechanism whereby legislation can be challenged through the courts on the grounds that it infringes one or more of the rights recognized by a constitution. Judges will evaluate whether, in fact, the legislation does so, and will be empowered to invalidate the law in question, or the offending part of the law, if the case is proven.

jurisdiction Refers to the right to exercise legal authority and the limits within which that right may be exercised.

jus ad bellum The conditions that determine whether one may justly declare war.

jus in bello The moral conditions that govern the fighting of war.

jus post bellum The moral considerations that arise in the aftermath of a war.

just war An account of how war should conform to moral regulation. Cf. **pacifism**, **realism**, and **romantic militarism**.

law of nature A way of thinking about political matters that is derived from ancient Greek thought and Roman law, whereby the content of law is given by nature and has universal validity.

Law of Peoples A law to govern relations between liberal and non-liberal peoples of the world. In Rawls' version, this law consists of principles acknowledging peoples' independence, their equality, their right to self-defence, and their duties of non-intervention, to observe treaties, to honour a limited set of rights, to conduct themselves appropriately in war, and to provide limited assistance for peoples living in certain kinds of unfavourable conditions.

legal positivism The view that rights are creations of positive law or conventional **social norms** that set out what is acceptable behaviour in particular societies. Positivists hold that these rights are subject to evaluation, criticism, and moral legitimation, but contend that this is a matter of deciding whether rights serve important human values and interests, rather than of acquiring knowledge of pre-existing natural or moral rights.

levelling down objection This refers to the commitment of those who endorse the principles of comparative egalitarianism to thinking that it would be *in one way* better if everybody were to be poor or blind, rather than if only some were to be rich or sighted, because then there would be more equality.

lexical, or lexicographical, order A Rawlsian technical term, using an analogy with the strict order of priority with which words are arranged in a dictionary, so that whatever begins with 'a' always precedes whatever begins with 'b', to refer to the prioritizing of principles. When one principle has lexical priority over another, it may not be compromised to any degree to realize the other principle better.

libertarian This refers to an ideology that celebrates freedom and is suspicious of government. The term was originally associated, and in some circles still is associated, with the anarchist vision of a non-coercive, egalitarian society, based on social cooperation. Its more common usage in contemporary political theory is to refer to a right-wing ideology that advocates, for both economic and moral reasons, a minimal role for government and a maximal role for the market in economic affairs.

liberty An individual has liberty in a purely **descriptive** sense in relation to a given domain of acts and omissions if, and only if, he or she can do as he or she wishes within that domain. If the individual chooses whatever act or omission he or she likes, then it follows that other people are not preventing that individual from acting, or omitting to act, as he or she chooses. The domain of conduct in relation to which an individual has liberty may be extensive or narrow, depending on the context. As long as he or she can choose even a single act or omission, however, that individual is at liberty in relation to that particular act or omission. It is a separate question whether the individual's liberty has value in a given context.

liberty rights These are rights that involve no more than the absence of a duty on the part of the right holder.

minimal state Introduced by Robert Nozick, the term refers to a state that restricts itself to enforcing basic property rights and rights against harm. A minimal state exercises sole **authority** in a given territory to arbitrate in judicial matters and enforce its judgements. Its protection is afforded to all who live within that territory.

moderate prioritarianism See **prioritarianism**.

modus vivendi An extemporary and contingent accommodation between two conflicting parties to supersede their contrasts, at least temporarily, for prudential and pragmatic reasons.

moral autonomy An individual has moral autonomy if, in addition to having **autonomy**, his or her conduct satisfies ethical standards of right conduct prescribed by a given theory of morality. The ethical standards might be incorporated within a thick concept of rationality, or they might be assumed to constitute a concept of **reasonableness** that is independent of a thin concept of rationality. Ethical standards may vary across different moral theories and, in some instances, may overlap with standards of beauty established by aesthetic theories.

multiculturalism This term can refer to the fact of cultural diversity in countries ranging from the former Yugoslavia to the UK, and may also describe the coexistence of different kinds of cultural group within a country.

nationalism The political doctrine that each nation is entitled to **self-determination**.

national minority A group that perceives itself to constitute a nation apart from the majority within that political community.

natural rights These are rights that exist in nature independently of any actual human laws or customs.

neoliberalism An approach to **democracy** that minimizes the scope of the **authority** of the state and turns most decisions over to the market or voluntary organization. Cf. **elite theory** and **interest group pluralism**.

neutralist liberalism A strand of contemporary liberal theory for which neutrality is not only a guideline for the public treatments of citizens, but also the central feature of liberal institutions, which ought to be designed independently from any substantive moral outlook, so as to be recognized as legitimate by people who widely disagree about values and morals.

neutrality The bracketing of religious and personal convictions, opinions, and corresponding practices in the **political sphere**, so as to avoid discrimination concerning religious and moral beliefs.

normative Concerned with how things ought to be or what people ought to do. Cf. **descriptive**.

norm of reciprocity The requirement that citizens refrain from making claims that require other citizens to adopt their sectarian way of life.

operative public values These refer to important ideas held in society that regulate how people behave. Operative public values in most liberal societies include the principles of **freedom of expression** and **sexual equality**.

opportunity cost When one devotes resources to a given option, one does not devote them to alternative options. The opportunity cost of going for a given option (e.g. studying philosophy rather than management) is the difference between the gains from one option and the gain for the best alternative option.

option luck A technical term that has been widely employed since Dworkin used it, which refers to luck in the choices that individuals make rather than that of the conditions into which an individual is born or brought to for reasons independent of his or her will. Cf. **brute luck**.

original position A hypothetical situation, employed by Rawls, to compare competing **principles of social justice** by asking which would be chosen by rational individuals were they to be situated behind a **veil of ignorance** that deprives them of knowledge of their fortunes in the social and natural lottery, as well as of their conception of well-being.

overlapping consensus A kind of consensus in which individuals agree only on a proper subset of their moral and political ideas, while disagreeing on other elements.

pacifism The view that it is always wrong to use violence, even in the face of violence or to prevent greater violence.

participatory justice This form of justice ensures the fair distribution of rights to take part in collective decisions that affect one's interests.

passive consent See **tacit consent**.

patriarchy This literally means 'rule of the father'. It is used in feminist philosophy to mean a society that is structured according to sexual inequality, with men being advantaged and women disadvantaged. Patriarchies, in this feminist sense, need not have male political leaders, although men usually occupy more positions of political power than do women.

philosophical anarchism This refers to the view that no states enjoy legitimate **authority** and that no one is obliged to obey the law. Philosophical anarchists do not necessarily call for the abolition of the state, because they think that—for the moment at least—there are good prudential reasons to preserve the state.

political liberty An individual's political liberty may be viewed as a component of his **civil liberty**. From this perspective, political liberty consists of a set of political rights that enable the individual to participate, to some extent, in his or her society's political process by voting, for example, or running for office. In some social contexts, some individuals might lack political liberty in this sense, yet have some civil liberty—that is, their civil rights may not include any political rights. Nevertheless, the term remains ambiguous. In addition to political rights, it seems to connote living under a constitutional government, the power of which to abuse civil and political rights is effectively limited by a system of checks and balances.

political sphere See **public sphere**.

politics of recognition These refer to campaigns and policies that are designed to secure equal respect for devalued **cultural identities** in society. The politics of **recognition** can include the notion of **cultural rights**, but are broader than this.

popular sovereignty The view that **sovereignty** belongs to the people and, therefore, that **authority** is legitimate when it rests (directly or indirectly) on the consent of those subject to it.

positive rights These are rights that are posited in law or social mores, which can be identified by empirical observation of the source of the rules in question.

post-structuralist A group of French thinkers who critically distanced themselves from structuralism, an approach that focused on rules and norms independent of agency, in order to explore the interaction of agents and structures across a wide range of disciplines. Foucault and Derrida are the most prominent post-structuralist thinkers.

power–knowledge A term, introduced by Michel Foucault, to register the point that practices of power involve forms of knowledge that give shape and direction to the exercise of power, as well as producing effects that are objects of knowledge. This is not to assert the identity of power and knowledge, but to note that they stand in relationship to one another and, hence, the analysis of power must attend to the forms of knowledge presupposed by exercises of power and the forms of knowledge that these exercises of power make possible.

power rights These rights enable their holders to change the rights and duties both of themselves and of others, as when two people enter into a contract.

primary good A good that any rational person would want, whatever else he or she might want.

principle of equal basic liberty See **equal basic liberty, principle of**.

principle of social justice See **social justice, principle of**.

prioritarianism A distributive principle according to which the moral value of a benefit or disvalue of a burden *diminishes* as an individual becomes better off. The standard form of this view requires attaching non-absolute priority to the interests of the less advantaged and is not comparative, although forms of **comparative prioritarianism**, **moderate prioritatianism**, and **extreme prioritarianism** also exist.

private sphere This refers to areas of life, such as the family, that are thought, in **classical liberalism**, to be separate from political influence and interference. Feminists have criticized the idea that the private sphere is immune from political consideration. Cf. **public sphere**.

public equality A kind of equality that is realized in society such that everyone can see that he or she is being treated as an equal.

public reason The common reason that all citizens in a pluralistic **democracy** use to advance their justifications of public policies. Usually contrasted with **sectarian reason**.

public sphere Defined in contrast to the **private sphere**. The public sphere refers to areas of life that are properly subject to political interference and which should be regulated by principles of justice. The public sphere is sometimes referred to as the **political sphere**.

realism The view that war is or should be governed by national interests, and falls outside of the sphere of morality.

reasonableness Reasonable persons will only offer principles for the regulation of their society that other reasonable persons can reasonably accept.

recognition This refers to the positive assertion of differences in the public space and it is seen as the first symbolic step towards the full inclusion of minority groups.

retributivist theories Theories of punishment according to which wrongdoers deserve to suffer in proportion to the gravity of the wrong they have committed.

right to exit This refers to a person's freedom to leave his or her culture if he or she is dissatisfied by it.

romantic militarism A reaction to warfare that sees it as morally uplifting. Cf. **pacifism** and **realism**.

rule utilitarianism A moral theory that states that we should choose that set of rules which,

if consistently followed, would maximize the amount of collective utility of all persons, or even sentient beings (for example, given a hedonistic conception of utility, that set of rules that would maximize the amount of pleasure and minimize the amount of pain in the world). We should then judge the moral acceptability of actions by reference to these rules. This two-stage approach introduces some distance between the moral acceptability of an act and its consequences, thereby overcoming some of the objections faced by **act utilitarianism**.

secession This describes the process in which a portion of a political community divorces itself from the rest of the community to form its own state—that is, a group's act of breaking away from a larger nation to establish its own system of government. For example, the Basques wish for secession from Spain's rule, because they see themselves as culturally distinct from the Spanish.

sectarian reason The kind of reasoning that can only have weight for people who already accept a world view that many reasonable citizens reject—for example, appeals to scripture and to self-interest. Cf. **public reason**.

security An individual's security is another name for his or her **civil liberty** and **political liberty**, where political liberty is conceived broadly to include living under a constitutional government that has no **authority** to violate basic rights, and which is suitably constrained by a system of checks and balances to prevent abuses of authority. Arguably, security is maximized under some form of constitutional **democracy**, which recognizes a basic right to absolute **liberty** of self-regarding conduct.

segregation Literally, this means the separation of a group (or an individual) from other groups (or individuals). Racial segregation was enforced by the 'Jim Crow' laws in the USA (1876–1965) and was a central feature of the apartheid regime in South Africa (1948–94).

self-determination The view that each people or nation should have its own set of political institutions to enable it to decide collectively on matters that are of primary concern for its members.

self-regarding conduct An individual's conduct is *purely self-regarding* in Mill's sense if, and only if, it does not directly and immediately affect other people, or if it only does so with those people's unforced and undeceived consent and participation.

sexual equality Literally, this refers to equality between the sexes, but the meaning and scope of this equality is disputed. For example, defenders of sexual equality may limit their claims to equal pay for equal work or may use them in arguments for the censorship of pornography.

social cleavage A factor that divides members of society into groups that have different status or resources. Examples of social cleavages are sex, race, and class.

social construction This refers to the process by which **social norms** affect our lives, either by shaping the options that are available to or appropriate for us, or by affecting the way in which we interpret society, understand ourselves, and form preferences.

social contract An agreement between persons in a **state of nature** that establishes the terms for a common society and/or government.

social justice, principles of The norms that provide uncompromising, or especially weighty, moral standards for resolving individuals' competing claims on the design of influential social and political institutions.

social norms These are informal rules about how people ought to behave in a society. Examples of social norms include rules of etiquette, clothing, and social interaction. Social norms can become internalized, such that people prefer to comply with them—for example, many people feel embarrassed about passing wind in public and do not wish to do so.

Society of Peoples This term refers to all of those peoples who follow the principles of the **Law of Peoples** (discussed by Rawls) in their relations with one another.

sovereignty The supreme **authority** within a given geographical territory.

state of nature This term refers to a condition of human life in which there is no society larger than the family grouping, or, if there is a larger society, no government or positive laws.

statism A view of society that supports the concentration of economic and political power in the state. Cf. **anarchy**.

Stoicism An Ancient Greek school of philosophy that emphasized the will as the source of virtue, and taught the development of self-control as the route to happiness. Stoics also rejected the idea that one should be importantly defined by one's city of origin, insisting instead that all were '*citizens of the world*'.

structural injustice A form of injustice that arises when the combined, unplanned actions of a plurality of actors in institutions put large categories of persons under a systematic threat of domination or deprivation of the means to develop and exercise their capacities, at the same time as they enable others to dominate or give them access to an abundance of resources.

sufficiency principles These are moral principles, assuming there are non-instrumentally morally relevant thresholds. They are often employed to claim that, when evaluating distributions, what matters is whether individuals have enough to escape absolute deprivation or to live above some critical threshold.

tacit consent Consent that is expressed by doing something that you would not otherwise be permitted to do, because someone has a right that you not do that thing without thereby consenting. An example would be tacitly consenting to pay for a meal in a restaurant by eating the meal. Also sometimes called **implicit consent** or **passive consent**. Cf. **explicit consent**.

territorialism The first doctrine that attempted to provide a political solution to the religious wars in sixteenth- and seventeenth-century Europe. It states that the religion of a given country should conform to that of the sovereign, hence allowing for religious pluralism and breaking the monopoly of the Church of Rome over Christianity. Yet it fell short of toleration, because it compelled religious minorities to emigrate to where the official Church corresponded to their faith. This solution could work only as a first compromise because it could not secure internal stability in contexts containing religious minorities, and it could not provide reasons why the religious beliefs of the sovereign were the right ones to secure the salvation of one's own soul.

Tobin Tax This is the popular name of a currency transaction tax, proposed by James Tobin in the 1970s as a means of reducing destabilizing trades, slowing down speculation, and promoting more long-term investing.

universal jurisdiction Criminal jurisdiction exercised on the basis of the principles of universality, which gives states the right to prosecute certain crimes regardless of where they have been committed and regardless of the nationality of the victims or the perpetrators.

usufruct In the civil law tradition, a full right to an object involves the right to enjoy its benefits (usus), to consume its fruits (fructus), and to sell or destroy it (abusus). Usufruct only includes the former two prerogatives. Moreover, it usually does not extend beyond the beneficiary's death. To illustrate, the usufructuary of a house can live in the house (usus) and/or rent it and pocket the money (fructus). However, he or she is neither allowed to destroy the house, nor entitled to sell it (abusus).

utilitarianism The doctrine, of which there are many versions, that social institutions and practices should be organized so as to maximize general welfare or common good as the sole ultimate ethical value, and that individual actions ought also to aim at this end. Mill's version holds that a code of justice and rights is more valuable for this purpose than any competing considerations.

utopian political theorizing Such theorizing advocates an ideal society, independent of the likelihood of our actually being able to achieve it. Plato's vision of an ideal republic, ruled by philosopher-kings, and Marx's conception of each giving according to their means and taking according to their needs, are examples.

veil of ignorance A phrase coined by Rawls to refer to the limited knowledge of characteristics— for example, sex, race, and class—that can be (dis) advantaging in the real world, but which ought not to be (dis)advantaging in the just society.

voluntarism The view that political authority and obligation is justified, because citizens have voluntarily agreed to obey the law. Often used interchangeably with the terms **consent theory** and **contract theory**, although, strictly speaking, voluntarism includes other ways of agreeing to do something, such as promising.

war crimes Violations of the rules of war, i.e. the rules that regulate the way in which wars can be permissibly fought. War crimes typically involve the use of unjustified violence against subjects who are not liable to be attacked, or the employment of prohibited methods and means of warfare.

References

Abbey, R. (2011) *The Return of Feminist Liberalism*, Durham: Acumen Publishing.

Ackerman, B. (1980) *Social Justice in the Liberal State*, New Haven, CT: Yale University Press.

Ackerman, B. (1994) 'Political liberalisms', *Journal of Philosophy*, 91(7): 364–86.

Ackerman, B. and Fishkin, J. (2002) 'Deliberation Day', *Journal of Political Philosophy*, 10: 129–52.

Ackerman, B., and Fishkin, J. (2004) *Deliberation Day*, New Haven: Yale University Press.

Addison, T. (2009) 'War on tax havens', *Indiana Journal of Global Legal Studies*, 16(2): 703–27.

Agar, N. (2001) *Life's Intrinsic Value*, New York: Columbia University Press.

Agarwal, A. and Narain, S. (1991) *Global Warming in an Unequal World: A Case of Environmental Colonialism*, New Delhi: Centre for Science and Environment.

Allievi, S. (ed.) (2010) *Mosques in Europe. Why a Solution has Become a Problem*, London: Alliance Publishing Trust.

Allievi, S. and Nielsen, J. (eds) (2003) *Muslim Networks and Transnational Communities in and Across Europe*, Leiden: Brill.

Alstott, A. (2004a) *No Exit: What Parents Owe Their Children and What Society Owes Parents*, Oxford: Oxford University Press.

Alstott, A. (2004b) 'What we owe to parents', *Boston Review*, April/May, available online at http://bostonreview.net/BR29.2/alstott.html.

Altman, A. and Wellman, C. H. (2011) *A Liberal Theory of International Justice*, Oxford: Oxford University Press.

Amnesty International (2004) *It's in Our Hands: Stop Violence Against Women*, available online at www.amnesty.org.

Anderson, E. (1999) 'What is the point of equality?', *Ethics*, 109(2): 287–337.

Anderson, E. (2010) *The Imperative of Integration*, Princeton: Princeton University Press.

Apel, K.-O. (1997) 'Plurality of the good? The problem of affirmative tolerance in a multicultural society from an ethical point of view', *Ratio Juris*, 10(2): 199–212.

Archibugi, D., Keonig-Archibugi, M., and Marchetti, R. (2011) (eds) *Global Democracy: Empirical and Normative Perspectives*, Cambridge: Cambridge University Press.

Aristotle (350 BC; 1987) 'Politics', in J. L. Ackrill (ed.) *A New Aristotle Reader*, Oxford: Clarendon Press, pp. 507–39.

Arneson, R. (1989) 'Equality and equal opportunity for welfare', *Philosophical Studies*, 56(1): 77–93.

Arneson, R. (2002) 'Democratic rights at the national level', in T. Christiano (ed.) *Philosophy and Democracy*, Oxford: Oxford University Press, pp. 95–116.

Arrhenius, G. (1999) 'Mutual advantage contractarianism and future generations', *Theoria*, vol. 65(1): 25–35.

Asheim, G. (2010) 'Intergenerational equity', *Annual Review of Economics*, 2: 197–222.

Assiter, A. (1989) *Pornography, Feminism and the Individual*, London: Pluto Press.

Bachrach, P. and Baratz, M. S. (1962) 'The two faces of power', *American Political Science Review*, 56: 941–52.

Badinter, E. (1989) 'Interview with L. Joffin', *Le Nouvel Observateur*, 1–5 November: 30–31.

Baghramian, M. (1994) *Relativism*, London: Routledge.

Balko, R. (2006) *Overkill: The Rise of Paramilitary Police Raids in America*, Washington DC: Cato Institute.

Barry, B. (1991) *Liberty and Justice: Essays in Political Theory 2*, Oxford: Clarendon Press.

Barry, B. (1995) *Justice as Impartiality*, Oxford: Oxford University Press.

Barry, B. (2001) *Culture and Equality*, Oxford: Polity Press.

Barry, B. (2005) *Why Social Justice Matters*, Cambridge: Polity Press.

Barry, J. (1999) *Rethinking Green Politics*, London: Sage.

Bartlett, K. T. (1990) 'Feminist legal methods', *Harvard Law Review*, 103(4): 829–88.

Baum, D. (1996) *Smoke and Mirrors: The War on Drugs and the Politics of Failure*, New York: Little, Brown and Co.

Bazargan, S. (2014) 'Varieties of contingent pacifism' in H. Frowe and G. Lang (eds.) *How We Fight: Ethics in War*, Oxford: Oxford University Press.

Bedi, S. (2009) *Rejecting Rights*, Cambridge: Cambridge University Press.

Beitz, C. (1979) *Political Theory and International Relations*, Princeton, NJ: Princeton University Press.

Beitz, C. (1989) *Political Equality: An Essay on Democratic Theory*, Princeton, NJ: Princeton University Press.

Beitz, C. R. (2009) *The Idea of Human Rights*, Oxford: Oxford University Press.

Bellamy, A. (2008) 'The responsibilities of victory: *jus post bellum* and the just war', *Review of International Studies*, 34: 601–5.

Bennett, C. (2010) *The Apology Ritual: A Philosophical Theory of Punishment*, Cambridge: Cambridge University Press.

Bentham, J. (1789; 1970) *An Introduction to the Principles of Morals and Legislation*, J. H.Burns and H. L. A.Hart (eds), London: Athlone Press.

Bentham, J. (1789; 1996) *An Introduction to the Principles of Morals and Legislation*, J. H. Burns and H. L. A. Hart (eds), Oxford: Oxford University Press.

Benton, T. (1993) *Natural Relations: Ecology, Animal Rights and Social Justice*, London: Verso.

Berlin, I. (1969) *Four Essays on Liberty*, Oxford: Oxford University Press.

Berlin, I. (2002) *Liberty*, H. Hardy (ed.), Oxford: Oxford University Press, pp. 1–251.

Bianchi, H. (2010) *Justice as Sanctuary: Toward a New System of Crime Control*, Eugene: Wipf & Stock Publishers.

Billig, M. (1995) *Banal Nationalism*, London: Sage.

Blake, M. (2005) 'International justice', *Stanford Encyclopedia of Philosophy*, available online at http://plato.stanford.edu/entries/international-justice/.

Bookchin, M. (1982) *The Ecology of Freedom*, Palo Alto, CA: The Cheshire Press.

Boonin, D. (2008) *The Problem of Punishment*, Cambridge: Cambridge University Press.

Bou-Habib, P. (2006) 'Compulsory insurance without paternalism', *Utilitas*, 18(3): 243–63.

Braithwaite, J. and Pettit, P. (1990) *Not Just Deserts*, Oxford: Oxford University Press.

Brandt, R. (1992) *Morality, Utilitarianism, and Rights*, Cambridge: Cambridge University Press.

Bridges, A. J., Wosnitzer, R., Scharrer, E., Sun, C., and Liberman, R. (2010) 'Aggression and sexual behaviour in best selling pornography videos: a content analysis update', *Violence Against Women*, 16(10): 1065–85.

Brown, W. (2008) *Regulating Aversion: Tolerance in the Age of Identity and Empire*, Princeton, NJ: Princeton University Press.

Browne, A. (2007) 'Muslims who seek Sharia as bad as BNP', *The Times*, 30 January, available online at http://www.timesonline.co.uk/tol/news/politics/article1299130.ece.

Brownmiller, S. (1977) *Against Our Will: Men, Women and Rape*, Harmondsworth: Penguin.

Bryson, V. (1999) *Feminist Debates: Issues of Theory and Political Practice*, Basingstoke: Palgrave.

Buchanan, J. and Tullock, G. (1965) *The Calculus of Consent: Logical Foundations of Constitutional Democracy*, Ann Arbor, MI: University of Michigan Press.

Burke, E. (1790; 1993) *Reflections on the Revolution in France*, F. P. Lock (ed.), Oxford: Oxford University Press.

Calder, G. and Zuolo, F. (eds.) (2014) *How Groups Matter*, London: Routledge.

Callicott, J. (1989) *In Defense of the Land Ethic*, Albany, NY: State University of New York.

Campbell, T. (2006) *Rights: A Critical Introduction*, London: Routledge.

Caney, S. (2005) *Justice Beyond Borders: A Global Political Theory*, Oxford: Oxford University Press.

Carson, R. (1962; 2002) *Silent Spring*, Boston, MA: Mariner Books.

Carter, I., Kramer, M. H., and Steiner, H. (2006) *Freedom: A Philosophical Anthology*, Oxford: Blackwell.

Casal, P. (1999) 'Environmentalism, procreation, and the principle of fairness', *Public Affairs Quarterly*, 13(4): 363–76.

Casal, P. (2003) 'Is multiculturalism bad for animals?', *Journal of Political Philosophy*, 11(1): 1–22.

Casal, P. (2007) 'Why sufficiency is not enough', *Ethics*, 117(2): 296–326.

Casal, P. and Williams, A. (2004) 'Equality of resources and procreative justice', in J. Burley (ed.) *Dworkin and His Critics*, Oxford: Blackwell, pp. 150–70.

Castellion, S. (1553; 1935) *Concerning Heretics: Whether They Are to Be Persecuted and How They Are To Be Treated*, R. H. Bainton (ed.), New York: Columbia University Press.

Castiglione, D. and McKinnon, C. (2003) *Toleration, Neutrality and Democracy*, Dordrecht: Kluwer Academic.

Chambers, C. (2008) *Sex, Culture, and Justice: The Limits of Choice*, University Park, PA: Penn State University Press.

Christensen, J. and Hampton, M. P. (1999) 'All good things come to an end', *The World Today*, 55(8/9): 14–17.

Christian Aid (2005) *The Shirts Off their Backs: How Tax Policies Fleece the Poor*, September, available online at: http://www.christianaid.org. uk/images/the_shirts_off_their_backs.pdf

Christiano, T. (1995) 'Democratic equality and the problem of persistent minorities', *Philosophical Papers*, 23(3): 169–90.

Christiano, T. (1996) *The Rule of the Many: Fundamental Issues in Democratic Theory*, Boulder, CO: Westview Press.

Christiano, T. (ed.) (2002) *Philosophy and Democracy*, Oxford: Oxford University Press.

Christiano, T. (2004) 'The authority of democracy', *Journal of Political Philosophy*, 12(3): 266–90.

Christiano, T. (2008a) 'Must democracy be reasonable?', *Canadian Journal of Philosophy*, 39(1): 1–34.

Christiano, T. (2008b) *The Constitution of Equality: Democratic Authority and its Limits*, Oxford: Oxford University Press.

Christie, N. (1977) 'Conflicts as property', *British Journal of Criminology*, 17(1): 1–15.

Clayton, M. and Williams, A. (eds) (2000) *The Ideal of Equality*, London: Macmillan.

Coady, C. A. J. (2006) 'The moral reality in realism', in C. A. J. Coady (ed.) *What's Wrong with Moralism?*, Oxford: Blackwell, pp. 21–36.

Cohen, B. (1967) 'An ethical paradox', *Mind*, 76: 250–9.

Cohen, G. A. (1978) *Karl Marx's Theory of History: A Defence*, Princeton, NJ: Princeton University Press.

Cohen, G. A. (1989) 'On the currency of egalitarian justice', *Ethics*, 99(4): 906–44.

Cohen, G. A. (1991) '*Incentives, Equality and Community*', Lecture delivered at Stanford University as part of The Tanner Lectures on Human Values, 21–3 May.

Cohen, G. A. (1994) 'Back to socialist basics', *New Left Review*, I(207): 3–16.

Cohen, G. A. (1997) 'Where the action is: on the site of distributive justice', *Philosophy and Public Affairs*, 26(1): 3–30.

Cohen, G. A. (1999) 'Socialism and equality of opportunity', in M. Rosen and J. Wolff (eds) *Political Thought*, Oxford: Oxford University Press, pp. 354–7.

Cohen, G. A. (2000) *If You're an Egalitarian, How Come You're So Rich?*, Cambridge, MA: Harvard University Press.

Cohen, G. A. (2004) 'Expensive taste rides again', in J. Burley (ed.), *Dworkin and His Critics*, Oxford: Blackwell, pp. 3–30.

Cohen, J. (2002) 'Procedure and substance in deliberative democracy', in T. Christiano (ed.) *Philosophy and Democracy*, Oxford: Oxford University Press.

Cohen, J. (2009) *Philosophy, Politics, Democracy: Selected Essays*, Cambridge, MA: Harvard University Press.

Cole, D. (2003) *Enemy Aliens: Double Standards and Constitutional Freedoms in the War on Terrorism*, New York: The New Press.

Cole, D. and Dempsey, J. X. (2006) *Terrorism and the Constitution*, revd edn, New York: The New Press.

Commission on Social Justice (1994) *Social Justice: Strategies for Renewal*, London: Vintage.

Commoner, B. (1980) *The Closing Circle: Nature, Man, and Technology*, New York: Knopf.

Condorcet, N. (2012) *Condorcet: Political Writings*, (ed. S. Lukes and N. Urbinati), Cambridge: Cambridge University Press.

Connolly, W.E. (1974) *The Terms of Political Discourse*, Lexington, Mass. : D. C. Heath and Co.

Crick, B. (1971) 'Toleration and tolerance in theory and practice', *Government and Opposition*, 6: 144–71.

Crisp, R. (2003) 'Equality, priority and compassion', *Ethics*, 13(4): 745–63.

Dagger, R. (2008) 'Punishment as fair Play', *Res Publica*, 14(4): 259–75.

Dahl, R. (1956; 1959) *A Preface to Democratic Theory*, Chicago, IL: University of Chicago Press.

Dahl, R. (1958) 'A critique of the ruling elite model', *American Political Science Review*, 52: 463–9.

Dahl, R. (1961) *Who Governs? Democracy and Power in an American City*, New Haven: Yale University Press.

Dahl, R. (1989) *Democracy and its Critics*, New Haven, CT: Yale University Press.

Dahl, R. (1999) 'Can international organizations be democratic? A skeptic's view', in I. Shapiro and C. Hacker-Cordon (eds) *Democracy's Edges*, Cambridge: Cambridge University Press.

Daniels, J. (2001) 'Justice is good for our health', *Boston Review*, 25(1): 4–19.

Daniels, N. (1988) *Am I My Parents' Keeper? An Essay on Justice between the Young and the Old*, New York/Oxford: Oxford University Press.

Darwall, S. (1995) *Equal Freedom: Selected Tanner Lectures in Human Values*, Ann Arbor, MI: University of Michigan Press.

Darwall, S. (2011) 'Authority, accountability, and preemption' *Jurisprudence*, 2: 103–19.

De Beauvoir, S. (1949) *The Second Sex* (*Le Deuxième Sexe*), Paris: Gallimard.

De Tocqueville, A. (1835) *De la démocratie en Amérique*, Brussels: L. Hauman.

Dershowitz, A. (2002) 'Want to torture? Get a warrant', *San Francisco Chronicle*, 22 January 2002.

Dershowitz, A. (2003) *Why Terrorism Works*, New Haven: Yale University Press.

Deveaux, M. (2001) *Cultural Pluralism and Dilemmas of Justice*, Ithaca, NY: Cornell University Press.

Dines, G. (2010) *Pornland: How Porn has Hijacked our Sexuality*, Boston, MA: Beacon Press.

Dobson, A. (2000) *Green Political Thought*, London: Routledge.

Dobson, A. (2003) *Citizenship and the Environment*, Oxford: Oxford University Press.

Dobson, A. and Eckersley, R. (eds) (2007) *Political Theory and the Ecological Challenge*, Cambridge: Cambridge University Press.

Dolinko, D. (1991) Some Thoughts About Retributivism, *Ethics*, 101: 537–59.

Donnelly, J. (2003) *Universal Human Rights in Theory and Practice*, 2nd edn, London: Cornell University Press.

Dorling, D. et al. (2007) *Poverty and Wealth Across Britain 1968–2005*, Bristol: Joseph Rowntree Foundation/The Policy Press.

Dowding, K. M. (1996) *Power*, Minneapolis: University of Minnesota Press.

Downs, A. (1957) *An Economic Theory of Democracy*, New York: Harper and Row.

Dryzek, J. (2000) *Deliberative Democracy and Beyond*, Oxford: Oxford University Press.

Dryzek, J. and Schlosberg, D. (1998) *Debating the Earth*, Oxford: Oxford University Press.

Duff, R. A. (1986) *Trials and Punishments*, Cambridge: Cambridge University Press.

Duff, R. A. (1990) *Intention, Agency, and Criminal Liability*, Oxford: Blackwell.

Duff, R. A. (1996) *Criminal Attempts*, Oxford: Oxford University Press.

Duff, R. A. (2000) *Punishment, Communication and Community*, Oxford: Oxford University Press.

Duff, R. A. (2001) *Punishment, Communication, and Community*, New York: Oxford University Press.

Duff, R. A. (2007) *Answering for Crime*, Oxford: Hart.

Duff, R. A. and Garland, D. (1994) *A Reader on Punishment*, Oxford: Oxford University Press.

Duff, R. A., Farmer, L., Marshall, S., Renzo, M., and Tadros, V (forthcoming), *Criminalization: The Political Morality of the Criminal*, Oxford: Oxford University Press.

Dunlap Jr, C. J. (2013) 'Forum: the moral responsibility of volunteer soldiers', *Boston Review*, 6 November 2013.

Dunn, J. (1979) *Western Political Theory in the Face of the Future*, Cambridge: Cambridge University Press.

Dworkin, A. (1981) *Pornography: Men Possessing Women*, New York/London:Putnam's/Perigee/ The Women's Press.

Dworkin, A. (1987) *Intercourse*, New York: The Free Press.

Dworkin, A. (1997) *Life and Death*, New York: The Free Press.

Dworkin, R. (1977) *Taking Rights Seriously*, London: Duckworth.

Dworkin, R. (1978) 'Liberalism', in S. Hampshire (ed.) *Private and Public Morality*, Cambridge: Cambridge University Press, pp. 113–43.

Dworkin, R. (1981*a*) 'What is equality? Part 1: Equality of welfare', *Philosophy and Public Affairs*, 10(3): 185–246.

Dworkin, R. (1981*b*) 'What is equality? Part 2: Equality of resources', *Philosophy and Public Affairs*, 10(4): 185–243.

Dworkin, R (1986) *Law's Empire*, London: Fontana Press.

Dworkin, R. (1986) *Law's Empire*, Cambridge, MA: Harvard University Press.

Dworkin, R. (1993) *Life's Dominion: An Argument about Abortion and Euthanasia*, London: Harper Collins.

Dworkin, R. (2000) *Sovereign Virtue: The Theory and Practice of Equality*, Cambridge, MA: Harvard University Press.

Dworkin, R. (2002) 'Sovereign virtue revisited', *Ethics*, 113(1): 106–43.

Dworkin, R. (2004) 'Replies to critics', in J. Burley (ed.), *Dworkin and His Critics*, Oxford: Blackwell, pp. 339–50.

Dworkin, R. (2011) *Justice for Hedgehogs*. Cambridge, MA: Harvard University Press.

Eckersley, R. (1992) *Environmentalism and Political Theory*, London: UCL Press.

Economic Policy Institute (2007) *State of Working America 2006–07*, Ithaca, NY: Cornell University Press.

Ehrlich, P. (1968) *The Population Bomb*, New York: Ballantine Books.

Ellis, D. (2000) *Women of the Afghan War*, Westport, CO: Praeger.

Elster, J. (2002) 'The market and the forum: three varieties of political theory', in T. Christiano (ed.) *Philosophy and Democracy*, Oxford: Oxford University Press, pp. 138–60.

Ely, J. H. (1980) *Democracy and Distrust: A Theory of Judicial Review*, Cambridge, MA: Harvard University Press.

Erasmus, D. (1511; 1970) *In Praise of Folly*, A. H. T. Levi (ed.), Princeton, NJ: Princeton University Press.

Eskridge, W. N. (1996) *The Case for Same-Sex Marriage*, New York: The Free Press.

Estlund, D. (2007) *Democratic Authority*, Cambridge: Cambridge University Press.

Estlund, D. (2011) 'Human nature and the limits (if any) of political philosophy', *Philosophy and Public Affairs*, 39(2): 209–37.

Ettelrick, P. (1993) 'Since when is marriage a path to liberation?', in W. Bubenstein (ed.) *Lesbians, Gays and the Law*, New York: The Free Press, pp. 401–5.

Ettinger, Y. and Cohen, G. (2012) 'Israel's High Court rules Tal Law unconstitutional, says Knesset, cannot extend it in present form', *Haaretz*, 21 February 2012.

EUMC (2006) *Perception of Discrimination and Islamofobia. Voices from Members of Muslim Communities in European Union*, Vienna: European Monitoring Centre on Racism and Xenophobia.

Fajnzylber, P., Lederman, D., and Loayza, N. (2002) 'Inequality and violent crime', *Journal of Law and Economics*, 45(1): 1–40.

Falk, R. and Strauss, A. (2000) 'On the creation of a global people's assembly: legitimacy and the power of popular sovereignty', *Stanford Journal of International Law*, 36: 191–220.

Feinberg, J. (1970*a*) 'Justice and personal desert', in *Doing and Deserving: Essays in the Theory of Responsibility*, Princeton: Princeton University Press.

Feinberg, J. (1970*b*) 'The Expressive Function of Punishment', in *Doing and Deserving: Essays in the Theory of Responsibility*, Princeton: Princeton University Press, pp. 95–118.

Feinberg, J. (1973) *Social Philosophy*, Englewood Cliffs, NJ: Prentice Hall.

Feinberg, J. (1984–88) *The Moral Limits of the Criminal Law. Vols. 1-4*, New York: Oxford University Press.

Feinberg, W. (1995) 'Liberalism and the aims of education', *Journal of the Philosophy of Education*, 29(2): 203–16.

Finnis, J. (1980) *Natural Law and Natural Rights*, Oxford: Oxford University Press.

Fletcher G. (1978) *Rethinking Criminal Law*, Boston: Little, Brown

Forst, R. (2001) 'Towards a critical theory of transnational justice', *Metaphilosophy*, 32: 160–79.

Forst, R. (2013) *Toleration in Conflict. Past and Present*, Cambridge: Cambridge University Press.

Foucault, M. (1977) *Discipline and Punish*, A. Sheridan (trans.), Harmondsworth: Penguin.

Foucault, M. (1982) 'The subject and power', *Critical Inquiry*, 8(4): 777–95.

Foucault, M. (1988) *Philosophy, Politics, Culture*, L. Kritzman (ed.), London: Routledge.

Fox, W. (1990) *Toward a Transpersonal Ecology*, Boston, MA: Shambhala Publications.

Frankfurt, H. (1987) 'Equality as a moral ideal', *Ethics*, 98(1): 21–43.

Fraser, N. (1995) 'From redistribution to recognition? Dilemmas of justice in a 'post-socialist' age', *New Left Review*, I(212): 68–93.

Fraser, N. (1997) *Justice Interruptus*, London: Routledge.

Fraser, N. (1998) 'Social justice in the age of identity-politics', in G. Peterson (ed.), *The Tanner Lectures on Human Values*, Vol. XIX, Salt Lake City, UT: University of Utah Press, pp. 1–67.

Fraser, N. (2000) 'Rethinking recognition, *New Left Review*, 2(3); 107–20.

Fraser, N. (2003) Recognition without ethics?', in C. McKinnon and D. Castiglione (eds) *The Culture of Toleration in Diverse Societies*, Manchester/New York: Manchester University Press, pp. 86–110.

Freeman, S. (2007) *Rawls*, London: Routledge.

Friedan, E. (1963) *The Feminine Mystique*, New York: Norton.

Friedman, M. (1962) *Capitalism and Freedom*, Chicago, IL: University of Chicago Press.

Frowe, H. (2011) *The Ethics of War and Peace: An Introduction*, New Abington: Routledge.

Frowe, H. and Lang, G. (eds) (2014) *How We Fight: Ethics in War*, Oxford: Oxford University Press.

Galeotti A. E. (2001) 'Do we need toleration as a moral virtue?', *Res Publica*, 7(3): 273–92.

Galeotti A. E. (2002) *Toleration as Recognition*, Cambridge: Cambridge University Press.

Galeotti, A. E. (2014) 'Toleration and purpose-built mosques: contestations in contemporary Europe' in G. Calder and F. Zuolo (eds), *How Groups Matter*, London: Routledge.

Gallie, W.B. (1956) ' Essentially contested concepts', *Proceedings of the Aristotelian Society*, 56: 167–98.

Galston, W. (2001) *Liberal Pluralism*, Cambridge: Cambridge University Press.

Galston, W. (2005) *The Practice of Liberal Pluralism*, Cambridge: Cambridge University Press.

Gardiner, S. (2003) 'The pure intergenerational problem', *The Monist*, 86(3): 481–500.

Gardiner, S. (2011) *A Perfect Moral Storm: The Ethical Tragedy of Climate Change*, Oxford: Oxford University Press.

Gaspart, F. and A. Gosseries, (2007) 'Are generational savings unjust?', *Politics, Philosophy & Economics*, vol. 6(2): 193–217.

Gauthier, D. P. (1986) *Morals by Agreement*, Oxford: Clarendon Press.

Geras, N. (2011) *Crimes Against Humanity: Birth of a Concept*, Manchester: Manchester University Press.

Gewirth, A. (1982) *Human Rights: Essays on Justification and Applications*, Chicago, IL: University of Chicago Press.

Gilbert, M. (1993) 'Group Membership and Political Obligation', *The Monist* 76, 119–31.

Gilligan, C. (1982; 1993) *In A Different Voice*, Cambridge, MA: Harvard University Press.

Giordano, R. (2007) 'Germans split over a mosque and the role of Islam', *New York Times*, 5th July 2007.

Glazer, N. (1997) *We Are All Multiculturalists Now*, Cambridge: Harvard University Press.

Glendon, M. A. (1991) *Rights Talk: The Impoverishment of Political Discourse*, New York: Free Press.

Godwin, W. (1793; 1976) *An Enquiry Concerning Political Justice, and its Influence on Modern Morals and Happiness*, I. Kramnick (ed.), London: Penguin.

Goodin, R. (1992) *Green Political Theory*, London: Polity.

Goodin, R. E. (2003) *Reflective Democracy*, Oxford: Oxford University Press.

Goodin, R. E. (2008) *Innovating Democracy: Democratic Theory and Practice After the Deliberative Turn*, Oxford: Oxford University Press.

Gordon, S. (1999) *Controlling the State: Constitutionalism from Ancient Athens to Today*, Cambridge, MA: Harvard University Press.

Gosseries, A. (2008) 'On future generations' future rights', *Journal of Political Philosophy*, 16(4): 446–74.

Gosseries, A. and Meyer, L. (2009) *Intergenerational Justice*, Oxford: Oxford University Press.

Gould, C. (2004) *Globalizing Democracy and Human Rights*, Cambridge: Cambridge University Press.

Gray, J. (2013) *Isaiah Berlin: An Interpretation of His Thought*, Princeton: Princeton University Press.

Greer, G. (1970; 1991) *The Female Eunuch*, London: Flamingo.

Griffin, J. (2008) *On Human Rights*, Oxford: Oxford University Press.

Grotius, H. (1925) *The Rights of War and Peace (De Jure Belli ac Pacis), Vol. 2*, F. W. Kelsey (trans.), Oxford: Clarendon Press.

Grotius, H. (2004) *On the Law of War and Peace*, Belle Fourche, South Dakota: Kessinger Publishing.

Gutmann, A. (1989) *Democratic Education*, Princeton, NJ: Princeton University Press.

Gutmann, A. (2004) *Identity in Democracy*, Princeton, NJ: Princeton University Press.

Gutmann, A. and Appiah, K. A. (1996) *Color Conscious: The Political Morality of Race*, Princeton, NJ: Princeton University Press.

Hampshire, S. (1972) 'A special supplement: a new philosophy of the just society', *New York Book Review*, 18(3), available online at http://www.nybooks.com/articles/10296.

Hampton, J. (1984) 'The moral education theory of punishment', *Philosophy & Public Affairs*, 13: 208–38.

Hansard (2003) 9 April, col. 288, available online at http://www.publications.parliament.uk/pa/cm200203/cmhansrd/vo030409/debtext/30409-04.htm.

Hardin, G. (1968) 'The tragedy of the commons', *Science*, 162(3859): 1243–8.

Hare, R. M. (1989) 'Punishment and retributive justice', in *Essays on Political Morality*, Oxford: Clarendon, pp. 203–16.

Harrison, G. (1979) 'Relativism and tolerance', in P. Laslett and J. Fishkin (eds) *Philosophy, Politics and Society*, Oxford: Blackwell, pp. 273–90.

Hart, H. L. A. (1955) 'Are there any natural rights?', *Philosophical Review*, 64: 175–91.

Hart, H. L. A. (1963) *Law, Liberty, and Morality*, Stanford: Stanford University Press.

Hart, H. L. A. (1982; 2011) *Essays on Bentham: Jurisprudence and Political Theory*. Oxford: Clarendon Press.

Hart, H. L. A (2008) *Punishment and Responsibility: Essays in the Philosophy of Law*, John Gardner (ed.), Oxford: Oxford University Press.

Haugaard, M. (1997) *The Constitution of Power: A Theoretical Analysis of Power, Knowledge and Structure*, Manchester: Manchester University Press.

Hayward, C. (2000) *De-facing Power*, Cambridge: Cambridge University Press.

Hayward, C. and Lukes, S. (2008) 'Nobody to shoot? Power, structure, and agency: a dialogue', *Journal of Power* 1: 5–20.

Hayward, T. (2005) *Constitutional Environmental Rights*, Oxford: Oxford University Press.

Heilbroner, R. (1980) *An Inquiry into the Human Prospect: Updated and Reconsidered for the 1980s*, New York: Norton and Co.

Held, D. (1995) *Democracy and the Global Order: From the Modern State to Cosmopolitan Governance*, Stanford, CA: Stanford University Press.

Held, D. (2004) *Global Covenant: The Social Democratic Alternative to the Washington Consensus*, Cambridge: Polity Press.

Heyd, D. (1992) *Genethics. Moral Issues in the Creation of People*. Princeton, NJ: Princeton University Press.

Heyd, D. (ed.) (1996) *Toleration: An Elusive Virtue*, Princeton, NJ: Princeton University Press.

Hindess, B. (1996) *Discourses of Power: From Hobbes to Foucault*, Oxford: Blackwell Publishing.

Hinsch, W. (2001) 'Global distributive justice', *Metaphilosophy*, 32: 58–78.

Hobbes, T. (1651; 1968) *Leviathan*, C. B. MacPherson (ed.), Harmondsworth: Penguin.

Hobbes, T. (1651; 1994) *Leviathan*. Indianapolis, IN: Hackett Publishing Co.

Hobbes, T. (1651; 1996) *Leviathan*, Cambridge: Cambridge University Press.

Hohfeld, W. N. (1919) *Fundamental Legal Conceptions as Applied to Legal Reasoning*, New Haven: Yale University Press.

hooks, b. (1982) *Ain't I a Woman? Black Women and Feminism*, London: Pluto Press.

Horton, J. (1985) 'Toleration, morality and harm', in S. Mendus and J. Horton (eds) *Aspects of Toleration*, London: Methuen, pp. 113–35.

Horton, J. (1996) 'Toleration as a virtue', in D. Heyd (ed.) *Toleration: An Elusive Virtue*, Princeton, NJ: Princeton University Press, pp. 28–43.

Horton, J. (2006) 'In defense of associative political obligations: Part one', *Political Studies*, 54: 427–43.

Horton, J. (2007) 'In defense of associative political obligations: Part two', *Political Studies*, 55: 1–19.

Horton, J. and Nicholson, P. (eds) (1992) *Toleration: Philosophy and Practice*, London: Avebury.

Hume, D. (1748; 1947) 'Of the original contract', in E. Barker (ed.) *Social Contract: Essays by Locke, Hume and Rousseau*, Oxford: Oxford University Press, pp. 207–36.

Hume, D. (1748; 1998) 'Of the original contract', in *Essays, Moral and Political* (3rd edn), S. Brittan (ed.), Edinburgh: Edinburgh University Press.

Hume, D. (1748; 1975) *Enquiries Concerning Human Understanding and Concerning the Principles of Morals*, Oxford: Clarendon Press.

Hume, D. (1994) *Hume: Political Essays*, (ed. K. Haakonssen), Cambridge: Cambridge University Press.

Hurd, H. M. (1996) 'The moral magic of consent', *Legal Theory*, 2: 121–46.

Hurrell, A. (2001) 'Global inequality and international institutions', *Metaphilosophy*, 32: 34–57.

Husak, D. N. (2008) *Overcriminalization: The Limits of the Criminal Law*, New York: Oxford University Press.

Hyams, K. (2004) 'Nozick's real argument for the minimal state', *Journal of Political Philosophy*, 12(3): 353–64.

IPCC (2013) *Climate Change 2013: The Physical Science Basis. Contribution of Working Group I to the Fifth Assessment Report of the Intergovernmental Panel on Climate Change*, (eds) T. F. Stocker et al., Cambridge: Cambridge University Press.

Itzin, C. (ed.) (1992) *Pornography*, Oxford: Oxford University Press.

Ivison, D. (1997) *The Self at Liberty*, Ithaca, NY: Cornell University Press.

Ivison, D. (2008) *Rights*, Stocksfield: Acumen.

Jamieson, D. (2002) *Morality's Progress*, Oxford: Oxford University Press.

Jamieson, D. (2008) *Ethics and the Environment: An Introduction*, Cambridge: Cambridge University Press.

Jamieson, D. (2014) *Reason In a Dark Time: Why the Struggle Against Climate Change Failed— And What It Means for Our Future*, Oxford: Oxford University Press.

Jefferson, T. (1789) 'Letter to J. Madison', 6 September, available online at http://memory.loc.gov/cgi-bin/query/r?ammem/mtj:@field(DOCID+@lit(tj060008))

Jeffreys, S. (2005) *Beauty and Misogyny: Harmful Cultural Practices in the West*, London: Routledge.

Johnasson, W. and Percy, W. (1994) *Outing: Shattering the Conspiracy of Silence*, New York/London: Hawarth Press.

Johnstone, G. (2012) *A Restorative Justice Reader*, Abingdon, Oxon: Willan.

Jones, C. (1999) *Global Justice: Defending Cosmopolitanism*, Oxford: Oxford University Press.

Kant, I. (1784; 1991) 'Idea for a universal history with a cosmopolitan purpose' in *Kant: Political Writings*, (ed.) H. Reiss, Cambridge: Cambridge University Press.

Kant, I. (1998) *Groundwork of the Metaphysics of Morals*, Cambridge: Cambridge University Press.

Kelly, E., Lovett, J., and Regan, L. (2005) *A Gap or a Chasm? Attrition in Reported Rape Cases*, Home Office Research Study 293, London: Home Office Research, Development and Statistics Directorate, available online at http://www.homeoffice.gov.uk/rds/pdfs05/hors293.pdf.

King, P. (1976) *Toleration*, London: Allen and Unwin.

Kingsnorth, P. (2003) *One No, Many Yeses: A Journey to the Heart of the Global Resistance Movement*, London: Free Press.

Klosko, G. (1992) *The Principle of Fairness and Political Obligation*, Lanham, MD: Rowman and Littlefield.

Klosko, G. (2005) *Political Obligations*, Oxford: Oxford University Press.

Knowles, D. (2010) *Political Obligation: A Critical Introduction*, New York: Routledge.

Kramer, F M. (1998) 'Rights without trimmings' in *A Debate Over Rights* (M. H. Kramer, N. E. Simmonds, and H. Steiner), Oxford: Oxford University Press, pp. 7–111.

Kramer, M. H. (2003) *The Quality of Freedom*, Oxford: Oxford University Press.

Kramer, M. H., Simmonds, N. E., and Steiner, H. (1998) *A Debate Over Rights*, Oxford: Oxford University Press.

Kukathas, C. (2003) *The Liberal Archipelago: A Theory of Diversity and Freedom*, Oxford: Oxford University Press.

Kukathas, C. (2006) 'The mirage of global justice', *Social Philosophy and Policy*, 23(1): 1–25.

Kuper, A. (2000) 'Rawlsian global justice: beyond the Law of Peoples to a cosmopolitan law of persons', *Political Theory*, 28(5): 640–74.

Kuper, A. (2004) *Democracy Beyond Borders: Justice and Representation in Global Institutions*, Oxford: Oxford University Press.

Kutz, C. (2005) 'The difference uniforms make: collective violence in criminal law and war', *Philosophy and Public Affairs*, 38, No. 2: 148–80.

Kymlicka, W. (1989) *Liberalism, Community, and Culture*, Oxford: Clarendon.

Kymlicka, W. (1995) *Multicultural Citizenship: A Liberal Theory of Minority Rights*, Oxford: Oxford University Press.

Kymlicka, W. (2002) 'Multiculturalism', in W. Kymlicka (ed.) *Contemporary Political Philosophy: An Introduction*, Oxford: Oxford University Press, pp. 327–76.

Kymlicka, W., Banting, K., Johnston, R., and Soroka, S. (2006) 'Do multiculturalism policies erode the welfare state? An empirical analysis', in K. Banting and W. Kymlicka (eds) *Multiculturalism and the Welfare State: Recognition and Redistribution in Contemporary Democracies*, Oxford: Oxford University Press, pp. 49–91.

Laborde, C. (2008) *Critical Republicanism: The Hijab Debate and Political Philosophy*, Oxford: Oxford University Press.

Lane, M. (2012) *Eco-Republic: What the Ancients Can Teach Us About Ethics, Virtue, and Sustainable Living*. Princeton: Princeton University Press.

Larmore, C. (1987) *Patterns of Moral Complexity*, Cambridge: Cambridge University Press.

Larudee, M. (2009) 'Sources of polarization of income and wealth: offshore financial centres', *Review of Radical Political Economics*, 41(3): 324–51.

Leader, S. (1996) 'Three faces of toleration', *Journal of Political Philosophy*, 4(1): 45–67.

Leiter, B. (2013) *Why Tolerate Religion*, Princeton: Princeton University Press.

Lenard, P. T. (2012) *Trust, Democracy and Multicultural Challenges*, Pennsylvania: University of Pennsylvania Press.

Leopold, A. (1987) *A Sand County Almanac, and Sketches Here and There*, New York: Oxford University Press.

Locke, J. (1685; 1991) *A Letter Concerning Toleration*, J. Horton and S. Mendus (eds) London: Routledge.

Locke, J. (1690; 1924) *Two Treatises of Government*, London: Dent and Sons.

Locke, J. (1690; 1952) *The Second Treatise of Government*, Indianapolis, IN: Bobbs-Merrill Co.

Locke, J. (1690; 1980) *The Second Treatise of Government*, Indianapolis, IN: Hackett.

Locke, J. (1690; 1988) 'The second treatise on civil government', in P. Laslett (ed.) *Two Treatises of Civil Government*, Cambridge: Cambridge University Press, pp. 265–428.

Lovelace, L. and McGrady, M. (1981) *Ordeal*, London: W. H. Allen.

Lowe, R. (1993) *The Welfare State in Britain since 1945*, London: Palgrave McMillan.

Lukes, S. (2005) *Power: A Radical View* (2nd edn), New York: Palgrave Macmillan.

MacKinnon, C. A. (1987) *Feminism Unmodified*, Cambridge, MA: Harvard University Press.

MacKinnon, C. A. (1989) *Towards a Feminist Theory of the State*, Cambridge, MA: Harvard University Press.

MacKinnon, C. A. (2006) *Are Women Human? And Other International Dialogues*, Cambridge, MA: Belknap Press.

MacKinnon, C. A. and Dworkin, A. (1997) *In Harm's Way: The Pornography Civil Rights Hearings*, Cambridge, MA: Harvard University Press.

Madison, J. (1981; rev. edn) 'The nature of the union: a final reckoning 1835-36', in M. Meyers (ed.) *The Mind of the Founder: Sources of the Political Thought of James Madison*, Lebanon, NH: University Press of New England, pp. 417–42.

Madison, J., Hamilton, A., and Jay, J. (1788; 1987) *The Federalist Papers*, I. Kramnick (ed.), Harmondsworth: Penguin.

Malthus, T. (1999) *An Essay on the Principle of Population*, Oxford: Oxford University Press.

Mandle, J. (2006) *Global Justice*, Cambridge: Polity Press.

Mansbridge, J. (ed.) (1990) *Beyond Self-Interest*, Chicago, IL: University of Chicago Press.

Marsh, G. (2003) *Man and Nature: Or, Physical Geography as Modified by Human Action*, Seattle, WA: University of Washington Press.

Martin, R. and Reidy, D. (2006) *Rawls's Law of Peoples: A Realistic Utopia?*, Malden, MA: Blackwell.

Marx, K. (1982) *Capital: A Critique of Political Economy, Vol. 1—The Process of Capitalist Production*, New York: International Publishers.

Matravers, M. (2011) 'Duff on hard treatment', in R. Cruft, M. H. Kramer, and M. R. Reiff (eds) *Crime, Punishment, and Responsibility: The Jurisprudence of Antony Duff*, Oxford: Oxford University Press, pp. 68–86.

Mavrodes, G. (1975) 'Conventions and morality of war', *Philosophy and Public Affairs*, 4(2): 117–31.

May, L. (2005*a*) *Crimes against Humanity: A Normative Account*, New York: Cambridge University Press.

May, L. (2005*b*) 'Killing naked soldiers: distinguishing between combatants and non-combatants', *Ethics and International Affairs*, 19, No. 3: 39–53.

McCubbins, M. D. and Rodriguez, D. B. (2006) 'When does deliberating improve decision making?', *Journal of Contemporary Legal Issues*, 15: 9–50.

McFerson, H. (2009) 'Governance and hyper corruption in resource-rich African countries', *Third World Quarterly*, 30(8): 1529–49.

McGreal, C. (2009) 'We are creating suicide bombers from the sons of the dead', *The Guardian*, 17 January 2009.

McKerlie, D. (2013) *Justice: the Young and the Old*, Oxford: Oxford University Press.

McKinnon, C. (2006) *Toleration: A Critical Introduction*, London: Routledge.

McKinnon, C. (2012) *Climate Change and Future Justice: Precaution, Compensation and Triage*, London: Routledge.

McKinnon, C. and Castiglione, D. (2003) *The Culture of Toleration in Diverse Societies*, Manchester/New York: Manchester University Press.

McMahan, J. (2006) 'On the moral equality of combatants', *Journal of Political Philosophy*, (14)4: 377–93.

McMahan, J. (2007) 'Collectivist defences of the moral equality of combatants', *Journal of Military Ethics* 6(1): 50–9.

McMahan, J. (2008) 'Torture in principle and practice', *Public Affairs Quarterly*, 22: 111–28.

McMahan, J. (2009) *Killing in War*, New York: Oxford University Press.

McMahan, J. (2013) 'The moral responsibility of volunteer soldiers', *Boston Review*, 6 November 2013.

Meadows, D., Meadows, D., Randers, J., and Behrens, III, W. (1972) *The Limits to Growth*, New York: Universe Books.

Mendus, S. (ed.) (1988) *Justifying Toleration*, Cambridge: Cambridge University Press.

Mendus, S. (1989) *Toleration and the Limits of Liberalism*, London: Macmillan.

Mendus, S. (ed.) (1999) *The Politics of Toleration*, Edinburgh: University of Edinburgh Press.

Mendus, S. and Edwards, D. (eds) (1987) *On Toleration*, Oxford: Clarendon Press.

Mendus, S. and Horton, J. (eds) (1985) *Aspects of Toleration*, London: Methuen.

Mernissi, F. (1991) *The Veil and the Male Elite*, London: Basic Books.

Mill, J. S. (1859; 1972) *On Liberty*, H. B. Acton (ed.), London: Dent Dutton.

Mill, J. S. (1859; 1977) 'On liberty', in J. M. Robson (ed.) *Collected Works, Vol. XVIII*, Toronto, ON/London: University of Toronto Press/Routledge and Kegan Paul, pp. 203–310.

Mill, J. S. (1861; 1962) *Utilitarianism*, M. Warnock (ed.) London: Fontana.

Mill, J. S. (1861; 1969) 'Utilitarianism', in J. Robson (ed.) *Collected Works, Vol. XVIII*, Toronto, ON/London: University of Toronto Press/Routledge and Kegan Paul, pp. 203–59.

Mill, J. S. (1861; 1991) *Considerations on Representative Government*, Buffalo, NY: Prometheus Books.

Mill, J. S. (1910) *Utilitarianism, On Liberty and Representative Government*, London: Everyman.

Mill, J. S. (1874; 1969) 'Nature', in *Three Essays on Religion*, New York: Greenwood Press.

Mill, J. S. (1859; 1996) *On Liberty and the Subjection of Women*, Ware: Wordsworth.

Miller, D. (1994) 'Complex equality', in D. Miller and M. Walzer (eds) *Pluralism, Justice and Equality*, Oxford: Oxford University Press, pp. 197–225.

Miller, D. (2006) *The Liberty Reader*, Edinburgh: Edinburgh University Press.

Milton, J. (1644; 1973) *Areopagitica*, J. W. Hales (ed.), Oxford: Clarendon Press.

Modood, T. (2005) *Multicultural Politics*, Edinburgh: Edinburgh University Press.

Modood, T. (2007; 2013) *Multiculturalism: A Civic Idea*, London: Polity Press.

Moellendorf, D. (2002a) *Cosmopolitan Justice*, Boulder, CO: Westview Press.

Moellendorf, D. (2002b) 'Is the war in Afghanistan just?', *Imprints*, 6, No. 2.

Moellendorf, D. (2008) 'Jus ex bello', *Journal of Political Philosophy*, 16(2): 123–36.

Mookherjee, M. (2009) *Women's Rights as Multicultural Claims: Reconfiguring Gender and Diversity in Political Philosophy*, Edinburgh: Edinburgh University Press.

Moore, M.S. (1997), *Placing Blame: A Theory of the Criminal Law*, Oxford: Oxford University Press.

Morris, A. D. (1984) *The Origins of the Civil Rights Movement*, New York: Free Press.

Morris, H. (1968) 'Persons and punishment', *Monist*, 52: 475–501

Morriss, P. (2002) *Power: a philosophical analysis*, (2nd edn), Manchester: Manchester University Press.

Morse, B. and Berger T. (1992) *Sardar Sarovar: The Report of the Independent Review*, Ottawa, ON: Resource Futures International.

Muir, J. (1997) *Nature Writings*, New York: New American Library.

Mulgan, T. (2001) 'A minimal test for political theories', *Philosophia*, vol. 28: 283–96.

Murphy, J. G. (1973) 'Marxism and retribution' *Philosophy and Public Affairs*, 2: 217–43.

Murphy, J. G. and Hampton, J. (1988) *Forgiveness and Mercy*, Cambridge: Cambridge University Press.

Musgrave, R. (1986) 'A reappraisal of financing social security', in *Public Finance in a Democratic Society. Vol. II : Fiscal Doctrine, Growth and Institutions*, New York: New York University Press.

Nagel, T. (1987) 'Moral conflict and political legitimacy', *Philosophy and Public Affairs*, 16(3): 215–40.

Nagel, T. (1991) *Equality and Partiality*, Oxford: Oxford University Press.

Nagel, T. (2005) 'The problem of global justice', *Philosophy and Public Affairs*, 33(2): 113–47.

Newey, G. (2000) *Virtue, Reason and Toleration: The Place of Toleration in Ethical and Political Philosophy*, Edinburgh: Edinburgh University Press.

Newey, G. (2013) *Toleration in Political Conflict*, Cambridge: Cambridge University Press.

Nicholson, P. (1985) 'Toleration as a moral ideal', in S. Mendus and J. Horton (eds) *Aspects of Toleration*, London: Methuen, pp. 158–73.

Nickel, J. W. (1987) *Making Sense of Human Rights*, Berkeley, CA: University of California Press.

Norman, R. (1995) *Ethics, Killing and War*, Cambridge: Cambridge University Press.

Norman, R. (1998) 'The social basis of equality', in A. Mason (ed.) *Ideals of Equality*, Oxford: Blackwell.

Nozick, R. (1974) *Anarchy, State, and Utopia*, New York/Oxford: Basic Books/Blackwell.

Nozick, R. (1981) *Philosophical Explanations*, Oxford: Clarendon.

Nozick, R. (1989) *The Examined Life*, New York: Simon and Schuster.

Nussbaum, M. (1996) 'Patriotism and cosmopolitanism', in J. Cohen (ed.) *For Love of Country: Debating the Limits of Patriotism*, Boston, MA: Beacon Press.

Nussbaum, M. (1999a) 'A plea for difficulty', in S. Okin et al. (eds) *Is Multiculturalism Bad for Women?*, Princeton, NJ: Princeton University Press, pp. 105–14.

Nussbaum, M. (1999b) *Sex and Social Justice*, Oxford: Oxford University Press.

Nussbaum, M. (2000) *Women and Human Development: The Capabilities Approach*, Cambridge: Cambridge University Press.

Nussbaum, M. (2006) *Frontiers of Justice: Disability, Nationality, Species Membership*, Cambridge, MA: Belknap Press.

Okin, S. M. (1989) *Justice, Gender and the Family*, New York: Basic Books.

Okin, S. M. (1999) 'Is multiculturalism bad for women?', in S. Okin et al. (eds) *Is Multiculturalism Bad for Women?*, Princeton, NJ: Princeton University Press, pp. 7–24.

Olsen, W., Gash, V., Vandecasteele, L., Walthery, P., and Heuvelman, H. (2010) *The Gender Pay Gap in the UK 1995-2007: Research Reports Parts 1 and*

2, Manchester: Cathie Marsh Centre for Census and Survey Research, University of Manchester/ Government Equalities Office (GEO).

Ophuls, W. (1977) *Ecology and the Politics of Scarcity: Prologue to a Political Theory of the Steady State*, New York: W. H. Freeman.

Orend, B. (2007) 'Jus post bellum', *Leiden Journal of International Law*, 20: 571–91.

Orwell, G. (2000) *Essays*, London: Penguin.

Ostrom, E. (1990) *Governing the Commons*, New York: Cambridge University Press.

Otsuka, M. (2003) *Libertarianism Without Inequality*, Oxford: Clarendon Press.

Oxfam (2000) *Tax Havens: Releasing The Hidden Billions for Poverty Eradication*, Briefing paper, available online at http://publications.oxfam. org.uk/oxfam/display.asp?K=20040623_23 16_000034&aub=Oxfam&sort=sort_date/ d&m=30&dc=86.

Paine, T. (1791; 1969) *The Rights of Man*, Harmondsworth: Pelican.

Paine, T. (1791; 1989) 'The rights of man: part 1', in B. Kuklick (ed.) *Political Writings*, Cambridge: Cambridge University Press.

Parekh, B. (2002; 2008) *Rethinking Multiculturalism: Cultural Diversity and Political Theory*, Basingstoke: MacMillan.

Parfit, D. (1983) 'Energy policy and the further future: the social discount rate' in D. MacLean and P. Brown (eds), *Energy and the Future*, Totowa NJ: Rowman & Allanheld, pp. 31–7.

Parfit, D. (1984) *Reasons and Persons*, Oxford: Oxford University Press.

Parfit, D. (1998) 'Equality and priority', in A. Mason (ed.) *Ideals of Equality*, Oxford: Blackwell.

Parfit, D. (2000) 'Equality or priority?', in M. Clayton and A. Williams (eds) *The Ideal of Equality*, London: Macmillan, pp. 81–126.

Passmore, J. (1974) *Man's Responsibility for Nature*, New York: Scribner's.

Pateman, C. (1988) *The Sexual Contract*, Cambridge: Polity Press.

Patterson, O. (1982) *Slavery and Social Death: A Comparative Study*, Cambridge, MS: Harvard University Press.

Paul, J. and Wahlberg, K. (2002) *Global Taxes for Global Priorities*, Global Policy Forum paper, available on line at http://www.globalpolicy.org/ socecon/glotax/general/glotaxpaper.htm.

Perkins Marsh, G. (1864) *Man and Nature*, New York: Scribner and Co.

Persson, I. (2001) 'Equality, priority and person-affecting value', *Ethical Theory and Moral Practice*, 1(4): 23–39.

Pettit, P. (1997) *Republicanism: A Theory of Freedom and Government*, Oxford: Oxford University Press.

Phillips, A. (1991) *Engendering Democracy*, University Park, PA: Penn State University Press.

Phillips, A. (1993) *Democracy and Difference*, Cambridge: Polity Press.

Phillips, A. (1997) *The Politics of Presence*, Oxford: Oxford University Press.

Phillips, A. (2007) *Multiculturalism without Culture*, Princeton, NJ: Princeton University Press.

Piketty, T. and Saez, E. (2003) 'Income inequality in the US 1913-1998', *Quarterly Journal of Economics*, 118(1): 1–39.

Plamenatz, J. P. (1968) *Consent, Freedom and Political Obligation*, (2nd edn), Oxford: Oxford University Press.

Plato (360 BC; 1892) 'Crito', in H. Cary (trans.) *The Works of Plato, vol. 1*, London: George Bell and Sons.

Plato (360 BC; 1974) *The Republic*, (2nd edn), D. Lee (trans.), Harmondsworth: Penguin.

Plumwood, V. (1993) *Feminism and the Mastery of Nature*, London: Routledge.

Pogge, T. (1989) *Realizing Rawls*, Ithaca, NY: Cornell University Press.

Pogge, T. (1994) 'An egalitarian law of peoples', *Philosophy and Public Affairs*, 23(4): 195–224.

Pogge, T. (2001) 'Priorities of global justice', *Metaphilosophy*, 32: 6–24.

Pogge, T. (2002) *World Poverty and Human Rights*, Cambridge: Polity Press.

Pojman, L. P. and Westmoreland, R. (1997) *Equality: Selected Readings*, New York: Oxford University Press.

Postman, N. (1985) *Amusing Ourselves to Death*, New York: Viking.

President's Review Group on Intelligence and Communications Technologies (2013) *Liberty and Security in a Changing World: Report and Recommendations*, available online at www. whitehouse.gov.

Primoratz, I. (1989) 'Punishment as language', *Philosophy*, 64(248): 187–205.

Privacy and Civil Liberties Board (2014) *Report on the Telephone Records Program Conducted under Section 215 of the USA Patriot Act and on the Operations of the Foreign Intelligence Surveillance Court*, available online at www.fas.org.

Proudon, P. J. (1851; 1923) *General Idea of the Revolution in the Nineteenth Century*, J. B. Robinson (trans.), London: Freedom Press.

Pufendorf, S. (2005) *Of the Law of Nature and Nations: Eight Books*, Clark, NJ: The Lawbook Exchange.

Radcliffe Richards, J. (1998) 'Equality of opportunity', in A. Mason (ed.) *Ideals of Equality*, Oxford: Blackwell.

Rakowski, E. (1993) *Equal Justice*, Oxford: Clarendon Press.

Ramsay, P. (2012) *The Insecurity State: Vulnerable Autonomy and the Right to Security in the Criminal Law*, Oxford: Oxford University Press.

Raphael, D. D. (1988) 'The intolerable', in S. Mendus (ed.) *Justifying Toleration*, Cambridge: Cambridge University Press, pp. 137–53.

Ratner, S. R., Abrams, J. S., and Bischoff, J. L. (2009) *Accountability for Human Rights Atrocities in International Law: Beyond the Nuremberg Legacy*, (3rd edn), New York: Oxford University Press.

Rawls, J. (1964) 'Legal obligation and the duty of fair play', in S. Hook (ed.) *Law and Philosophy*, New York: New York University Press, pp. 3–18.

Rawls, J. (1971) *A Theory of Justice*, Cambridge, MA/Oxford: Harvard University Press/Oxford University Press.

Rawls, J. (1971) *A Theory of Justice*, Oxford: Oxford University Press.

Rawls, J. (1971; 1999) *A Theory of Justice*, (revd edn), Cambridge, MA: Harvard University Press.

Rawls, J. (1988) 'The priority of the right and ideas of the good', *Philosophy and Public Affairs*, 17(4): 251–76.

Rawls, J. (1992; 1993; 1996) *Political Liberalism*, New York: Columbia University Press.

Rawls, J. (2005) *Political Liberalism* (expanded edn), New York: Columbia University Press.

Rawls, J. (1999) *The Law of Peoples, with the Idea of Public Reason Revisited*, Cambridge, MA: Harvard University Press.

Rawls, J. (2000) 'Reply to Alexander and Musgrave', in M. Clayton and A. Williams (eds) *The Ideal of Equality*, London: Macmillan, pp. 21–41.

Rawls, J. (2001) *Justice as Fairness. A Restatement*, Cambridge, MA: Harvard University Press.

Rawls, J. (2002; 2005) *Political Liberalism*, (expanded edn), New York: Columbia University Press.

Raz, J. (1986) *The Morality of Freedom*, Oxford: Clarendon Press.

Raz, J. (1988) 'Autonomy, toleration and the harm principle', in S. Mendus (ed.) *Justifying Toleration*, Cambridge: Cambridge University Press, pp. 155–75.

Regan, T. (1983) *The Case for Animal Rights*, Berkeley, CA: University of California Press.

Renzo, M. (2010) 'A criticism of the international harm principle', *Criminal Law and Philosophy*, 4(3): 267–82.

Renzo, M. (2012) 'Crimes against humanity and the limits of international criminal law', *Law and Philosophy*, 31(4): 443–76.

Renzo, M. (2013) 'Responsibility and answerability in the criminal law', in R. A. Duff, L. Farmer, S. Marshall, M. Renzo, and V. Tadros (eds) *The Constitution of the Criminal Law*, Oxford: Oxford University Press, pp. 209–36.

Riker, W. (1980) *Liberalism Versus Populism*, San Francisco, CA: W. H. Freeman.

Riley, J. (1998) *Mill: On Liberty*, London: Routledge.

Riley, J. (2007) *Mill's Radical Liberalism*, London: Routledge.

Riley, J. (2013) 'Isaiah Berlin's "Minimum of Common Moral Ground"', *Political Theory*, 41(1): 61–89.

Riley, J (2014*a*) 'Isaiah Berlin's "Pelagian Soul": a reply', *Political Theory*, 42(3): forthcoming.

Riley, J. (2014*b*) *Mill: On Liberty*, (2nd edn), London: Routledge.

Riley, J. (2014c) *Mill's Radical Liberalism*, London: Routledge.

Roberts, M. and Wasserman, S. (2009) (eds) *Harming Future Persons: Ethics, Genetics and the Non-Identity Problem*, Dordrecht: Springer.

Robeyns, I. (2008) 'Ideal theory in theory and practice', *Social Theory and Practice* 24(3): 341–62.

Roemer, J. (1995) 'Equality and responsibility', *Boston Review*, April/May, available online at http://www.bostonreview.net/BR20.2/roemer.html.

Roemer, J. (1998) *Equality of Opportunity*, Cambridge, MA: Harvard University Press.

Rolston, III, H. (1988) *Environmental Ethics*, Philadephia, PA: Temple University Press.

Rousseau, J.-J. (1762; 1947) *Of the Social Contract*, C. Frankel (trans.), New York: Hafner Publishing Co.

Rousseau, J.-J. (1762; 1968) *Of the Social Contract*, London: Penguin.

Rousseau, J.-J. (1750, 1754; 1997) '*The Discourses' and Other Early Political Writings*, V. Gourevitch (ed.), Cambridge: Cambridge University Press.

Routley, R. (1973) 'Is there a need for a new, an environmental, ethic?', *Proceedings of the XVth World Congress of Philosophy*, 1: 205–10.

Roy, A. (1999; 2002) 'The greater common good', in *The Algebra of Infinite Justice*, London: Flamingo, pp. 39–126.

Ruskin, J. (1992) *Selected Writings*, K. Clark (ed.), New York: Penguin Classics.

Saltford, J. (2003) *The United Nations and the Indonesian Takeover of West Papua, 1962-1969*, Abingdon: Routledge Curzon, ch. 10.

Sandler, R. L. (2007) *Character and Environment: A Virtue-Oriented Approach to Environmental Ethics*, New York: Columbia University Press.

Scanlon, T. M. (1986), 'The significance of choice', in S. M. McMurrin (ed.), *The Tanner Lectures on Human Values*, Salt Lake City, UTAH: University of Utah Press.

Scanlon, T. M. (1991) ''The moral basis of interpersonal comparison', in J. Elster and J. Roemer(eds), *Interpersonal Comparisons of Well-Being*, Cambridge: Cambridge University Press, pp. 17–44.

Scanlon, T. M. (2000) 'The diversity of objections to inequality', in M. Clayton and A. Williams(eds), *The Ideal of Equality*, London: Macmillan, pp. 41–60.

Scanlon, T. M. (2003*a*) *The Difficulty of Tolerance*, Cambridge: Cambridge University Press.

Scanlon, T. M. (2003*b*) 'Punishment and the rule of law', in *The Difficulty of Tolerance: Essays in Political Philosophy*, New York: Cambridge University Press, pp. 219–33.

Scaramuzzi, I. (2004) 'France trips on the veil', *Confronti*, February, available online at http://www.confronti.net/oldconfronti/english/archives/feb04.htm.

Scheffler, S. (1999) 'Conceptions of cosmopolitanism', *Utilitas*, 11(3): 255–76.

Scheid, D. E. (ed.) (2014) *The Ethics of Armed Humanitarian Intervention*, Cambridge: Cambridge University Press.

Schmidt, R. (2008) *The Currency Transaction Tax: Rate and Revenue Estimates*, New York: United Nations University Press.

Schumpeter, J. (1956) *Capitalism, Socialism and Democracy*, New York: Harper and Row.

Schweitzer, A. (1987) *The Philosophy of Civilization*, Buffalo, NY: Prometheus.

Scott, J. C. (1990) *Domination and the Arts of Resistance*, New Haven: Yale University Press.

Scott, J. (2001) *Power*, Cambridge: Polity Press.

Sen, A. (1992) *Inequality Re-examined*, Cambridge, MA/Oxford: Harvard University Press/Clarendon Press.

Sen, A. (1999) *Development as Freedom*, New York/Oxford: Knopf/Oxford University Press.

Sen, A. (2006) *Identity and Violence: The Illusion of Destiny*, New York: W. W. Norton.

Sen, A. (2009) *The Idea of Justice*, London: Allen Lane.

Shachar, A. (2001) *Multicultural Jurisdictions: Cultural Differences and Women's Rights*, Cambridge: Cambridge University Press.

Shacknove, A. (1985) 'Who is a refugee?', *Ethics*, 95(2): 274–84.

Shanley, M. L. and Pateman, C. (eds) (1991) *Feminist Interpretations and Political Theory*, Cambridge: Polity Press.

Shapiro, I. (2003) *The State of Democratic Theory*, Princeton, NJ: Princeton University Press.

Sher, G. (1987) *Desert*, Princeton, N.J.: Princeton University Press.

Shiffrin, S. V. (2004) 'Egalitarianism, choice-sensitivity, and accommodation', in R. J. Wallace et al. (eds) *Reason and Value: Themes from the Moral Philosophy of Joseph Raz*, Oxford: Oxford University Press, pp. 270–302.

Sher, G. (1987) *Desert*, Princeton, NJ: Princeton University Press.

Shue, H. (1996) *Basic Rights: Subsistence, Affluence and US Foreign Policy*, Princeton, NJ: Princeton University Press.

Shue, H. (1999) 'Conditional sovereignty', *Res Publica*, 8(1): 1–7.

Shue, H. (2006) 'Torture in dreamland: disposing of the ticking bomb', *Case Western Reserve Journal of International Law*, 37: 231–40.

Sidgwick, H. (1898) 'The morality of strife', in *Practical Ethics*, London: Swann Sonnenschein and Co., pp. 83–112.

Sikka, P. (2003) 'Transfer pricing: how to get 160 missile launchers for the price of a ballpoint pen', *Tax Justice Network Newsletter*, September, pp. 10–11, available online at http://www.taxjustice.net/cms/upload/pdf/e_ns_0903.pdf.

Sikora, R. and Barry, B. (1978) (eds) *Obligations to Future Generations*, Philadelphia, PA: Temple University Press.

Simmons, A. J. (1979) *Moral Principles and Political Obligations*, Princeton, NJ: Princeton University Press.

Simmons, A. J. (1999) 'Justification and legitimacy', *Ethics*, 109(4): 739–71.

Simmons, A. J. (2001) 'On the territorial rights of states', *Philosophical Issues*, 11: 300–326.

Singer, P. (1973) *Democracy and Disobedience*, Oxford: Oxford University Press.

Skinner, Q. (1998) *Liberty Before Liberalism*, Cambridge: Cambridge University Press.

Steiner, H. (1994) *An Essay on Rights*, Oxford: Blackwell.

Steiner, H. (1998) 'Working rights', in M. H. Kramer, N. E. Simmonds, and H. Steiner *A Debate Over Rights*, Oxford: Oxford University Press, pp. 233–301.

Steinhoff, U. (2013) *On the Ethics of Torture*, Albany, NY: State University of New York Press.

Strasser, M. (1997) *Legally Wed: Same Sex Marriage and the Constitution*, Ithaca, NY: Cornell University Press.

Strossen, N. (2000) *Defending Pornography: Free Speech, Sex and the Fight for Women's Rights*, New York: New York University Press.

Suarez, F. (1944) *Selections from Three Works of Francisco Suarez, Vol. 2*, Oxford: Oxford University Press.

Suarez, F. (1994) *Selections from Three Works of Francisco Suarez*, trans. G.L. Williams, A. Brown, and J. Waldron, Oxford: H. Milford.

Sunstein, C. (1992) 'Neutrality in constitutional law, with special reference to pornography, abortion, and surrogacy', *Columbia Law Review*, 92: 1–52.

Sunstein, C. (2002) 'The law of group polarization', *Journal of Political Philosophy*, 10: 175–95.

Sutcliffe, B. (2002) *100 Ways of Seeing an Unequal World*, London: Zed Books.

Swift, A. (2001) 'Part 2: Liberty', in *Political Philosophy*, Cambridge: Polity Press, pp. 51–90.

Swift, A. (2008) 'The value of philosophy in nonideal circumstances', *Social Theory and Practice*, 34(3): 363–89.

Tadros, V. (2011), *The Ends of Harm: the Moral Foundations of Criminal Law*, Oxford: Oxford University Press.

Tamir, Y. (1993) *Liberal Nationalism*, Princeton: Princeton University Press.

Tamir, Y. (1995) 'Two concepts of multiculturalism', *Journal of the Philosophy of Education*, 29(2): 161–72.

Tan, K.-C. (2004) *Justice Without Borders: Cosmopolitanism, Nationalism and Patriotism*, Cambridge: Cambridge University Press.

Tasioulas, J. (2006) 'Punishment and repentance', *Philosophy*, 81(2): 279–322.

Tawney, R. H. (1920) *The Acquisitive Society*, New York: Harcourt, Brace and Co.

Tawney, R. H. (1926) *Religion and the Rise of Capitalism*, New York: Harcourt, Brace and Co.

Tawney, R. H. (1931) *Equality*, London: George Allen and Unwin.

Taylor, C. (1992) *Sources of the Self: The Making of the Modern Identity*, Cambridge, MA: Harvard University Press.

Taylor, C. (1993) 'The politics of recognition', in A. Gutmann (ed.) *Multiculturalism and the Politics of Recognition*, Princeton, NJ: Princeton University Press, pp. 25–73.

Taylor, P. (1986) *Respect for Nature*, Princeton, NJ: Princeton University Press.

Temkin, L. (1993) *Inequality*, Oxford: Clarendon Press.

Temkin, L. (2000) 'Equality, priority, and the levelling down objection', in M. Clayton and A. Williams (eds) *The Ideal of Equality*, London: Macmillan, pp. 126–62.

Titmuss, R. (1971) *The Gift Relationship*, London: HarperCollins.

Thompson, J. (2002) *Taking Responsibility for the Past: Reparation and Historical Injustice*, Cambridge: Polity Press.

Tocqueville, A. (1835; 2003) *Democracy in America*, London: Penguin.

Tomasi, J. (1995) 'Kymlicka, liberalism and respect for cultural minorities', *Ethics*, 105(3): 580–603.

Tully, J. (1995) *Strange Multiplicity: Constitutionalism in an Age of Diversity*, Cambridge: Cambridge University Press.

Tyler, A. (2008) *Islam, the West and Tolerance: Conceiving Coexistence*, London: Palgrave Macmillan.

United Nations (1985) *United Nations Report of the World Conference to Review and Appraise the Achievements of the United Nations Decade for Women: Equality, Development and Peace*, Nairobi, 15–26 July 1985, UN Doc A/CONFA 16/27/Rev. 1 UN Sales No. E.85.IV.1.0 (1986).

United Nations Development Programme (1998) *Human Development Report 1998*, New York: Oxford University Press.

United Nations, Department of Economic and Social Affairs, Population Division (2009) *Trends in International Migrant Stock: The 2008 Revision* (United Nations database, POP/DB/MIG/Stock/Rev.2008).

United States Census Bureau (2005) 'Historical income table: families', Table F-3, available online at http://www.census.gov/hhes/www/income/histinc/f03ar.html.

Vallentyne, P. (2002) 'Equality and the duty of procreators', in D. Archard and C. Macleod (eds) *The Moral and Political Status of Children*, Oxford: Oxford University Press, pp. 195–211.

Van Parijs, P. (1995) *Real Freedom for All*, Oxford: Clarendon Press.

Van Parijs, P. and van der Veen, R. (1986) 'A capitalist road to communism', *Theory and Society*, 15: 635–55.

Varner, G. (1998) *In Nature's Interests?*, New York: Oxford University Press.

Von Hayek, F. (1944) *The Road to Serfdom*, London: Routledge.

Von Hayek, F. (1944; 1960) *The Constitution of Liberty*, Chicago, IL: University of Chicago Press.

Von Hayek, F. (1973; 1978; 1979) *Law, Legislation and Liberty*, (3 vols), Chicago, IL: University of Chicago Press.

Von Hirsch, A. (1995) *Censure and Sanctions*, Oxford: Clarendon.

Von Hirsch, A. (ed.) (2003) *Restorative Justice and Criminal Justice: Competing or Reconcilable Paradigms?*, Oxford: Hart.

Wahl, P. and Waldow, P. (2001) *Currency Transaction Tax: A Concept with a Future— Chances and Limits of Stabilising Financial Markets Through the Tobin Tax*, Bonn: WEED.

Waldron, J. (1988) 'Toleration and the rationality of persecution', in S. Mendus (ed.) *Justifying Toleration*, Cambridge: Cambridge University Press, pp. 61–86.

Waldron, J. (1995) 'Minority cultures and the cosmopolitan alternative', in W. Kymlicka (ed.) *The Rights of Minority Cultures*, Oxford: Oxford University Press, pp. 93–119.

Waldron, J. (1999a) *Law and Disagreement*, Oxford: Oxford University Press.

Waldron, J. (1999b) *The Dignity of Legislation*, Cambridge: Cambridge University Press.

Waldron, J. (2003) 'Reasonableness', in C. McKinnon and D. Castiglione (eds) *The Culture of Toleration in Diverse Societies*, Manchester/New York: Manchester University Press.

Walker, B. (1997) 'Plural cultures, contested territories: a critique of Kymlicka', *Canadian Journal of Political Science*, 30(2): 211–54.

Walter, N. (1998) *The New Feminism*. London: Little, Brown & Co.

Walter, N. (2010) *Living Dolls: The Return of Sexism*, London: Virago

Walzer, M. (1973) 'Political action: the problem of dirty hands', *Philosophy and Public Affairs*, 2: 60–80.

Walzer, M. (1977; 2000) *Just and Unjust Wars: A Moral Argument with Historical Illustrations*, (3rd edn), New York: Basic Books.

Walzer, M. (1983) *Spheres of Justice*, New York: Basic Books.

Walzer, M. (1994) *Thick and Thin: Moral Arguments at Home and Abroad*, Notre Dame, IN: University of Notre Dame Press.

Walzer, M. (2004) *Arguing About War*, New Haven, CT/London: Yale University Press.

Ward, C. (1996) *Anarchy in Action*, London: Freedom Press.

Warnock, M. (1987) 'The limits to toleration', in S. Mendus and D. Edwards (eds), *On Toleration*, Oxford: Clarendon Press, pp. 123–39.

Weale, A. (1985) 'Toleration, individual differences and respect for persons', in S. Mendus and J. Horton (eds), *Aspects of Toleration*, London: Methuen, pp. 16–35.

Wellman, C. H. (1997) 'Associative allegiances and political obligations, ' *Social Theory and Practice*, 23: 181–204.

Wellman, C. H. (2012), 'The rights forfeiture theory of punishment', *Ethics*, 122: 371–93.

Wenz, P. (1988) *Environmental Justice*, Albany, NY: State University of New York Press.

Weston, K. (1991) *Family We Choose: Lesbians, Gays, Kinship*, New York: Columbia University Press.

Wilkinson, R. and Pickett, K. (2009) *The Spirit Level*, London: Allen Lane.

Williams, A. (2004) 'Equality, ambition and insurance', *Aristotelian Society*, Supplementary Volume LXXVIII: 131–50.

Williams, B. (1972) *Morality: An Introduction to Ethics*, Harmondsworth: Penguin Books.

Williams, B. (ed.) (1981) *Obscenity and Film Censorship: An Abridgement of the Williams Report*, Cambridge: Cambridge University Press.

Williams, B. (1996) 'Toleration: an impossible virtue', in D. Heyd (ed.) *Toleration: An Elusive Virtue*, Princeton, NJ: Princeton University Press, pp. 3–18.

Williams, M. and Waldron, J. (eds) (2008) *Toleration and Its Limits*, Nomos XVIII New York: New York University Press.

Wintemute, R. (1996) *Sexual Orientation and Human Rights*, Oxford: Clarendon Press.

Wolff, J. (1991; 2000) 'Political obligation: a pluralistic approach', in M. Baghamrian and A. Ingram(eds), *Pluralism: The Philosophy and Politics of Diversity*, London: Routledge; pp. 179–96.

Wolff, J. (1998) 'Fairness, respect and the egalitarian ethos', *Philosophy and Public Affairs*, 27 (2): 97–122.

Wolff, J. and de-Shalit, A. (2007) *Disadvantage*, Oxford: Oxford University Press.

Wolff, R. P. (1970) *In Defense of Anarchism*, New York: Harper and Row.

Wollstonecraft, M. (1792) *A Vindication of the Rights of Woman* (many editions available).

World Commission on Environment and Development (1987) *Report of the World Commission on Environment and Development: Our Common Future*, Oxford: Oxford University Press.

World Health Organization (2001) *The World Health Report 2001*, Geneva: WHO Publications.

Yoo, J. C. and Ho, J. C. (2003) 'The status of terrorists', *Virginia Journal of International Law*, 44: 207–28.

Young, I. M. (1983) 'Justice and hazardous waste', *The Applied Turn in Contemporary Philosophy: Bowling Green Studies in Applied Philosophy*, 5: 171–83.

Young, I. M. (1990; 1993; 1995) *Justice and the Politics of Difference*, Princeton, NJ: Princeton University Press.

Young, I. M. (1997) *Intersecting Voices: Dilemmas of Gender, Political Philosophy and Policy*, Princeton, NJ: Princeton University Press.

Young, I. M. (2000) *Inclusion and Democracy*, Oxford: Oxford University Press.

Young, I. M. (2001) 'Activist challenges to deliberative democracy', *Political Theory*, 29: 670–90.

Young, I. M. (2004) *On Female Body Experience*, Oxford: Oxford University Press.

Young, I. M. (2007) 'Structural injustice and the politics of difference' in A, Laden and D. Owen (eds), *Multiculturalism and Political Theory*, Cambridge: Cambridge University Press, pp. 60–88.

Young, I. M. (2011) *Responsibility for Justice*, Oxford: Oxford University Press.

Zagorin, P. (2005) *How the Idea of Toleration Came to the West*, Princeton, NJ: Princeton University Press.

Zimmerman, M. J. (2011) *The Immorality of Punishment*, New York: Broadview Press Ltd.

Index